ENTERTAINING ALL' ITALIANA

ENTERTAINING ALL' ITALIANA

Anna Del Conte

BANTAM PRESS

LONDON · NEW YORK · TORONTO · SYDNEY · AUCKLAND

TRANSWORLD PUBLISHERS LTD
61–63 Uxbridge Road, London W5 5SA

TRANSWORLD PUBLISHERS (AUSTRALIA) PTY LTD
15–23 Helles Avenue, Moorebank, NSW 2170

TRANSWORLD PUBLISHERS (NZ) LTD
Cnr Moselle and Waipareira Aves,
Henderson, Auckland

Published 1991 by Bantam Press
a division of Transworld Publishers Ltd
Copyright © Anna Del Conte 1991
Line illustrations © Marilyn Day

A cataglogue record for this book is available from the British Library.
ISBN 0593 021800

Typeset in 11/12 Plantin by
Chippendale Type Ltd, Otley, West Yorkshire
Printed in Great Britain by
Mackays of Chatham, plc, Chatham, Kent.

FOR MY MOTHER

at whose table I learnt the basic principles
that have guided me when writing this book.

Contents

Introduction   ix
Notes on Quantities and Equipment   xiv

Spring Menus   1
Regional Menus   47
Summer Menus   85
Harmonious Menus   141
Autumn Menus   169
Historical Menus   215
Winter Menus   251
Special Occasion Menus   295
My Five Favourite Menus   335
Basic Recipes   365

Index   383

I would like to thank Georgina Morley, my editor at Bantam Press, for the contribution she has made to this book by her meticulous and helpful editing.

My thanks also go to Annie Lee, my copy-editor, for her help and her patience in deciphering my illegible corrections.

Introduction

'*La cosa più importante quando si dà un pranzo è avere un menù equilibrato*' ('The most important thing when giving a dinner party is to have a well-balanced menu'). Thus spake Signora Oppi half a century ago while popping delicious little bon-bons between her scarlet lips. I was listening and watching through a crack in our drawing-room door as my mother's friends were having tea. Signora Oppi was very chic and beautiful, and anything she said made a great impression on me. This pronouncement of hers has echoed in my mind for years, so that when I give a dinner party I spend a lot of time planning my '*menù equilibrato*'. Another endorsement of her edict is the fact that remarkably often, when I have come back from a dinner party with the impression that something was wrong, the something in question was not the food itself, which was good, but the menu.

When you plan a dinner you should think of it as a whole and not as a succession of dishes. This is regarded as of great importance in Italy. You want, above all, to avoid a series of jarring contrasts. I do not mean by this that all the courses should have a similar taste, rather that their flavours should be in harmony. I have sometimes been given a most delicious creamy pudding after a hot spicy dish which left my taste-buds unable to appreciate the delicacy of the pudding that followed, no matter how much wine or water I drank in between. At other times, after two nutritious and rather heavy courses, the pudding has been far too rich. On one such occasion I can remember longing for a clean fruit salad while trying to swallow a spoonful of the sweetest and richest chocolate mousse. It is just as bad when I am given vegetables that clash with the meat or fish with which they are served, or when a bowl of salad is passed to me while I am enjoying something that would be ruined in close proximity with the oil and vinegar in the salad. More on this subject in the introduction to the section on Harmonious Dinners.

It is also very important to plan your menu so that you are totally at ease and ready to enjoy yourself. To this end, choose dishes that you know you can do well. Your friends would prefer to eat time after time the lamb casserole you make to perfection rather than a new, esoteric dish which you have had no time to test properly, and which imposes a visible strain on your nerves.

The majority of my dishes come from Italian home cooks rather than restaurateurs. Restaurant food is usually last-minute food because the chef and/or owner cooks to order, not wanting to waste anything. The easiest and most traditional Italian home cooking, and often the best, is based on slow cooking, generally involving large pieces of meat, whole fish, vegetable stews or other dishes that may have to be prepared well in advance and are best made in reasonably large quantities. In Italy the food is usually brought to the table on a large serving dish rather than being served on individual plates. After all, you are not a restaurateur who wants to produce the exact amount and no more; on the contrary, you would like your friends to have second helpings, a sure sign of appreciation. To make serving easier, you may like to place portions of the meat or the fish on individual plates, but after that hand round the vegetables and the salads in dishes and bowls. Do not put in front of each diner an exquisite plate with three mange-tout and four slivers of carrot surrounding in perfect symmetry a slice of meat in its pool of pinky sauce. Frills and bows have never been a characteristic of the Italian scene. The only dishes that might at times be served on individual plates are some kinds of antipasto and some puddings.

I have sometimes been told by friends that the quantities in my recipes are too large for the number of people specified. For one thing, it is very difficult to judge people's appetite, but more importantly, it is essential to have enough food to allow most people to have a second helping. No doubt only a few of your guests will have that second helping, which means that you will finish up today's dinner tomorrow. But you cannot be sure in advance. Another point is that it makes a lot of sense to taste your dishes the day after, because it is only then, rested and undistracted, that you will be able properly to judge your cooking. Besides, you will enjoy a rest from going into the kitchen and from having to think about what to eat.

How many people make the perfect number at a dinner party? Brillat-Savarin wrote that they should be not less than the Graces nor more than the Muses. Between three and nine stands six, and I would argue that this is a very good number. There is usually a single conversation round the table, mainly carried on by the two more articulate diners, to whom everyone else is quite happy to listen. The only danger with six people is that two of them may take an instant dislike to each other, or may disagree violently about some important topic. I shall always remember fireworks exploding around our dining-room table at the time of the Suez crisis, when Britain and France invaded Egypt. The two men at the table held totally opposed views about the rights and wrongs of what was happening, and my perfect *timballo di tagliatelle* and *manzo alla California* were swallowed unnoticed during hot exchanges and vitriolic glares. Meanwhile the wives, feeling more and more embarrassed, were looking at me with a mixture of apology and resentment at my unhappy choice of guests.

From this point of view a dinner for eight or ten is safer, but it demands considerably more effort. For these numbers I have tried to choose dishes that need the minimum of last-minute preparation. Fish, for instance, appears more in the menus for six, because it usually needs to be cooked just before serving, while large braising joints of meat, or casseroles, are the obvious answer for a large party.

The book is divided into ten sections, of which four represent the four seasons and contain the bulk of the recipes. Seasons . . . I begin to wonder if they still exist. As far as food and produce are concerned, they hardly do, and in the last few years even the seasons themselves seem to have changed. Here I am, writing this at the beginning of November on an amazingly warm and sunny day, and I am in London, not Rome. My *mentuccia*, special mint from Tuscany, has survived the last two winters in the garden, and the new rocket is already large enough to be picked. Even if I did not have it growing in my garden, I could easily go to a good supermarket and buy it. Less tasty, for sure, but still rocket in November. In the same way, I could buy courgettes, tomatoes and other 'out of season' vegetables too numerous to mention.

I suppose you could say how lucky we are, yet I regret the time when the months were marked by the different produce that appeared in the shops and markets. And just as there were seasonal vegetables, so there were seasonal dishes. In Italy there still are. In April, *brasati* and *umidi* – braised meats – are forgotten in favour of roasts and sautéed meat. Polenta slowly gives way to the more frequent appearance of pasta, and by the summer it has disappeared from the table, as have risotto and pasta with heavy meaty sauces. I remember the joy of seeing, again in April, the first peas of the season, and at Easter the *soncino* – lamb's lettuce. These were followed by all the glories of the summer fruit and vegetables.

As much as the food itself, the expectation was a keen pleasure. But although there is little of that left, we can still prepare a dinner suitable for the season. Some of the menus fall obviously into a particular season, others were more difficult to classify. It was the feel of the menu that was the decisive factor.

Four sections of the book are devoted to menus with a single theme running through them: regional, colour or flavour, historical and special occasions. A fifth section lists my five favourite menus, while the last contains what I have called basic recipes. These vary from how to make pasta to the standard Italian method for preparing the vegetables that are the most common accompaniments in all the menus.

Here and there in the book you will find vegetarian menus. Italian cuisine has a marvellous range of vegetarian dishes, thanks partly to the superb quality of the sun-ripened vegetables. A few of these, among so many, are the succulent tomatoes, the sweet onions, the meaty peppers, the really tasty potatoes and, of course, the marvellous range of salads. The other reason for the wealth of vegetarian dishes is that vegetables combine so well with both pasta and rice, both staples of Italian cuisine.

Italian cooking is also very rich in ways of using pulses, which are widely cultivated and of outstanding quality. Particularly good are the buttery beans of Lamon, in Veneto, the tiny lentils of Castelluccio in Umbria and the sweet broad beans of Tuscany.

The only snag with good vegetarian dishes is that many of them need time and some of them a certain cooking expertise. The vegetables, after all, are no longer a mere accompaniment, they are the centrepiece of the dish. Finally, my oft-repeated advice: buy the freshest vegetables, and whenever possible buy seasonal vegetables – they have a deeper, yet sweeter, flavour.

By and large all the menus are designed on the traditional pattern of a three-course dinner consisting of a *primo* (first course), a *secondo* (main course) and a *dolce* (pudding). Some lunches or informal dinners have only a *primo* and a *secondo*, plus cheese and fruit, very *all'Italiana*. It is also very *all'Italiana* to have four courses at very formal parties or on special occasions, as I have done in my menus for Christmas, the New Year and Easter. A four-course meal does not necessarily mean that more food is eaten, just that the food must be prepared in smaller quantities and be more varied.

The antipasto usually consists of something bought from the nearby delicatessen, be it a lovely platter of pink prosciutto or a light and colourful *insalata di pesce* – fish salad. These days, with the renaissance of the *cucina povera* – *cuisine du terroire* – the antipasto may well be a garlicky *bruschetta* (page 109) or a platter of *crostini* (page 69), something appetizing and informal. My first courses are mainly Italian *primi*: pasta, risotti and soups. There is a sprinkling of other dishes for those who think a dish of pasta or a risotto would be too heavy for a first course. The *secondi* are mostly meat or fish, as tradition demands, although a few menus are constructed in an unorthodox way. A pudding is usually the finale at formal dinner parties, but if you are too busy, tired or just fed up with being in the kitchen, do not hesitate to plump for fruit. A bowl of velvety peaches accompanied by a bottle of good wine, a mixture of soft fruits served with a lovely white chunk of ricotta or with a bowl of creamy mascarpone can be a better ending than some of my more elaborate puddings. But it is my job to write the recipes, and I leave the choice to you. Cheese is rarely served at dinner in Italy, being considered too heavy for the evening meal, while at lunch it is very often part of the dessert.

My last piece of advice is: keep it simple, and make it perfect by buying first-class ingredients.

Notes on Quantities and Equipment

The measurements for the ingredients are given in metric and imperial form. Although the difference between each system is very small, I would advise you to use the same set throughout any one recipe.

Tablespoons, meant to be level = 15 ml

Teaspoons, meant to be level = 5 ml

A set of measuring spoons is a great help to any cook.

Wherever necessary, I have suggested the best type of saucepan to use. To cook *all'Italiana* you will certainly need a large, heavy saucepan in which, as well as boiling your pasta, you can cook a good risotto and some polenta. You will also need a heavy sauté pan, about 25 cm/10 in in diameter, with a close-fitting lid.

In addition you would do well to have an earthenware stockpot for beans and soups, and a small round earthenware dish for slow cooking sauces. Both should be of the type that can be put directly on the heat. Earthenware is the perfect material for dishes that need long slow cooking, as it retains heat and moisture well. Earthenware dishes convey a sense of homely food and abundance, and they look very good if brought to the table.

Over my many cooking years I have learnt the wisdom of buying only the minimum of equipment and tools. Many of them, acquired years ago on impulse, sit there simply cluttering up my cupboards. But there are a few without which I could not cook.

The first is my food mill, a tool which I regret to say is not popular in this country. Most cooks here have a food processor but not a food mill. Yet the food mill can do more than the processor, and all without noise. With it I make the most delicious potato purée, tomato sauces and bean purées, all preparations that a food processor cannot do as well. The only drawback with a food mill is that you have to work it yourself.

Another tool I could not live without is a large colander for properly draining pasta, rice, potatoes and any other vegetables that have been boiled. A colander has the advantage over a large strainer that the water drains more slowly, so that the cooked rice or pasta does not become a sticky mass and vegetables are less likely to break. You need only a shake or two at the end for the little water left among the holes to run away.

With the large saucepan and the colander you will also need a cheese grater to make the necessary trio for a perfect pasta dish.

There are, of course, a few other tools I am attached to. My mortar and pestle is invaluable for crushing herbs and spices and for making pastes of any sort, allowing the deeper flavour of the ingredients to come through. If you prefer fresh pasta to dried, I suggest you buy a pasta machine, the inexpensive hand-cranked type that clamps on to the table. The other tool I like, although it is not vital, is the ice-cream machine. I find it solves the 'which pudding?' problem.

The symbol at the top of each recipe is indicative of the ease, or difficulty, of preparing the dish.

*   means the dish is easy to prepare
**   means the dish is not difficult, but requires some time and care
***   is for dishes that are more complicated and time-consuming, some calling for the skills of an experienced cook

There is never more than one recipe of the latter kind in any one menu.

ENTERTAINING ALL' ITALIANA

Spring Menus

A LUNCH FOR 6

Linguine coi piselli alla panna
FLAT SPAGHETTI WITH PEAS AND CREAM

Costolettine di agnello alla griglia
GRILLED LAMB CUTLETS

L'insalata bianca e verde
LAMB'S LETTUCE, ROCKET AND FENNEL SALAD (page 153)

Granita al caffé
COFFEE GRANITA

In Italy the vegetable that announces the arrival of spring is the pea. The spring peas are small and sweet in tender pods, which are themselves often used by thrifty housewives to make soups.

In Venice, in the old days, a purée of pea pods was added to *risi e bisi*, rice and peas, the dish served at the Doge's banquet every year on St Mark's day, 25 April. When we had a flat in Venice we spent many Easter holidays there, and I realized then why the pods were used as well as the peas. The peas that arrive at Rialto market from the islands in the lagoon are closer to mange-tout than to the garden peas sold in English shops. But, never mind, we cannot all move to Venice for the lovely peas.

In this country peas arrive later, and when they are first on the market it is not too difficult to find lovely small ones with shiny unblemished pods. Buy them, and welcome the spring with this easy dish of pasta in which the sweetness of the peas and of the cream is livened by the vermouth and the stock.

As peas are the spring vegetable, so lamb is the spring meat. The recipe in this menu comes from Rome, where the lamb – *abbacchio* – is slaughtered when still milk-fed and the cutlets are therefore of a pale pink colour and quite small. You can find small lamb cutlets here too, although the lamb would already have been weaned and its meat would be of a darker colour. These cutlets are richer in flavour than those from *abbacchio*, and they are excellent prepared as in the Roman recipe.

With the lamb I would serve the lamb's lettuce, rocket and fennel salad on page 153. You could even leave out the fennel and rocket and serve only the traditional spring salad of lamb's lettuce. It should be tossed with your best olive oil, and lemon juice instead of vinegar, which blends better with the subtle flavour of lamb's lettuce.

If you want a hot vegetable, serve bunch spinach, first boiled and then sautéed in olive oil, sharpened by lemon juice – *spinaci all'agro* (page 373) – and/or the potatoes on page 370.

Spring does not offer an array of fruit. It is, after all, the season of flowers, which we admire while eating last year's apples. So after these two courses I would plump for a coffee granita. It might be 'old hat' but it is still one of the best Italian sweets.

*   *Linguine coi piselli alla panna*

FLAT SPAGHETTI WITH PEAS AND CREAM

Linguine can be bought in Italian shops. If you cannot find them, use dried egg tagliatelle or *fettuccine*.

---

450 g/l lb linguine	*freshly grated Parmesan for*
salt	*serving*

For the sauce

45 g/1½ oz unsalted butter	*1 tbsp flour*
4 shallots, very finely chopped	*6 tbsp dry white vermouth*
1 tsp sugar	*120 ml/4 fl oz meat stock, or ¼*
1 tsp salt	*bouillon cube dissolved in the*
225 g/½ lb fresh garden peas,	*same quantity of water*
podded, or frozen peas,	*150 ml/¼ pint single cream*
thawed	*freshly ground white pepper*

If you are using fresh peas, plunge them in a saucepan of boiling water and cook them for 5 minutes. Frozen peas do not need this blanching.

Choose a large sauté or frying pan into which you can later transfer the drained pasta. Put the butter and shallots in the pan and sprinkle with the sugar and salt. Sauté the shallots until soft and then add the peas. Coat them in the butter for 1 minute, sprinkle with the flour and cook for a further minute, stirring the whole time. Stir in the vermouth, boil for 1 minute and then add the stock. Cover the pan and regulate the heat so that the liquid will simmer gently for the peas to cook. They must be tender, not just *al dente*. Stir in the cream, cook for a couple of minutes. Add pepper, taste and check seasoning.

Meanwhile put a large saucepan of water on the heat and bring to the boil. Add 1½ tablespoons of cooking salt and when the water has come back to a roaring boil, slide in the *linguine*, all at once, pushing them in gently with your hands. Stir with a long fork, put the lid back on the pan until the water is boiling again, then remove the lid and cook at a steady boil until the *linguine* are done. Drain, but do not overdrain, and transfer immediately to the pan with the sauce. Stir-fry, using two forks, and stirring with a high movement so that all the pasta strands are well coated with the sauce.

Now, if your frying pan is a good-looking one, bring the pan directly to the table. The less pasta is transferred from one container to another, the better; it keeps hotter. But if you do not like to bring saucepans to the table, turn the pasta into a heated bowl and serve, handing round the Parmesan in a bowl.

PREPARATION
The sauce can be prepared up to 2 hours in advance, but add the cream at the last moment, when you are reheating the sauce before adding the pasta.

✳✳ *Costolettine di agnello alla griglia*
GRILLED LAMB CUTLETS

12–18 lamb cutlets, depending on size	1 tbsp green peppercorns, crushed
6 tbsp chopped herbs: thyme, mint and marjoram	10 tbsp extra virgin olive oil
	the juice of 1½ lemons
2 garlic cloves, chopped	2 tsp French mustard
	salt

Ask your butcher to remove the backbone from the cutlets, leaving only the rib, and to flatten them to a thickness of about 1 cm/½ in.

Coat the chops with the chopped herbs, the garlic and the

peppercorns, pressing the mixture in on both sides. Place the chops in a grill pan and dribble with 3 tablespoons of the oil and half a tablespoon of the lemon juice. Leave to marinade for 1–2 hours.

Heat the grill and when hot cook the chops. Grill one side for about 3 minutes and then turn them over and grill the other side for a further 2 minutes. Do not overcook them or they will become dry.

While the chops are cooking, make the sauce. Pour 1 tablespoon of the lemon juice into a small bowl and stir in the mustard and some salt. Gradually add the rest of the oil while beating with a fork or a small wire balloon whisk to thicken the sauce. Taste and add more lemon juice and/or salt, if necessary.

When the chops are cooked, transfer them to a heated platter and sprinkle them with salt. Serve at once, with the lemon sauce either spooned over the meat or handed separately in a bowl.

PREPARATION

You can prepare the sauce up to 2 days in advance, but the chops must be cooked at the last minute.

**   *Granita al caffé*

COFFEE GRANITA

---

*900 ml/1½ pints freshly brewed   200 ml/7 fl oz whipping cream
   espresso coffee   2 tbsp icing sugar
6 tbsp sugar*

Heat the coffee, add the sugar and stir to dissolve. Taste and add a little more sugar to your taste. Pour the coffee into freezing trays and, when cold, freeze until solid.

Plunge the bottom of the tray in a bowl of hot water for a few seconds, then break up the coffee ice into chunks and process until it forms small crystals. Return to the trays and place back in the freezer.

Before serving, place six long-stemmed wine glasses in the refrigerator to chill.

Whip the cream and stir in the icing sugar to sweeten very slightly.

Remove the granita from the freezer. If it is too solid, process again for a few seconds just before serving. Spoon the granita into the chilled glasses and top with the whipped cream.

PREPARATION
The coffee granita can be prepared up to 1 week in advance.

A DINNER FOR 6

Risotto con le verdure in forma
MOULDED RISOTTO WITH VEGETABLES

Pollastrelli all'aceto balsamico
ROAST POUSSINS WITH BALSAMIC VINEGAR

Pomodori in teglia
BAKED TOMATOES (page 372)

Zabaione con la puré di fragole
ZABAGLIONE WITH STRAWBERRY PURÉE

Six is a good number of people to sit round the table. It does not demand too much on the part of the hostess, who can really enjoy her friends and take part in the conversation without having to jump up every two minutes to attend to something or other. I find it is also a good number for all concerned, since most of the time there will be one general conversation, and this is usually much more interesting than the social chit-chat you tend to have with your neighbour to the left or right at a larger dinner party.

The risotto in this menu is made entirely with seasonal vegetables. If you want to make it later in the year, use French beans or other vegetables instead. Choose vegetables with the same type of flavour and avoid a clash such as, for instance, peppers or cauliflower would produce. I make the risotto in a mould because in this way I can cook it beforehand, put it in the mould and reheat it in the oven for 20 minutes. It looks great and it tastes good.

The next course is a tribute to one of my favourite ingredients, *aceto balsamico*. This special vinegar is used a lot in Emilia-Romagna to baste roast meat, poultry, game birds, etc. Its sweet-and-sour flavour and its honeyed yet spiced aroma seem to give an edge to the gravy, while blending harmoniously with the meat.

With the poussins I like to serve the baked tomatoes on page 372 and/or the sautéed mushrooms on page 371.

Zabaglione is lovely, but I find it very tiresome to have to get up from the table and retire into the kitchen to make it. I prefer cold zabaglione, which is also less rich, especially when mixed with the tanginess of fresh fruit. You can leave the strawberries whole and mix them in just before serving, but I prefer to purée them beforehand. The flavour of the fruit is better distributed and the zabaglione looks stunning. If you are careful not to blend the purée in too thoroughly the result is much prettier, looking like Verona marble, pink and yellow. You can then garnish it with a few whole strawberries.

*** *Risotto con le verdure in forma*

MOULDED RISOTTO WITH VEGETABLES

150 g/5 oz fresh peas, podded, or
   frozen peas, thawed
150 g/5 oz courgettes
300 g/10 oz ripe firm tomatoes,
   peeled
1.5 litres/2½ pints vegetable stock
   or Italian broth (see page 378)
5 tbsp extra virgin olive oil
large bunch of parsley, chopped
2 garlic cloves, peeled and bruised

75 g/2½ oz unsalted butter
3 shallots, chopped
350 g/12 oz arborio or other Italian
   risotto rice
150 ml/¼ pint dry white wine
half a dozen basil leaves, torn
45 g/1½ oz freshly grated
   Parmesan
salt and pepper
450 g/1 lb asparagus

For the mould

15 g/½ oz butter

3 tbsp dried breadcrumbs

Boil the fresh peas in lightly salted water until just tender. If you are using frozen peas, blanch for about 2 minutes. Blanch the courgettes, drain and cut into small cubes. Cut the tomatoes in half, squeeze out the seeds and then cut into short strips.

Heat the stock until just simmering. Keep it simmering.

Meanwhile put half the oil with the parsley and the garlic in a sauté pan, sauté for 1 minute and then stir in all the vegetables. Season lightly with salt and sauté over low heat for 2 minutes. Remove and discard the garlic.

Put the rest of the oil and about a third of the butter in another heavy saucepan. Add the shallots and sauté until tender. Add the rice, cook for 2 minutes and then splash with the wine. Boil rapidly, stirring constantly, until the rice has absorbed the wine. Add 1 ladleful of stock and let the rice absorb it while you stir constantly. Continue to add the stock gradually, while you stir, until the rice is nearly, but not quite, cooked – about 15 minutes from the moment you begin to add the stock.

Draw the rice off the heat and add the vegetables, the basil, half the remaining butter cut into small pieces and the Parmesan. Stir thoroughly but gently, then taste and check seasonings. Spread the risotto on a cold surface to cool.

Snap off all the tough butt ends of the asparagus. For this dish you want only the tips, plus about 5 cm/2 in of the stalks. Remove any tiny leaves sprouting below the tips. Wash the asparagus and place it in a large sauté pan. Cover it with boiling water, season with a little salt and add the rest of the butter. Cook until tender but firm. Drain and transfer to a dish. Cover with foil and keep warm. Do not throw away the cooking water; you can use it to make a soup with the rest of the stalks.

Heat the oven to 200°C/400°F/Gas 6.

Generously butter a 1 litre/1¾ pint ring mould and sprinkle the breadcrumbs all over the surface. Shake off excess crumbs. Spoon the cold risotto into the mould and place in the oven. Bake for 20 minutes until the risotto is heated through.

To unmould, run a palette knife round the sides, place a round dish over the mould and turn it upside down. The mould should lift off quite easily.

Place the asparagus tips in the central hole and around the risotto. Serve at once.

PREPARATION
Both the risotto and the asparagus can be cooked a few hours in advance. Reheat the risotto in the oven, as directed above, and the asparagus in a bain-marie.

✳✳   *Pollastrelli all'aceto balsamico*

ROAST POUSSINS WITH BALSAMIC VINEGAR

---

6 small or 3 large poussins
salt and pepper
10–12 thin rashers of lean
  pancetta *or unsmoked lean*
  streaky bacon

60 g/2 oz unsalted butter
3 tbsp olive oil
9 tbsp balsamic vinegar

Trim, wash and dry the poussins. Rub them with salt and pepper, seasoning the cavities as well.

Heat the oven to 200°C/400°F/Gas 6.

Wrap each poussin in two slices of *pancetta* and tie with a string to keep it in place. If the poussins are large, use three slices.

Heat half the butter and the oil in a heavy roasting tin. When the fats are hot, brown the birds all over for 10 minutes. Splash with half the balsamic vinegar and put in the oven until cooked. They will take 25–40 minutes, depending on their size. Baste two or three times during the cooking.

Transfer the poussins to a heated dish, cut and remove the string and keep warm.

Add the remaining balsamic vinegar to the roasting tin. Scrape the pan with a metal spoon and when the liquid begins to simmer add, little by little, the remaining butter. As soon as the last bit of butter has been incorporated, draw off the heat. Season with salt and pepper to taste. Pour the sauce into a heated bowl.

Lay the poussins on individual heated plates. If you have used large poussins, cut each one in half down the back and through the breast bone with poultry shears.

PREPARATION

The poussins can be prepared, all neatly tied up for cooking, up to 1 day in advance and refrigerated. They can be cooked up to half an hour in advance. They will keep warm, well wrapped in foil, in the oven with the heat turned off. Reheat the sauce before serving.

** *Zabaione con la puré di fragole*
ZABAGLIONE WITH STRAWBERRY PURÉE

---

4 egg yolks
150 g/5 oz caster sugar
150 ml/¼ pint Moscato or sweet
   white wine

150 ml/¼ pint whipping cream
450 g/1 lb strawberries
4 tbsp orange juice
3 tbsp icing sugar

Beat the yolks with 100 g/3½ oz of the sugar. Add 120 ml/4 fl oz of the Moscato and cook, whisking constantly, in a bain-marie until thick and frothy. Do not boil or the yolks will curdle. Set aside to cool.

Whip the cream and fold into the zabaglione.

Blend two-thirds of the strawberries with the icing sugar in a food processor and then purée through a sieve to eliminate the seeds. Marinate the rest of the strawberries with the remaining sugar, the orange juice and the remaining wine.

Fold the strawberry purée into the zabaglione and mix a little so that the mixture is marbled. Transfer to six chilled glasses and decorate with the marinated strawberries.

PREPARATION
The fruit purée can be made up to 2 days in advance and refrigerated. It also freezes well. Make the zabaglione and fold in the purée up to 1 day in advance and keep in the fridge. Do not marinate the strawberries for longer than 2 hours or they will become mushy.

A VEGETARIAN DINNER FOR 4

Cappelletti alle erbe
RAVIOLI STUFFED WITH HERBS AND RICOTTA

Asparagi alla milanese
ASPARAGUS WITH FRIED EGGS AND PARMESAN

Pere alla crema del Lario
PEARS STEWED IN RED WINE WITH LIQUEUR-FLAVOURED CREAM

Vegetarian meals are often thought of as being ethnic and peasant (none the worse for that!). Not this one. It is quite an elegant meal which requires time and a certain amount of skill.

As with all stuffed pasta, you should make the *cappelletti* a few times before you serve it to your friends. Making pasta is a job that needs practice, and stuffing the pasta is an extra task to learn. In spite of that, however, the whole procedure is very well worth the time and effort. The result is so much nicer than bought ravioli, whose stuffing always seems to taste the same.

The asparagus is served in the Milanese way, with fried eggs, into the yolks of which you dip the spears. I have no qualms about including this recipe here even though it has already appeared in my previous book, *Secrets from an Italian Kitchen*, since it is the perfect dish for this vegetarian menu.

A note about cooking asparagus. Lately, at a Guild of Food Writers lunch, I had to leave the asparagus because they were what I call raw. The inner part was still hard and the asparagus had had no time to develop its full flavour. This was no doubt due to the *al dente* mania which has infected Britain and the USA in the last few years. I am certainly not campaigning for the return of overcooked, tasteless, mushy vegetables such as used often to be served before the *al dente* craze. I am saying only that cooked vegetables should be properly cooked, i.e. cooked long enough for them to develop their full flavour, even at the expense of appearance. Harold McGee, the American food scientist, in his latest book, *Curious Cook*, writes that flavour and colour evolve from two different chemical reactions. Chlorophyll breaks down quickly, but flavour compounds take time to develop. Asparagus, like green beans, releases its aroma as soon as it begins to be properly cooked. When asparagus is ready, the green tip should bend gracefully so that you have to lift your head up and open your mouth wide to receive it. It should not be like stiff green sticks. The correct cooking time depends entirely on its quality and age. I have had asparagus that cooked in 5 minutes and others that took 20 minutes. Just lift a spear out of the pan when you can smell the asparagus aroma; if it bends, taste it. It is probably ready.

The dinner closes with stewed pears with liqueur-flavoured cream. *Crema del Lario* is an unusual hybrid of Italian and English cooking. Lario is another name for Lake Como, the lake that was such a fashionable resort for British people up to the time of the First World War. They must have taught their local cook to prepare their beloved syllabub, and she, like any self-respecting cook, wanted to add her personal touch. In this case it was pears, and cream flavoured with the local pear *eau-de-vie* instead of English sherry or Madeira.

✳✳✳ *Cappelletti alle erbe*

RAVIOLI STUFFED WITH HERBS AND RICOTTA

---

15 g/½ oz parsley, preferably flat-leaf
15 g/½ oz of a mixture of these fresh herbs: rosemary, sage, thyme, marjoram, basil and borage (2 leaves), if available
15 g/½ oz unsalted butter
1 garlic clove, peeled and bruised
180 g/6 oz fresh ricotta
2 tbsp grated pecorino (if you cannot find good pecorino, double the quantity of Parmesan)
3 tbsp freshly grated Parmesan
¼ tsp grated nutmeg
salt and pepper
1 egg yolk
1 tbsp olive oil
pasta made with 2 eggs and 200 g/7 oz unbleached white flour

For the dressing
200 ml/7 fl oz double cream
20 g/¾ oz unsalted butter
salt and pepper
60 g/2 oz Parmesan

Chop all the herbs by hand or in a food processor. Heat the butter with the garlic in a small frying pan, add the herbs and sauté for a minute. Remove and discard the garlic. Transfer the herbs to a bowl, scraping up all the lovely bits stuck to the bottom of the pan. Add the ricotta, pecorino, Parmesan and nutmeg to the bowl. Add salt, if necessary, and a good grinding of pepper. Mix very thoroughly and then blend in the egg yolk. Mix again so that everything is properly amalgamated. Cover the bowl with clingfilm and refrigerate while you make the pasta.

Prepare the basic dough as directed on page 374. If you are rolling out by hand, roll out about one third of the dough as thin as you can, keeping the rest of the dough, covered by a bowl, to use later. If you are using a hand-cranked machine, cut and stuff each strip of pasta as soon as you have thinned it out, stopping at the last but one notch.

Cut into strips of about 3.5 cm/1½ in and then cut the strips across to form 3.5 cm/1½ in squares. Put about ½ teaspoon of the filling in the centre of each square, then fold the square across diagonally to form a triangle. Press the edges down firmly to seal them, moistening them with a little cold water if necessary. (If you are making *cappelletti* in a very dry atmosphere, moisten a narrow strip all round the edges with a wet pastry brush before you fold the dough to form the triangle.) Pick the triangle up by one corner, with the point of the triangle pointing upwards, and wrap it round your index finger. Press the two ends firmly together. The peaked part of each *cappelletto* should stand upright. As you make them, place them in rows on a clean tea-towel. They are now ready to be cooked in plenty of salted boiling water, with a tablespoon of oil added to prevent them sticking to each other. Fresh *cappelletti* take about 5–7 minutes to cook, but if you have made them beforehand and they have dried out, they will take 15–20 minutes.

While the *cappelletti* are cooking, heat half the cream with the butter in a large, heavy, sauté pan. Simmer gently for 1 minute to thicken the sauce. Season with a little salt and plenty of black pepper. Draw off the heat while you drain the pasta.

Lift the *cappelletti* out of the water with a large slotted spoon or a large metal sieve and transfer to the pan containing the cream. Put the pan back on the heat, add the remaining cream and half the Parmesan and sauté for a couple of minutes, turning the *cappelletti* over and over to coat them evenly with the sauce. Transfer to a heated bowl and serve, handing the remaining Parmesan separately in a small bowl. You can keep them warm in a low oven, covered with foil.

PREPARATION

As the *cappelletti* contain ricotta, they must be eaten within a maximum of 24 hours. I don't like freezing pasta, as pasta that has been frozen does not taste as good. However, I have tested freezing these *cappelletti* and it can be done if absolutely necessary. Freeze in single layers interleaved with clingfilm. Cook while still frozen. Do not keep in the freezer for longer than 1 week.

** Asparagi alla milanese

ASPARAGUS WITH FRIED EGGS AND PARMESAN

1.35 kg/3 lb asparagus	4 tbsp freshly grated Parmesan
salt	8 eggs
60 g/2 oz unsalted butter	freshly ground black pepper

First scrape the ends of the asparagus stems and snap off or cut off the hard part. Wash thoroughly. Tie the asparagus in small bundles. Tie them in two places, at the top near the tips and at the bottom above the butts.

If you haven't got an asparagus boiler, use a tall narrow saucepan, half full of boiling water. Remember to add salt to the water before you add the asparagus. Stand the bundles of asparagus, tips upward, in the water. If necessary, put some potatoes in the saucepan to keep the bundles upright. If the saucepan is not tall enough to put the lid on without damaging the tallest spears, make a domed lid from a sheet of foil and tie it under the rim of the saucepan.

When the asparagus are cooked, lift the bundles out and place them on kitchen paper to drain properly before you divide them and place them on four individual plates. Keep warm.

Melt three-quarters of the butter in a non-stick frying pan and pour it over the asparagus spears. Sprinkle with cheese.

Melt the remaining butter in the same pan and break the eggs into the pan. When fried, slide two eggs on to each plate next to the asparagus tips. Grind some pepper over them and serve immediately, with plenty of crusty bread.

PREPARATION
You can cook the asparagus up to 1 hour in advance and reheat them in a bain-marie in the oven, covered with foil.

*   *Pere alla crema del Lario*

PEARS STEWED IN RED WINE WITH
LIQUEUR-FLAVOURED CREAM

---

2 ripe but firm pears, preferably
   Williams
grated rind and juice of ½ a lemon
165 g/5½ oz caster sugar
cinnamon stick, about 2.5 cm/1 in
   long

200 ml/7 fl oz good red wine
4 tbsp Poire William eau-de-vie or
   Italian Grappa alla Pera
300 ml/½ pint whipping cream

Peel the pears, cut them in quarters and remove the cores. To prevent discoloration, drop them immediately into a bowl of cold water to which a few drops of lemon juice have been added.

Put half the sugar and the cinnamon in the wine and heat gently until the sugar has dissolved. Add the pears and cook until tender, about 10–15 minutes.

While the pears are cooling, mix the remaining sugar and the lemon rind and add the lemon juice and the liqueur. Stir until the sugar has dissolved. Whip the cream until it forms stiff peaks and then slowly fold the liqueur mixture into it.

Lift the pears out of the wine syrup (you can use the syrup to flavour a fruit salad) and place two quarters in each individual glass bowl. Spoon over the cream and chill for 1 hour.

PREPARATION
The pears can be cooked up to 3 days in advance and refrigerated. They can also be frozen. The pudding must be finished no more than 1 hour before serving.

A DINNER FOR 8

Minestrina delicata
CLEAR SOUP WITH HARD-BOILED EGGS AND PARSLEY

Salame di pollo e spinaci al sapor di basilico
CHICKEN AND SPINACH ROLL FLAVOURED WITH BASIL

Prugne al vino col gelato di mascarpone
PLUMS BAKED IN WINE WITH MASCARPONE ICE-CREAM

T he *minestrina* is a recipe I devised one evening when I felt in need of a delicate meal. On such an occasion I always go back to the food of my childhood, a dish of spaghetti or rice *all'inglese* – dressed with fresh butter and Parmesan – or a light soup. I had a friend, Marisa, who whenever tired, fed up or under stress would head for the kitchen, saying, *'Vado a farmi una minestrina'* ('I am going to make myself a light soup'). In my case, on the evening in question, I went to the kitchen and found I had some good broth in the fridge. As I put it on the heat I suddenly remembered how much I used to like a particular soup my mother's cook Maria sometimes made. I could still picture the colour of the soup in the bowl . . . but that was all. So I had to improvise. I hard-boiled an egg, grated some Parmesan and chopped a lovely bunch of parsley. I added to the stock two *pugnetti* – small handfuls – of *pastina*, little pasta stars, which in Italy are often used to make soups more nourishing. The resulting soup certainly looked like Maria's *minestrina*, and – more importantly – it tasted very good. I have also tried the soup with rice because I thought not all my readers would find *pastina* easily. It is good, with the more toothsome texture of the rice grain. Both versions are quick and easy to make, but don't attempt to make it unless you have some very good stock.

The second course, by way of contrast, is neither quick nor particularly easy. The good thing about it is that it is cheap, and yet *fa una bellissima figura* – it makes a good impression. It goes without saying that it is also very good.

The pudding consists of plums stewed in wine served hot with a rich mascarpone ice-cream. Some health-conscious people might prefer to have only the plums, which are perfect by themselves. With the mascarpone ice-cream, however, the pudding rises to a different plane and becomes an exquisite combination of flavours. The ice-cream melts in contact with the hot fruit, so that the plums float in a rich, velvety, white sauce. This ice-cream has the further advantage that it can be made without an ice-cream machine. I prefer to bake the plums instead of stewing them in a pan because they keep their shape much better; they swell up during the cooking and look very round and smooth. To preserve this look you should catch them just before the skin bursts, and for this reason it is a good idea to cook them in advance when you are not too busy and have time to keep an eye on them. You can then reheat them in a low oven before serving.

*　　　　　*Minestrina delicata*

CLEAR SOUP WITH HARD-BOILED EGGS AND PARSLEY

---

2 litres/3½ pints Italian broth (see page 378)	3 hard-boiled eggs
	8 tbsp chopped parsley
120 g/4 oz pastina (small pasta shapes such as stelline or puntine) or long grain rice	60 g/2 oz freshly grated Parmesan
salt	freshly ground pepper, preferably white

Heat the broth and when it boils add the rice or *pastina*. Stir very thoroughly from time to time during the cooking. The method for cooking pasta in soup differs slightly from that for cooking pasta to be eaten *asciutta* – drained. The stock in which the *pastina* or rice is cooking must boil gently or they will stick to the bottom of the pan. When I cook *pastina* or rice in a soup I put a lid askew on the saucepan to prevent the broth evaporating too much.

While the *pastina* or rice is cooking, purée the eggs through the small-hole disc of a food mill, or push them through a wire sieve into a bowl. Gently mix in the parsley, Parmesan, a teaspoon of salt and a generous grinding of pepper. Mix with a fork, rather than a spoon, because it will keep the egg lighter. Spoon the mixture into one or two bowls.

When the *pastina* or rice is cooked, ladle into individual soup bowls and serve, handing round the egg mixture separately.

PREPARATION

Both *pastina* and rice must be cooked just before serving. The garnish can be prepared a few hours in advance.

*** *Salame di pollo e spinaci al sapor di basilico*

CHICKEN AND SPINACH ROLL FLAVOURED WITH BASIL

1 fresh chicken, about 1.8 kg/4 lb
4 tbsp dry Marsala or dry sherry
60 g/2 oz unsmoked ham, cut in a
    single slice
180 g/6 oz cooked spinach or frozen
    spinach, thawed
a dozen fresh basil leaves

2 eggs
salt and pepper
¼ tsp grated nutmeg
pinch of powdered cinnamon
pinch of ground cloves
30 g/1 oz unsalted butter, melted

For the sauce

250 ml/9 fl oz chicken stock
30 g/1 oz unsalted butter
15 g/½ oz flour
150 ml/5 fl oz double cream

the juice of 1 lemon
a dozen fresh basil leaves, torn
salt and pepper
a pinch or two of cayenne pepper

For the stock

1 onion, cut in half and stuck with
    1 clove
1 carrot, cut into chunks
1 clove of garlic
1 celery stalk cut into pieces

1 bay leaf
a few parsley stalks
1 ripe tomato
5 or 6 peppercorns, bruised
a little salt

First remove the skin from the chicken. To do this, start by cutting through the skin down the back. Work first on one side and then on the other, using a boning knife or a small pointed knife. Keep the point of the knife away from the skin, since you need to preserve it without holes. Work the skin away from the flesh. When you reach the drumsticks cut them off and keep them for another meal. Cut off the wings and use them in the stock. Remove all the meat from the carcass, beginning with the breast.

Put the carcass, the wings, the neck and all the ingredients for the stock in a saucepan. Cover with cold water and bring slowly to the boil, then turn the heat down so that the liquid is just simmering. Skim off the scum that rises to the surface during the first 5 minutes or so. Simmer for 2 hours, then drain into a bowl.

Slice one breast of the chicken into strips, put them in a bowl and pour over the Marsala. Leave to marinate for at least 1 hour.

Cut the ham in similar long strips.

Put the rest of the chicken meat in a food processor and grind to a coarse purée. Transfer to a bowl.

Squeeze all the liquid out of the spinach. Put the spinach in the food processor, add the basil and process to a coarse purée. Add to the chicken purée.

Mix in the eggs, salt and pepper, the spices and the melted butter. Work the mixture very thoroughly with your hands until everything has blended.

Heat the oven to 200°C/400°F/Gas 6.

Lay a rectangular sheet of foil on a board and place the chicken skin on it. Trim the skin into a rectangle and use the trimmings to patch any holes you may have made while removing the skin. Sprinkle with salt and pepper.

Spread the chicken and spinach mixture over the skin. Lay the chicken and ham strips over it and then roll the skin up along the length of the rectangle to form a large sausage. Wrap the foil loosely round it and close each end firmly.

Lay the roll in a tin and bake in the oven for 1½ hours.

Remove the roll from the oven and place on a carving board while you make the sauce.

Measure 250 ml/9 fl oz of the stock and heat it. Melt the butter in a heavy saucepan and stir in the flour. Cook for 2 minutes, stirring constantly. Draw the saucepan off the heat and add the stock a few tablespoons at a time while beating constantly. When all the stock has been incorporated, return the pan to a low heat and simmer for 10 minutes, stirring frequently. Add the cream, half the lemon juice, the basil and the juices from the roasting tin and bring back to the boil. Simmer for 2 minutes and then add the two peppers and salt if necessary. The sauce should have the consistency of single cream. Taste and check seasoning, adding a little more lemon juice according to your taste.

Unwrap the roll. Using a sharp knife, flat-bladed if possible, or an electric knife, carve into 6 mm/¼ in slices, laying them neatly on a heated platter. Spoon a little of the sauce along the middle of the slices and serve the rest of the sauce separately in a heated bowl or sauce-boat.

Serve with the potatoes on page 370 and the baked tomatoes on page 372.

PREPARATION

You can prepare the roll and wrap it in foil ready for baking up to 1 day in advance, and refrigerate it. The roll can be carved up to 30–40 minutes in advance and kept warm, well covered with foil. Do not lay out the slices but keep them tight together in the roll shape, so that they will not dry out. Prepare the sauce when you carve the meat and reheat up to simmering point before serving.

**   *Prugne al vino*

PLUMS BAKED IN WINE

1 kg/2 lb red plums	10 peppercorns
300 ml/½ pint dry white wine	2 bay leaves
200 g/7 oz sugar	½ tsp ground cinnamon

Heat the oven to 170°C/325°F/Gas 3

Wash the plums and put them in a shallow ovenproof dish large enough to contain them in a single layer.

In a saucepan heat the wine, sugar, peppercorns, bay leaves and cinnamon. It is difficult to give the right amount of sugar, but if the plums are ripe and good, this amount should be enough. When the wine is just boiling, pour it over the plums. Cover the dish with foil and tie the foil under the rim of the dish. Put the dish in the oven and bake for 20–30 minutes. Check after 20 minutes; the plums should be just soft, but whole, and beautifully plumped up. When they are ready, taste one plum and if not sweet enough add a little more sugar.

PREPARATION

The plums can be refrigerated for up to 5–6 days, or you can freeze them. Reheat in a moderate oven for 10 minutes just before serving.

Gelato di mascarpone

MASCARPONE ICE-CREAM

---

400 g/12 oz mascarpone	*3 egg yolks*
120 g/4 oz icing sugar	*4 tbsp* amaretto *liqueur*

Beat the mascarpone with the icing sugar. Beat in the egg yolks and the *amaretto*. Mix thoroughly until well blended.

Spoon the mascarpone cream into the bowl in which you want to serve it, and cover with clingfilm. Freeze for at least 6 hours.

Remove from the freezer and put in the fridge about 1 hour before serving.

PREPARATION

This ice-cream can be made up to 2 weeks in advance.

A DINNER FOR 8

*Insalata di zucchine e pomodori all'aceto balsamico
e alla menta*
COURGETTE AND TOMATO SALAD DRESSED WITH BALSAMIC
VINEGAR AND FLAVOURED WITH MINT

Bocconcini di coda di rospo alla puré di lenticchie
MONKFISH MORSELS WITH LENTIL PURÉE

Spinaci all'agro
LEMON-FLAVOURED SPINACH (page 373)

Macedonia di frutta con la neve al limone
FRUIT SALAD WITH LEMON GRANITA

I find that it is always reassuring and relaxing for the host or hostess to serve a first course that can be totally prepared in advance, tasted, adjusted and then forgotten until it is time to serve it. As a matter of fact this menu is ideal for the last-minute cook; everything except the fish can be made in advance.

A courgette and tomato salad is a natural. It is a delicious, classic dish, prepared in most Italian homes. By adding the balsamic vinegar and the mint, and by spending a little longer on the preparation, you can make it more interesting and more attractive. Serve plenty of good bread with it – a *ciabatta* is ideal.

The second course might seem *nuova cucina* but, as far as I'm concerned, it is very *vecchia cucina* – *vieille cuisine* – since a similar dish of fish and lentils was made in my home in Milan as long ago as I can remember. The fish was *baccalà*, salt cod, and the lentils were not puréed, but the principle and the coupling of the two elements was the same. Here I substitute monkfish for the salt cod. Good salt cod is very hard to come by in this country, and monkfish has the necessary firm and rather chewy texture.

A word about the lentils. I decided that the little slate-coloured Puy lentils from France are worth the extra pennies they cost over the brown or green lentils that are imported from Canada or Turkey. The taste of the Puy lentils is sweeter yet deeper, the skin is softer and there is much less waste. The other lentils I recommend are the Italian ones from Castelluccio in Umbria, but they are very difficult to find outside Italy. If you use Puy lentils or *lenticchie di Castelluccio* you do not need to soak them or to purée them, since their skin is not of that unpleasant papery consistency that gets stuck between your teeth. Just cook them (30–40 minutes is usually enough), drain them, dress them with the oil and spoon them around the fish. The lemon-flavoured spinach on page 373 is an ideal accompaniment.

The last course, like the first, is an embellishment of a classic dish. Not only that, it is also an improvement. After all, fruit salad is already a good dessert and the addition of the frozen granita provides a perfect combination of sorbet and fruit salad. It is rather like eating a sorbet of mixed summer fruit dressed with lemon juice. An added bonus is the fact that the bowl looks stunning all covered with greeny icicles.

If you want some biscuits to hand round with the fruit salad, I would recommend the delicate almond crescents on page 380.

* *Insalata di zucchine e pomodori all'aceto balsamico e alla menta*

COURGETTE AND TOMATO SALAD DRESSED WITH BALSAMIC VINEGAR AND FLAVOURED WITH MINT

---

1 kg/2 lb small young courgettes	1 garlic clove, very thinly sliced
salt	4 tomatoes, preferably plum
6 tbsp extra virgin olive oil	tomatoes
3 tbsp balsamic vinegar	3 tbsp chopped mint
freshly ground black pepper	

Wash and scrub the courgettes thoroughly, but leave the ends on to prevent water getting inside. Cook them in boiling salted water until tender, but not soft. Take them out of the saucepan and refresh under cold water. Leave them to cool a little, dry them and cut off the ends. Cut the courgettes in half lengthwise and lay them neatly on a dish.

Mix together the oil, balsamic vinegar, pepper and salt and spoon over the courgettes, reserving 2 tablespoons of the dressing. Sprinkle the garlic slivers on top. Cover with clingfilm and set aside for about 1 hour.

Blanch and skin the tomatoes. Cut them in half and squeeze out the seeds and some of the liquid. Cut each half into 1 cm/½ in cubes. Before serving, place the tomatoes over the courgettes, sprinkle lightly with salt and pepper and spoon over the remaining dressing.

PREPARATION
Courgettes are best eaten the day they are cooked. The tomatoes can be blanched and cubed and kept in a covered container in the fridge for up to 1 day in advance. Remember to take them out of the fridge at least 2 hours before serving, so that they are at room temperature when eaten.

** *Bocconcini di coda di rospo alla puré di lenticchie*

MONKFISH MORSELS WITH LENTIL PURÉE

1.35 kg/3 lb monkfish
6 sage leaves
2 rosemary sprigs, about 10 cm/4 in long
1 garlic clove
3 tbsp olive oil

125 ml/¼ pint dry white wine
4 tomatoes, preferably plum tomatoes, skinned, seeded and cut into very small cubes
salt and pepper
4 tbsp chopped parsley

For the lentil purée
400 g/14 oz lentils
8 garlic cloves, washed but unpeeled
½ onion, stuck with 1 clove

2 bay leaves
2 tbsp wine vinegar
5 tbsp extra virgin olive oil
salt and pepper

First prepare the lentil purée. Spread the lentils on a plate, a few at a time, and pick out any tiny stones or pieces of grit. Although not always necessary, it is better to soak lentils in cold water for 3–4 hours, since sometimes they have been in storage for a long time and their skin has become tough. However, if you buy Puy lentils or *lenticchie di Castelluccio*, read my note in the introduction to this menu on pages 24–5.

After you have soaked the lentils, rinse them under running

water and put them in a saucepan – ideally it should be an earthenware pot. Add all the other ingredients, except the oil, salt and pepper, and add enough water to cover the lentils by about 2½ cm/1 in. Bring to the boil, turn down the heat so that the water simmers gently and cook until the lentils are very tender. How long this will take depends on the quality of the lentils and on the length of time they have been in storage. But they should be ready well within 1 hour. Drain, reserving the liquid. Remove and discard the bay leaves and purée the lentils through a food mill set with the small hole disc, or rub through a sieve. I do not recommend using a food processor because it will not get rid of the skin of the lentils. Add enough of the lentil cooking liquid for the purée to be quite soft. Transfer to a clean saucepan and add the oil, salt and plenty of pepper. Taste, check seasonings and keep warm over a flame disperser or in a bain-marie while you prepare the fish.

Trim all the grey skin and the membrane from the fish. (If left on they will cause the fish to shrink.) Cut the monkfish into 2½ cm/1 in morsels and pat dry with kitchen paper.

Chop the herbs and the garlic and put into a large non-stick pan with the oil. Sauté for 1 minute and then add the fish and cook over moderate heat for 2 minutes, shaking the pan frequently. Turn the fish over and cook for a further minute. Splash with the wine and let it bubble away for a minute or so while turning the fish over once or twice. Add the tomato and cook for 2 minutes. Season with salt and plenty of pepper to taste.

To serve, heat a large dish (a round one is prettier) and spoon the lentil purée round the outside of the dish. Transfer the fish into the middle of the lentil ring. Sprinkle the parsley over the fish and serve at once.

PREPARATION

The lentil purée can be made up to 3 days in advance and refrigerated, tightly covered. It can also be frozen. Heat it up very slowly either in a bain-marie or on a flame disperser. The fish must be cooked just before you sit down at the table. Keep it warm in the pan with the lid firmly on.

** *Macedonia di frutta con la neve al limone*

FRUIT SALAD WITH LEMON GRANITA

---

*1 kg/2 lb assorted fruit: bananas,
  pears, peaches, apricots, plums,
  grapes, cherries*
4 passion fruits

*3 tbsp sugar, more or less,
  according to taste*
*150 ml/¼ pint freshly squeezed
  orange juice*

For the lemon granita

2 large lemons

120 g/4 oz caster sugar

Peel the bananas and peel and core the pears. Slice the bananas and cut the pears into 1 cm/½ in cubes and put them in a glass bowl.

Wash, peel and stone the peaches, and wash and stone the apricots and plums. Cut into similar sized pieces and add to the bowl with all the juices that have come out while cutting the fruit. Wash the grapes, remove the seeds, if necessary, and if the grapes are too large cut them in half. Wash and stone the cherries and add to the bowl with the grapes. Cut the passion fruits in half, scoop out the inside and add to the other fruit. Sprinkle with the sugar and pour over the orange juice.

Cover the bowl with clingfilm and refrigerate for at least 3 hours. Mix two or three times during the chilling.

To make the granita, wash 1 lemon and grate the rind. Squeeze both lemons. Bring to the boil 450 ml/¾ pint of water with the sugar and the lemon juice. Add the grated rind and boil for 3 minutes. Leave aside to cool and then transfer the mixture into a shallow metal tin. Freeze until almost set.

Break the mixture into chunks and process until it forms small crystals. Return to the freezer. After about 2 hours break the mixture up again with a fork and then return to the freezer. Just before serving, break up the granita with a fork and spread it all over the top of the fruit salad. Serve at once.

PREPARATION

Both the fruit salad and the granita can be prepared up to 24 hours in advance. The fruit salad, however, is best made no more than 4–5 hours in advance.

A VEGETARIAN DINNER FOR 8

Pasta e fagioli alla contadina
BEAN AND PASTA SOUP WITH RADICCHIO

Scarpazzone lombardo
SPINACH *TOURTE*

Cassata siciliana
SICILIAN *CASSATA*

After years of eating various versions of *pasta e fagioli*, I recently came across an excellent recipe in the Trattoria Veneta in Milan, where peasant dishes from Veneto are served to the sophisticated Milanese. The *pasta e fagioli* was decorated with leaves of red radicchio, over which was laid half a hard-boiled egg. I was surprised by both. The owner told me that the *soffritto* (fried mixture) in the soup was based on radicchio, hence the decoration, while the egg was 'for nourishment'. After all, it was a *contadina* – a peasant soup – which would have been the only course for the *contadini* of Veneto. He also told me to mash the egg into the soup and mix it up. So I tasted, and once again I was pleasantly surprised, this time by a slightly tart flavour. 'Aceto,' the owner said. 'Aceto?' I queried. 'Eh si, signora' – vinegar to counteract the fattiness of the lard with which the *soffritto* was traditionally made. Now the lard has been replaced by olive oil for health and diet reasons, but the vinegar has survived because of the sharp lift it gives to the sweet heaviness of the *borlotti* beans.

My suggestion for the second course is a spinach *tourte*, an ancient recipe from Lombardy which incorporates some sweet flavourings, something often done in the past. Recipes for spinach *tourtes* can also be found in old English recipe books, and here again spinach is combined with sultanas, biscuits and spices, plus a small quantity of sugar added not so much to sweeten the food as to enhance its flavour. A recipe by Patrick Lamb, a royal chef active in the early eighteenth century, is very similar to this Italian one, as my friend the food historian Michelle Berriedale-Johnson pointed out to me. Lamb spread a similar mixture on toasted bread, which he then brushed with white of egg and baked in the oven. These spinach toasts were flavoured at the end with orange juice. I sometimes hand round a warm tomato sauce (page 89), which gives a good combination of taste and colour, but this is not essential.

The pudding will be the *pièce de résistance* of your dinner party. It is, to paraphrase the words of the song, 'lovely to look at, delightful to eat'. This is the authentic *cassata siciliana*, which has nothing to do with the ice-cream that has stolen its name. Alternatively, for a lighter dessert, choose the oranges and dried apricots in wine syrup on page 256, doubling the quantities.

The whole meal can be prepared totally beforehand, apart from cooking the pasta, which must be done just before serving the soup.

* *Pasta e fagioli alla contadina*
BEAN AND PASTA SOUP WITH RADICCHIO

---

450 g/1 lb dried borlotti *beans*
2 floury potatoes, cut into large chunks
2.25 litres/4 pints vegetable stock or water
salt
1 head of red radicchio, about 200 g/7 oz
150 ml/¼ pint extra virgin olive oil
1 celery stalk with its leaves, finely chopped

1 small onion, finely chopped
3 tbsp chopped parsley, preferably flat-leaf
4 tbsp good red wine vinegar
freshly ground black pepper
225 g/8 oz small tubular pasta, such as ditalini
90 g/3 oz Parmesan, freshly grated
4 hard-boiled eggs, shelled and cut in half

Soak the beans overnight in cold water.

Rinse and drain the beans and put them in a stockpot, preferably earthenware, with the potatoes. Cover with the stock or water and bring very slowly to the boil with the lid tightly on. Dried beans will take at least 1 hour to cook.

When the beans are soft, purée about two-thirds of the beans and the potato in a food mill or a food processor and return the purée to the pot. Taste, add salt and bring the soup back to the boil.

Remove 8 of the larger outside leaves from the radicchio head and wash them. Set aside. Cut the rest of the radicchio into small strips, and wash and dry them.

Put about two-thirds of the oil, the celery, onion, parsley and shredded radicchio in a frying pan, add a pinch of salt and sauté over low heat until the vegetables are soft, about 10 minutes. Add to the soup together with the vinegar and cook for 15 minutes. Season with a good grinding of pepper.

Add the pasta to the soup. If the soup is too thick, add a little hot water before adding the pasta, but remember that this type of soup should be quite thick and very creamy.

When the pasta is just done, draw off the heat, mix in half the cheese and allow the soup to stand for 5 minutes before dishing it out. Pasta in this kind of soup does not need to be *al dente*. Ladle the soup into soup plates and pour over the remaining oil. Float the reserved radicchio leaves on the soup and lay half a hard-boiled egg over each leaf. Serve with the remaining Parmesan separately in a bowl.

PREPARATION

The soup, without the pasta, is best prepared 1 or 2 days in advance and refrigerated. It also freezes very well. The pasta must be added just before serving.

** *Scarpazzone lombardo*

SPINACH *TOURTE*

100 g/3½ oz good-quality stale white bread, crusts removed	60 g/2 oz digestive biscuits, crushed
450 ml/¾ pint full-cream milk	45 g/1½ oz pine nuts
1.5 kg/3¼ lb bunch spinach or young leaf spinach, or 600 g/1¼ lb frozen leaf spinach	45 g/1½ oz almonds, blanched, peeled and chopped
salt and pepper	2 tsp sugar
45 g/1½ oz sultanas	1 tsp fennel seeds, crushed
the juice of ½ an orange	½ tsp ground cinnamon
150 g/5 oz unsalted butter	½ tsp ground nutmeg
5 eggs	9 tbsp freshly ground Parmesan
	butter and flour for the tin

Put the bread in a bowl, cover with the milk and leave for half an hour or so. Then break it up with a fork and beat to a paste.

Meanwhile, pick the spinach; if you are using bunch spinach, remove the roots, or if you are using leaf spinach remove the thicker part of the stem. Wash in several changes of cold water until no more soil settles on the bottom of the sink or basin. Bunch spinach has a much better taste than the leaf variety, but it does need more careful washing.

Put the spinach in a saucepan with no more water than that which clings to the leaves. Add 1 teaspoon of salt and cook, covered, until tender. Drain in a colander and set aside. If you are using frozen spinach, allow to thaw.

Heat the oven to 200°C/400°F/Gas 6.

Put the sultanas in a bowl, cover with the orange juice and set aside. Melt the butter in a saucepan, add the bread and milk mixture and cook over very low heat for 5 minutes, stirring constantly.

Squeeze all the water out of the spinach with your hands. Chop coarsely by hand (a food processor would liquefy it) and add to the bread mixture. Cook for a couple of minutes, stirring constantly, then transfer to a bowl and allow to cool a little.

Beat the eggs lightly and mix thoroughly into the spinach mixture. Add the sultanas and all the other ingredients. Taste and adjust the seasonings.

Butter a 25 cm/10 in spring-clip cake tin. Line the bottom with greaseproof paper and butter the paper. Sprinkle with a little flour and then shake off the excess. Spoon the mixture into the tin and cover with foil.

Bake for 20 minutes, then remove the foil and bake for a further 25 minutes or so, turning down the heat to 185°C/350°F/Gas 4. The *tourte* is ready when a toothpick inserted in the middle comes out dry. Allow to cool and then remove from the tin and serve at room temperature, set in a lovely round dish.

PREPARATION

The tourte can be made totally up to 2 days in advance and refrigerated. I have never tried freezing it (I'm not keen on freezing dishes, because they lose their freshness), but I'm sure it could be done. If you freeze the *tourte*, take it out of the freezer and leave in the kitchen for at least 6 hours in advance. Do not serve chilled.

*** *Cassata siciliana*

SICILIAN *CASSATA*

Make your own sponge cake or follow my recipe on page 381, doubling the quantities. Buy fresh ricotta from a reputable shop with a quick turnover. Ask to taste it before you buy: ricotta should have no bitter flavour. Otherwise use the UHT ricotta now sold in pots in most supermarkets. I have added a little cream to the filling. This is not in the traditional recipe, but I feel that the ricotta available here needs it.

450 g/1 lb ricotta
150 ml/¼ pint whipping cream
120 g/4 oz caster sugar
225 g/½ lb candied peel, chopped
1 tsp ground cinnamon
75 g/2½ oz bitter chocolate,
  chopped

30 g/1 oz pistachio nuts, blanched,
  skinned and chopped
120 ml/4 fl oz Marsala or rum
450 g/1 lb sponge cake, cut into
  1 cm/½ inch thick slices
225 g/8 oz glacé fruits

For the icing

375 g/13 oz icing sugar
2 tbsp water

1 tbsp lemon juice

Mix the ricotta thoroughly in a large bowl until smooth. Lightly whip the cream and fold into the ricotta with the sugar. Add the candied peel, cinnamon, chocolate, pistachios and half the Marsala or rum. Mix very thoroughly.

Line the base of a 20 cm/8 in spring-clip tin with greaseproof paper. Cover the base with slices of cake, plugging any holes with bits of cake. Moisten with some of the remaining Marsala or rum, using a pastry brush. Line the sides of the tin with the sliced cake and moisten with some more spirit. Spoon in the ricotta mixture, cover with a layer of sliced cake and moisten with the rest of the spirit. Cover with clingfilm and chill for at least 3 hours.

To make the icing, put 45 g/1½ oz of icing sugar and the water in a small heavy saucepan and bring slowly to the boil, stirring constantly. This stock syrup, as it is called, helps make the icing run evenly. Put the rest of the sugar in the top of a double-boiler, or into a saucepan that can fit inside a larger pan half full of simmering water. Add very gradually enough stock syrup to moisten and dilute to the consistency of double cream, working it well in with a wooden spoon. Add the lemon juice and continue cooking in the bain-marie until just warm.

Unmould the cake and slowly pour the icing on to the centre, letting it run all over the surface and down the sides.

Put the cake back in the refrigerator to allow the icing to set.

Just before serving, place the cake on a dish and decorate with the glacé fruits. Serve chilled.

If you have neither time nor inclination to make the icing, simply cover the cake with a lavish layer of sifted icing sugar just before serving and decorate with the reserved fruit.

PREPARATION

Cassata must be made at least 8 hours before serving. If it is made with fresh ricotta it can be prepared up to 1 day in advance; if you are using UHT ricotta, you can make it up to 3 days in advance.

A DINNER FOR 8

Tagliatelle coi carciofi
TAGLIATELLE WITH ARTICHOKES

Agnello arrosto alla moda del rinascimento
ROAST LEG OF LAMB WITH A SAFFRON AND
BALSAMIC VINEGAR SAUCE

Arancie e kiwi
ORANGES AND KIWI FRUIT

This is a dinner that needs the hand of an experienced cook. It is well worth the time and effort, however, and I know it will be a great success with your guests. It has the advantage that the first and last courses, and much of the second course too, can be prepared in advance.

Apart from the preparation of the artichokes, which is a lengthy and rather demanding job, the first course is quick and easy if you buy the tagliatelle as opposed to making it yourself. If you make your own tagliatelle it is, of course, less easy and certainly not so quick, but the result is so much better that it is worth every minute of your time.

The roast lamb is an interesting and excellent dish which I have adapted from a recipe in Maestro Martino's *Libro de Arte Coquinaria*, published in 1450. Maestro Martino was the chef to the Patriarch of Aquileia, a town near Venice. Little is known about the man, but fortunately his manuscript was incorporated in full in the book *De Honesta Voluptate et Valetudine* by Platina, first published in Latin in 1475, which became well known throughout continental Europe.

In those days, spices were used with great liberality. They came from the Middle East via one of Italy's maritime republics and were sold at very high prices; their use was thus a sign of wealth. Saffron was especially popular because of its golden colour. In this dish the colour does not come through the rich brown of the gravy, but the slight metallic and highly aromatic taste of the spice certainly does.

If you have a butcher who knows his job, ask him to saw off the bone at the extremity of the shin, just above the knuckle joint.

The section of pelvic bone can then be removed, making the carving much easier. Also ask your butcher to remove any excess surface fat. The cooking time is a question of personal taste, but my strong recommendation is not to overcook lamb. 15 minutes per 450 g/1 lb is enough. I serve this roast with the potato and carrot timbales on page 272.

After these two very nourishing dishes, the only fitting way to end the meal is with a light dessert based on fruit. I chose the salad of oranges and kiwi fruit because of its beautiful appearance. Kiwis are not my favourite fruit, but I have found that the slightly unripe ones have an attractively tingling acidity which goes well with the orange, and none of the mushy texture of the mature fruits. I like the fruit salad *au nature*, but if you wish you can spoon over half a glass or so of dry white wine; or, indeed, of champagne if you are opening a bottle before dinner.

*** *Tagliatelle coi carciofi*
TAGLIATELLE WITH ARTICHOKES

---

*tagliatelle made with 500 g/1 lb
2 oz unbleached white flour and
5 eggs, or 1.25 kg/2½ lb shop-
bought fresh tagliatelle, or
600 g/1¼ lb dried egg tagliatelle*
*6 or 7 globe artichokes, according
to size*
4 garlic cloves, peeled

4 tbsp olive oil
salt and pepper
450 ml/¾ pint single cream
60 g/2 oz unsalted butter
*4 tbsp freshly grated Parmesan
cheese*
225 ml/8 fl oz milk

If you are making your own tagliatelle, turn to page 374 and follow the instructions.

Trim and prepare the artichokes as directed on page 341. Cut them into quarters lengthwise and remove the beard and the prickly purplish leaves at the base. Slice the artichokes into very thin wedges, about ½ cm/⅛ in thick, so that the cut-up leaves remain attached to the bottom. Put in the bowl of acidulated water. Remove all the tough outside part of the stalks, keeping only the tender marrow inside. Cut it into rounds and add to the bowl. Now at last the artichokes are ready to be cooked.

Thread a wooden cocktail stick through the garlic cloves. (This is to make it easier to fish them out when the artichokes are cooked.) Put them in a large sauté pan with the oil and add the artichokes. Fry them gently for about 5 minutes, turning them over to *insaporire* – make them tasty – and then add enough water to come one-third of the way up the side of the pan. Season with salt and pepper.

Put the lid tightly on the pan and cook, over very low heat, for 35–45 minutes, until the artichokes are very tender. Add a little more water whenever all the liquid has evaporated.

Set aside while you cook the tagliatelle in plenty of boiling salted water. Remember that if the tagliatelle are fresh they take no longer than 2 minutes to cook.

Heat the oven to 190°C/375°F/Gas 5.

While the pasta is cooking, heat the cream. Drain the tagliatelle, but do not overdrain, and put immediately back into the pan. Toss with the butter and the hot cream. Add the artichokes and the Parmesan and mix thoroughly.

Butter a large and shallow oven dish and pour the tagliatelle into it. Before baking heat the milk and pour it over the tagliatelle. You may not need to add it all, but remember that the dish will dry while baking.

Put the dish in the oven and bake for about 20 minutes. Let it rest out of the oven for a few minutes before you bring it to the table, so that the flavours will settle and combine, and to ensure that your guests will be able to appreciate the delicacy of this dish without burning their mouths.

PREPARATION

The tagliatelle can be made up to 2 days in advance. Leave them on trays to dry and cover them with a cloth as soon as they are thoroughly dry. The artichokes can also be cooked 1 or 2 days in advance and refrigerated, covered with clingfilm. The whole dish can be prepared up to 1 day in advance, except for the hot milk, covered with clingfilm and refrigerated. Bring back to room temperature before baking, and add the hot milk before you put the dish in the oven.

** *Agnello arrosto alla moda del rinascimento*

ROAST LEG OF LAMB WITH A SAFFRON AND BALSAMIC VINEGAR SAUCE

2–2.25 kg/4½–5 lb leg of lamb
4 or 5 garlic cloves
2 tbsp mixed fresh herbs
  (rosemary, sage, thyme,
  marjoram, parsley, lovage or
  celery leaves)
salt and pepper
75 g/2½ oz pancetta *or unsmoked*
  streaky bacon, in a single slice

2 tbsp olive oil
450 ml/¾ pint dark meat stock
¼ tsp saffron powder or saffron
  strands
60 ml/2 fl oz balsamic vinegar
1 egg yolk
30 g/1 oz unsalted butter

See page 35 for details about the preparation of the joint.

Heat the oven to 220°C/425°F/Gas 7.

Chop the garlic and herbs and add salt and pepper. Cut the *pancetta* into strips, coat with the herb mixture and lard the lamb joint with the coated strips. Rub the joint with the oil and any left-over mixture of garlic and herbs and place it on a rack.

Heat the stock. If you are using saffron strands, pound them in a mortar. (You will find this easier to do if you sprinkle a pinch of granulated sugar in with the saffron.) Dissolve the saffron into half the stock, then beat in half the balsamic vinegar and the egg yolk. Add a little salt and pepper and pour the mixture into a roasting tin. Place in the oven. Place the meat on the rack above, so that the juices from the meat drip into the tin.

Cook for 15 minutes and then turn down the heat to 190°C/375°F/Gas 5 and cook until the meat is done. (If you like the meat pink, allow about 1½ hours from the time you put it into the oven.) Baste the joint with the sauce in the tin every 20 minutes or so. Remove the meat from the oven and leave it in a warm place for 15–30 minutes.

Meanwhile make the sauce. Strain the contents of the roasting tin into a saucepan and add the remaining stock. Bring to the boil and then add the rest of the balsamic vinegar and the butter little by little, swirling the pan until completely dissolved. Taste and check seasonings. Pour into a heated sauce-boat. Carve the meat into fairly thick slices and hand round the sauce.

PREPARATION

The lamb can be larded a few hours beforehand, but like any other roast it cannot be cooked long in advance. Both the meat and the sauce can be kept warm for up to 30 minutes.

*   *Arancie e kiwi*

ORANGES AND KIWI FRUIT

---

12 *large oranges*   *caster sugar to taste*
8 *kiwi fruit*

Cut both ends off the oranges and stand them on one end. Placing each orange on a plate to collect the juice, remove the skin and white pith with a small sharp knife by cutting off the skin downwards. Then slice the oranges horizontally.

Set aside the smaller slices for another occasion. Allowing 3–4 slices per person, lay the large central slices on a large round dish.

Peel the kiwi fruits and slice them across. Lay a slice of kiwi fruit on each orange slice, matching the sizes as much as you can.

Pour over the juice that has collected from the oranges and sprinkle with a little sugar, if you wish. Cover the dish with clingfilm and refrigerate.

PREPARATION

I like to make this dessert not more than 8 hours before serving it, keeping it covered in the fridge.

A DINNER FOR 12

Anello di tagliolini in salsa di zucchine
TAGLIOLINI RING IN A CREAMY COURGETTE SAUCE

Petti di cappone alla Stefani
CHICKEN BREASTS IN A SEVENTEENTH-CENTURY
SWEET-AND-SOUR SAUCE

Mascarpone alle due salsine
MASCARPONE WITH ELDERFLOWER AND
ROSE GERANIUM SAUCES

BOWLS OF *AMARETTI*, SWEETMEATS AND CANDIED FRUITS

A sit-down dinner for twelve people is quite demanding, so the menu must be well thought out as to its feasibility, but none the less elegant for that. If you have no one to help serve at the table I suggest you divide each course between two dishes, so that each end of the table can pass one around. Another excellent method is to put the dishes on the sideboard and let everyone help themselves. Although you could dish the pasta out beforehand, this would deny you the opportunity of showing the very pretty ring of *tagliolini* to your guests. It would also mean that those waiting to start while everyone was served would end up eating cold pasta.

It is perhaps because I am Italian that I have never taken to the idea of handing round plates on to which the food has already been placed in carefully (often wrongly) measured portions. It is not done in Italy, except with some special antipasti and a few puddings, so if you are entertaining *all'Italiana* you should allow your guests to serve themselves.

The only demanding part of preparing this meal is making your own *tagliolini*. However, you can make them well in advance, and once dried you can store them in an airtight container. If you do make your own pasta, make it in two batches of 3 eggs each unless you are quite experienced. If you use ready-made pasta, buy it fresh from an Italian shop, or buy one of the best brands of dried pasta such as the Cipriani *tagliolini*. The sauce is easy and can also be prepared in advance.

The second course is based on a seventeenth-century recipe by

Bartolomeo Stefani. I first had it at the restaurant Il Cigno in Mantova, where it has been recreated with great success. Stefani was chef to Ottavio Gonzaga, and his book *L'Arte di Ben Cucinare* was published in 1662. He was a great cook who had a flair for adapting traditional Mantovano country recipes to suit the table of his patron. He was also the first cook to discard the heavily spiced food of the Middle Ages and early Renaissance in favour of cooking with a lighter touch, flavoured with herbs and flowers. It was cooking of a brilliant inventiveness, and one that modern Italian chefs are keen to revive.

The original recipe is for capon breasts, capon being a tastier and less dry meat than chicken. As it is now illegal in this country to caponize cocks, I decided to use large chicken breasts instead. It works very well as long as you buy fresh chicken from a good supplier.

With them I serve boiled green beans or boiled carrots and cauliflower, dressed with enough extra virgin olive oil to give them a shine. Do cook the vegetables properly, please, which does not mean overcooking them. This applies particularly to the green beans, about which see my note on page 80.

The last course is simply a question of buying mascarpone, picking the rose geranium leaves and the elderflowers and making the sauces. Pick your elderflowers in full bloom from the south-facing side of the bush because they will be more scented. It would be a mistake to underrate this sweet because of its simplicity. The two sauces are very different from one another, yet each combines deliciously with the richness of the cream cheese. The geranium leaf sauce has a deeper, sweeter and darker flavour, reminiscent of Arabian nights, while the elderflower sauce – my favourite – is lighter and fresher. It seems to encapsulate the scent of the English countryside on a warm evening in May.

I like to scatter pretty dishes of *amaretti* round the table, as well as little meringues, candied fruits, quince cheese or whatever I have got in the cupboard, plus some fresh fruit. The fresh fruit for this occasion must be small, such as grapes, cherries or large strawberries, fruit that can be picked up in one's hand and put straight in the mouth.

***   *Anello di tagliolini in salsa di zucchine*

TAGLIOLINI RING IN A CREAMY COURGETTE SAUCE

Tagliolini *made with 600 g/1¼ lb unbleached white flour and 6 eggs, or 1.25 kg/2½ lb fresh tagliolini, or 780 g/1¾ lb dried*   *egg* tagliolini *or tagliatelle*
90 g/3 oz unsalted butter
100 g/3½ oz freshly grated Parmesan

For the sauce

600 g/1¼ lb fresh young courgettes
salt
90 g/3 oz unsalted butter
1½ tbsp flour

120 ml/4 fl oz dry white wine
1 bouillon cube
300 ml/½ pint double cream
300 ml/½ pint single cream
freshly ground black pepper

First make the *tagliolini*, following the instructions on page 375.

For the sauce, wash the courgettes thoroughly and boil them in plenty of salted boiling water until tender but not soft. Process to a coarse purée or put through a food mill fitted with a large-hole disc. Set aside.

Melt the butter in a saucepan, blend in the flour and cook for 1 minute, stirring constantly. Add the wine and cook for a further minute. Crumble the bouillon cube between your fingers so that the pieces fall into the pan. Add about 150 ml/¼ pint of hot water while you continue stirring to prevent lumps forming. Blend in the two creams and then the purée of courgettes. Add pepper and salt to taste. Bring to the boil and simmer very slowly while you cook the pasta.

Generously butter two ring moulds of 1 litre/1¾ pint capacity each.

Boil the *tagliolini* in plenty of hot salted water. If they are fresh or home-made they will cook in less than 1 minute. Scoop out a cupful or so of the water and reserve. Drain the pasta and put it quickly back in the saucepan. Dress with the butter and Parmesan and pour over about half a cupful of the reserved pasta water. Spoon the pasta into the prepared moulds and press down with a spoon.

Put a heated round platter over each mould, turn the mould

upside down and give the platter a shake. Remove the mould, which should lift away very easily.

If your saucepan is not large enough to cook the *tagliolini* all together, cook and drain half, spoon into one of the moulds and keep it in a warm oven while you prepare the other half.

If the sauce looks too thick, thin it down with a few tablespoons of the reserved pasta water.

Spoon some of the sauce into the hole in the middle of the ring and hand the rest around in two heated sauce-boats or pretty small bowls.

PREPARATION

The *tagliolini* can be made well in advance, allowed to dry thoroughly and stored in tins or plastic containers, each layer interleaved with kitchen paper. The courgettes can be puréed up to 1 day in advance and refrigerated, but the sauce, which takes only a few minutes, is better when made no more than 3 or 4 hours in advance. Reheat it slowly in a bain-marie. If necessary the whole dish can be prepared up to 1 hour in advance and reheated in a hot oven for 15 minutes.

*   *Petti di cappone alla Stefani*

CHICKEN BREASTS IN A SEVENTEENTH-CENTURY
SWEET-AND-SOUR SAUCE

---

10 large chicken breasts, boned and skinned	1 litre/1¾ pints light stock 300 ml/½ pint dry white wine

For the sauce

4 tbsp soft brown sugar	4 tbsp balsamic vinegar
100 ml/3½ oz dry white wine	2 tsp salt
75 g/2½ oz sultanas	freshly ground black pepper
the grated rind of 2 lemons	100 ml/3½ fl oz extra virgin olive oil

---

Wipe the chicken breasts and remove any fat. Put them in a large sauté pan and cover with the stock and the wine. If you have not got a large enough pan for the chicken to lie in a single layer, use two pans, dividing the stock and wine accordingly. The pieces should fit closely together. Poach until the breasts are cooked through – about 30 minutes, depending on their size. Leave to cool in the liquid.

Prepare the sauce. Put the sugar and the wine in a small saucepan and bring very slowly to the boil. Simmer until the sugar has completely dissolved. Draw off the heat and add the sultanas and the lemon rind. Leave aside to cool and then strain over a bowl.

Add the balsamic vinegar, salt and pepper to the liquid in the bowl. Now pour in the oil gradually, whisking with a small wire whisk to form an emulsion. When you have added all the oil, mix in the sultana and lemon rind mixture. Taste and adjust seasoning.

Three hours or thereabouts before you want to serve the dish, lift the cold chicken breasts out of the stock and place them on a board. (Keep the stock for a soup; it's quite delicious.) Cut the chicken into thin slices, about 1 cm/½ in thick, and lay the slices on a very large dish, or preferably two smaller ones. Spoon the sauce over the chicken and cover the dish with clingfilm. Do not refrigerate, since the chicken is best at room temperature. Before serving, I put green beans and cauliflower florets alongside the chicken if I am using an oval dish, or in a mound in the middle if I am using a round dish.

PREPARATION
The chicken breasts can be poached up to 2 days in advance and refrigerated, covered, in their liquid. Before cutting, wipe off any solidified fat that may have stuck to the joints. The sauce can be prepared up to 1 week in advance and kept covered in the fridge.

Mascarpone alle due salsine

MASCARPONE WITH ELDERFLOWER AND ROSE GERANIUM SAUCES

---

1 kg/2 lb mascarpone

For the elderflower sauce

2 dozen elderflowers
150 ml/¼ pint dry white wine
caster sugar
the rind of 1½ lemons, the yellow
    part only

1 tsp fennel seeds
4 peppercorns

For the rose geranium sauce

about half a dozen rose geranium
    leaves
the juice of 1 lemon

4 peppercorns
caster sugar

Divide the mascarpone between twelve individual small bowls. Cover with clingfilm and refrigerate.

To make the elderflower sauce
Wash the elderflowers in a basin of cold water. Put them in a bowl, cover with boiling water and leave to infuse for at least 6 hours. Strain the liquid. Measure the liquid and pour it into a saucepan with sugar, the 'poundage' of which should be half the 'pintage' of the liquid; e.g. to 300 ml/½ pint of liquid you should add 125 g/¼ lb of sugar. Add the lemon rind, fennel seeds and peppercorns and bring slowly to the boil, stirring constantly to dissolve the sugar. Simmer for 10 minutes, then strain the sauce into a jug. When cold, cover the jug and refrigerate. Serve with the mascarpone.

To make the rose geranium sauce
Rinse the rose geranium leaves and crush them gently in your hands to release their aroma. Put them immediately in a bowl and cover with boiling water. Leave to infuse for 6 hours, then strain. Measure the liquid and pour it into a clean saucepan. Add half the amount of sugar, as for the elderflower sauce. Pour in the lemon

juice, add the peppercorns, and bring slowly to the boil. Simmer gently for a few minutes. Taste and add more lemon juice if necessary, to give a slight sharp edge. Strain into a jug and when cold, cover and refrigerate. Serve with the mascarpone.

PREPARATION

Both sauces can be made up to 1 week in advance and kept in the refrigerator.

Regional Menus

There is, in effect, no such thing as 'Italian' cooking. Italy, after all, was united politically only a little over 130 years ago, and still to this day the country is by no means united gastronomically. So it seems to me more to the point to speak of Milanese, Venetian, Neapolitan or Sicilian cooking rather than of Italian cooking. It is the regional cuisines that have produced the *pièces de résistance* of Italian cooking, the pizza and *spaghetti al sugo* from Naples, the *bagna caûda* and the *bollito misto* from Piedmont, the risotto with saffron and *ossobuco* from Milan, to mention but a few.

I like, sometimes, to prepare a dinner with a regional basis. In winter my mind and my palate are geared towards northern Italian dishes – a joint of beef braised in Barolo with a steaming golden polenta to mop up the rich sauce, or a warm, comforting risotto with sausages. In the summer I draw more from southern Italian cooking, rich in tomatoes, peppers and fish, simply grilled or steamed. And the wintry, creamy puddings of Turin or Milan will give way to ice-creams from Naples and Sicily and fruit salads.

In the following section I have listed six menus from six regions, the region being the theme. The menus cover six different occasions, from a Bolognese pasta feast for twenty people to a late Roman supper for four friends, the ideal menu for an after-theatre meal. Or it might be fun to ask your friends to a Tuscan lunch in the middle of London, a lunch in which you will reproduce the food you had when you were on holiday in Chianti or Lucchesia. A bit of a gimmick, perhaps, but food and eating do not always have to be taken too seriously, as my husband and some of my friends have cause to remind me quite often!

A VENETIAN LUNCH FOR 4

Risotto coi peoci
RISOTTO WITH MUSSELS

Radicchio alla trevisana
GRILLED RADICCHIO AND CHICORY

Formaggio e frutta
CHEESE AND FRUIT

When we had a flat in Venice, I used to go every morning on a pilgrimage by gondola-ferry across the Canal Grande from Ca' d'Oro to the Rialto market. The Rialto market is a sight that should not be missed by anyone visiting Venice. It stretches along a few *calli* (alleys) and *campielli* (squares), around the bridge and along the Canal Grande. For the tourists there are stalls selling lace and tablecloths, and others selling bags, wallets and purses, but for the Venetians there are stalls piled high with the choicest fruits and the greatest selection of vegetables you have ever seen, as well as fish stalls with crawling crustaceans and slender silvery fish, so many different species and kinds that you can spend the morning in a study of ichthyology. But then, standing there, entranced by the sheer abundance and variety of it all, I would be reminded by the jostlings of more down-to-earth Venetian house-wives that I had a lunch to cater for.

After searching for whatever looked best, I would finish up, as often as not, giving in to my longing for seafood, and would return home with bags of molluscs for lunch and dinner. In the tradition of the local cuisine, rice was the natural accompaniment to the seafood.

The risotto was followed by *radicchio alla trevisana* whenever it was in season. The radicchio was the *radicchio di Treviso*, the best radicchio for grilling, with its slight bitter flavour brought out by the heat. I have never seen *radicchio di Treviso* outside Italy, but I love grilled radicchio so much that I make it in this country with the round *radicchio di Chioggia* that is sold here, together with one or two heads of Belgian chicory, which goes beautifully with it.

The cheese platter would certainly include the delicious Asiago, a semi-fat cheese made principally in the province of Vicenza.

Asiago is sometimes available in specialized Italian shops. A bowl of seasonal fruit would make an informal end to the meal.

**   *Risotto coi peoci*

RISOTTO WITH MUSSELS

1.35 kg/3 lb mussels
200 ml/7 fl oz dry white wine
6 tbsp olive oil
3 shallots or 1 medium onion, very finely chopped
salt
1 litre/1¾ pints light fish stock or vegetable stock

1 stalk of celery, with the leaves if possible
1 garlic clove
300 g/10 oz arborio, or other Italian risotto rice
4 tbsp chopped parsley, preferably flat-leaf
salt and pepper

First clean the mussels. Scrape off the barnacles, tug off the beard and brush thoroughly with a stiff brush under running water. Throw away any mussel that remains open after you have tapped it on a hard surface; this means it's dead.

Put the wine in a large sauté or frying pan, add the mussels and cover the pan. Cook over high heat until the mussels are open, which will take only 3–4 minutes. Shake the pan every now and then.

As soon as the mussels are open, remove the meat from the shells and discard the shells. Do not force the mussels open or the muscle around them will break and they will lose their shape and look messy. Strain the cooking liquid through a sieve lined with muslin, pouring it slowly and gently so that most of the sand and debris is left at the bottom of the pan.

Pour the oil into a wide heavy saucepan, add the shallots or onion and a pinch of salt, and sauté until they are soft and just beginning to colour.

Heat the stock to simmering point and keep it just simmering all through the cooking.

While the shallots are cooking, chop the celery and garlic together and then add to the pan. Sauté for a further minute or so.

Now add the rice and, as we say in Italian, *tostatelo* – 'toast it' in the oil, turning it over and over for a couple of minutes. Pour over the mussel liquid and stir well. When the liquid has been absorbed add the rest of the stock, one ladleful at a time. Stir very frequently. When the rice is done, draw the pan off the heat, stir in the mussels and the parsley, and season with salt, if necessary, and with plenty of black pepper. Transfer to a heated dish and serve immediately.

PREPARATION

The mussels can be cleaned and opened up to 1 day in advance. They must be kept in the refrigerator. The risotto should be made just before serving. However, you can half cook the risotto, up to the point when you add the first ladleful of stock. Bring to the boil, stir, and turn off the heat. The risotto can now be left until you want to finish the dish. When you come back to it you will find the risotto already half cooked, having absorbed all the stock. Stir in a knob of butter and continue cooking, gradually adding the remaining stock. The risotto will not be quite so perfectly cooked, but on the other hand you won't have to be banished to the kitchen by yourself for so long, and resent the making of it.

* *Radicchio alla trevisana*
GRILLED RADICCHIO AND CHICORY

450 g/1lb red radicchio	6 tbsp extra virgin olive oil
225 g/½ lb chicory	salt and pepper

Wash the radicchio and the chicory carefully. Dry very thoroughly. Cut the radicchio into quarters and the chicory in half, both lengthwise.

Oil the grill pan and lay the vegetables in it. Pour over the olive oil and season with salt and a lot of pepper. Leave for 20 minutes and then cook under a slow, pre-heated grill until the leaves soften, taking care to turn the radicchio and chicory pieces so that they cook all round.

PREPARATION

You can wash and dry the radicchio and chicory up to 1 day in advance and refrigerate, wrapped in a tea-towel. The vegetables can be grilled a few hours in advance and kept, covered, in the kitchen, not in the fridge.

A ROMAN LATE SUPPER FOR 6

Finocchi in pinzimonio
FENNEL WEDGES WITH OLIVE OIL

Coda alla vaccinara
OXTAIL AND CELERY BRAISED IN WHITE WINE

Frutta o gelato
FRUIT OR ICE-CREAM

In Rome the evening meal is often eaten as late as ten o'clock. People stay out till that time, and when they get home they like to sit down to a meal as soon as possible. For this reason I have found that quite a few Roman dishes are suitable to serve when you come home after the theatre or cinema with a few friends.

The first course of this meal is a fresh *pinzimonio*. In a *pinzimonio* everyone is given a little bowl full of the best olive oil. They then help themselves from a dish in the middle of the table, which may contain a variety of raw vegetables but in this case contains fennel, and dip the vegetables in the oil. It is a dish as gregarious and cheerful as the Romans and therefore characteristic of Roman cuisine.

While you and your guests are enjoying the *pinzimonio*, the second course is heated in the oven. It is an earthy peasant dish whose name, *alla vaccinara*, means cooked in the butcher's way, *vaccinaro* being the old name for a butcher in Roman dialect. *Coda alla vaccinara* is best made a day in advance, which means that it will need only to be heated up the following evening. In Rome, *coda alla vaccinara* is served by itself; no vegetables, just plenty of bread.

After these two courses I would put a bowl of fruit in the middle of the table, although a sorbet might be equally agreeable and just the right thing to help you digest a late meal. In the past the health-giving properties of iced drinks were well known; they were extolled by a certain Filippo Baldini, a professor of medicine, who wrote an essay in 1784 totally devoted to sorbets. For a good ice-cream turn to page 106, where you will find a basil-flavoured lemon sorbet, or to page 138 for a delicious ricotta ice-cream.

*

Finocchi in pinzimonio

FENNEL WEDGES WITH OLIVE OIL

---

3 medium to large fennel bulbs,
  preferably the squat round type
180 ml/6 fl oz extra virgin olive oil

salt and freshly ground black
  pepper
2 dozen Greek black olives

Cut off the top of the fennel and any part of the stalk that is bruised or discoloured. Trim the base, then cut the fennel vertically into quarters. Cut each quarter into wedges, about 2.5 cm/1 in thick. Wash in two or three changes of water, drain and pat dry with kitchen paper. Place the fennel wedges neatly on a dish.

Mix the seasoning into the oil and then divide the oil between six small bowls. Pile the olives in the middle of the fennel or scatter them on top. Place the dish in the middle of the table and give each person a bowl of olive oil into which to dip the fennel.

PREPARATION
The fennel can be cut and washed up to a few hours in advance. Wrap in a tea-cloth, put the bundle in a plastic bag and keep in the fridge.

**

Coda alla vaccinara

OXTAIL AND CELERY BRAISED IN WHITE WINE

---

225 g/½ lb pork rind
60 g/2 oz pancetta *or* unsmoked
  streaky bacon, cut in a single
  thick slice and chopped
3 tbsp olive oil
2 tbsp chopped parsley, preferably
  flat-leaf
1 garlic clove, peeled and chopped
1 onion, finely chopped

1 carrot, finely chopped
1.5 kg/3¼ lb oxtail, cut into joints
200 ml/7 fl oz dry white wine
250 ml/9 fl oz meat stock
2 tbsp tomato purée
salt and freshly ground black
  pepper
350 g/¾ lb celery

Blanch the pork rind in boiling water for a couple of minutes. Drain, refresh under cold water and cut into large strips.

Put the *pancetta*, oil, parsley, garlic, onion and carrot in a casserole and sauté over low heat, stirring frequently, until the vegetables are soft but not brown.

Heat the oven to 170°C/325°F/Gas 3.

Add the oxtail and the pork rind to the *soffritto* – the vegetable mixture – and sauté these as well, turning them over in the *soffritto*. Heat the wine and pour over the meat. Let it bubble for a couple of minutes, while you turn the meat over once.

Heat the stock in the saucepan in which you heated the wine. Stir the tomato purée into the casserole and then add the hot stock. Season with salt and pepper. Cover the casserole and put it in the oven for about 2–2½ hours. Turn the meat over every half hour. Skim off as much fat as you can from the surface of the cooking liquid.

Wash the celery and remove the strings from the outside leaves of the stalks. Cut the stalks and leaves into pieces and add to the casserole. Continue cooking for about half an hour until the celery is done – it should be still just slightly crunchy – and the meat comes away from the bone.

Skim off as much fat as you can from the surface of the cooking liquid. Taste and check seasonings and serve at once.

PREPARATION

Coda alla vaccinara should be prepared 2–3 days in advance and refrigerated, so that the fat can be removed easily. Do not put the celery in then. When cold, remove the solidified fat. Put the casserole on the heat (it doesn't need to go in the oven) and add the celery when the liquid is simmering. You can also freeze the dish, but remember to add the celery when reheating.

A MILANESE DINNER FOR 8

Minestra mariconda
EGG, PARMESAN AND PARSLEY DUMPLINGS IN STOCK

Manzo alla California con la puré di patate
BEEF BRAISED IN VINEGAR AND CREAM WITH POTATO PURÉE

Il panettone col mascarpone
PANETTONE WITH MASCARPONE

Lombardy offers quite a number of delicate and attractive-looking soups. These are based on properly made stock, richly yet delicately flavoured, with the right proportion of meat to bone (see the recipe on page 378). *Minestra mariconda*, one of these soups, contains little cheese-flavoured dumplings. I have adapted the recipe from a book, *Il Cucoco Senza Pretese* (*The Unpretentious Cook*), a collection of Lombard recipes published in 1834. The original recipe suggests using fish stock for fasting days. What fascinates me in this book is that at the end of each recipe there is a list of costs for each ingredient, and the total. This soup, with quantities for at least twelve people, cost *Lire* 53, equal, today, to 2½ pence!

The California in the name of the meat course is, unexpectedly, a locality to the north of Milan. It is tempting to think that the other one was named by emigrants from Lombardy, but this is unlikely, as California USA was originally a Spanish colony. The cooking of northern Italy is rich in braised meat dishes, and these are traditional for dinner parties and Sunday lunches. They are ideal for a large dinner party because the meat, which is cooked in a single piece, needs little attention and can even be cooked in advance. The best accompaniments are a soft potato purée and a bowl of spinach sautéed in butter and flavoured with freshly grated nutmeg.

For pudding I thought nothing could be more suitable than *panettone*, the Milanese cake *par excellence*. It used to be eaten in Lombardy only at Christmas time, but now it is eaten in most parts of Italy all year round. This dome-shaped cake has also conquered the world with its light texture and buttery taste. The tall, cylindrical shape created by Angelo Motta in 1921 has given way in the last decade to the original shape of a squat dome, much to the satisfaction of all true Milanese.

This was the sweet bread which became a big seller in the fifteenth century and made Toni, the poor baker, wealthy, and his daughter happy. A local nobleman wanted to marry the beautiful daughter and so he gave her father money to buy the best eggs, flour and butter, as well as sultanas and candied orange and citron. The delicious sweet bread the baker was able to make became known as *pan di Toni* and the prosperous Milanese ladies flocked to Toni's bakery to buy it. Or so it is said! For this is just one of the many stories surrounding the origin of *panettone*. It certainly is an ancient bread, possibly dating from the Middle Ages. A less romantic, and perhaps more plausible, explanation of the odd name lies in the Milanese penchant for diminutives. Thus *pane* became *panett* and, being bigger than usual, it became *panettone*.

As a true Milanese, I love my *panettone*. I like it for breakfast or for tea, or with sweet white wine or *vinsanto*, but I like it best for dinner with another notable Lombard product, mascarpone. When I want to serve it at the end of the meal, I just buy a good *panettone*, put a few slices in a moderate oven for 10 minutes, and serve it hot with the mascarpone, which voluptuously melts in contact with the hot *panettone*. You will need a 500 g/1 lb 2 oz tub of mascarpone. Put it into a bowl and hand it round.

There is now a *panettone* on the market which contains bits of chocolate as well as the traditional dried fruit. When I eat it by itself I prefer the old-fashioned *panettone*, but I find that the new chocolate-studded variety is ideal with mascarpone.

✱✱✱ *Minestra mariconda*

EGG, PARMESAN AND PARSLEY DUMPLINGS IN STOCK

---

200 g/7 oz fresh white
   breadcrumbs, with crust
   removed
200 ml/7 fl oz full-cream milk
120 g/4 oz unsalted butter
2 eggs

4 tbsp chopped parsley
60 g/2 oz freshly grated Parmesan
half a nutmeg, grated
salt and pepper
2 litres/3½ pints Italian broth (see
   page 378)

Soak the breadcrumbs in the milk for 10 minutes or so, then squeeze the milk out very thoroughly. Heat the butter in a small frying pan, add the breadcrumbs and sauté for 10 minutes, until the mixture is very dry, like dry paste. Transfer to a bowl.

Add the eggs to the bowl and then add all the other ingredients except the broth. Mix thoroughly with a fork, cover the bowl with clingfilm and refrigerate for at least 2 hours.

Bring the broth slowly to the boil in a large saucepan. Taste and adjust seasoning.

Pick up a small teaspoonful of the bread mixture and, with the back of another teaspoon, push it down into the broth. If the mixture is hard enough, you can make little pellets, the size of hazelnuts, with your hands. To prevent the dumplings breaking, keep the heat low so that the broth just simmers. Cook gently for 5 minutes and then ladle the soup into heated soup bowls. Serve with more Parmesan handed separately.

PREPARATION

You can prepare the dumpling mixture up to 1 day in advance and keep it covered in the fridge. Ideally the dumplings should be cooked shortly before serving, but I have successfully cooked them about 1 hour before and reheated the soup very slowly.

✱✱   *Manzo alla California*

BEEF BRAISED IN VINEGAR AND CREAM

---

120 g/4 oz unsalted butter	*1.8 kg/4 lb lean chuck steak or top*
2 onions, very finely chopped	*rump in one piece, neatly tied*
2 celery stalks, very finely chopped	*120 ml/4 fl oz red wine vinegar*
2 carrots, very finely chopped	*salt and pepper*
1 tbsp vegetable oil	*600 ml/1 pint single cream*

Melt the butter in a deep casserole. Add the vegetables and sauté gently for 10 minutes, stirring frequently.

Heat the vegetable oil in a non-stick pan and seal the meat on all sides. Transfer the meat on to the bed of vegetables.

Pour the vinegar into the non-stick pan and deglaze rapidly. Pour over the meat and season with salt and pepper.

Heat the cream and, when just beginning to show bubbles at the edge, pour into the casserole. Bring slowly to the boil and simmer over a very low heat for about 3 hours, until the meat is very tender when pricked with a fork. Turn the meat three or four times during the cooking. When the meat is ready, remove to a side plate and keep warm, covered with foil. Skim off as much fat as you can from the surface of the sauce. Purée in a food processor or liquidizer until smooth. Transfer to a clean saucepan and heat slowly. Taste and adjust seasoning.

If the sauce is not tasty enough – nowadays some meat contains a lot of water – boil briskly to reduce.

Slice the meat across the grain into 1 cm/½ in thick slices and lay them, slightly overlapping, in a heated dish. Cover with some of the sauce and serve the rest in a heated bowl.

PREPARATION
The dish can be prepared up to 3 days in advance and refrigerated. Skim the fat off the sauce – it is much easier to do this when the sauce is cold. Slice the meat and reheat very gently in the sauce. The dish can also be frozen.

A SICILIAN DINNER FOR 6

Caponatina di melanzane
SWEET AND SOUR AUBERGINE

Il timballo del Gattopardo
MACARONI PIE

Insalata di finocchi, cicoria belga e arancie
FENNEL, BELGIAN CHICORY AND ORANGE SALAD

Cassata siciliana
SICILIAN *CASSATA* (page 33)

*C*aponatina, one of the peaks of Sicilian cooking, demonstrates very clearly a main characteristic of that cuisine. A simple local ingredient, in this case the aubergine, is taken as the basis of the dish, and it is then embellished and enriched until the end result is an opulent and almost baroque achievement. In some areas of Sicily tiny octopus, or *bottarga* (dried roe of tuna or grey mullet), or even a small lobster is added. In Palermo *caponatina* becomes more Arab in concept by the addition of almond and cinnamon. And to make it even more grandiose, in Catania it is often covered with *'la salsa di San Bernardo'*, a sauce based on toasted bread mixed with grated chocolate, toasted almonds, sugar and vinegar. It is a sauce allegedly created by the Benedictine monks in their monastery.

Caponatina, or *caponata*, is usually served as an antipasto, although in that case it would not precede the *timballo* that follows here. In fact, in a truly Sicilian meal the *timballo* would be served first. But I can hardly imagine, in this day and age, anyone wanting to start the meal with such a substantial dish before going on to the main course, and for this reason I have introduced the *timballo* as the *secondo*.

It is indeed a grand *secondo*, being my interpretation of the *timballo* offered in 1860 by the Prince Fabrizio Salina to the notables of the town of Donnafugata in Sicily. This is how Giuseppe Tomasi di Lampedusa describes it in his famous novel, *The Leopard*: 'The burnished gold of the crusts, the fragrance exuded by the sugar and cinnamon, were but preludes to the delights released from the inside of the pie when the knife broke the crust. First came a spice-laden haze, then chicken livers, hard-boiled eggs, sliced ham, chicken and truffles in masses of piping hot, glistening macaroni, to which the meat juice gave an exquisite hue of suede.' I have seldom seen a dish described in such beautiful language and yet with such gastronomic accuracy.

This *timballo* will always be a *tour de force* on the part of the cook. It takes time and a certain knowledge of pastry-making and baking, though the filling is quite easy.

After that I suggest a salad, and when I think of Sicily I immediately think of this one. It is based on the most Sicilian of all produce, the orange. It is a fresh, astringent salad, perfect after the voluptuous *timballo*.

I end the meal with the Sicilian *cassata*. This is the traditional Easter sweet in Sicily, which shares only its name with the industrially made frozen concoction.

* ## *Caponatina di melanzane*

SWEET AND SOUR AUBERGINE

1.5 kg/3¼ lb aubergines	*plum tomatoes, drained and*
salt	*puréed*
vegetable oil for frying	*1 tbsp grated chocolate*
1 celery head	*black pepper*
125 ml/4 fl oz olive oil	*150 ml/¼ pint red wine vinegar*
2 onions, sliced	*100 g/3½ oz capers, rinsed*
1 tbsp sugar	*90 g/3 oz sweet green olives*
400 g/14 oz tomato passata *or*	

Peel the aubergines, cut them into 2 cm/¾ in cubes, place them in a colander and sprinkle with salt. Put a weight on top and leave them to drain for at least 1 hour. Squeeze them out, rinse, and dry with kitchen paper.

Heat 2.5 cm/1 in of vegetable oil in a wok or a frying pan. When the oil is very hot (it should be hot enough to make a small piece of stale bread turn brown in 40 seconds), slip in as many aubergine cubes as will fit in a single layer and fry until golden brown on all sides, turning them over with a fish slice half-way through the cooking. Adjust the heat if the aubergines begin to burn. Lift them out of the oil and drain on kitchen paper. Repeat until all the aubergine cubes are fried.

Remove the outer sticks and the leaves from the celery head and keep them for another dish. Use only the heart. Remove the coarse outside threads with a potato peeler, if necessary, and cut the sticks into 3.5 cm/1½ in long matchsticks. Fry the celery sticks in the same oil as the aubergine until golden and crisp. Drain on kitchen paper.

Heat the olive oil in a clean sauté or frying pan and add the onion, 2 pinches of salt and 1 pinch of the sugar. Cook for about 5–7 minutes, until soft and just coloured. Add the tomatoes, the rest of the sugar, the grated chocolate, a little salt and a generous grinding of pepper. Cook over a lively heat for about 2 minutes and then add the vinegar and the capers.

Stone the olives, cut them into quarters and add to the pan together with the aubergine and the celery. Cook over low heat for a further 30 minutes. Taste and adjust seasonings. Spoon the *caponatina* into a serving bowl and allow to cool. Serve at room temperature with plenty of good bread.

Caponatina looks stunning dished out into a large loaf of *pugliese* bread which is cut in half with the soft inner crumb hollowed out. Spoon it into the bread just before serving.

PREPARATION

Caponatina is better made at least 1 day in advance. For 1 day it does not need to be refrigerated. You can prepare it up to 3 days in advance and keep it in the fridge, but remember to bring it back to room temperature before serving, so that the subtle flavour can be fully appreciated.

*** *Il timballo del Gattopardo*

MACARONI PIE

---

30 g/1 oz dried porcini
75 g/2½ oz unsalted butter
90 g/3 oz **luganega** *or other sweet,*
coarse-ground, pure pork
sausage, skinned and cut into
small pieces
150 g/5 oz boneless chicken breast,
skinned and cut into 1 cm/½ in
cubes
120 g/4 oz chicken livers, trimmed
and cut into small pieces
150 ml/¼ pint dry white wine
salt and pepper
pinch of ground cloves

pinch of ground cinnamon
generous pinch of grated nutmeg
1 tbsp truffle paste
60 g/2 oz prosciutto, thickly sliced
120 g/4 oz cooked garden peas
60 g/2 oz Parmesan, freshly grated
300 g/10 oz **penne** *or short*
macaroni
150 ml/¼ pint strong meat stock
1 tbsp white flour
3 tbsp dried breadcrumbs
2 hard-boiled eggs, shelled
1 egg yolk and 2 tbsp of milk for
glazing

For the pastry

250 g/9 oz plain flour
1 tsp salt
1 egg plus 1 egg yolk

100 g/3½ oz caster sugar
120 g/4 oz unsalted butter, diced

First make the pastry. Sift the flour with the salt into a mound on a work surface. Make a well in the middle and add the egg, the egg yolk, 2 tablespoons of water and the sugar. Mix lightly, then add the butter. Blend together by pushing small pieces of dough away from you, using the heel of your hand. If the dough is too dry, add a little more cold water. Gather the dough into a ball and wrap in foil or clingfilm lightly dusted with flour. Chill in the refrigerator for at least 1 hour. The pastry may also be made in a food processor.

Soak the dried porcini in a cupful of hot water for 30 minutes. Lift them out carefully and rinse gently under cold running water. Dry them and cut them into small pieces. Strain the soaking liquid through a sieve lined with kitchen paper.

Put 40 g/1½ oz of the butter and the *luganega* in a small heavy frying pan and sauté for 7 minutes, breaking the sausage up with a fork. Add the chicken and sauté for 2 minutes, stirring frequently, then mix in the chicken livers. Cook for 2 minutes or so, then add the wine and boil fast for 1 minute to evaporate the alcohol. Add salt and pepper to taste and about 4 tablespoons of the porcini soaking liquid.

Reduce the heat and cook until nearly all the liquid has evaporated. Add a couple of tablespoons of hot water and continue cooking for about 5 minutes, stirring occasionally. The meat should cook in very little liquid but should not be allowed to cook dry. Check the seasonings.

Meanwhile melt 15 g/½ oz of the remaining butter in a small heavy saucepan. Add the chopped porcini and cook over a low heat for about 2 minutes. Add the cloves, cinnamon, nutmeg and salt and pepper to taste, and a couple more tablespoons of the porcini soaking liquid. Cook, stirring occasionally, for 5 minutes, then pour the sauce into the pan with the sausage and chicken mixture. Mix well and cook for a further 5 minutes. Transfer the contents of the pan with all the cooking juices to a bowl, add the truffle paste and mix well. Cut the prosciutto into thin short strips and add to the bowl together with the peas and all but two tablespoons of the Parmesan. Mix well. Set aside for the flavours to combine.

Now cook the pasta in plenty of boiling salted water until very *al dente*. It will finish cooking later, in the oven.

While the pasta is cooking, heat the stock. Blend the remaining butter with the flour and add it bit by bit to the simmering stock. Do not add the next teaspoonful of the mixture until the previous one has been completely incorporated. When all the mixture has been added, withdraw the pan from the heat and set aside.

Drain the pasta and turn it into a large bowl. Toss with the stock and butter mixture.

About 1 hour before you want to cook the dish, remove the dough from the refrigerator and allow to become pliable at room temperature.

Heat the oven to 220°C/425°F/Gas 7.

Generously butter a 20 cm/8 in spring-form cake tin.

Roll out about one-third of the dough into a 20 cm/8 in circle on a piece of greaseproof paper. Turn the sheet of paper over on to the bottom of the tin and peel off the paper. Rolling the dough out on to greaseproof paper makes it much easier to transfer. Roll out half the remaining dough into a wide strip and use this to line the sides of the tin. Seal the joins with cold water. Sprinkle the remaining cheese and the breadcrumbs over the base. Cover with a layer of pasta and then a layer of filling. Build up these alternate layers until you have used up all the ingredients. Cut the eggs into segments and push them here and there into the filling.

Roll out the remaining dough into a circle and cover the pasta. Seal the dough lid to the side strip. Brush the top of the pie with the egg yolk beaten with 1 teaspoon of salt. If you wish, make a few decorations with the dough trimmings, brush with egg yolk and milk glaze and fix to the top of the pie. Pierce the top with the prongs of a fork in several places to let the steam escape. Bake for about 10 minutes, then turn the oven down to 165°C/325°F/Gas 3 and bake for a further 25 minutes.

Remove from the oven and leave to stand for about 10 minutes. Unclip the tin and carefully transfer the pie to a serving dish. Don't try to lift the pie off the bottom of the tin; being heavy, and still hot, it could easily break.

PREPARATION

The pastry dough can be prepared up to 3 days in advance and refrigerated. It can also be frozen. The filling can be made up to 1 day in advance and refrigerated. The *timballo* must be assembled no longer than 30 minutes before being baked.

* *Insalata di finocchi, cicoria belga e arancie*

FENNEL, BELGIAN CHICORY AND ORANGE SALAD

---

2 medium-sized fennel bulbs,
   preferably the round bulbs which
   are sweeter than the long ones
2 oranges
4 chicory heads

the juice of 1½ lemons
5 tbsp olive oil
salt
2 dozen black olives

Remove the stalk, green foliage and any bruised or brown parts from the fennel bulbs. (Keep them for a soup, except, of course, the brown bits.) Cut the bulbs in quarters lengthwise, then cut them across into thin slices. Wash the slices, drain and dry them thoroughly, then put them in a bowl.

Peel the oranges to the quick and slice them across thinly on a plate so as not to waste any of the juice. Cut the smaller slices in half and the larger slices into quarters. Add to the fennel in the bowl together with the juice collected on the plate.

Cut the chicory into rings. Wash and dry thoroughly and then add to the bowl.

Beat the lemon juice and the olive oil together, add salt and pour over the prepared vegetables. Toss very well. Taste and adjust salt. (Pepper is never added to this kind of salad in Sicily: its hotness would clash with the sweetness of the fennel and the orange.)

Transfer the salad to a deep dish and scatter the olives over it, or serve straight from the bowl.

PREPARATION

The vegetables can be sliced up to 1 day in advance and kept, wrapped in a tea-towel, in the fridge. The oranges, too, can be prepared up to 1 day in advance and refrigerated in a covered bowl.

A TUSCAN LUNCH FOR 12

Crostini alla toscana
CHICKEN LIVER CANAPÉS

Arista alla toscana con fagioli all'uccelletto
TUSCAN ROAST PORK WITH *CANNELLINI* BEANS AND
TOMATOES SAUTÉED IN OIL

Insalate di stagione
SEASONAL SALADS

Fave e pecorino
BROAD BEANS AND PECORINO CHEESE, OR A PLATTER
OF CHEESES

Panforte e vinsanto
SIENESE FRUIT AND SPICE CAKE WITH *VINSANTO*

For about ten years in the 70s we had a little house on a hill in Chianti and spent many happy holidays there. Then one morning when I was shopping in Gaiole, our local village, I realized to my dismay that there were no fewer than seven British cars in the little village square. Chianti had become Chiantishire! We decided that somewhere which had become the playground of the British upper class was not for us, so we sold Cornia, our house, and bought a flat in Venice, where the residents, at least, are Italian.

While we were in Tuscany we had many pleasant times with the locals, always over a glass or two, or more, of *vinsanto*. Sometimes we had lunch with them, and my menu here is typical of that sort of occasion. There is, I must confess, one fewer course in my menu than in those authentic Tuscan feasts because I have omitted the tagliatelle that used to follow the antipasto. So the antipasto becomes our first course.

I give a recipe for the *crostini* that are part of the antipasto, but you should also serve two or three of the following dishes: a platter of salame, prosciutto, mortadella and other pork meats with a bowl of figs or a dish of slices of yellow melon as accompaniment, some *bruschetta* (page 109) and/or a rustic salad of lentils cooked with all the *odori* (onion, garlic, celery and herbs), garnished with rocket and dressed only with the best olive oil.

The main course, the *arista*, can be served hot or cold; in Tuscany, traditionally, it is served cold. The strange name of this dish is a mystery. Many cookery writers, myself included, have subscribed to the theory that it comes from an episode that took place at a banquet during the Ecumenical Council in Florence in 1439. A Greek patriarch who was there, having tasted the dish, is supposed to have expressed his approval by exclaiming, 'Aristos!' – the best. The story, however charming, has proved to be unfounded, since the dish *arista* is mentioned in a novella written by Franco Sacchetti some hundred years before the Council.

Another odd name is that of the *fagioli all'uccelletto*, *uccelletto* meaning little bird. Many theories have been advanced as to its origin. The only one I find convincing is that beans prepared in this way are the traditional accompaniment to *uccelletti*, which the Tuscans are passionate about shooting and inordinately fond of eating. *Fagioli all'uccelletto* can also be made *in bianco* – without tomato. The two versions are equally good.

The salad I leave to you, but whatever it is, make a lot and dress it with plenty of extra virgin olive oil. My recipe is on page 368. Another good dish is the tomatoes with basil on page 363.

If your lunch takes place in the spring, you can put on the table a bowl of young broad beans and a whole Tuscan pecorino cheese. Do not bother to pod the beans. Let your guests do it and invite them to cut a wedge of pecorino to eat with the beans. It is a perfect marriage as long as the broad beans are really young and tender.

If broad beans are already past their best, serve the pecorino with other Italian cheeses. At the same time put on the table two *panforti*, the deliciously spiced and honeyed cakes from Siena. Although I have made *panforte* at home, I am convinced that the ready-made *panforte* available in many Italian shops is better. Pass round a glass of sweet *vinsanto*, fortified wine, as the Tuscans do on such an occasion.

*

Crostini alla toscana

CHICKEN LIVER CANAPÉS

---

400 g/14 oz chicken livers
4 tbsp olive oil
½ celery stalk, very finely chopped
1 shallot, very finely chopped
2 small garlic cloves, peeled and
  chopped
3 tbsp fresh parsley, chopped
1 tbsp tomato purée
6 tbsp dry white wine

salt and freshly ground black
  pepper
15 ml/1 tbsp capers, rinsed and
  chopped
4 anchovy fillets, chopped
30 g/1 oz unsalted butter
3 tbsp extra virgin olive oil
1 or 2 French bread sticks

Remove the fat, gristle and any greenish bits from the chicken livers. Wash, dry and cut into small pieces.

Put the oil in a saucepan and, when just hot, add the celery, shallot, garlic and parsley and cook for 5–10 minutes until soft. Add the chicken livers and cook very gently – they must not fry – until they have lost their raw colour. Mix in the tomato purée and cook for 1 minute. Raise the heat, pour over the wine and reduce until nearly all the wine has evaporated. Lower the heat and add a little salt and plenty of pepper. Simmer gently for 10 minutes.

Remove the pan from the heat and add the capers and anchovies. Transfer the mixture to a chopping board and chop coarsely. If you use a food processor, be very careful not to reduce the mixture to a purée. Return the mixture to the saucepan and add the butter. Cook slowly for 2 minutes, stirring constantly.

Cut the French bread in slices and brush with olive oil. Toast in a hot oven, 200°C/400°F/Gas 6, for 6–7 minutes until crisp. When cool, spread with the chicken liver mixture and serve.

NOTE: the bread can be moistened with chicken stock mixed with *vinsanto*, instead of oil.

PREPARATION
The chicken liver mixture can be made up to 1 day in advance. Cover and refrigerate.

*   # *Arista alla toscana*

TUSCAN ROAST PORK

---

6 garlic cloves, peeled
4 rosemary sprigs, about 10 cm/
*   3½ in long*
2 tsp fennel seeds
salt and pepper

2 kg/4½ lb boned and rindless loin
*   of pork (boneless weight)*
4 cloves
120 ml/4 fl oz olive oil
150 ml/¼ pint dry white wine

Ask the butcher to give you the bones of the joint and to tie the joint into a neat roll.

Chop together the garlic, rosemary and fennel seeds, add salt and pepper and mix well. Make small deep incisions in the meat, along the grain, and push the mixture into the meat. Pat the rest of the mixture all over the meat and stick with the cloves. Rub with half the oil and place the joint in a bowl. Allow to stand for 4–5 hours, outside the fridge, covered with a plate.

Heat the oven to 180°C/350°F/Gas 4.

Put the meat and the bones in a roasting tin and pour in the rest of the oil. Roast in the oven for 2½–3 hours, basting every 20 minutes or so. The meat is ready when it is very tender.

Turn the oven up to 220°C/425°F/Gas 7 for the last 10 minutes to brown the meat, then transfer it to a wooden board. Remove and discard the bones.

Remove as much fat as you can from the surface of the cooking liquid. Deglaze with the wine and 150ml/¼ pint of hot water, boiling briskly while scraping the bottom of the tin to loosen the tasty nuggets of residue. Reduce to about a third. This is a very concentrated juice that can also be eaten with the meat when it is cold. Remove the fat which will have solidified on the top and you will find a delicious soft jelly underneath.

If you want to serve the pork hot, remove the string from the meat, carve and place neatly on the serving dish. Spoon the deglazing liquid over it.

PREPARATION

Like any other roast joint, if you want to serve it hot you cannot cook it ahead of time. If you prefer to serve the *arista* cold, as the Tuscans do, you can cook it up to 2 days in advance and refrigerate it, well wrapped in foil. Remove from the fridge at least 2 hours before serving to bring back to room temperature.

*

Fagioli all'uccelletto

CANNELLINI BEANS AND TOMATOES SAUTÉED IN OIL

6 tbsp extra virgin olive oil
2 sprigs of fresh sage
2 sprigs of fresh rosemary
4 garlic cloves, chopped
450 g/1 lb ripe tomatoes, preferably plum tomatoes, blanched and skinned

salt and pepper
4 tins cannellini *beans, 400 g/ 14 oz size, or 1.5kg/3½lb cooked beans*

Put three-quarters of the oil, the sage, rosemary and garlic in a pot, preferably an earthenware one of the type you can put directly on the heat. Sauté until the herbs begin to sizzle.

Meanwhile chop the tomatoes coarsely and then add them to the pan. Season with salt and pepper and cook until the oil separates, about 20 minutes. Now rinse and drain the *cannellini*. Add to the pan and continue cooking for about 15 minutes, until everything is well blended.

Before serving, pour over the remaining olive oil and check seasoning.

PREPARATION

The dish can be prepared up to 2 days in advance. Cover and refrigerate and gently reheat, or bring back to room temperature if you want to serve the dish cold with the cold *arista*.

A BOLOGNESE FEAST FOR 30

Maccheroni gratinati con la luganega e l'aglio
BAKED MACARONI WITH SAUSAGE AND GARLIC

Lasagne verdi al forno
BAKED GREEN LASAGNE

Penne ai quatro formaggi
PENNE WITH FOUR CHEESES

Tagliatelle gratinate al prosciutto cotto e piselli
BAKED TAGLIATELLE WITH HAM AND PEAS

Insalata di fagiolini e pomodori
GREEN BEAN AND TOMATO SALAD

Insalata di finocchio al parmigiano
FENNEL AND PARMESAN SALAD

Crostata di conserva di amarena
MORELLO CHERRY JAM TART

La bonissima
WALNUT AND HONEY PIE (page 274)

Pasta is fashionable, pasta is nourishing, pasta is easy. To any Italian living abroad, pasta is also the food that, more than any other, brings back nostalgic memories of so many meals enjoyed over the years in so many places. A charming anecdote about Rossini, 'the greatest composer among gourmets and the greatest gourmet among composers', illustrates how pasta can linger in the memory. A man sat next to Rossini at a dinner party one day and said, 'You remember me, I'm sure, Maestro. I met you at that dinner given in your honour when there was a splendid macaroni pie'. Rossini thought for some time, then slowly shook his head. 'I certainly remember the macaroni pie,' he said, 'but I'm afraid I don't remember you.'

Fifteen years ago I wrote a book, *Portrait of Pasta*, to try and make this marvellous food better known and understood. As well as mouth-watering recipes it had hard facts on the non-fattening and health-giving properties of pasta. Since then I have written two other books on the same much-loved subject, but no matter how many pasta recipes I have to test, I am always pleased to eat the results. I think I must be the original pastaholic.

Bologna is the home of many of the best pasta dishes and pasta is the ideal food for a large party. Thus you will find that this Bolognese pasta feast avoids those two torments, the pre-prandial banishment to the kitchen and the nagging worry as to whether the dish will taste the way it should. The pasta dishes I have chosen are all baked ones, which means that they can be prepared in advance. You can even taste and correct them in advance and thus be sure of bringing to the table just what you had in mind. You only need to heat them in the oven before serving them. By the time everyone begins to help themselves the dishes will have been out of the oven long enough for the flavours to blend. And as these four pasta dishes go well together, four small portions can happily share the same plate. Put a few bowls full of freshly grated Parmesan here and there for your guests to help themselves.

After that you need a few different salads, but please, serve them after and not with the pasta. Not only does pasta need no accompaniment (especially true in the case of these dishes based on cream and béchamel), but also the sauces would jar with the acidity of the vinegar and the fruitiness of the oil in the salad dressing. And if you clear the table of the pasta dishes and bring in the salad bowls it will help to give the feeling of another course – and more food!

The green salad should be a mixture of round or Cos lettuce, lamb's lettuce, chicory, endive and radicchio. On page 368 you will find the recipe for my kind of *insalata verde*. Make two large bowls of green salad because everybody will take some.

With the green salad I suggest you serve two or three other salads. The green bean and tomato salad in this menu is a classic. Another classic is the courgette and tomato salad on page 25, which you might prefer if the courgettes in the shops are better than the beans. The other salads I would recommend are the celeriac and radicchio on page 284 and the tomato, cucumber and peppers on page 129.

The fennel and Parmesan salad is the perfect transition between the salads and the cheeses to follow, or to be eaten with them. Serve at least four different cheeses, with plenty of good bread. In Italy we never serve butter with cheese, and it would be wrong to put butter on the table when you serve the cheese with the salad.

For pudding I would choose two sweets based on fruit and two traditional sweets from Emilia-Romagna, a sharp morello cherry tart and a rich walnut and honey pie, for which you will find the recipe on page 274. Instead of morello cherry jam, I have sometimes used damson jam, which is delicious when – as so often – it is home-made. Whatever you use, the jam must be sharp and fruity.

Prepare a cleansing, refreshing sweet based only on fruit, such as your favourite fruit salad, any seasonal fruits and one or two of my fruit desserts. Choose the Sharon fruits with lime juice (page 192), the oranges and kiwi fruit (page 39) or the peaches with raspberry sauce (page 117), according to the season.

✳✳   *Maccheroni gratinati con la luganega e l'aglio*

BAKED MACARONI WITH SAUSAGE AND GARLIC

2 heads of garlic, peeled	*180 g/6 oz butter, 150 g/5 oz*
1 kg/2 lb luganega or other coarse-	*white flour*
grained, pure pork sausage such	*90 g/3 oz Parmesan, grated*
as Toulouse	*90 g/3 oz Gruyère, grated*
2 tbsp oil, vegetable, corn or olive	*salt and pepper*
a dozen fresh sage leaves	*¼ of a nutmeg*
a sprig of fresh rosemary	*1 kg/2 lb penne, macaroni or any*
a thin béchamel sauce made with	*other large tubular pasta shape*
2.25 litres/4 pints full-fat milk,	*40 g/1½ oz butter*

Put the peeled garlic cloves in a small saucepan and cover with about 300 ml/½ pint of water. Bring the water to the boil, cover the pan tightly and cook very gently for about 1 hour. Check that there is always some water in the pan and add some boiling water if necessary. At the end there should be no more than 3 or 4 tablespoons of water left.

Purée the contents of the pan through a chinois or a food mill or in the food processor. Alternatively it is quite easy to mash them with a fork, which saves washing-up.

While the garlic is boiling, skin the sausage, crumble it and put it into a non-stick frying pan with the oil. Chop the herbs and add to the sausage. Fry over low heat until the fat runs out, then turn the heat up to medium and fry until the meat is lovely and brown, about 20 minutes. Remove the sausage meat from the pan with a slotted spoon, leaving the fat behind.

To make the béchamel sauce, heat the milk until it just begins to bubble at the edge. Meanwhile melt the butter in a heavy-based saucepan over low heat. Blend in the flour, stirring vigorously. Now draw the pan off the heat and add the hot milk, a few tablespoons at a time. You must let the flour mixture absorb each addition thoroughly before going on to the next stage.

When all the milk has been absorbed, return the pan to the heat. Add salt to taste and bring to the boil. I recommend cooking the sauce for at least 20 minutes, setting the pan either in a bain-marie or over a flame disperser. Long, slow cooking makes the sauce more velvety and delicate. Mix in the garlic purée and the grated cheeses. Season with a lot of pepper and with the nutmeg. Taste and add salt, bearing in mind that the sausage might well be on the salty side.

Generously butter a large oven dish or a lasagne tin.

Cook the pasta in plenty of boiling salted water. If you do not have a large enough saucepan, cook it in two batches. Always cook pasta in plenty of water. Drain it when still slightly under-cooked and dress it immediately with about three-quarters of the béchamel and with the sausage meat. Turn it into the prepared dish. Spread the remaining béchamel all over the top and dot with butter.

Heat the oven to 200°C/400°F/Gas 6 about three-quarters of an hour before you want to serve the dish. When the oven is hot, put the pasta dish into it and bake until hot. To test if it is hot enough, insert a knife in the middle of the dish and feel the bits that stick to the blade. Let the dish stand for a few minutes outside the oven before bringing it to the table.

PREPARATION
The whole dish can be prepared up to 1 day in advance, covered with clingfilm and refrigerated. It can also be frozen, although I find that freezing pasta alters its flavour slightly.

*** *Lasagne verdi al forno*
BAKED GREEN LASAGNE

---

lasagne verdi *made with 3 eggs,*
330 g/12 oz unbleached white
flour and 200 g/7 oz cooked or
frozen leaf spinach, or
700 g/1½ lb fresh lasagne

verdi, *or 500 g/1 lb 2 oz dried*
lasagne verdi
1 tbsp vegetable oil
150 g/5 oz freshly grated Parmesan
30 g/1 oz butter, melted

For the ragù

60 g/2 oz unsalted butter
100 ml/3½ fl oz olive oil
100 g/3½ oz pancetta *or*
unsmoked streaky bacon, finely
chopped
2 small onions, finely chopped
1 carrot, finely chopped
2 celery stalks, finely chopped
2 garlic cloves, finely chopped

2 bay leaves
2 tbsp tomato purée
450 g/1 lb lean chuck or braising
steak, minced
300 ml/½ pint dry white wine
300 ml/½ pint meat stock
salt and freshly ground black
pepper

For the béchamel sauce

1.5 litres/2½ pints full-fat milk
150 g/5 oz unsalted butter
120 g/4 oz flour

salt
3 pinches of grated nutmeg

First make the *ragù*. Heat the butter and oil in a saucepan and cook the *pancetta* for 2 minutes. Add the onion, and when it has begun to soften add the carrot, celery, garlic and bay leaves. Cook for a couple of minutes, stirring constantly. Add the tomato purée and cook over a low heat for 30 seconds. Put in the minced steak and cook briskly for 3–4 minutes, until the meat has lost its raw colour, stirring with a fork to break up the lumps. Splash with the wine and boil for 2 minutes or so, until the liquid has almost evaporated. Fish out and discard the bay leaf and pour in the stock. Mix well, season and simmer, uncovered, for about 2 hours, adding a little warm water if the sauce gets too dry. The heat should be at its lowest, so that just a few bubbles break the surface of the sauce.

To make the béchamel sauce, heat the milk until it begins to bubble at the edge. Meanwhile melt the butter in a heavy-based saucepan over low heat. Blend in the flour, stirring vigorously. Now draw the pan off the heat and add the hot milk, a few tablespoons at a time. You must let the flour mixture absorb each addition thoroughly before going on to the next stage.

When all the milk has been absorbed, return the pan to the heat. Add salt to taste and bring to the boil. Cook over the gentlest heat for 20 minutes, stirring frequently. You can put the pan over a flame disperser or in a bain-marie to save the worry of frequent stirring. Add the nutmeg and check seasonings. The sauce should have the consistency of thin double cream.

If you are making your own lasagne, turn to page 374 for making the pasta dough, and to page 376 for cutting the lasagne. If your lasagne are home-made, bring a large saucepan of salted water to the boil. Add the vegetable oil. Place a large bowl of cold water near the cooker and lay some clean and dry kitchen cloths nearby. When the water boils, drop in 5 or 6 rectangles of pasta and stir with a wooden spoon. Cook for about 1 minute after the water has come back to the boil, then lift each sheet of pasta out with a fish slice and plunge it into the bowl of cold water. Lift it out and lay it on the cloths. Repeat this operation until all the pasta is cooked. Pat the top of the cooked lasagne dry.

If you are using bought lasagne, cook according to the directions on the packet.

Heat the oven to 200°C/400°F/Gas 6.

Butter a 35 × 25 cm (14 × 10 in) ovenproof dish generously. Spread 2 tablespoons of the *ragù* over the bottom, cover with a layer of lasagne and spread over a little *ragù* and some béchamel. Sprinkle with grated Parmesan. Cover with another layer of lasagne and repeat until all ingredients are used, finishing with a layer of béchamel. Sprinkle with the remaining Parmesan and dribble the melted butter all over the top.

Bake in the oven for 15–20 minutes, until the top has formed a golden crust. Allow the dish to settle for at least 5 minutes before serving.

PREPARATION

The dish can be prepared totally up to 1 day in advance and refrigerated, covered with clingfilm. The meat sauce can be made up to 3 days in advance and refrigerated. It also freezes well.

*   # Penne ai quattro formaggi

PENNE WITH FOUR CHEESES

---

700 g/1½ lb penne *or other*
    tubular pasta
salt
90 g/3 oz Gruyère
90 g/3 oz Bel Paese

150 g/5 oz mozzarella
125 g/4 oz unsalted butter, melted
75 g/2½ oz freshly grated
    Parmesan
cayenne pepper

Drop the pasta into rapidly boiling salted water.

While the pasta is cooking, cut the Gruyère, Bel Paese and mozzarella into small pieces.

Heat the oven to 200°C/400°F/Gas 6.

Drain the pasta when it is still slightly undercooked and return it immediately to the saucepan. Add half the butter, the Parmesan, all the other cheeses and 2 or 3 pinches of cayenne. Mix thoroughly.

Smear an ovenproof dish with a little of the melted butter and transfer the pasta into it. Dribble the remaining butter all over the top and bake for about 15 minutes.

PREPARATION

The dish can be prepared up to 1 day in advance. Dribble the butter on the top just before you put the dish in the oven, and bake for a little longer to heat the pasta through.

** *Tagliatelle gratinate al prosciutto cotto e piselli*

BAKED TAGLIATELLE WITH HAM AND PEAS

Tagliatelle made with 4 eggs and 400 g/14 oz unbleached white flour, or 1 kg/2 lb fresh shop-bought tagliatelle, or 500 g/1 lb 2 oz dried egg tagliatelle	*salt* 300 g/10 oz *best ham, unsmoked* 450 g/1 lb *cooked garden peas or* frozen petits pois, *thawed* 600 ml/1 pint *single cream*
60 g/2 oz *unsalted butter* 2 shallots, *very finely chopped*	*pepper* 60 g/2 oz *Parmesan, freshly grated* 120 ml/4 fl oz *full-fat milk*

If you are making your own tagliatelle, do this first, following the instructions on page 374, and then prepare the sauce.

Melt a knob of butter in a frying pan. Add the shallots and a pinch of salt and sauté until soft. The salt helps to release the moisture from the shallots, thus preventing them from browning.

Meanwhile cut the ham into thin short strips and add to the shallots. Cook for a minute or so and stir in the peas. Let them *insaporire* – take up the flavour – for a minute or two and then pour in the cream. Bring slowly to the boil and simmer for 5 minutes. Add salt and pepper to taste. The sauce is now ready.

Cook the pasta in plenty of boiling salted water. Drain when very *al dente*, but do not overdrain. Return the pasta immediately to the cooking pot and dress with the remaining butter and the cheese. Spoon over the sauce and toss thoroughly.

Heat the oven to 200°C/400°F/Gas 6.

Choose an oven dish large enough for the tagliatelle to spread loosely and not pile up too thickly. Butter the dish generously and fill it with the pasta. Just before you want to put the dish in the oven, heat the milk and dribble a few tablespoons all over the dish. (This is to keep the tagliatelle moist while baking.) Bake for about 15–20 minutes, until hot all through.

PREPARATION

The dish can be prepared, apart from the milk, up to 1 day in advance and refrigerated, covered with foil. Add the milk before baking and bake for a little longer to heat the pasta properly. This dish does not freeze well.

Insalata di fagiolini e pomodori

GREEN BEAN AND TOMATO SALAD

---

1 kg/2 lb green beans
salt
7 tbsp olive oil
450 g/1 lb firm ripe tomatoes

6 garlic cloves, bruised
2 tbsp lemon juice
freshly ground black pepper
a dozen fresh basil leaves

Top and tail the beans. Wash well and cook uncovered in plenty of boiling salted water until *al dente*. I find the *al dente* point easy to catch, since the beans give off a characteristic smell when they are nearly cooked. Remember to add a good deal of salt to the water, as green beans are very insipid. Drain and refresh quickly under cold water. Blot with kitchen paper, heap them in the middle of a dish and dress with a third of the oil while they are still warm.

While the beans are cooking, drop the tomatoes into the beans saucepan. Count up to eight, then retrieve them with a slotted spoon and plunge them immediately into a bowl of cold water. Skin them and cut them into wedges or slices, discarding the seeds.

Put the rest of the oil, the garlic, lemon juice and plenty of pepper in a bowl and leave to infuse for at least 1 hour.

Lay the tomatoes all round the beans and season them with salt and pepper. Remove and discard the garlic from the little sauce and spoon the sauce over the beans and the tomatoes. Scatter the basil leaves over the salad.

PREPARATION

The beans can be cooked up to 2 days in advance and refrigerated in a closed container. The tomatoes can be skinned and cut a few hours in advance, but they must be dressed at the last minute.

* *Insalata di finocchio al Parmigiano*

FENNEL AND PARMESAN SALAD

The best Parmesan for this salad is a young cheese. You can also use *grana padano*, which is cheaper than the authentic Parmesan, properly known as Parmigiano-Reggiano. The best fennel is the kind with round bulbs as it is sweeter than the long fennel.

---

6 *fennel bulbs*	4 *tbsp lemon juice*
120 *ml/8 tbsp extra virgin olive*	*salt and pepper*
oil	120 *g/4 oz good fresh Parmesan*

Remove the stalks and any outside brown leaves from the fennel. Cut the bulbs vertically into quarters and then cut them across into very thin strips. Wash in plenty of water, drain and dry well.

Put the fennel in a salad bowl and dress with the oil, lemon, salt and pepper. Do not put in too much salt, since you have to add the cheese, which is salty. Toss thoroughly and taste. Leave for about 30 minutes.

Cut the Parmesan into slivers and lay on top of the fennel.

PREPARATION
The fennel can be sliced and washed the day before and kept in the refrigerator. It should be wrapped in a clean tea-cloth or a small clean pillow-case.

✳✳✳   *Crostata di conserva di amarena*

MORELLO CHERRY JAM TART

For the Pastry

225 g/8 oz flour
½ tsp salt
100 g/3½ oz granulated sugar

the grated rind of ½ lemon
125 g/4 oz cold unsalted butter
2 egg yolks

For the filling

4 tbsp ground almonds
350 g/12 oz morello cherry or
  damson jam

the juice of ½ lemon
1 egg yolk and 2 tbsp of milk for
  glazing

To make the pastry, pile the flour on a work surface. Mix in the salt, sugar and lemon rind and rub in the butter. Add the egg yolks and work quickly to form a ball. If you prefer, make the pastry in a food processor. Wrap in foil and chill for at least 30 minutes.

Heat the oven to 200°C/400°F/Gas 6.

Butter a 20 or 22 cm (8 or 9 in) tart tin with a loose bottom and sprinkle with 1 tbsp of flour. Shake off excess flour.

Remove the dough from the fridge. Put aside about one-third and roll out the rest into a circle. Line the prepared tin with the circle of dough and press it down firmly into the angle between the base and the side. Sprinkle the ground almonds over the bottom.

Put the jam in a bowl and mix in the lemon juice. Spread the jam over the circle of dough. Roll out the reserved dough and cut several strips about 1 cm (a little under ½ in) wide. Place these strips over the tart to form a lattice that goes right across the tart. Don't worry if you have to make one or two joins in the strips; once the tart is baked the joins won't show. Brush the pastry lattice with the egg yolk and milk glaze.

Bake in the preheated oven for about 10 minutes. Turn the heat down to 180°C/350°F/Gas 4 and bake for a further 20 minutes until the pastry turns a lovely light golden brown. Remove from the tin and transfer to a wire rack to cool. In Italy, as in France, tarts are served without cream.

PREPARATION

Make the *crostata* on the day you want to eat it. The pastry can be made up to 2 days in advance and refrigerated, wrapped in foil. It also freezes well.

Summer Menus

A LUNCH FOR 6

Pasta al sugo
PASTA WITH TOMATO SAUCE

Pollo all'aglio
CHICKEN WITH GARLIC

Formaggio e frutta
CHEESE AND FRUIT

O f all the dishes with which to start a meal in Italy, *pasta al pomodoro* is surely the most common. In millions of Italian families, when the children come home from school at lunchtime – few children eat at school – the mother *mette giù la pasta*, drops the pasta into a large pot of boiling water. The sauce is the usual sauce, called simply *il sugo* or *la salsa*, since the *di pomodoro* is understood.

Just as there are millions of families, so there are millions of *sughi*. Some of the ones I have had in various homes have stuck in my mind particularly. One such is made by Micki di San Giuliano, a Sicilian friend. She puts about a dozen cloves of peeled garlic with the tomatoes and the oil, and nothing else. Then, when the sauce is eventually cooked, she takes all the garlic out. 'Eventually' is the key word: her sauce cooks slowly for an hour and a half. In Italy, tomato sauces are usually cooked for a long time – 35 minutes is the minimum, while an hour is usually regarded as the optimum cooking time. Admittedly there are a few kinds of *sughi* that are hardly cooked at all, but they are of a different generation; they are of recent birth, children of *la nuova cucina* and not part of the tradition of family cooking.

I have two or three favourite *sughi* of my own, but recently I have adopted two given to me by two of my children: *il sugo di Guy* and *il sugo di Julia*. Guy used not to be interested in food, even though I prepared it for him with great love and care. Up to his school days he was the most difficult eater any mother ever came across. He had perfected two special tricks. One was to keep little pellets of food tucked away somewhere in his mouth, pellets which we later found dotted around the house or in the garden. The second trick was to be able to regurgitate on the spot any food which I finally managed to make him swallow.

So for years Guy and good food were poles apart. Then, a few years ago, he went to live in Pavia, in southern Lombardy, and it has been pleasant to see the change that has resulted from living in a country where food has a high priority. Guy has now developed an excellent palate; he loves to talk about food, to exchange recipes and even to cook for me. His tomato sauce is a northern Italian one, by which I mean that it is more complex than tomato sauces from the south, one of which is that made by his sister Julia.

Julia has always been a 'happy eater', and as such developed a discerning palate from the day she tasted her first solid meal. She now cooks very well, and when she went to be an *au pair* with some Neapolitan friends she came back with excellent recipes for vegetable *tourtes*, fish soups and, of course, pasta sauces.

I prefer Guy's sauce for large tubular pasta and for tagliatelle, while Julia's is certainly best for spaghetti. The oregano in Julia's sauce consists of the dried flowers of oregano plants, just as it does in southern Italy, where it is collected on the mountain slopes already dried on the plant. Oregano is the only herb sold and used dried in Italy; I cannot remember ever having heard of dried basil there. The unusual touch in this sauce lies in the fact that the basil is added at the beginning of the cooking. Julia was specifically told by her Neapolitan hostess that the basil flavour should not be all-pervading, as it would be if the basil were added at the end. It should just be an unidentifiable whiff.

Both recipes make enough sauce for about 450 g/1 lb of pasta, equal to 5–6 helpings. Both sauces are better if puréed through a food mill, because the occasional tomato seeds and pieces of skin are not minced into the sauce as they would be in a food processor. However, if you have not got a food mill, use a food processor.

My *pollo* with garlic is light and fresh and quite garlicky, though not too much so. The garlic loses its strength through being cooked a long time in its skin, an unusual method in Italian cooking. It is then puréed and spread on bread, which is a perfect accompaniment to the chicken. I like to surround the chicken joints with the sautéed mushrooms on page 371.

A bowl of salad on a side plate or served with a platter of cheeses afterwards would be ideal, and fresh fruit to follow in the real Italian manner.

*

Il sugo di Julia

JULIA'S TOMATO SAUCE

---

2 Spanish onions
6 tbsp extra virgin olive oil
3 garlic cloves, peeled
2 tbsp oregano, or a dozen fresh
    basil leaves

800 g/1¾ lb Italian tinned plum
    tomatoes
1 scant tsp sugar
salt and pepper

Slice the onions coarsely and put them into a saucepan with a very heavy bottom. I use a shallow, round earthenware pot with a long handle, of the kind that can be put directly over the heat. Earthenware keeps the heat well and cooks evenly at the lowest heat.

Add the oil, the garlic and the oregano or basil. Chop the tomatoes coarsely and add to the pan with their juice. (The easy way to chop tinned tomatoes is to pour out some of the juice and then to cut the tomatoes through with a pair of kitchen scissors.) Season with sugar, salt and pepper and bring to the boil.

Cook very gently for 1 hour, then purée the sauce through a food mill. Taste and check seasonings. The sauce is now ready to be spooned over 450 g/1 lb of spaghetti cooked *al dente*. Cook the pasta in plenty of salted boiling water in the usual way, or use the Agnesi method (see page 376) which allows you to leave the kitchen.

PREPARATION
The sauce keeps very well in the refrigerator for up to 4 days, and it freezes very well.

* # *Il sugo di Guy*

GUY'S TOMATO SAUCE

---

800 g/1¾ lb Italian tinned plum tomatoes	2 celery sticks, chopped
	5 tbsp extra virgin olive oil
2 tsp tomato purée	salt and pepper
1 tsp sugar	4 tbsp good red wine
2 onions, chopped	30 g/1 oz butter

Chop the tomatoes coarsely. This is best done by cutting the tomatoes with kitchen scissors while still in the tin, having first poured a little of the liquid into a heavy-based saucepan. Put them in a saucepan, together with the tomato purée, sugar, onion, celery, olive oil, salt and pepper. Cook for 15 minutes or so, then purée the sauce through a food mill.

Return the sauce to the pan and add the wine. Continue cooking for a further 40 minutes. Mix in the butter, taste and check seasoning.

Cook 450 g/1 lb of *penne* or other large tubular pasta in plenty of fast-boiling salted water until *al dente*. Drain and dress immediately with the sauce. If you prefer, cook the pasta using the method described on page 376, which is less demanding as there is no need to stay in the kitchen.

PREPARATION

The sauce can be made up to 4 days in advance and kept in the refrigerator. It can also be frozen.

** *Pollo all'aglio*

CHICKEN WITH GARLIC

---

1 fresh roasting chicken, about 1.5 kg/3¼ lb	2 large garlic heads
4 tbsp olive oil	150 ml/¼ pint dry white wine
2 sprigs of fresh rosemary	45 g/1½ oz butter
salt	3 tbsp chopped parsley
freshly ground black pepper	1 French bread stick, cut into slices 1 cm/½ in thick

---

Ask the butcher to cut the chicken into ten pieces: two wings, two drumsticks, two thighs, two pieces from each breast and two pieces from the back.

When you get home, remove and discard some of the loose fatty skin. Dry the chicken pieces with kitchen paper.

Heat the oil with the rosemary in a large sauté pan that can hold the chicken pieces in a single layer. When the oil is hot, slip in the pieces, skin side down, and sauté over lively heat until brown. Turn the pieces over and brown the other side. Season with salt and pepper.

While the chicken is browning, remove the outer skin from the garlic heads, separate the cloves and add them to the chicken. When the chicken pieces are nicely brown all over, splash with the wine and turn down the heat. Cook gently for 20 minutes, turning the pieces over two or three times during the cooking. Leave the pan uncovered so that the water that today's chickens often contain can evaporate. However, if the liquid has all dried up, add a couple of tablespoons of hot water.

When the chicken is done, fish out the garlic and reserve. Transfer the chicken to a heated platter and spoon over the cooking juices. Cover with foil and keep warm.

Heat the oven to 200°C/400°F/Gas 6.

Peel the garlic cloves and purée them through a food mill, a chinois or in a food processor. Blend in the butter with a fork and spread on the bread. Place the bread on a baking tray and bake in the oven for 8 minutes.

Sprinkle the chicken with the parsley and serve, surrounded by the garlicky toasts.

PREPARATION

The chicken can be cooked up to 2 days in advance. Keep in the fridge, in the saucepan if you can, and then reheat slowly. The garlic purée can also be prepared in advance. Reheat it in a bain-marie and add the butter before serving.

A DINNER FOR 6

Soffiato di capelli d'angelo
VERMICELLI SOUFFLÉ

Filetti di pesce con le scaglie di patate
FISH FILLETS WITH POTATO SCALES

Budino alla pesca
PEACH MOULD

The vermicelli soufflé is one of my oldest recipes, but this version has been revised, and improved, by a good friend and excellent cook. This soufflé is an elegant dish, yet it is quick and easy to make and, being supported by the vermicelli, there is little danger of it appearing at the table as a *soufflé tombé*.

I cannot remember how the fish dish came into my repertoire. I can only say that each time I make it I get the same enthusiastic reaction from my guests. This is one of the few dishes which I place directly on my guests' plates, as it is rather difficult to handle. I find it enough of a worry to transfer the fish once, from the cooking dish to the plate, without inflicting this worry on my friends, with the attendant risk of the fish finishing up on their laps. It is easy to do in the kitchen with two fish slices and no one watching.

I have found brill the best fish for this recipe, because of its size and the firmness of its flesh. Dover sole is good too, but it must be large enough for one sole to serve two people. Both fish give firm, thick fillets and their flavour is quite delicious, so that they lend themselves to simple treatment as in this recipe, where the only flavouring is melted butter and dill. Try to buy whole fish, and ask the fishmonger to fillet them. Bring home the heads, bones and skin for making a fish stock. Serve a good green salad after, not with the fish.

I love the peach mould, but then I love peaches. I am not sure to what degree my love of peaches is tied up with memories of my Italian childhood, but, be that as it may, this delicious pudding is not on the menu merely to assuage my nostalgia. It calls for peaches that are full of flavour, so buy white peaches if you can. They are usually more fragrant than yellow ones, but unfortunately they are rarer.

✶✶   ## *Soffiato di capelli d'angelo*

VERMICELLI SOUFFLÉ

---

100 g/3½ oz unsalted butter	60 g/2 oz Bel Paese
75 g/2½ oz freshly grated	½ tsp grated nutmeg
Parmesan	4 eggs, separated
600 ml/1 pint full-fat milk	2 egg whites
45 g/1½ oz flour	salt and pepper
60 g/2 oz Gruyère	200 g/7 oz dried egg vermicelli

Generously butter a 2 litre/3½ pint soufflé dish and sprinkle the buttered surface with a little grated Parmesan.

Prepare the béchamel. Heat the milk to simmering point. Melt 60 g/2 oz of the butter, blend in the flour and cook for 30 seconds. Draw the pan off the heat and gradually add the milk, beating vigorously with a wooden spoon. When all the milk has been incorporated, transfer the sauce to the top of a double boiler and cook with the lid on for at least half an hour. Stir occasionally. If you do not have a double boiler put the saucepan into another pan half full of simmering water.

Meanwhile grate the Gruyère and the Bel Paese through the large holes of a grater. When the béchamel is ready, mix in the cheeses and the nutmeg. Allow to cool a little and then add the egg yolks. Mix very thoroughly and add seasonings to taste, with emphasis on the pepper.

Heat the oven to 400°F/200°C/Gas 6.

Drop the vermicelli nests one at a time into plenty of salted boiling water to which you have added 15 ml/1 tbsp of oil. Mix quickly with a fork to prevent the pasta strands sticking together. Drain when very *al dente*, reserving 1 cupful of the water. Return the pasta immediately to the pan, adding the remaining butter and a couple of tablespoons of the reserved water. Mix thoroughly, then add the béchamel and cheese sauce. Toss well.

Whisk the egg whites until stiff but not dry and fold, by the spoonful, into the pasta mixture. Turn the mixture into the prepared soufflé dish and bake for 25 minutes, until the top is golden brown. Serve at once.

PREPARATION

The dish can be prepared up to 1 day in advance, but do not add the egg whites more than 1 hour before cooking the soufflé. It does not need to be kept in the fridge.

*** *Filetti di pesce con le scaglie di patate*

FISH FILLETS WITH POTATO SCALES

---

6 waxy potatoes, medium size	salt and pepper
6 large sole or brill fillets of about	90 g/3 oz unsalted butter
200 g/7 oz each	3 tbsp chopped dill

Wash the potatoes and boil them in their skins for 5 minutes. Peel them as soon as you can handle them and set aside to cool.

Skin the fillets if necessary and wash and dry them with kitchen paper. Sprinkle with salt and pepper and lay them in an oven dish, preferably metal, greased with 15 g/½ oz of the butter.

Heat the oven to 200°C/400°F/Gas 6.

When the potatoes are cold (they slice better when cold), cut them into very thin slices.

Sprinkle the dill over each fillet. Cover each fillet with the potatoes, laying them down like the scales of the fish. Sprinkle with salt and pepper. Melt the remaining butter and pour it over the potatoes, using a brush to cover all the gaps and corners.

Bake for 15–20 minutes, basting two or three times, until the potatoes are tender.

Pass the dish under a very hot grill to brown the surface of the potatoes. Place the fillets on individual heated plates and spoon over the cooking juices. Serve at once, handing round a bowl of steamed courgettes or mange-tout, lightly dressed with butter.

PREPARATION

The dish can be prepared, but not baked, up to 1 hour in advance, but no more.

**   *Budino alla pesca*

PEACH MOULD

---

700 g/1½ lb ripe peaches,
    preferably white
150 g/5 oz caster sugar
150 ml/¼ pint sweet white wine
4 gelatine leaves or 20g/¾ oz
    gelatine powder

1 lemon
200 ml/7 fl oz double cream
225 g/½ lb strawberries for
    garnish

If the peaches are really ripe they should peel quite easily. Otherwise, put them in a bowl and cover them with boiling water. Leave them for about 20 seconds and then refresh them under cold water. Peel them and cut them in half.

Poach the peaches with the sugar in the wine until tender. Leave to cool and then purée them coarsely in a food mill set with a large-hole disc. Alternatively, you can mash them up with a fork.

Soak the gelatine leaves in cold water until soft and then dissolve them in 2 tablespoons of the lemon juice over low heat. If you are using gelatine powder, sprinkle it over the lemon juice, leave to 'sponge' for a minute or so and then dissolve over very low heat until the liquid is clear.

Partly whip the cream and add to the peach purée. Mix a couple of tablespoons of the cream and peach mixture into the dissolved gelatine and then spoon this into the cream and peach mixture. Fold in very thoroughly with a metal spoon.

Wet a 1.2 litre/2 pint ring mould with cold water. Spoon the peach mixture into the mould and chill for at least 4 hours.

Wash and dry the strawberries. Put them in a bowl and sprinkle with 1 tablespoon of sugar and the remaining lemon juice. Cover the bowl and chill.

To unmould, run a palette knife down the side of the mould. Put a round dish over the mould and turn the mould over. If the pudding does not drop, place a cloth soaked with hot water over the mould and give the mould a few sharp jerks. You should now be able to lift the mould off the pudding.

Put some strawberries in the middle of the hole and others around the dish for garnish.

PREPARATION

The pudding can be prepared up to 1 day in advance and refrigerated. The strawberries must be prepared no longer than 2–3 hours in advance or they will 'cook' in the lemon juice.

A DINNER FOR 6

I ricchi e i poveri
PRAWN AND BEAN SALAD

Cannelloni di melanzane in salsa
AUBERGINE CANNELLONI WITH TOMATO SAUCE

Formaggio
CHEESE

Coppette di pompelmo con l'uva
GRAPEFRUIT BOWLS WITH GRAPES

I often serve meatless dinners, especially on informal occasions, perhaps because meat is far from being my favourite food.

The name of the first course, *I ricchi e i poveri*, means the rich and the poor, and it is easy to see why. It is a recent development from the tunny fish and bean salad, and was created by Tuscan restaurateurs who, though not afraid to alter old recipes, like to keep within their cuisine's tradition of simplicity. The dish is better made with raw prawns, which are slowly becoming more easily available. My fishmonger, John Nicholson of Chiswick, assures me that 'any good fishmonger now has them'. They are often frozen, but they are very much tastier than frozen cooked prawns. Allow them to thaw completely before you blanch them.

The *secondo* was given to me by a friend and superb cook, Betsy Newell, who runs a cookery school in Kensington, London. I seem to remember she had the aubergine cannelloni somewhere in Italy; to them she has added her special touch, the tomato sauce. Remember to buy plenty of good bread to mop up the tomato sauce, or prepare some potato purée.

Being a cosy informal dinner, it would be just right to bring to the table a platter of cheeses. This should contain at least three different cheeses, ranging from a strong blue cheese to one that is mild and soft.

· For pudding I suggest one based on fruit. Choose the peaches with raspberry sauce on page 117, or this delightfully fresh mixture of grapefruit and grapes. Hand round a dish of lemon-flavoured meringues (page 381) or the delectable almond crescents on page 380.

* *I ricchi e i poveri*

PRAWN AND BEAN SALAD

---

450 g/1 lb dried cannellini *beans,*
  or 4 tins cannellini *beans*
  (400 g/14 oz size)
2 *onions, cut in half*
2 *bay leaves*
9 *tbsp extra virgin olive oil*
450 g/1 lb *shrimps or prawns,*
  preferably raw

4 *tbsp lemon juice*
1 *tbsp wine vinegar*
a good pinch of cayenne pepper
salt
6 *tbsp chopped parsley, preferably*
  flat-leaf
1 *garlic clove, chopped (optional)*

If you are using dried *cannellini*, put them in a bowl and cover with cold water. Leave overnight. Drain and rinse them and put them in a stockpot (earthenware is best) with the onions and the bay leaves. Do not add salt, as it may make the beans burst. Cover with water by about 5 cm/2 in and cook at a slow and steady simmer until done. I cannot give you an exact time because it depends on the quality of the *cannellini* and how long they have been in storage, but it should take no longer than 1½ hours. Drain them (you can keep the liquid for a soup for another occasion) and fish out the onions and the bay leaves.

If you are using tinned *cannellini*, drain them into a pasta colander and rinse them.

Transfer the beans to a large bowl, toss with half the oil and, only if you are using dried *cannellini*, season with 2 teaspoons of salt. (The tinned ones are already salted.)

Now prepare the seafood. When I use tiny shrimps, which are usually sold already cooked, I remove only the heads, leaving the carapace on. The carapace has a lot of flavour and, in the small specimens, can be chewed quite easily. You can, of course, peel them if you prefer. The prawns, however, must be shelled. Place the seafood in a second bowl and toss with the lemon juice. If you use raw prawns, which are, of course, better, put them in a saucepan, cover with cold water and add 1 teaspoon of salt and 1 tablespoon of wine vinegar. Bring to the boil and cook until a white foam forms on the surface. Drain the prawns and shell them while they are still hot. Raw prawns are usually large, so I suggest you cut them into small pieces.

Half an hour before serving, mix the shrimps or prawns gently into the beans.

Bring a saucepan of water to the boil, place the bowl over it, cover the bowl with a lid and heat the beans and seafood in this form of bain-marie. When the mixture is warm, dress with the remaining oil, season with the cayenne and with salt if necessary and sprinkle with the chopped parsley and the optional garlic. Serve the salad while it is still warm.

PREPARATION

The beans can be cooked up to 2 days in advance and refrigerated, but the shrimps or prawns must be served the day they are bought.

*** *Cannelloni di melanzane in salsa*

AUBERGINE CANNELLONI WITH TOMATO SAUCE

---

450 ml/³⁄₄ pint tomato sauce	*100 g/3½ oz fresh white*
2 aubergines, each weighing about	*breadcrumbs*
350–400 g/12–14 oz	*2 tbsp chopped herbs: a mixture of*
salt and pepper	*rosemary, thyme, oregano,*
200 g/7 oz celery	*parsley*
200 g/7 oz leeks, white part only	*2 garlic cloves, finely chopped*
450 g/1 lb courgettes	*7 tbsp olive oil*
200 g/7 oz Emmental	

First make the tomato sauce on page 90 (Guy's tomato sauce).

Wash and dry the aubergines, leaving the skin on. Cut them lengthwise into 6 mm/¼ in thick slices. Salt the slices and place in a colander for at least 30 minutes to drain off the bitter juices.

Wash and dry the celery, leeks and courgettes and cut them into 5 cm/2 in julienne strips. Sauté the vegetables lightly in 3 tablespoons of the oil, beginning with the celery alone, as it takes a little longer to cook, then the courgettes and finally the leeks. Season with salt and pepper. Do not overcook the vegetables, but just cook enough to become tender. This takes about 6 minutes in all. Season well and set aside to cool.

Cut the Emmental into similar juliennes and mix into the vegetables. Mix together the breadcrumbs, herbs and garlic.

Rinse the aubergine slices well and pat dry. Brush each side with a light coating of olive oil. Cook quickly under or on a hot grill until soft, but not overcooked. Set aside.

Heat the oven to 200°C/400°F/Gas 6.

Choose an ovenproof serving dish into which the aubergine cannelloni will fit snugly in a single layer. Spread half the well-seasoned tomato sauce over the bottom of the serving dish. Season each slice of aubergine with salt and pepper. Place a rounded tablespoon of the vegetable/cheese mixture in the middle of each slice and wrap the aubergine round the filling along the length of the slice. Place the cannelloni in the dish and sprinkle with the herbed breadcrumb mixture. Dribble over the remaining oil. Place in the pre-heated oven for 10–15 minutes, until the cheese begins to melt and the cannelloni are thoroughly heated.

Remove from the oven and let the dish rest for 5 minutes before serving, for the flavours to blend. Serve the bundles with the remaining tomato sauce.

PREPARATION

The entire dish can be prepared 2 days in advance and refrigerated in the covered oven dish. Heat through just before serving.

*   *Coppette di pompelmo con l'uva*

GRAPEFRUIT BOWLS WITH GRAPES

---

3 grapefruit	*caster sugar to taste*
450 g/1 lb seedless grapes	*3 tbsp maraschino or kirsch*

Wash and dry the grapefruit and cut them in half. Prepare each half as you usually do, removing all the thin skin between the segments, and the central pith. Put the clean pieces of grapefruit in a bowl. Chill the shells.

Wash and dry the grapes and add to the bowl. Sprinkle with 3–4 tablespoons of sugar and splash with the liqueur. Taste and adjust the sugar, according to the sourness of the grapefruit.

Cover the bowl with clingfilm and chill for 2–3 hours, stirring the mixture two or three times while it chills. Put half a grapefruit shell on each plate and fill with the fruit mixture.

PREPARATION

If necessary you can prepare the grapefruit 1 day in advance and keep, covered, in the fridge. Mix the fruits together and add the liqueur and the sugar not more than 3 hours before serving.

A DINNER FOR 6

Pasticcio di pasta e melanzane in bianco
BAKED PASTA AND AUBERGINE

Filetti di San Pietro in salsa di broccoli
JOHN DORY FILLETS WITH BROCCOLI SAUCE

Sorbetto di limone al basilico
BASIL-FLAVOURED LEMON SORBET

The excellent *pasticcio* in this menu is another testimony to the aubergine's rare ability to blend with other flavours while retaining its own. Here, the aubergine, so often treated in a rustic and earthy manner, is combined with a delicate cheese-flavoured béchamel, a sauce usually connected with elegant dishes. The pasta shape I like best for this pasticcio is *ziti*; being thick and hollow they hold the béchamel, and they match the size of the aubergine. The only snag is that you have to break them into pieces.

I had the second course years ago at the Ristorante Dante in Bologna. I still remember my surprise at being offered such an unlikely combination as fish and broccoli in a restaurant in Bologna, where dishes outside the traditional, yet excellent, range of local cooking are viewed with suspicion. Here a fish is combined with a broccoli purée made mellow with cream.

The fish is the very fine but rather ugly John Dory, a fish with a very large head which accounts, with the backbone, for two-thirds of its weight. It has two black marks on each side, these being responsible for its name in both Italian and French – San Pietro and Saint Pierre. These marks, the legend says, are the fingerprints of Saint Peter who, taking pity on it after it was caught, threw the fish back into the sea. If I ever caught a John Dory I fear I should not throw it back into the sea. I find it one of the best fish, with its firm white flesh, suitable for cooking in most ways from the simplest to the most elaborate.

As accompaniment, a few buttered new potatoes would be very welcome, although not necessary, and afterwards a green salad, for which my favourite recipe is on page 368.

I really think that after these two courses, which are quite demanding, you will need only a sorbet with a sharp edge to cleanse the palate. I suggest this lemon sorbet, which I had at the Carraro restaurant in London. As well as being delicious, it looks very pretty, the pale lemon green being speckled with the dark green of the basil. While the flavour of the lemon is immediately identifiable, the basil seems to blend in so well as to be indistinct. Yet it is the basil that transforms an everyday lemon sorbet into a conversation stopper.

✳✳ *Pasticcio di pasta e melanzane in bianco*

BAKED PASTA AND AUBERGINE

700 g/1½ lb aubergines	*a bunch of parsley*
salt	*5 tbsp olive oil*
1 small dried chilli, seeded	*pepper*
2 garlic cloves	*350 g/12 oz* penne *or* ziti

For the béchamel

600 ml/1 pint full-fat milk	*30 g/1 oz flour*
2 bay leaves	*60 g/2 oz Gruyère*
60 g/2 oz unsalted butter	*60 g/2 oz Parmesan*

Wash and peel the aubergines. Cut them into thick slices and then into strips. Cut the strips to a length of about 4 cm/1¾ in, the same length as the pasta you are using. Put the aubergine in a colander, layered with salt, and leave to drain for about 1 hour. Rinse and dry with kitchen paper.

Now make the béchamel. Heat the milk with the bay leaves to boiling point and leave to infuse for about 30 minutes, if you can spare the time. Melt the butter, add the flour and cook for 1 minute or so, stirring constantly. Bring the milk back to simmering and add a little at a time to the roux, having removed the pan from the heat. Beat hard to incorporate. When all the milk has been added return the pan to the heat, add salt and pepper to taste and bring to the boil. Set the pan on a flame disperser or in a bain-marie and continue cooking for 20 minutes or so. Remove and discard the bay leaves.

Chop the chilli, garlic and parsley together and put in a frying pan with the oil. Fry gently for 1 minute and then add the aubergines. Sauté over low heat for about 7–10 minutes until soft, turning them over frequently. Taste and adjust seasonings. Turn off the heat and set aside.

Heat the oven to 200°C/400°F/Gas 6.

If you are using *ziti*, break them into 4–5 cm/1¾–2 in pieces. Boil the pasta in plenty of salted boiling water. Drain when very *al dente* and transfer to the pan with the aubergines.

Sauté the pasta for 2–3 minutes, mixing it well with the aubergines.

Butter a shallow dish of the right size for the pasta to come about 5–7 cm/2–3 in up the sides. Turn the pasta and aubergine mixture into it.

Cut the cheeses into pieces and process or grate them. Add to the béchamel. Taste and check seasonings. Pour the béchamel over the pasta and bake for 20 minutes until a light crust has formed at the top. Leave out of the oven for 5 minutes before serving, for the flavours to blend.

PREPARATION
The dish can be prepared 1 day in advance and covered with clingfilm. It does not need to be refrigerated. Bake for a little longer in the oven until hot all through.

** *Filetti di San Pietro in salsa di broccoli*

JOHN DORY FILLETS WITH BROCCOLI SAUCE

---

60 g/2 oz unsalted butter	*225 ml/8 fl oz fish broth (page 379)*
2 shallots, finely chopped	*1 kg/2 lb John Dory fillets*
salt and pepper	*4 tbsp double cream*
600 g/1¼ lb broccoli	

Heat the oven to 190°C/375°F/Gas 5

Put half the butter in a sauté pan. Add the shallots and a little salt and sauté for 5–7 minutes until soft.

Remove the tough outside layer of the broccoli stalks. Wash the broccoli thoroughly, cut them into small pieces and add to the shallots with a cupful of the fish broth. Cook until quite tender, not just *al dente*, adding a small ladleful of the broth whenever the broccoli are cooking with no liquid. They will take about 20 minutes. Season with salt and pepper to taste.

While the broccoli are cooking, butter an oven dish with the remaining butter and lay the fish fillets in it. Season with salt and pepper, cover the dish with foil and bake for 10 minutes.

When the broccoli are done, put them with all the cooking juices in the food processor and purée them. Spoon the purée into a clean saucepan and add the cream. Bring slowly to the boil and cook over very low heat for 5 minutes, stirring frequently. Taste and check seasoning. Keep the sauce warm.

Transfer the fish fillets to a heated serving dish and surround them with the broccoli sauce. Pour the cooking juice from the fish over the dish and serve at once. If you find it easier for serving, place the fish on to individual heated plates and spoon a couple of tablespoons of sauce around each fillet.

PREPARATION

The broccoli sauce can be prepared a few hours in advance and refrigerated, tightly covered with clingfilm. The fish must be cooked at the last minute.

*
with an
ice-cream
machine

***
without

Sorbetto di limone al basilico

BASIL-FLAVOURED LEMON SORBET

---

8 lemons	350 g/12 oz caster sugar
2 oranges	2 dozen large basil leaves, chopped

It is essential to use leaves from a *young* basil plant.

Scrub, wash and dry the fruit. Remove the rind, without chipping into the white pith, and put it into a saucepan. Add 600 ml/1 pint of water and the sugar. Bring slowly to the boil and simmer until the sugar has dissolved. Turn the heat up to moderate and boil rapidly for 3–4 minutes. Draw off the heat and allow the syrup to cool completely.

Meanwhile squeeze the lemons and the oranges. Strain the juice and add to the cold syrup, together with the basil leaves. If you have an ice-cream machine, pour the mixture into it and freeze according to the manufacturer's instructions.

If you do not have an ice-cream machine, pour the mixture into a metal bowl and freeze for about 2 hours, until the mixture is half frozen. Remove from the freezer, put the bowl in the sink (because the mixture might splatter everywhere) and beat with a hand-held electric beater or a whisk. This will break down the crystals. You can use a food processor. Freeze again and then whisk once more. Return the bowl to the freezer until the sorbet is ready.

PREPARATION

Sorbets, especially those based on fruit, lose their flavour if made longer than 24 hours in advance.

A LUNCH FOR 8

Bruschetta toscana
GRILLED BREAD WITH OLIVE OIL, GARLIC AND TOMATO

Tagliatelle di Guido
TAGLIATELLE WITH MOZZARELLA, ANCHOVY FILLETS
AND PARSLEY

Peperoni all'aceto
PEPPERS IN VINEGAR

Noci, uva e grana
WALNUTS, GRAPES AND PARMESAN

*B*ruschetta is the Mediterranean answer to French garlic bread, yet, apart from the garlicky flavour, it is quite different. *Bruschetta* originated in Rome, and the word derives from *bruscare*, which in the local dialect means to burn slightly. The Roman *bruschetta* is usually made without tomatoes, while the Tuscan version has a few ripe tomatoes sprinkled on top. This is the version I prefer, provided I can find good tomatoes. A 'good' tomato (a tall order these days) should be ripe but not mushy and juicy but not watery, with plenty of firm pulp, few seeds and a tomatoey scent. If you can't find these, forget about *bruschetta* and settle for a *frittata* (pages 330–32), which you can equally well serve cold with the drinks. I suggest you serve *bruschetta* with the pre-prandial wine – a Chianti, of course – and then go into the kitchen to prepare the pasta, which must be done at the last minute.

My brother Guido is a great gourmet; never one to follow recipes slavishly, he always improves on them, or so he claims. The dressing for the tagliatelle is one of his creations. It certainly needs no further improvements, and yet it is simplicity itself. The strong aromatic flavour of the parsley *soffritto* is softened by the addition of the delicate egg mixture. If you can, buy salted anchovies as they have more flavour than tinned anchovy fillets.

After two such positive courses a tasty vegetable dish seems the right follow-on, and these peppers fill the bill perfectly.

The last course, if it could be called such, was a favourite of my father's. In spite of his sophisticated tastes in other matters, the food that he loved best was peasant food. I remember him telling me that the dish he usually had at Savini, the famous restaurant in Milan where he often went for supper after an evening at La Scala, was *polenta e baccalà* (polenta and salt cod) or *polenta pasticciata* (polenta baked in layers with béchamel and *luganega*, a coarse-ground sausage). And if truffles were in season, the chef would add a few slices to the polenta; peasant food no longer!

In the real peasant tradition, my father used to eat bread with everything. My children, brought up in England where bread is eaten only with particular foods, were amazed to see *Nonno* eating bread with huge bunches of grapes at the end of the meal. Although I find bread and grapes rather dull, I find the mixture of walnuts, grapes, Parmesan and bread a perfect blend of different flavours, the bread being the unifying note. The grapes should be white and tasty, not the bland variety tasting only of water and sugar too often sold here under the name 'Italia'.

*　　　　　## *Bruschetta toscana*

GRILLED BREAD WITH OLIVE OIL, GARLIC AND TOMATO

---

6 ripe firm tomatoes, preferably
   plum tomatoes
a handful of fresh basil leaves
8 slices good crusty bread, about
   1 cm/½ in thick

4 garlic cloves, peeled and crushed
salt
black pepper
4 tbsp extra virgin olive oil

Blanch and skin the tomatoes, cut them in half lengthwise, and remove as many seeds as you can. Dice the tomatoes into 1.5 cm/¾ in cubes.

Wash and dry the basil. Tear the leaves into small pieces.

Grill the bread slices on both sides and then rub them on each side with the garlic. Cut each slice in half, to make them easier to eat.

Spoon some tomato cubes and some basil leaves over each slice and sprinkle with a little salt and a generous grinding of pepper. Dribble the olive oil over the bread and serve at once.

PREPARATION

The tomatoes can be cubed and refrigerated, in a covered bowl, up to a few hours in advance.

*

***

if you make
your own pasta

Tagliatelle di Guido

TAGLIATELLE WITH MOZZARELLA,
ANCHOVY FILLETS AND PARSLEY

---

*Tagliatelle made with 5 eggs and
    500 g/1 lb 2 oz plain flour, or
    1.2 kg/2½ lb fresh tagliatelle, or
    600 g/1¼ lb dried tagliatelle
300 g/10 oz Italian mozzarella
4 eggs
150 ml/¼ pint single cream*

*salt and pepper
12 anchovy fillets or 6 salted
    anchovies
a large bunch of parsley, preferably
    flat-leaf
3 garlic cloves, peeled
120 ml/4 fl oz extra virgin olive oil*

If you are making your own tagliatelle, do this first, following the directions on page 374.

Put a large saucepan full of salted water on the heat and while the water is coming to the boil prepare the sauce. Grate the mozzarella through the coarse holes of a grater or cut into small cubes. Put it in a bowl and add the eggs, one at a time, to incorporate thoroughly. Stir in the cream and add a good deal of pepper. Set aside.

If you are using anchovy fillets, let the oil drip away and pat them dry with kitchen paper. Salted anchovies must be cleaned, rinsed under cold water and dried with kitchen paper. Chop together the anchovies, parsley and garlic and put them in a frying pan that will be large enough to hold all the pasta. Add the oil and sauté for 1 minute, stirring very frequently.

When the tagliatelle are *al dente*, drain them through a colander or use a spaghetti lifter to transfer them directly into the frying pan. If you use the colander, reserve a cupful of the water in which the pasta has cooked.

Stir-fry for 1 minute and then add the egg mixture. Fry for a further minute, lifting the tagliatelle high into the air so that the strands of pasta coat evenly. Taste and check seasonings. If the dish appears too dry, add a little of the reserved water.

If your pan is presentable, serve straight from it at the table, otherwise transfer the pasta into a heated bowl and serve at once. For this type of pasta I bring a small jug full of pasta water to the table – pasta dressed with eggs, and especially homemade pasta, tends to become very dry while it cools, and the jug of hot pasta water is the ideal solution, as any Neapolitan knows.

PREPARATION
You can grate the mozzarella and chop the parsley, anchovies and garlic in advance, but no more than that. The dish must be made shortly before eating.

* ## *Peperoni all'aceto*

PEPPERS IN VINEGAR

---

2 Spanish onions
5 tbsp extra virgin olive oil
salt and pepper
8 meaty peppers, red, yellow and
   green

4 tbsp sugar
4 tbsp red wine vinegar

Coarsely chop the onions and sauté slowly in the oil. Add 1 teaspoon of salt to release the moisture in the onion, thus preventing it from browning too quickly. Cover the pan and cook gently for 45 minutes, until the onion is very soft indeed. Add a couple of tablespoons of hot water if it begins to stick to the bottom of the pan.

Wash and dry the peppers, cut them in quarters and remove the seeds, cores and white ribs. Cut them into 1½ cm/½ in pieces.

Add the peppers to the onion and sauté for 5 minutes, stirring frequently. Turn the heat up a little, add the sugar and leave it to caramelize for 10 minutes or so, stirring frequently. Pour over the vinegar, add salt and pepper and cover the pan tightly. Cook over very low heat for a further hour, checking every now and then that the peppers do not burn. Add a couple of tablespoons of hot water whenever necessary. If, on the other hand, there is too much liquid at the end of the cooking, uncover the pan and boil fast to reduce until the juices are tasty and syrupy.

Serve warm or at room temperature, but neither piping hot nor straight from the fridge.

PREPARATION
The dish can be prepared up to 8 days in advance, covered and refrigerated. It also freezes well.

*   *Noci, uva e grana*

WALNUTS, GRAPES AND PARMESAN

This is the sort of dish you must provide in generous proportions. After all, whatever is left over will not be wasted. Buy 1 kg/2 lb of walnuts, 1.35 kg/3 lb of white grapes, a good wedge of Parmesan of at least 450 g/1 lb and some crusty Italian bread (a *ciabatta* is ideal) or French bread.

Divide the grapes into small bunches. Put the bunches in a colander and place under cold water. Dry them thoroughly with kitchen paper. Put the Parmesan in the middle of a large round dish and surround it with the walnuts and the grapes.

Put the dish in the middle of the table for everybody to help themselves. If your table is oval or rectangular, make two smaller dishes to place at each end of the table.

A SUMMER DINNER FOR 8

Fusilli e fagiolini al pomodoro
FUSILLI AND GREEN BEANS IN TOMATO SAUCE

Carpaccio di salmone
SALMON CARPACCIO

Insalata di pomodori, cetrioli e peperoni
TOMATO, CUCUMBER AND PEPPER SALAD (page 129)

Pesche al sugo di lampone
PEACHES WITH RASPBERRY SAUCE

Green beans are in the shops all the year round, whether from Spain, France, Kenya or Zimbabwe. But to me green beans are still summer vegetables, bringing back memories of Italian summers, when they appear in all their different shapes and colours: the buttery Meraviglia di Venezia, with a name that promises so much, the long and snake-like Stringa, the deliciously bitter Fagiolino di Sant'Anna, so called because it is ready around the saint's day, 26 July, the beautiful bluey-green Re dei Blu, king of the blues, and Bobis, bobby beans, to mention but a few of the most popular.

I find that all green beans available in this country have a similar flavour, so that the really important thing is their freshness. Green beans should reach the pan soon after they are gathered, a very tall order. You can, to a certain extent, tell how fresh they are. Fresh beans look stiff and shiny, with a bright colour. If possible, break one: it should be hard and snap with a clean break. Once you are home with your fresh beans, wash them thoroughly before you cook them.

On the subject of cooking green beans, I would like to insert a short parenthesis inspired by a pen and telephone friend from across the ocean, Corby Kummer of Boston. In the September 1990 issue of the magazine *The Atlantic* he wrote an article titled 'An End to al Dente', explaining why green beans, more than any other vegetable, must be well cooked, which does not mean overcooked. 'Green beans are immature beans in their casings, bred to be edible . . . All these casings contain lignin, a substance found in wood, hemp and linen, but in few other green vegetables. Boiling seems best at breaking down the lignin, better than braising, steaming or microwaving.' As I told Corby Kummer, I boil my beans until their particular smell rises. That is when I taste them; they may be ready or they may need a few more minutes.

I first had this excellent combination of *fusilli* and green beans at the Pensione Giuseppina in Scala, a delightful spot near Ravello, where we ate many southern Italian dishes like this, simple yet delicious.

The Carpaccio of my second course is just as fresh-tasting and just as delicious, but more elegant. The name Carpaccio is now used to define any dish that features raw meat or raw fish. As is usually the case in gastronomy, there is no patent to protect the name or recipe from changes, embellishments or plagiarism. The original Carpaccio, made with raw fillet of beef, was created by Giuseppe Cipriani at Harry's Bar for his customer the Countess Nani Mocenigo. Some later versions that have sprung up in the last decade share nothing but the name with the original. In this recipe of mine, although there is fish instead of meat, the fish is finely sliced like the beef in the original Carpaccio. The other similarity is that a salmon Carpaccio like this one can certainly be as good as its famous progenitor. To be at its best it should be made with wild salmon. The rest is easy: good extra virgin olive oil, lemon juice and the right length of time for the marinade. I have also made it with farmed salmon and with salmon trout fillets. These I left whole and they were excellent. The tomato, cucumber and peppers salad on page 129 would be a perfect seasonal accompaniment.

I think that during the summer fresh fruit is the best ending to any meal. I like to serve raspberries when they are in season. I sprinkle them with lemon juice and 2–3 tablespoons of sugar 1 hour before serving, and then I serve them with cream. The lemon juice brings out their flavour. If you prefer a more exotic sweet, I suggest the peaches with raspberry sauce as in my recipe. Sometimes I add 2 or 3 sweet geranium leaves to the raspberry sauce; they add an intriguing touch with their flower-scented flavour.

The almond crescents on page 380 are delicious both with the raspberries and with the peaches.

✳✳   *Fusilli e fagiolini al pomodoro*
FUSILLI AND GREEN BEANS WITH TOMATOES

---

600 g/1¼ lb green beans
salt
1 onion, finely chopped
8 tbsp extra virgin olive oil
8 medium size ripe tomatoes,
    blanched and skinned

pepper
600 g/1¼ lb fusilli
a dozen basil leaves
freshly grated Parmesan

Top and tail the beans and wash well. Cook in plenty of salted boiling water for 5 minutes. Drain and refresh under cold water. Do remember that green beans need to cook in water that is quite salty, more so than any other vegetable. Cut the beans into pieces of the same length as the *fusilli*, and set aside.

Put the onion and half the oil in a sauté or frying pan large enough to contain the beans and the pasta. If necessary use two smaller sauté pans, dividing the ingredients in half and using a little more oil. Add a sprinkling of salt, which will help the onion to release its moisture, thus preventing it from burning. Cook for about 10 minutes, stirring frequently and pressing the onion down to squeeze out its juices, then add the beans.

Cut the tomatoes in half and squeeze out the seeds and water. Chop coarsely and add to the onion and beans. Season with plenty of pepper and cook over very low heat until the beans are tender, adding a couple of tablespoons of hot water twice during the cooking, which will take about 20–25 minutes. Stewed beans should be cooked until they are tender; they should not be crunchy.

While the beans are cooking, cook the pasta in plenty of boiling salted water. Drain well – *fusilli* keep enough water in their spirals – and transfer to the pan with the beans. Add the rest of the oil and stir-fry for a minute or two. Serve at once, preferably from the pan. If you do not want to bring the pan to the table, transfer to a heated dish. Hand a bowl of Parmesan round separately.

PREPARATION
The beans can be cooked in the tomato sauce up to 2 days in advance and kept covered in the refrigerator. Heat slowly before you add the pasta, which must be cooked at the last minute.

*   # Carpaccio di salmone

SALMON CARPACCIO

---

1 kg/2 lb salmon fillets or salmon trout fillets	salt and pepper
	225 ml/8 fl oz single cream
5 tbsp extra virgin olive oil	cayenne pepper to taste
6 tbsp lemon juice	1 fennel bulb

If you are using salmon fillets cut them across into thin strips, but if you are using salmon trout fillets leave them whole.

Place the fish on a dish and dress with the olive oil, 2 tablespoons of the lemon juice, salt and pepper. Cover the dish with clingfilm and leave to marinate for 3–4 hours in the refrigerator.

Put the cream in a bowl and beat in 2 tablespoons of lemon juice, salt and cayenne pepper to taste. Add more lemon juice according to your taste.

About 1 hour before serving, transfer the fish, but not the juice at the bottom of the dish, into a clean dish and dribble over the cream mixture. Do not refrigerate any more, as Carpaccio is better eaten at room temperature.

Remove the stalks and any bruised part of the fennel. Keep any feathery top the fennel may have. Cut the fennel bulb into quarters lengthwise and then across into very thin strips. Wash, drain and dry the fennel and the feathery top.

Sprinkle the fennel strips and feathery top over the Carpaccio and serve.

PREPARATION
As explained in the method, above.

* *Pesche al sugo di lampone*

PEACHES WITH RASPBERRY SAUCE

---

8 or 9 large yellow peaches, ripe
  but firm

7 tbsp dry white wine
4 tbsp caster sugar

For the sauce

450 g/1 lb fresh raspberries
150 g/5 oz icing sugar, sifted
the juice of 1 lemon

4 young sweet geranium leaves,
  torn into small pieces (optional)

Peel the peaches with a small sharp knife. If the skin does not come away easily, plunge the peaches into boiling water for 30 seconds and then straight into cold water. Cut the peaches into segments of about 2 cm/¾ in each. Lay the segments, overlapping, in a deep dish.

Mix together the wine and the sugar and spoon over the peaches. Cover with clingfilm and refrigerate for at least 2 hours.

Now make the sauce by simply blending together the raspberries, icing sugar, lemon juice and the optional sweet geranium leaves in the food processor or blender. Taste and add more sugar and/or lemon juice according to taste. If you want a smooth sauce, strain it through a fine sieve, pushing the purée with a spoon. I like it as it is, with a coarser consistency. Transfer the sauce to a bowl, cover with clingfilm and chill.

Just before serving, mask the peach segments with some sauce and serve the rest of the sauce separately in a bowl.

PREPARATION

The raspberry coulis can be prepared up to 2 days in advance and kept in the fridge in an airtight container. It also freezes very well, but do not leave it for longer than 2 months.

I prefer to prepare the peaches no longer than 4 hours in advance because I do not like their appearance if they stay too long in the wine.

A DINNER FOR 8

La bresaola con la ruccola
CURED FILLET OF BEEF WITH ROCKET

Rotolo di spinaci al burro e formaggio
SPINACH AND PASTA ROLL WITH MELTED BUTTER AND
PARMESAN

Torta di patate e mandorle
POTATO AND ALMOND CAKE

Ciliege cotte al vino
CHERRIES STEWED IN WINE

*B*resaola is raw fillet of beef that has been cured in salt and air-dried for 2–4 months. It is a speciality of Valtellina, an Alpine valley in Lombardy. It has a flavour similar to prosciutto, though a little sharper. *Bresaola* is served thinly sliced and lightly dressed with olive oil and lemon juice. Or at least, this is the modern way to serve it. The old-fashioned way, still observed by the purists, is to eat *bresaola* as it is. Last year the food historian Massimo Alberini and his wife took me to the Ristorante Peck in Milan. He ordered *bresaola* and the *maître* asked, 'Così, al naturale?' Alberini was shocked and replied, 'E me lo domanda? Ma certamente.' ('How could you ask me? Certainly.')

My mother is another purist as far as *bresaola* goes, and at home in Milan I still have *bresaola* as it used to be served, by itself with fresh bread. But the perfect *bresaola* one can buy in Milan is hard to come by anywhere else. The *bresaola* I buy here is not of such exceptional quality, so a dribble of good olive oil improves it a lot. I sometimes add a bunch of rocket dressed with olive oil and lemon juice, and here is the recipe, if it can be called such. The slight peppery flavour of the rocket is a good foil to the meat. Buy *bresaola* – thinly sliced – the day you want to eat it, or it will become dark and leathery.

Having had a good portion of meat in the easy first course, my *secondo* is an elegant vegetarian dish consisting of a roll of home-made pasta stuffed with spinach and ricotta, the most traditional of all vegetarian pasta fillings. The pasta must be rolled out by hand, but it is not too difficult to handle, being made with only 2 eggs. I recommend adding a teaspoon of oil to the dough to make it easier to stretch and roll thin. For the same reason I also suggest making a dough that is slightly more moist than the dough you would roll out by machine. Once cooked, allow the *rotolo* to cool, if you have time, because like any other food it becomes easier to slice. I use an electric carving knife, which I find one of the most useful tools. It is as invaluable for carving roast meat as it is for slicing a roulade like this, or a stuffed fish, or a piece of braised meat that would otherwise tend to crumble.

After experimenting with different sauces to serve with the *rotolo*, I have come to the conclusion that the best, as so often, is the simplest: melted butter and Parmesan. However, if you should prefer a more positive-tasting sauce, I suggest this sauce of cream and fontina. If you cannot find fontina, use Swiss raclette, which is similar both in its flavour and its melting properties.

The deliciously moist potato and almond cake comes from the Hotel Mar y Vent in Bañalbufar on Majorca. Nothing Italian about it. But the way it was served at the hotel, lavishly covered with icing sugar, by itself at the end of the meal was very Italian indeed. It reminded me of all the different *torte* covered with icing sugar that are on display at most bakeries and patisseries in central Italy. Falling in line with the British tradition that sweets at the end of a meal should not be eaten dry – something I totally agree with – I have served the cake with various ice-creams or stewed fruit. The cherries as prepared in this recipe are ideal, the anise flavour of the fennel seeds blending with the flavour of the almonds.

*   ## *La bresaola con la ruccola*

CURED FILLET OF BEEF WITH ROCKET

---

225 g/½ lb rocket
75 ml/5 tbsp extra virgin olive oil
20 ml/1½ tbsp lemon juice

salt and pepper
450 g/1 lb bresaola

Pick and wash the rocket. Dry it very thoroughly and put it in a bowl. Dress with the oil, lemon juice and salt and pepper to taste. Toss well. Taste and add a little more lemon juice, if necessary.

Place the *bresaola* in the centre of a serving dish and surround it with the rocket. If you prefer to prepare individual plates, divide the rocket between the 8 plates and place the *bresaola* over it.

PREPARATION

The rocket can be prepared up to 1 day in advance and kept in the fridge, loosely wrapped in a kitchen towel.

*** *Rotolo di spinaci al burro e formaggio*
SPINACH AND PASTA ROLL WITH MELTED BUTTER AND PARMESAN

---

450 g/1 lb frozen leaf spinach, thawed, or 1 kg/2 lb fresh bunch spinach
salt
2 tbsp shallots, finely chopped
150 g/5 oz unsalted butter
50 g/1¾ oz chopped prosciutto or mortadella
200 g/7 oz fresh ricotta

100 g/3½ oz freshly grated Parmesan
¼ tsp nutmeg
1 egg yolk
a sheet of home-made pasta dough, made with 2 eggs, 200 g/7 oz plain flour and 1 tsp olive oil
2 garlic cloves, peeled and bruised
a small sprig of fresh sage

If you are using frozen spinach, cook the thawed spinach in a covered pan with salt for 3 minutes. Drain and squeeze to remove all the liquid. If you are using fresh spinach, discard any wilted or discoloured leaves, the roots and the long stems. Wash in a basin in several changes of cold water until the water shows no trace of grit. Cook with just the water that clings to the leaves in a covered pan with salt for 10 minutes, or until tender, then drain. Squeeze the spinach lightly to remove most of its moisture. Set aside.

In a frying pan, sauté the shallot with 45 g/1½ oz butter over medium heat. Chop the spinach coarsely by hand (a food processor would liquefy it) and when the shallot turns pale gold in colour, add it to the pan with the chopped prosciutto. Sauté for 5 minutes, turning the spinach over and over to *insaporire* – take up the flavour. You will find that all the butter has been absorbed.

Transfer the contents of the frying pan to a mixing bowl, and add the ricotta, half the grated Parmesan, the nutmeg, and, last of all, the egg yolk. Mix all the ingredients with a fork until they are well combined. Check seasoning.

Make the pasta dough (see page 374), and roll out a piece about 30 cm/14 in diameter. Spread the filling over the pasta, starting about 5 cm/2 in in from the edge near you. The filling should cover all but a ½ cm/¼ in border all around the sheet, and the larger border near you. Fold this border over the filling, and continue to fold until you have rolled up all the pasta. Wrap the pasta roll tightly in muslin, tying the two ends securely with string.

Use a fish kettle or other long, deep pan that can hold the roll and 3–4 litres/5–7 pints of water. Bring the water to the boil, add 1 tablespoon of salt, then put in the pasta roll and cook at a gentle but steady boil for 25 minutes after the water has come back to the boil. Lift out the roll, using the fish retriever in the kettle or two fish slices, and place on a wooden board. Unwrap the roll as soon as you can without burning your hands and set aside to cool a little, which will make slicing easier.

Heat the oven to 200°C/400°F/Gas 6.

Cut the roll into 1 cm/½ in slices. Generously butter a large oven dish and lay the slices on it, overlapping a little.

Heat the butter in a heavy frying pan with the garlic cloves and the sage. When the butter begins to turn a lovely golden colour, draw off the heat. Remove and discard the garlic and the sage and spoon the butter evenly over the roll.

Cover the dish with foil and place in the oven until the roll is hot, about 20–30 minutes, depending on how hot it was when it went in the oven. Remove the dish from the oven and uncover it. Serve, handing the remaining Parmesan separately.

PREPARATION

The *rotolo* can be made up to 2 days in advance and refrigerated, wrapped in foil.

Here is the alternative sauce:

Fontina and cream sauce

600 ml/1 pint single cream	*salt and white pepper*
200 g/7 oz fontina or raclette cheese	

Bring the cream slowly to the simmer in a heavy-based saucepan and simmer over a low heat for 2 minutes. The cream must not boil; only a few bubbles should occasionally break the surface.

Meanwhile slice the cheese into very thin slices. Add the cheese to the cream and stir constantly until it is dissolved. Stir in 4 tablespoons of boiling water, which will dilute the sauce to the right consistency. Taste and add seasonings. The sauce should be very creamy and glossy.

Heat the oven to 200°C/400°F/Gas 6.

Spread 2 or 3 tablespoons of the sauce over the bottom of a large buttered oven dish. Cover with the sliced *rotolo* and coat with a few tablespoons of the sauce. Cover the dish with foil and heat for 20–30 minutes, depending on whether the *rotolo* was warm or cold when it went into the oven. Pour the remaining sauce into a heated sauce-boat and serve with the rest of the Parmesan in a separate bowl.

PREPARATION

The sauce can be prepared up to 30–45 minutes in advance and kept hot in a bain-marie, i.e. by sitting the pan in a larger saucepan half full of boiling water and putting a lid on.

**   *Torta di patate e mandorle*

POTATO AND ALMOND CAKE

200 g/7 oz old floury potatoes, such as King Edward	6 eggs, separated
200 g/7 oz almonds	200 g/7 oz caster sugar
1 white bread roll (a small bap is ideal)	the grated rind of 1 lemon
	salt
	icing sugar for decoration

Boil the potatoes in their skins and then peel and purée them through the small disc of a food mill.

While the potatoes are cooking, blanch the almonds for 20 seconds in boiling water. Peel them and dry them in kitchen paper. Chop them in the food processor, stopping before they become too finely ground.

Take out the soft inside of the bread roll and crumble it by hand or in the food processor.

Heat the oven to 240°C/475°F/Gas 9.

Put the egg yolks in a bowl. Add the sugar, almonds, bread-crumbs, lemon rind, a pinch of salt and the potato purée. Mix thoroughly. Whisk the egg whites until stiff but not dry and fold them gently into the mixture using a large metal spoon, with a high movement to incorporate air into the mixture.

Butter a 25 cm/10 in spring-clip cake tin. Sprinkle a large table-spoon of flour into the tin. Shake the tin to cover all the surface and then throw away the excess flour. Fill the tin with the mixture and place the tin in the oven. Turn the heat down to 170°C/325°F/Gas 3 and bake for about 50 minutes to 1 hour, until a cocktail stick inserted into the middle of the cake comes out dry. Loosen the band round the tin and turn the cake on to a wire rack, where it should be left to cool. Serve lavishly sprinkled with sifted icing sugar.

PREPARATION
The cake is best eaten the day it is cooked, but it can be made up to 2 days in advance.

* ## *Ciliege cotte al vino*

CHERRIES STEWED IN WINE

---

1 kg/2 lb cherries	*1–2 tsp fennel seeds*
600 ml/1 pint good red wine	*7.5 ml/½ tbsp peppercorns*
325 g/11 oz granulated sugar	*2 bay leaves*

Wash the cherries and remove the stalks. Make a syrup with the wine and the sugar in a large heavy sauté pan. Boil gently for 3 minutes. Pound the fennel seeds and add to the syrup with the peppercorns and bay leaves. Now stir in the cherries and cook gently for 20 minutes.

Remove the cherries with a slotted spoon and put them in a glass bowl. Taste the syrup and, if necessary, boil fast to make it stronger and more full of flavour. Leave to cool (or you might shatter the glass bowl) and then pour over the cherries through a strainer. Cover with clingfilm and refrigerate.

PREPARATION

The cherries are much tastier if stewed 2 or 3 days before serving. They also freeze very well, which is a bonus. When they are plentiful and good, prepare 2–3 kilos of these cherries and keep them in the freezer for the time when one is fed up with the monotony of the winter fresh fruit.

A DINNER FOR 8

Gnocchetti alla puré di fagioli bianchi
PASTA WITH BUTTER BEAN PURÉE

Triglie alla marchigiana
RED MULLET WITH PROSCIUTTO AND ROSEMARY

Insalata di pomodori, cetrioli e peperoni
TOMATO, CUCUMBER AND PEPPER SALAD

Pesche in camicia
MERINGUED PEACHES

Up to ten years ago I would never have served dried pasta at a dinner party; only home-made pasta or various timbales were considered right. Now, even in Italy, dried pasta is totally accepted at any meal, even, as here, pasta combined with humble beans. Pasta and pulses are a staple in southern Italy and Sicily. What is new is to purée the pulses, and what is mine is to do it with butter beans instead of broad beans or lentils.

My husband being something of a pulse addict, all sorts of beans appear regularly at our table. One day I had run out of my usual stock of chick-peas, lentils and *borlotti*, but it so happened that I had some butter beans in the larder. Having soaked and cooked them, I began to taste them and immediately, in my mind, I could taste them with pasta. I removed the tough skin, as I always do with chick-peas and broad beans, and then puréed them. The final result was quite delicious, creamy, delicate and buttery, even though the dish contained no butter. A perfect dressing for the pasta.

Gnocchetti sardi are a good shape of pasta to go with this sauce. They are available at Italian shops, but if you cannot find them, use shells, *ditali* or any medium-sized shape. The grated cheese should be a mature pecorino because it has a stronger flavour than Parmesan.

When you serve pasta at a dinner party, ask your guests to start sitting down before you go to the kitchen to drain the pasta. Pasta cannot wait, while the guests can.

The *secondo* is a classic dish from the Marches. It might seem odd to have prosciutto in a fish dish; it did indeed seem so to me when I first had these *triglie*. But the oddity turns out to be one of the most successful couplings of ingredients. The link between the fish and the prosciutto is the rosemary. Red mullet are easily available in Britain now. Unfortunately they are often frozen, but they seem to keep their flavour quite well. It seems strange to think that red mullet was a very common fish in the nineteenth century around the south coast of England. Whatever happened to the local red mullet?

The fish can be served with a few boiled or steamed potatoes, or just with bread. The salad is a classic Italian type of summer salad. It goes very well after these two dishes, and is just as Mediterranean as they are. Alternatively, serve the green bean and tomato salad on page 80.

The last course is a lovely-looking peach pudding. I am very partial to peaches and I am glad to say that there has been a great improvement in imported peaches in this country in recent years. A good tip is to put peaches on a sunny window-sill, where they will ripen and soften a little and will become much tastier. Whatever you do, don't put them in the fridge as that kills their flavour.

In this sweet, the poached peaches are *in camicia*, dressed in a white shirt, the shirt being the meringue covering. When you eat them you break through the lemony, sugary meringue into the flowery flavour of the peaches. For meringues, remember to use egg whites at room temperature, not straight from the fridge.

* *Gnocchetti alla puré di fagioli bianchi*

PASTA WITH BUTTER BEAN PURÉE

250 g/9 oz butter beans	salt and pepper
1 celery stick, preferably with its leaves	120 ml/4 fl oz extra virgin olive oil
	a large bunch of parsley, chopped
1 medium onion	700 g/1½ lb gnocchetti,
8 garlic cloves	conchiglie or other medium
2 bay leaves	sized pasta
2 rosemary sprigs	grated pecorino or Parmesan

Rinse the beans, cover them with water and leave to soak for 6–8 hours or overnight. Alternatively, cover them with boiling water and soak for 1 hour.

Drain the beans and put them in a pot with the celery, onion, garlic, bay and rosemary. Cover with water to come about 2.5 cm/ 1 in above the beans. Bring to the boil, add 1 teaspoon of salt, lower the heat and simmer gently until the beans are tender. Drain, reserving the liquid.

Now you can either peel the beans by hand and purée them with the flavouring vegetables in a food processor, or you can purée the beans and the vegetables through a food mill, in which case the skin of the beans will not go through the disc. Return the purée to the saucepan and add enough of the reserved cooking liquid to make a thin purée. Bring back to the simmer and pour in half the oil in a thin stream, while beating vigorously to incorporate it. Draw off the heat, add half the parsley, a generous amount of pepper and salt if necessary. Cover the pan and keep warm.

Cook the pasta in the usual way or use the Agnesi method described on page 376. I find this much easier when I have friends to supper, as you can leave the kitchen, quite confident that the pasta will cook beautifully without needing to be watched. When it is ready, drain, reserving a cupful of the pasta water. Transfer the pasta into a large heated bowl. Toss immediately with the remaining oil and dress with the bean purée. Add enough reserved pasta water to give the dish the right fluidity, and bring the rest of the water to the table in a jug. This sauce dries out pretty quickly and it may be necessary to add a drop or two later on. Mix very thoroughly, sprinkle with the remaining parsley and serve at once. Hand round a bowl of grated pecorino or Parmesan.

PREPARATION
The bean purée can be prepared up to 2 days in advance and refrigerated. It also freezes well. Add the oil when you reheat it.

**   *Triglie alla marchigiana*
RED MULLET WITH PROSCIUTTO AND ROSEMARY

---

8 red mullet, cleaned but with the
   heads on
the juice of 2 lemons
6 tbsp extra virgin olive oil
salt and freshly ground black
   pepper

2 tbsp chopped rosemary
1 garlic clove, peeled and chopped
6 tbsp dried breadcrumbs
8 large slices of prosciutto, not too
   thinly cut
2 lemons for garnish

Ask the fishmonger to scale and clean the fish, but to leave the liver inside as it is one of the best parts of a red mullet. Wash the fish and dry them thoroughly inside and out. Lay them on a dish. Mix together the lemon juice and 2 tablespoons of the oil. Add salt and pepper and dribble a little of the mixture into the cavity of each fish. Brush the rest of the lemon and oil mixture all over the fish and leave to marinate for 2 hours.

Heat the oven to 190°C/375°F/Gas 5.

Brush an oven dish with a little of the remaining oil.

Mix together the rosemary, garlic, breadcrumbs, a little salt and a generous amount of pepper. Coat the fish with the mixture, pressing the crumbs into it with your hands. Wrap a slice of prosciutto round each fish and lay the fish in the prepared dish. Dribble the remaining oil over and bake for 15–20 minutes, basting the fish twice during the cooking. Serve from the dish, handing round the lemons cut into wedges.

New potatoes are lovely with these fish.

There is no sauce in this dish, only a few tablespoons of the cooking juices. If you think your guests are going to miss a sauce (they shouldn't!) you can put a bottle of your best olive oil on the table; it is also the ideal dressing for the boiled or steamed potatoes.

PREPARATION
The fish can be wrapped in the prosciutto and laid ready in the oven dish up to 1 hour before serving.

* *Insalata di pomodori, cetrioli e peperoni*

TOMATO, CUCUMBER AND PEPPER SALAD

You must start this salad a day in advance.

---

2 large red onions	4 good tomatoes
the juice of 4 lemons	4 large peppers, red and yellow
2 tsp sugar	6 tbsp extra virgin olive oil
1 large cucumber	pepper
salt	

Peel the onions and slice them very thinly. Put them in a bowl and add 6 tablespoons of the lemon juice and the sugar. Mix well, cover the bowl and leave for 24 hours.

Peel the cucumber and slice it thinly. Put the slices in a bowl and sprinkle with salt. Leave for 1 hour.

Wash and dry the tomatoes, slice them thinly and put them in a salad bowl.

Wash and dry the peppers, cut them into quarters, remove the cores, ribs and pips and cut the quarters across into 8 mm/⅓ in strips. Add to the bowl.

Squeeze the liquid out of the cucumber and add to the bowl. Do the same with the onion.

Just before serving, toss with the olive oil and the remaining lemon juice and season with a generous amount of pepper and some salt. Taste and correct seasonings, adding a little more lemon juice, according to your taste.

PREPARATION

The tomatoes and peppers can be prepared up to 1 hour in advance, after you have sliced and salted the cucumber.

*** *Pesche in camicia*

MERINGUED PEACHES

---

8 firm but ripe peaches, all of the same size
120 g/4 oz sugar

150 ml/¼ pint sweet white wine
the juice of 1 lemon

For the meringue

2 egg whites
100 g/3½ oz caster sugar

the grated rind of 1 lemon

Peel the peaches. If they are rather hard, put them in boiling water for 20 seconds and then plunge them into a bowl of cold water.

Choose a large sauté pan in which the peaches can fit snugly.

Make a syrup with the sugar, wine, lemon juice and 150 ml/¼ pint of water. Boil the syrup for about 3 minutes. Add the peaches and cook over very low heat with the lid on until they are soft, about 10–15 minutes. Lift the peaches out of the juices and leave them to cool. Taste the juices and if necessary boil rapidly for a few minutes until rich and tasty. Pour the juices into a little jug. Chill the peaches for at least 2 hours.

About 1 hour before serving, heat the oven to 150°C/300°F/Gas 2. Whip the egg whites until stiff. Add about one-third of the caster sugar and whip again. The mixture will become beautifully shiny. Now fold in the remaining sugar and the grated lemon rind, using a large metal spoon.

Line an oven tray with baking parchment. Roll each peach in the meringue and place on the tray. Patch up any spots of naked peach with a little meringue. Place the tray in the oven and bake until the meringue has set and is golden on top, about 15–20 minutes.

Transfer the peaches to individual plates or to a serving dish and place a leaf of lemon balm or mint on each peach. Hand round the jug of peach syrup.

PREPARATION

The peaches can be cooked up to 4 days in advance and chilled in a covered box. They can also be frozen. You cannot bake the peaches in the meringue covering too long in advance or the meringue will be made soggy by the peach juices. Leave the baking of the meringue until about 1 hour before beginning the meal. Do not refrigerate the meringued peaches because the humidity in the fridge will spoil the meringue.

A BUFFET PARTY FOR 25

Vitello tonnato alla Milanese
VEAL IN A TUNA SAUCE

Mousse di prosciutto cotto della Signora Gay
TRUFFLE-FLAVOURED HAM MOUSSE (page 300)

I ricchi e i poveri
PRAWN AND BEAN SALAD (page 99)

Carpaccio di salmone
SALMON CARPACCIO (page 116)

Insalata di pasta, fontina, noci e sedano
PASTA, FONTINA, WALNUT AND CELERY SALAD

Conchiglie rosse ripiene di spaghettini in insalata
SALAD OF RADICCHIO LEAVES FILLED WITH THIN SPAGHETTI

Insalate varie
VARIOUS SALADS

Torta di patate e mandorle
POTATO AND ALMOND CAKE (page 122)

Gelato di ricotta
RICOTTA ICE-CREAM

La torta di cioccolato di Julia
CHOCOLATE AND NUT CAKE

Pere alla crema del Lario
STEWED PEARS WITH LIQUEUR-FLAVOURED CREAM (page 17)

Macedonia di frutta con la neve al limone
FRUIT SALAD WITH LEMON GRANITA (page 28)

There are now two kinds of supper party: one, rather informal, when only one or two large dishes, often hot, are served as a main course, and the other when quite a few dishes, usually cold, are put on the table for everyone to help themselves. This menu falls into the second category, which is the more old-fashioned and formal kind of buffet party. You will find some of the recipes in other menus. I have gathered them here to provide a good assortment and give the right balance to the buffet. But there are also a few recipes only to be found in this menu, of which the *vitello tonnato* is one.

Vitello tonnato is a very elegant summer dish – it is the dish most northern Italian hostesses would serve at a supper party. In the old days it was the traditional dish served on 15 August, Ferragosto, the feast of the Assumption of the Virgin. My recipe comes from my mother, and every time I make it I remember the occasion when her *vitel tonné* (as it was called in Milanese dialect) finished on the dining-room floor. It was at a lunch party at the beginning of the war, and my mother had managed to find the right joint of veal, a triumph at that time when meat was getting scarce. The beautiful dish was brought in by Augusta, our maid, who was a real exhibitionist when waiting at table. She loved to dress up with frilly apron, crest and white gloves, and would make her entry into the dining-room as if she was on stage, carrying large dishes poised delicately on one hand, and taking tiny elegant steps with her short fat legs. She tripped over the carpet, and the next thing I remember is the beige sticky mess on the floor. It was a family lunch with some aunts and uncles, and I remember my Aunt Esther getting up, scooping up the meat and saying, in Milanese dialect, *'Ma l'è trop bun e mi me lo magni istess'* ('But it's too good and I'm going to eat it just the same'). Augusta, by now in tears, was asked to collect the debris, clean off the sauce and tell cook to reconstruct the dish with the left-over sauce. The *vitel tonné* reappeared a few minutes later, beautifully decorated with lemon butterflies and cornichon fans, just as it had been before.

My mother's recipe is the traditional recipe from Milan, where the sauce is made with cream instead of mayonnaise; the version with mayonnaise being from Piedmont.

Because it is difficult to find the right cut of veal, I have often used chicken instead, cooking it whole in the same way and cutting it into pieces when cold. But what you really need is good tuna, not skipjack. Buy Italian or Spanish tuna preserved in olive oil or brine, available in specialist shops and best delicatessens or by post from The Oil Merchant, 3 Haarlem Street, London W 14.

The Signora Gay of the ham mousse (page 298) is the octogenarian mother of a great friend of mine in Milan. Ten years ago she moved to Milan from her native Turin to be nearer her daughter. But once a week she makes the 100-mile journey back to Turin to buy her poultry and meat, because, she says, '*La carne e i polli a Milano non sono buoni come a Torino*' ('Meat and chicken in Milan are not so good as in Turin'). This illustrates the high standard of Signora Gay's table, where the ingredients are her prime concern. And how right she is. Her cooking is light, but full of flavours, achieved through careful timing, absolute precision and great love, and not by the easy way out – that of adding cream and butter. The mousse is testimony to the lightness of her touch and the balance of the ingredients.

For this type of party you need many different salads, plus a large bowl of green salad. My version of this is on page 368. There are many other recipes for salads throughout this book, and I would suggest you choose the most seasonal.

I have also included recipes for my favourite pasta salads, or should I say for two out of the only four pasta salads I like. Pasta salads are all the rage outside Italy, but not with me, nor with most of my compatriots. We prefer our pasta hot, but at a large party like this, a few cold pasta dishes would be popular. My pasta salads are, I hope, a far cry from those porridge-like concoctions sold in many delicatessens, where overcooked pasta shapes stick to each other in a horrid mess of gluey sauce. Cold pasta must be slightly undercooked and tossed with an olive oil dressing, not with a mayonnaise-based or cream-based sauce.

The sweets also appear in other menus, but one that is particular to this menu is the ricotta ice-cream. It is a recipe kindly given to me by Caroline Liddell and Robin Weir and is included in their new book, *Ices*, published by New English Library. The authors write: 'Both the flavour and the texture are clearly ricotta' and indeed they are. I have tried the recipe both with fresh ricotta and with long-life ricotta, and the ice-cream is delicious with either.

The recipe for the melt-in-the-mouth chocolate cake comes from my daughter, the Julia of the title. It is one that even I, not a chocolate lover, find irresistible. It is perfect with the ricotta ice-cream, while the potato and almond cake (page 122) makes an ideal accompaniment to the fruit salad on page 28 or the stewed pears.

*** *Vitello tonnato alla Milanese*

VEAL IN A TUNA SAUCE

---

1 joint of veal, about 1.35 kg/3 lb	300 ml/½ pint chicken stock
1 carrot	225 g/8 oz best tuna, packed in
1 celery stick	olive oil or brine
1 medium onion, stuck with 2	6 anchovy fillets
cloves	6 tbsp double cream
1 bay leaf	1 tsp caster sugar
a few parsley stalks	the juice of 1 lemon
salt	4 tbsp extra virgin olive oil
6 peppercorns, bruised	2 tbsp fresh tarragon
150 ml/¼ pint dry white wine	

For the decoration

1 lemon	a few cornichons

Ask the butcher to tie the joint in a neat shape. Put it in a casserole with the carrot, celery, onion, bay leaf, parsley stalks, a little salt and the peppercorns. Pour in the wine and half the stock and bring slowly to the boil. Cover the pan tightly and cook for about 1½ hours until the meat is tender. Draw off the heat and leave to cool in the pan.

When the veal is cold, cut it into 1 cm/½ in slices and lay them, slightly overlapping, on a serving dish.

Remove the bay leaf and the parsley stalks from the cooking juices. Purée all the cooking juices and the vegetables in a food processor. Transfer the purée to a bowl.

Put the tuna and the anchovies in the food processor. Add a few tablespoons of the remaining stock and process for 1 minute or so. Scrape the bits down from the side of the bowl and add a few tablespoons of the purée, the cream and the sugar. Process again, while gradually adding the lemon juice and the olive oil. You might not need to add all the lemon juice, or you might want a little more. Taste a few times and correct the sauce to your liking, adding salt if necessary and a good grinding of pepper. The sauce should have the consistency of single cream. If necessary, add more stock. Coat the veal slices with a few tablespoons of the sauce. Cover with clingfilm and refrigerate.

When you are ready to serve the veal, spoon over a little more sauce and transfer the rest of the sauce to a bowl, to be handed round separately. Coarsely chop or cut the tarragon and scatter over the veal. Decorate with the lemon, cut into butterfly shapes, and with the cornichons, if you wish, and serve with a bowl of cold rice dressed with some extra virgin olive oil.

PREPARATION
The dish is best made a day or even 2 days in advance.

* *Insalata di pasta, fontina, noci e sedano*
PASTA, FONTINA, WALNUT AND CELERY SALAD

---

450 g/1 lb small macaroni or other medium-sized tubular pasta
salt
8 tbsp mild extra virgin olive oil
225 g/½ lb fontina
225 g/½ lb Bel Paese
225 g/½ lb Gorgonzola piccante (strong)

4 tbsp walnut kernels
the heart of 1 large celery head
1 tbsp walnut oil
freshly milled black pepper
a handful of celery leaves

Cook the pasta in plenty of salted boiling water and drain when very *al dente*. Refresh under cold water, drain again and transfer to a large bowl. Pat dry with kitchen paper. Toss with the olive oil and leave to cool completely.

Cut the three cheeses into small cubes and add to the pasta, together with the walnut kernels.

If you use the heart of the celery the stalks should not have any strings, but if there are still some, remove them with a knife or a swivel-action peeler. Cut the stalks into thin strips and add to the bowl. Toss with the walnut oil and with plenty of pepper. Taste and add salt if necessary. Leave aside for 1 hour or so for the flavours to combine.

Sprinkle the celery leaves over the top to make the salad look pretty.

PREPARATION
The pasta can be cooked and tossed with oil up to 6 hours in

advance. The other ingredients, which can be prepared up to 1 day ahead, must be added no longer than 2 hours in advance.

✳✳   *Conchiglie rosse ripiene di spaghettini in insalata*

SALAD OF RADICCHIO LEAVES FILLED WITH THIN SPAGHETTI

---

2 or 3 large radicchio heads	2 garlic cloves
450 g/1 lb spaghettini	2 dried chillies
salt	freshly milled black pepper
120 ml/4 fl oz extra virgin olive oil	225 g/½ lb black olives
60 g/2 oz parsley, preferably flat-leaf	5 tbsp capers
	8 hard-boiled eggs

Cut the core of the radicchio heads and unfurl the outside leaves very gently so that they remain whole. Keep the rest of the radicchio for the green salad. Wash the leaves, dry very thoroughly and place them on one or two large dishes. You will need about 15 leaves.

Cook the *spaghettini* in plenty of salted water. It cooks quite quickly, and when serving it cold you should drain it when you think it is still on the undercooked side. Drain and refresh it under cold water. Drain again and then transfer to a large bowl. Pat dry with kitchen paper. Toss with half the oil and allow to cool.

About 2 hours before you want to serve the pasta, chop together, by hand or in a food processor, the parsley, garlic and chillies. Add the mixture to the *spaghettini* and toss thoroughly with the rest of the oil. Taste and add salt and pepper if necessary.

Fill each radicchio leaf with a forkful or two of *spaghettini*. Sprinkle the olives and the capers over it. Cut the eggs in segments and decorate each shell or the dish with them.

PREPARATION
The radicchio leaves can be prepared up to 1 day in advance and kept in the fridge in a covered container. The pasta can be cooked and partly dressed with the oil up to 8 hours ahead, but it must be dressed no longer than 4 hours in advance.

***   # Gelato di ricotta

RICOTTA ICE-CREAM

400 ml/14 fl oz full-fat milk	*250 g/9 oz ricotta*
225 g/8 oz granulated sugar	*150 ml/¼ pint whipping cream*
3 egg yolks	*1 tbsp dark rum*

First make the custard. Combine the milk and half the sugar in a medium-sized saucepan and bring to boiling point. Meanwhile in a medium-sized heatproof bowl combine the egg yolks with the remaining sugar and beat, preferably with a hand-held electric mixer, until the mixture is pale and thick enough to hold the shape when a ribbon of mix is trailed across the surface. Pour the hot milk in a thin stream on to the egg yolks and sugar, whisking steadily as the milk is added.

The bowl can now be placed over a pan of simmering water, or the custard can be returned to the saucepan which should then be put on top of a heat diffuser mat so that it is not in direct contact with the heat. Only if you have an accurate thermometer, and/or are confident that you will not overheat the sauce, should you put the saucepan over a gentle direct heat.

Use a small wooden spoon or spatula to stir the custard. Heated over water, the custard will not suffer as long as it is stirred frequently; it will take 25–30 minutes to thicken sufficiently, or to reach 85°C/185°F. Over direct heat the custard needs constant attention and will take 8–10 minutes. Without a thermometer to judge if the custard has thickened sufficiently, remove the spoon and tilt the back of it towards you. Look first at the way the sauce coats the spoon. If it forms only a thin film, try drawing a horizontal line across the back of the spoon. This should hold a clear shape. If not, continue cooking the custard until it coats the back of the spoon more thickly and holds a clear line. As soon as the custard has reached the right temperature and thickened sufficiently, remove the pan from the heat and plunge the base in a few inches of cold water.

Gradually beat in pieces of the crumbled ricotta and continue to beat vigorously until the custard is almost smooth. (Do not worry if a few small lumps remain; these will be broken down in the churning process.) When cold, remove, cover and chill in the fridge.

When ready, start the ice-cream machine. Stir the chilled cream and rum into the custard, then pour into the machine and churn until the mixture has frozen to a consistency firm enough to serve or to store. Quickly scrape into plastic freezer boxes, cover with waxed paper and a lid. When frozen allow about 25–30 minutes in the fridge to soften sufficiently to serve.

** *La torta di cioccolato di Julia*

CHOCOLATE AND NUT CAKE

Make sure the nuts you buy are not stale; buy them from a reliable shop with a quick turnover. Use eggs that are at room temperature, not straight out of the refrigerator.

---

225 g/8 oz hazelnuts	*225 g/8 oz caster sugar*
225 g/8 oz walnuts	*5 large eggs, separated*
225 g/8 oz best-quality bitter chocolate	*1½ tbsp orange peel, very finely chopped*
75 ml/2½ fl oz brandy	*icing sugar*
1 tsp ground cinnamon	*pouring cream (optional)*
2 tbsp full-cream milk	

Heat the oven to 200°C/400°F/Gas 6.

Spread the hazelnuts in a baking tray and toast them for 5 minutes. Leave them to cool a little and then rub them between your hands, or with a rough cloth, to remove the papery skin. Do this in the sink or, better still, in the garden, to avoid having little bits of the brown skin flying all over the kitchen.

Put the hazelnuts and the walnuts in the food processor. Cut the chocolate into small pieces and add to the nuts. Pulse the machine on and off until the mixture is of a grainy consistency, not ground fine.

Transfer the mixture to a bowl and then stir in the brandy, cinnamon, milk and sugar. Mix thoroughly. Now add the egg yolks gradually, blending them in very well, and finally add the orange peel.

Butter generously a 20 cm/8 in spring-clip cake tin. Sprinkle with flour and then shake off any excess.

Whisk the egg whites until stiff but not dry. Ideally you should use a large wire balloon whisk or a hand-held electric beater that can be moved around the mixture. An electric table-mixer is not satisfactory, and a food processor is not at all suitable. If you have one, use a large copper bowl, copper being the most efficient material for feeding bubbles of air into the whites. Fold the egg whites into the chocolate mixture with a large metal spoon, a few tablespoons at a time, cutting through the mixture with a high movement to incorporate more air.

When all the egg whites have been lightly folded in, spoon the mixture into the prepared tin and bake in the oven for about 1 hour. The cake is ready when a cocktail stick inserted in the middle comes out dry. Unclip the band and turn the cake on to a wire rack. Remove the base and leave until cold.

Before serving, sprinkle lavishly with icing sugar. Cream is optional, but it certainly makes the cake even more luscious.

PREPARATION
The cake is better eaten as soon as it is cool. But you can satisfactorily make it up to 1 day in advance.

Harmonious Menus

Perhaps the title should be 'Even More Harmonious Menus', since, as I have often said, Italian meals are usually conceived as a whole so that the flavours in the various courses harmonize with each other. But the five menus in this section have a particular theme running through them. In the first two the theme is a colour, and in the other three it is a flavour.

Dinners based on a particular colour used to be very fashionable in 'high society' in the 1920s and 30s. With the war, and the austerity of the post-war years, such occasions were banished from the social scene, but in the 70s they began to come back. I was lucky enough to go to one of the most sophisticated, which took place in my native Milan. The invitation asked the guests to come in black and white for *'una cena in frac'* – a supper in white tie. I arrived in what I thought was quite a smart outfit, forgetting how Italian women are likely to rise to a challenge like that. They all appeared as if dressed by Poiret after drawings by Aubrey Beardsley. When the dining-room door opened, the elegance of the table competed with that of the guests. White everything, except for a few black, or rather very deep purple, tulips intermingled with cascades of white lilacs and strongly scented white tuberoses.

Here and there on the table lay white dishes containing black and white food. I remember hard-boiled eggs covered with caviar, small balls of cream cheese coated with black pepper, prunes stuffed with paté placed between *bocconcini* – morsels – of buffalo mozzarella. The first course was a sensational bowl of black tagliatelle made with cuttlefish ink in a creamy fish sauce, followed by chicken *chaud-froid*. The salads were tiny potatoes dressed with oil and covered with slivers of black truffle, and thin strips of fennel sprinkled with poppy-seeds. The pudding was equally arresting: white ice-cream made with lemon-flavoured cream surrounded by blackberries.

One of these days I shall try to recreate this menu. Meanwhile I have successfully produced golden dinners and green dinners, like those that follow, though I have never asked my guests to come dressed in gold or green. I pass the idea on to you.

Each of the other three menus in this section is based on a particular flavour. What is important, when devising such a meal, is that the flavour that is carried through should be of the right kind.

I can best illustrate what I mean by giving one or two examples of the wrong kind of flavour. A dinner based on onion or garlic, for instance, apart from the rather crude obviousness of the ingredient, would be very unpopular with some people. A dinner with two consecutive courses in which tomato was the main flavouring ingredient would be boring to the eye and to the palate, as would a meal of two courses strongly flavoured with Parmesan. An ingredient that has the right kind of flavour is one that can present itself in various ways. An example of this would be a dinner based on fish. This is usually most pleasing, and is something very well accepted in Italy. You will find a few such menus in this book.

The most elaborate 'flavour' dinner I have heard of was given by the Archbishop of Milan in 1529. On this occasion, as John MacPhee tells us in his book *Oranges*, there were served '16 courses that included caviar and oranges fried with sugar and cinnamon, brill and sardines with slices of orange and lemon, oysters with pepper and oranges, lobster with citrons, sturgeon in aspic covered with orange juice, fried sparrows with oranges, individual salads containing citrons into which the coat of arms of the diner had been carved, a soufflé of pine nuts and raisins covered with orange juice and candied peel of citron and orange'.

My most memorable meal of this kind was at the restaurant Miron in Nervesa delle Battaglia, a town to the north of Venice. The restaurant specializes in *funghi*. It was September, and our Venetian friends took us there for lunch. Every course was based on one kind of *funghi* or another, starting with porcini caps in different guises and ending with an *insalatina di ovuli e scaglie di parmigiano* – a little salad of *Amanita caesaria* very thinly cut and Parmesan slivers dressed with olive oil and lemon juice.

The other day I was invited to an even more remarkable occasion, *un pasto alle rane* – a meal based on frogs. The appointment was at a restaurant in Parma for the following June or July, when frogs are at their best. The meal apparently starts with a pâté of frog, followed by a risotto with frogs, and then various other frog dishes. So many, in fact, that I cheekily asked if the *tiramisù* was layered with a cream of mascarpone and frog purée. Much as I love frogs, I thought that might be going too far. The menus I have created here are based on more conventional ingredients, lemon, basil and balsamic vinegar.

A GOLDEN DINNER FOR 6

Risotto giallo con costolette di maiale
SAFFRON RISOTTO WITH BREADED PORK CHOPS

Insalata di carote, sedano di Verona e arancie
CARROT, CELERIAC AND ORANGE SALAD

Zabaione gelato
COLD ZABAGLIONE

At the time of the Renaissance there was a belief that gold, consumed with one's food, was good for the heart. Thus, at the wedding feast given in 1368 for the marriage of a Visconti lady to the Duke of Chiarenza, all the birds and the fish were served covered with gold leaf. Apart from the imagined therapeutic effects of gold, its use by the nobility and the wealthy meant that it became very fashionable to serve golden food. The problem was, of course, that few families were as rich as the Visconti, Dukes of Milan, so they had to content themselves with the pretence rather than the reality; they created dishes that looked as though they were coated with gold. It was in this way that certain of the characteristic dishes of Milanese cooking were born, one of them being the famous *costolette alla milanese*.

Costolette are often accompanied by a risotto with saffron, to enhance the golden effect, not to mention the feeling of wealth given by eating such a costly food (at the time of writing saffron costs £4 for 25 g – less than an ounce!). In my menu the yellow risotto is served with pork chops, which are easier to find than the veal chops which Milanese tradition would dictate. You can fry the chops while you cook the risotto, since both need constant attention.

My menu carries the golden theme into the salad and the pudding. Carrot and orange are a good combination, to which I add celeriac to moderate the sweetness given by the other two ingredients.

The zabaglione is served cold, which makes it much easier for the hostess, and kinder on the digestion. I suggest passing around with it a dish of the almond crescents on page 380.

** *Risotto giallo*

SAFFRON RISOTTO

1.5 litres/2½ pints Italian broth
  (page 378)
1 small onion, very finely chopped
60 g/2 oz beef marrow, chopped, or
  pancetta, chopped
60 g/2 oz unsalted butter
350 g/12 oz arborio, or other
  Italian risotto rice

150 ml/¼ pint dry red wine
¼ tsp powdered saffron, or about
  ¼ tsp saffron threads, dissolved
  in ½ cup of boiling stock
salt
freshly ground black pepper
30 g/1 oz freshly grated Parmesan

I have devised this unorthodox method of making a risotto so as to cut down on the last-minute cooking. It works quite well.

Bring the broth to simmering point and keep it at a very low simmer.

Put the onion, beef marrow or *pancetta* and half the butter in a large, wide saucepan. Sauté until the onion is soft and translucent, and then add the rice and stir for about 2 minutes until well coated with fat. Pour in the wine, boil for 1 minute, stirring constantly, then pour in 300 ml/½ pint of the stock. As soon as the broth is boiling again, turn off the heat and cover firmly with a lid. You can now leave it for half an hour while you go and have a drink with your guests.

When you go back to finish the dish you will find that the rice will have absorbed all the stock and will be half done. Reheat the broth to simmering point. Add a knob of the butter to the rice and pour in about 200 ml/7 fl oz of the broth.

Mix the saffron infusion thoroughly and add to the rice. Continue cooking and adding broth in small quantities, especially when the rice is nearly cooked. Do not add too much at a time or you may finish with perfectly cooked rice swimming in too much stock. The rice should cook at a steady, lively simmer the whole time.

When the rice is ready – *all'onda* as we say, i.e. soft and creamy – turn off the heat and add the rest of the butter and the Parmesan. Leave, covered, for 1 minute and then give the risotto a vigorous stir to mix in the butter and the cheese – to *mantecare* the risotto, to make it creamy. Taste and check seasoning.

Transfer the risotto to a large round dish, previously warmed, and pile it in a golden mound at the centre of the dish. Surround it with the chops and serve at once.

PREPARATION

As I explain above, you can half cook the rice up to 1 hour in advance and then finish the dish just before serving.

**   *Costolette di maiale*

BREADED PORK CHOPS

---

6 pork chops, about 18 mm/¾ in thick	1 garlic clove, peeled
milk	½ small dried chilli, seeded
salt and freshly ground black pepper	90 g/3 oz dried breadcrumbs
	4 tbsp freshly grated Parmesan cheese
2 eggs	90 g/3 oz unsalted butter
1 tbsp fresh rosemary	1 tbsp vegetable oil

Ask the butcher to knock off the corners and trim off the tail ends of the chops. Remove most of the fat from the chops and trim them. Put them in a dish, cover with milk and sprinkle with salt and pepper. Leave to marinate for about 2 hours to soften the meat and make it whiter.

Lift the chops out of the marinade and pat dry with kitchen paper. In a soup plate or a large shallow bowl, beat the eggs lightly with 1 teaspoon of salt.

Chop and pound the rosemary, garlic and chilli to a powder and mix thoroughly with the breadcrumbs and the Parmesan. Spread this mixture on a plate.

Coat the chops with the egg, letting the surplus drain back into the dish, and then with the breadcrumb mixture. Pat the mixture firmly into the chops with your hands and then, if you have time, place the chops in the refrigerator. This is not essential, but it will make them easier to fry. They can be chilled for as little as 30 minutes or as long as 5 or 6 hours.

Heat the butter and the oil in a large, heavy frying pan. When the butter begins to turn a light russet colour, slip as many chops into the pan as will fit in a single layer. If your frying pan is not large enough to hold all the chops in a single layer, use two frying pans, dividing the butter and the oil between the two pans and adding an extra knob of butter to each pan. Fry for about 5 minutes, and then turn them over and cook for about 3 minutes. Turn the heat down and continue cooking for a further 5 minutes or so. Be careful not to burn the butter. The chops are cooked when they are easily pierced by a fork near the bone. Transfer to the risotto dish and serve.

PREPARATION

While the chops can be prepared in advance, they must be fried no longer than 15 minutes before serving.

* *Insalata di carote, sedano di Verona e arancie*

CARROT, CELERIAC AND ORANGE SALAD

450 g/1 lb carrots	*1 tsp French mustard*
225 g/½ lb celeriac	*salt and pepper*
3 oranges	*4 tbsp extra virgin olive oil*
the juice of 1 lemon	

Peel and grate the carrots through a mandolin or in a food processor fitted with a grater disc. Put in a bowl. Peel the celeriac, cut into chunks and discard, if necessary, the spongy flesh in the middle. Grate the celeriac and add to the bowl.

Scrub one of the oranges and dry it. Grate the rind of half the scrubbed orange and squeeze the juice of the same orange. Pour half this orange juice and the lemon juice into a bowl and whisk in the mustard, the grated orange rind and salt and pepper to taste. Gradually add the olive oil while whisking constantly to emulsify the sauce. Taste and adjust seasonings, adding more lemon or orange juice, according to your taste. Spoon over the carrot and celeriac mixture. Toss thoroughly and then pile the grated vegetables on to a dish.

Peel the remaining two oranges to the quick and slice them. Place the slices around the vegetables. Cover with clingfilm and leave for 30 minutes or so.

PREPARATION
This is the kind of salad that must be grated and dressed about 1 hour before serving.

**   *Zabaione gelato*

COLD ZABAGLIONE

---

5 egg yolks	gelatine (I prefer gelatine leaves
120 g/4 oz caster sugar	to powdered gelatine – gelatine
¼ tsp ground cinnamon	leaves are totally tasteless and
150 ml/¼ pint sherry, preferably	they dissolve more
medium	homogeneously)
2 gelatine leaves or 1 tsp powdered	200 ml/7 fl oz whipping cream

---

Beat the yolks and the sugar together with a metal whisk or a hand electric beater, until the mixture holds the shape when a ribbon of mix is trailed across the surface. Add the cinnamon and the sherry and continue beating for 1 minute. Put the bowl over a saucepan one-third full of hot water or use a double boiler. Bring the water to the slowest simmer, certainly not to the boil, while you continue whisking until the mixture becomes very light and has doubled its original volume. Put the base of the bowl in a sink of cold water and continue beating until it begins to cool down.

If you are using gelatine leaves, soften them in 3 tablespoons of cold water and then dissolve gently over a low heat. If you are using the powder, sprinkle the gelatine over 3 tablespoons of hot water. Leave it for a couple of minutes to 'sponge' and then dissolve, stirring it over a very low heat. Do not let it come near the boil. Pour the liquid into the custard, while beating vigorously. Put the mixture in the fridge.

About 1 hour before you want to serve it, whip the cream to soft peaks and fold into the zabaglione. Whip for a further minute or so, then spoon the zabaglione into tall-stemmed wine glasses. Place the glasses in the fridge until you bring them to the table.

PREPARATION
The zabaglione can be made up to 1 day in advance and kept, covered, in the refrigerator. Add the cream an hour or so before serving.

A GREEN AND WHITE DINNER FOR 6

Pecorino con le fave
PECORINO CHEESE WITH RAW BROAD BEANS

Quaglie nel nido
BRAISED QUAILS IN A NEST OF *PAGLIA E FIENO*

Insalata bianca e verde
LAMB'S LETTUCE, ROCKET AND FENNEL SALAD

Panna cotta
MOULDED CREAM PUDDING

Green and white make a lovely combination of colours for the table. This is especially so in the spring, when you can decorate the table with a bouquet of young shoots in different shades of green intermingled with small white roses or a few branches of philadelphus. But green and white is not only a happy conjunction of colours, it also produces a very effective combination of foods.

In Italy pasta is almost always served as a first course, rather than a main course. I am particularly happy to adhere to this custom because once I sit at the table I want to stay put rather than having to dash into the kitchen to cook the pasta half-way through the meal. So, when serving this menu recently, I offered the pecorino and broad beans as a snack with the pre-prandial drinks, reversing the Tuscan habit of eating them at the end of the meal. The pecorino was a particularly good one which a friend had brought from Tuscany. The first broad beans had just arrived in the shops, so they were small and young, which is what they must be when you eat them raw. Otherwise forget about the broad beans and serve the pecorino with some green olives.

The *secondo* is my adaptation of a dish I had some years ago at the Ristorante Peck in Milan. You can use pigeons instead of quails, but I do find the pigeons in this country very tough and dry. Quails, being farmed, are now available all the year round. The joy about using quails is that you can pick them up in your hands and eat them like that, especially when cooked slowly, in the Italian manner, so that the succulent meat comes away easily from the tiny bones. The long cooking time, 45 minutes, might amaze some people, but I assure you it is not a mistake!

The quails look attractive in their nest of green and white *tagliolini*. You can use a large round dish and put all the quails in the middle with the pasta around, or you can put two quails surrounded by the *tagliolini* on each individual plate.

The salad is served afterwards, and I suggest a change of plates rather than serving it on a side plate. It is a salad with a slightly tart flavour that fits perfectly between the courses that come before and after.

The *dolce* is one of my favourites. It is a traditional pudding from Piedmont with a light, subtle flavour, traditionally served on its own. In modern times I have seen *panna cotta* served with a coulis of raspberries, or with an apricot sauce or with some fresh strawberries. Purists would cry out at the sacrilege. I am more open-minded, and I have dared to serve *panna cotta* with *crème anglaise*. It was heavenly. For this dinner I have simply decorated the dish with sweet geranium leaves, to keep in tune with the colour theme, but if you prefer you could decorate it with three or four slices of kiwi.

* *Pecorino con le fave*

PECORINO CHEESE WITH RAW BROAD BEANS

This is hardly a recipe. All you have to do is buy 450 g/1 lb of pecorino, preferably seasoned and Tuscan, and 1.5 kg/3¼ lb of young broad beans.

Cut the pecorino into wedges and put them on a dish. Put the unpodded broad beans in a bowl and let everybody get on with it. The drink must be red wine; a good Chianti Classico would be perfect.

*** *Quaglie nel nido*

BRAISED QUAILS IN A NEST OF *PAGLIA E FIENO*

---

12 quails
100 g/3½ oz prosciutto, chopped
1 tbsp tomato purée
150 ml/¼ pint double cream
450 g/1 lb dried green and white
  tagliolini, or 700 g/1½ lb fresh
  paglia e fieno

1 tbsp vegetable oil
75 g/2½ oz unsalted butter
4 tbsp grated Parmesan

For the marinade

150 ml/5 fl oz good red wine
  vinegar
75 ml/3 fl oz olive oil
4 bay leaves
2 lemon strips
1 sprig of rosemary
1 bunch of parsley with stalks

1 sprig of fresh sage
1 onion, cut in pieces
3 garlic cloves
2 tsp salt, preferably rock salt
6 juniper berries, bruised
½ tbsp peppercorns, bruised
a few celery leaves

Clean, wash and trim the quails. Put them in a pot, preferably earthenware, or in a casserole.

Heat all the ingredients for the marinade. Allow to cool, pour over the birds and leave for at least 6 hours. Turn the birds over as often as you can remember to.

Heat the oven to 170°C/325°F/Gas 3.

Put the casserole with the quails and the marinade on the heat and add the prosciutto and the tomato purée. Turn the birds over and over until the marinade is boiling. Lay the quails breast downwards. Cover the pot with a sheet of foil and put the lid on tightly. Place the pot in the oven and cook for 45 minutes.

Remove the quails from the pot and keep them warm, loosely covered with the foil.

Remove the bay leaves and any tough sprigs from the cooking juices and purée the juices in a food processor. Put the purée in a clean saucepan and add the cream. Taste and check seasoning, and keep it warm on a flame disperser placed over a very low heat, or in a bain-marie.

Cook the pasta in plenty of salted boiling water to which you have added the vegetable oil. Drain very quickly, reserving 1 cupful of the pasta water. Return the pasta to the pan and toss with the butter and the cheese. Add some of the pasta water to achieve the right fluidity.

Shape the pasta into a ring on a large round heated dish, or divide into six portions and place on individual heated plates. Put the quails in their large common nest, or two birds into each nest. Spoon all the sauce over the birds and serve at once.

PREPARATION

The quails can be prepared up to 2 days in advance and reheated in the oven. The sauce can be made up to half an hour in advance, while the quails are kept warm, covered with foil, in a low oven. But the pasta must be cooked at the last minute.

* *Insalata bianca e verde*

LAMB'S LETTUCE, ROCKET AND FENNEL SALAD

---

225 g/½ lb lamb's lettuce
120 g/4 oz rocket
1 large fennel bulb, preferably of
   the round kind which is sweeter
6 spring onions, the white part only
120 g/4 oz green olives in natural
   brine

4 tbsp soured cream
2 tbsp extra virgin olive oil
the juice of 1 lemon
5 ml/1 tsp caster sugar
salt and pepper

Pick and wash the two salads. Dry them well and put them neatly on a dish. Remove and discard any brown patches on the outside of the fennel. If the fennel has some feathery green attached, cut it off, wash and dry it and add it to the green salads.

Cut the fennel bulb into quarters lengthwise, and then across into very thin strips no more than ½ cm/¼ in thick. Wash and dry them and scatter them over the salad.

Trim and wash the spring onions. Cut the white part into thin rings and scatter them over the salad. Put the olives here and there on the dish.

Beat the soured cream, oil, lemon juice, sugar, salt and pepper to an emulsion and pour over the salad. Do this just before you bring it to the table or the green leaves will wilt.

PREPARATION
You can trim and wash all the different vegetables up to 1 day in
advance. Keep them wrapped in a clean cloth or in a closed
container in the fridge. The dressing can be made up to 3 days in
advance.

✳✳✳   *Panna cotta*

MOULDED CREAM PUDDING

---

180 g/6 oz caster sugar
1 tsp lemon juice
450 ml/¾ pint double cream
150 ml/¼ pint full-fat milk
piece of vanilla pod

4 tbsp peach eau-de-vie or white rum
10 g/⅓ oz powdered gelatine or
  gelatine leaves
a couple of dozen sweet geranium
  leaves, if available

First prepare the caramel. Heat the oven to 170°C/325°F/Gas 3 and
place six 120 ml/4 fl oz ramekins in it to heat for 5 minutes.

Put 75 g/2½ oz of the sugar, 3 tablespoons of water and the
lemon juice into a small saucepan and bring slowly to the boil.
The syrup will heat up very slowly at first and then it will begin to
turn very pale gold. It will turn dark brown quite quickly. At that
moment withdraw the pan from the heat and pour the caramel
into the heated ramekins. Tip the ramekins in all directions for the
caramel to slide and coat the surface evenly. Set aside and prepare
the pudding.

Heat the cream, milk, vanilla and spirit in a heavy saucepan.
Add the remaining sugar and bring slowly to the boil, stirring
constantly. Boil for 1 minute. Set aside to infuse for 1 hour or so
and then strain the mixture.

Sprinkle the gelatine powder into 4 tablespoons of warm water
and leave to 'sponge' for a few minutes. Heat the gelatine while
beating with a metal whisk until it has dissolved. If you are using
gelatine leaves, soften them in cold water and then squeeze them
and dissolve them in 4 tablespoons of hot water. Spoon a couple
of tablespoons of the cream mixture into the gelatine, stirring
rapidly. Now add this mixture to the cream mixture, stirring very
thoroughly to incorporate.

Pour the cream mixture into the ramekins. Allow to cool and then cover with clingfilm and chill for at least 2 hours.

Run a palette knife around the side of the ramekins and then unmould on to individual plates. Place the sweet geranium leaves around each mould as if they were the petals of a flower.

PREPARATION

The cream mixture can be prepared up to 1 day in advance. Keep in the ramekins and unmould just before serving.

A LEMON-FLAVOURED DINNER FOR 8

Stracciatella al sapor di limone
LEMON-FLAVOURED EGG AND PARMESAN SOUP

Vitello al limone con la puré di patate
VEAL WITH LEMON AND CREAM, AND POTATO PURÉE

Coppette di frutta al caramello
FRUIT SALAD IN A CARAMEL SAUCE

The theme here is lemon, used in all three dishes but in different ways. It is a flavour I like very much, not only in sweet things but also in savoury dishes. This menu is one of my favourites and, as it happens, everybody to whom I give it seems to be as enthusiastic about it as I am. It is an elegant and well-balanced menu and yet it is one of the easiest you could make.

The light soup needs a home-made Italian broth (my recipe is on page 378) made with meat and just a few bones, rather than the other way round.

The second course, I can only beg you to try. It is expensive, the veal being an expensive cut, but it goes a long way because you eat every bit of it. Go to a good butcher, preferably one who knows the different cuts, and ask for a joint suitable for roasting. I like to serve the veal with a buttery-soft potato purée, but I have also successfully served fresh tagliatelle as an accompaniment. I cook the pasta just before sitting at the table and keep it hot in the cooking pan, tossed with butter and a few tablespoons of the veal sauce. A dish of buttered spinach is the ideal vegetable.

The little fruit salad has a flavour all of its own, given by the lemony-orangy caramel.

*   ## Stracciatella al sapor di limone

LEMON-FLAVOURED EGG AND PARMESAN SOUP

---

3 eggs
4 tbsp semolina
6 tbsp freshly grated Parmesan
salt and freshly ground pepper,
   preferably white

the grated rind of 1 lemon
2.3 litres/4 pints Italian broth (see
   page 378)
a handful of fresh marjoram leaves

Beat the eggs lightly in a bowl. Add the semolina, Parmesan, salt and pepper and the grated lemon rind. Beat thoroughly with a fork.

Heat the broth to simmering point. Pour a couple of ladlefuls over the egg mixture, whisking with a fork or a balloon wire whisk.

Turn the heat down to low and pour the egg mixture into the broth. Cook for 5 minutes, whisking the whole time. Taste and adjust seasoning. The egg mixture will curdle and form soft flakes. Ladle the soup into individual bowls and add the washed and dried marjoram leaves.

PREPARATION
This soup takes only 2 or 3 minutes to make once the broth has come to the boil. You can mix the eggs, semolina and parmesan up to 1 hour in advance.

**   ## Vitello al limone

VEAL WITH LEMON AND CREAM

1.6 kg/3½ lb veal rump in a single
   piece, tied into a neat roll
2 large lemons
salt and pepper
1 sprig of rosemary
6 fresh sage leaves

2 sprigs of thyme
1 small bunch of parsley
a handful of celery leaves
1 garlic clove, peeled
90 g/3 oz unsalted butter
300 ml/½ pint double cream

Put the veal in a bowl and squeeze the juice of 1 lemon over it. Season with salt and pepper and marinade for about 2 hours. Chop all the herbs, the celery leaves and the garlic, and put in an oval casserole which will hold the piece of meat rather snugly. Add the butter and sauté the herbs for 1 minute.

Dry the veal thoroughly and add to the casserole. Sauté gently on all sides; the meat should just lose its raw colour.

While the veal is sautéing, peel the other lemon to the quick and slice it very thinly. Tuck the slices under the meat. Heat the cream and pour it over the meat. Sprinkle with salt and pepper. Cover the casserole, putting the lid slightly askew – this will intensify the flavour of the sauce by letting the vapours evaporate. Cook for 1½–2 hours, turning the veal over from time to time.

When the veal is cooked – the timing depends on the cut of the veal and the thickness of the joint, but it must be tender right through when pricked with a fork – taste and check the seasonings of the sauce. If it seems a little watery (it all depends on how much water the raw meat contained), remove the veal to a carving board and cover loosely with foil. Reduce the sauce by boiling it fast until rich and fully flavoured.

Let the veal rest for 5 minutes before carving it into 1 cm/½ in slices. An electric carving knife is a great help when carving a braised joint like this. Lay the slices, slightly overlapping, on a heated dish. Spoon some of the sauce over it and serve the rest separately in a sauce boat.

PREPARATION
The dish can be prepared up to 2 days in advance and refrigerated. It can also be frozen, but it must be thawed before reheating. Carve it before reheating it in the casserole.

**   *Coppette di frutta al caramello*

FRUIT SALAD IN A CARAMEL SAUCE

4 bananas	a lovely bunch of seedless white
the juice of 2 lemons, strained	grapes, about 450 g/1 lb
7–9 clementines, according to	5 tbsp granulated sugar
size	the juice of 1 orange, strained

Peel the bananas and cut into fairly thick rounds. Put in a bowl and sprinkle with a little lemon juice. Mix, cover the bowl with clingfilm and chill for half an hour.

Peel the clementines and remove as much of the stringy white pith as time and your patience will allow. Some clementines are quite difficult to clean properly. Put in a bowl, sprinkle with a little lemon juice, cover with clingfilm and chill.

Wash and dry the grapes and set aside.

For the caramel sauce, put the sugar and 3 tablespoons of cold water in a small aluminium or unlined copper saucepan. Put the pan over medium heat and heat until the mixture becomes a golden colour. Do not stir, in spite of the temptation to do so. It will take a good 5–7 minutes to begin to become golden and then it will quickly darken in colour. At that moment remove from the heat straight away.

While the sugar is melting, heat the juice of the orange and the remaining lemon juice slowly. Add the hot fruit juices to the caramel, stirring hard, as soon as you draw the caramel off the heat. I heat the juice to prevent any of the caramel going hard, but if this should happen, put the pan back on the heat and stir hard until all lumps of caramelized sugar have melted. Leave aside to cool.

About 1 hour before serving, divide the fruit between eight glass bowls. Spoon the sauce over and return to the fridge.

PREPARATION
The pudding can, if necessary, be prepared up to 1 day in advance. It is still good, but the bananas will have darkened. I suggest you prepare everything except the bananas the day before if you need to.

A BASIL-FLAVOURED DINNER FOR 8

Patate e fagiolini al pesto
POTATOES AND GREEN BEANS WITH PESTO

Dentice al forno
BAKED SEA BREAM WITH TOMATOES AND BASIL

Spinaci all'agro
LEMON-FLAVOURED SPINACH (page 373)

Sorbetto di limone al basilico
BASIL-FLAVOURED LEMON SORBET (page 106)

Basil has been known in Mediterranean countries since antiquity, when it was considered a sacred plant. In one of Boccaccio's stories, the heroine, Isabella, buries her murdered lover's head in a pot of basil. The story was made into a poem by Keats: 'And so she ever fed it with thin tears,/Whence thick and green and beautiful it grew.' A seventeenth-century visitor to Italy wrote, 'Amongst their Medicinall Plants scarce known amongst us, I took notice of one Odiferous Hearbe called Basilico.'

Basil is still very much associated with Italy, and especially with the cooking of Liguria. It is in Liguria that pesto was created, because that is where the best basil is to be found. The climate there is ideal, combining moist sea breezes with warm, dry sunshine. Basil needs those conditions to be at its best; in more northern climates it loses its sweetness and becomes too pungent and mint-like. In spite of that, however, basil is now all the rage in northern Europe and the USA, where people have discovered it at long last.

If you grow your own basil, don't keep the plants too long, as the taste becomes quite unpleasant. Basil plants are now so easily available that it is best to use them and then after a month or so buy a new one. For this reason I use basil mostly in the late spring and early summer, when it is quite sweet. I make my pesto for freezing then, but without the garlic or the cheese, which I add when I want to use it.

The warm potato and bean salad in this menu is based on the Genoese *trenette al pesto*, in which the *trenette*, a home-made kind of tagliatelle, are cooked with potatoes and French beans. Here I do without the pasta, which always needs cooking at the last minute, and serve the vegetables on their own. The pesto for this dish is made without cheese.

The fish course is very simple, but it must be cooked shortly before serving. The fish used in Italy for this dish is dentix, a Mediterranean fish of excellent quality. As dentix is seldom available here, I use sea bream, which is almost as good. You can get small sea bream of about 350 g/¾ lb each, or larger ones weighing more than 1–1.5 kg/2–3¼ lb. I prefer to buy two large fish rather than eight little ones; they are simpler to cook and the fish look grander when brought to the table. The basil in this course is just part of the overall Mediterranean flavour. The lemon-flavoured spinach on page 373 would be a perfect accompaniment to the fish.

The finale is the delicious sorbet on page 106.

* *Patate e fagiolini al pesto*

POTATOES AND GREEN BEANS WITH PESTO

---

1 kg/2 lb new potatoes	*5 tbsp extra virgin olive oil*
680 g/1½ lb green beans	*salt and pepper*

For the pesto

60 g/2 oz fresh basil leaves	*salt and pepper*
2 garlic cloves, peeled	*2 tbsp olive oil*
30 g/1 oz pine nuts	

To make the pesto, put all the ingredients in the food processor and process at high speed until they are completely blended. Taste and check seasonings.

Boil the potatoes in their skins. When ready, drain and peel them while still hot. Leave aside.

Top and tail the beans and wash them. Cook them in plenty of salted water until properly cooked, but not overcooked. (See my note about cooking green beans on page 80. When green beans are nearly ready they give off a characteristic smell. They usually need a few more minutes after that.) Drain the beans and transfer them to a piece of kitchen paper to dry. Cut them into 2.5 cm/1 in pieces.

While the beans are cooking, cut the potatoes into 2 cm/¾ in cubes, put them in a bowl and dress with the olive oil.

Add the beans and toss. Spoon the pesto into the salad and toss thoroughly but gently. Serve warm.

PREPARATION
You can cook the vegetables up to 2 hours in advance and dress them with the olive oil. Reheat them by placing the bowl, covered with a lid, over a saucepan of simmering water. It will take only 10 minutes to reheat. Mix thoroughly and then add the pesto. Pesto can be made in advance and frozen.

**   *Dentice al forno*

BAKED SEA BREAM WITH TOMATOES AND BASIL

---

*2 large sea bream weighing about
   1.35 kg/3 lb each
salt and pepper
6 garlic cloves, peeled and bruised
1 bunch of parsley, chopped
6 tbsp olive oil
150 ml/¼ pint dry white wine*

*8 ripe tomatoes, peeled, seeded and
   cubed
1 dried chilli
2 dozen fresh basil leaves, torn into
   small pieces
2 tsp anchovy purée*

Heat the oven to 200°C/400°F/Gas 6.

Wash the fish and check that the fishmonger has removed all the scales and the gills. Dry the fish thoroughly and season with salt and pepper inside and out. Place 1 garlic clove and half a tablespoon of parsley into each cavity.

Brush an ovenproof dish with 1 tablespoon of the oil and place the fish in it. Pour over the wine and 3 tablespoons of the remaining oil and place the dish in the oven. Bake for 25 minutes, basting occasionally. The fish is ready when the eye bulges out and the flesh parts easily from the bone. Keep warm while you prepare the sauce.

Put the rest of the oil, the tomato, chilli, basil, anchovy purée and the remaining garlic cloves in a frying pan and cook for 5 minutes.

When the fish is ready, spoon a few tablespoons of the cooking

When the fish is ready, spoon a few tablespoons of the cooking juices into the sauce and add salt to taste. Remove the garlic and the chilli and pour the sauce into a heated bowl. When you serve the fish, spoon a little of the cooking juices over each portion and hand round the sauce separately.

PREPARATION
I am afraid this is the sort of dish that must be cooked shortly before eating. You can keep the fish warm, covered with foil, in the oven with the heat turned off, while you serve the first course. The sauce can also be kept warm, or it can easily be reheated.

A BALSAMIC-VINEGAR-FLAVOURED DINNER FOR 6

Cicoria belga all'aceto balsamico
ROASTED CHICORY WITH BALSAMIC VINEGAR

Petti di anatra all'aceto balsamico
DUCK BREASTS WITH BALSAMIC VINEGAR

Gelato di fragola all'aceto balsamico
STRAWBERRY ICE-CREAM FLAVOURED WITH BALSAMIC
VINEGAR

After reading my previous book, *Secrets from an Italian Kitchen*, some of my friends suggested that balsamic vinegar must be one of my favourite ingredients. Well, yes, it is. So I really enjoyed designing a menu round it.

I find vinegar a good addition to many dishes. Balsamic vinegar has a sweeter and deeper flavour than other vinegars, as a result of the way it is made. While any wine vinegar is made from dry wine, balsamic vinegar starts from cooked white Trebbiano grapes which are picked very late. The result of the cooking of the 'must' is that most of the water is evaporated and thus the sugar content becomes much higher. The lovely amber syrup is then put in a wooden barrel from which, some long time later, it is decanted into a succession of at least five other barrels. This process of maturing must by law last for twelve years or more, and only then is the balsamic vinegar ready.

The expertise of the maker, the ideal climate of the provinces of Modena and nearby Reggio and, finally, the approval of the 'tasting masters' make this a very fine vinegar with a deep velvety sweetness and a complex mixture of aromas. No wonder it has been the most highly regarded condiment since the Middle Ages. This, the *aceto balsamico tradizionale*, can be bought only in specialized shops in Italy at stratospheric prices.

The balsamic vinegar you and I usually buy in shops outside Italy is something rather different. It is still made from the boiled must of the same Trebbiano grape, but it is produced in a much-reduced span of time and its particular flavour is sometimes emphasized by caramelized sugar. In spite of not being the 'genuine article', this balsamic vinegar is still a condiment that can, for instance, harmonize the symphony of flavours in a seafood salad, or blend with the robustness of the raw meat in a Carpaccio. Balsamic vinegar brings out aromas and scents with an intensity never previously detected.

This is what it does in the first and last courses of my menu. The delicious bitterness of the chicory is tempered, and yet enhanced, by the complex sweetness of the vinegar. Strawberries dressed with balsamic vinegar are a classic of Emilia-Romagna, for precisely the reasons given above. But, as far as I know, this *gelato* is my own creation. I certainly have never eaten it or heard of it before. As you might detect, I am rather proud of this recipe – I hope you will see why! If you want to serve a balsamic vinegar-flavoured dinner when strawberries are out of season, I suggest you make the mascarpone ice-cream on page 23 and simply put on the table a pretty little bottle full of balsamic vinegar. A teaspoon poured on each portion makes a lovely flavour contrast, and colour contrast, with the ivory richness of the ice-cream.

In the *secondo* the balsamic vinegar is used in the sauce to cut through the richness of the duck, much as brandy, port or Madeira are. I wrote this recipe for duck breasts, as they are easily available in many shops nowadays, though I prefer to buy a duck and remove the breasts, which are enough for my husband and myself. I then make a *ragù* for a dish of pasta with the rest of the meat, and I boil the carcass for a bowl of rich, well-flavoured stock. But this needs time, and time, today, is often the least easily available ingredient. So I suggest you buy the French *magrets de canard*, which are now sold in many butchers and better supermarkets. Some of these breasts are quite large, weighing 250 g/9 oz each, which is enough for two people. They are from Barbary ducks, which have leaner meat. These duck breasts go very well with the stewed lentils that accompany *cotechino* on page 268, or with the celery purée on page 225. A second *contorno* – accompanying vegetable – could be grilled polenta (page 378), which you can prepare beforehand and just reheat quickly in the oven for 5 minutes.

I have tried cooking the breasts beforehand and then warming them, cut into slices, in the sauce for half a minute. It does not work, however, because they cook too much and curl up, looking not very attractive. But cooking the duck is the only thing you have to do at the last minute, as the first course is already on the plates and the last is ready in the freezer or the fridge. In fact, this is another menu which might have been specially designed for the 'last-minute cook'.

* *Cicoria belga all'aceto balsamico*

ROASTED CHICORY WITH BALSAMIC VINEGAR

---

2 salted anchovies or 4 anchovy
   fillets
milk
8 fat, firm chicory heads of similar
   size
150 ml/¼ pint extra virgin olive
   oil

salt and pepper
2 tbsp pine nuts
4 tbsp balsamic vinegar
225 g/½ lb curly endive (frisée)
3 hard-boiled eggs

Rinse the salted anchovies under cold water or drain the oil from the anchovy fillets and pat them dry. Chop coarsely, put them in a small bowl and cover them with milk. This will bring out the strong flavour.

Remove a thin slice from the root end of each chicory head and any brown edges from the outside leaves. Slice the heads in half along their length and rinse them under cold water. Lay them on a slanting board, cut side down, to drain for half an hour. Dry them with kitchen paper.

Heat the oven to 230°C/450°F/Gas 8.

Grease an oven tray with a little of the oil. Lay the chicory halves, cut side up, on the tray, brush them with olive oil and season with salt and pepper. Bake for 10 minutes, until the inner core can be pierced with a fork. Transfer them to a dish.

Remove the anchovies from the milk and put them in a small frying pan with the remaining oil. Cook gently for 1 minute while mashing them with a fork. Keep the heat very low or the anchovies will acquire a bitter flavour. Stir in the pine nuts and the balsamic vinegar. Sauté for a further minute and then add salt, if necessary, and a good deal of pepper. Spoon three-quarters of the hot sauce over the chicory. Cover with clingfilm and set aside for 2 hours.

Wash the endive and dry it thoroughly.

Half an hour before you are ready to serve dinner, cut the endive into very thin strips. This is quite easy if you gather little bunches of the leaves and then shred them, the finer the better. Place the shredded endive on a serving dish, spoon over the remaining sauce, but do not mix the salad or you will spoil its appearance.

Place the chicory halves neatly on the bed of endive and pour over all the juices from the dish where it has been sitting.

Cut the hard-boiled eggs in half and take out the yolks (you can use the whites in a salad on another occasion). Press the yolks through a sieve or through a food mill fitted with the small-hole disc. Do this directly over the dish so that the egg mimosa will stay airy and light.

PREPARATION

The only thing that is better done at the last minute is the sieving of the egg yolks. The rest can be prepared up to 3 hours in advance. The chicory can be baked up to 1 day in advance and kept covered. It does not need refrigerating.

** *Petti di anatra all'aceto balsamico*

DUCK BREASTS WITH BALSAMIC VINEGAR

60 g/2 oz unsalted butter	*strong meat stock*
1 celery stalk, very finely chopped	*3 duck breasts, weighing about*
1 shallot, very finely chopped	*350 g/12 oz each*
salt and pepper	*1 tbsp olive oil*
4 tbsp dry white wine	*4 tbsp balsamic vinegar*
150 ml/¼ pint duck stock, or other	*1 tbsp flour*

Heat the oven to 220°C/425°F/Gas 7.

Heat half the butter with the celery and the shallot in a saucepan. Add 2 pinches of salt. When the vegetables are just soft but by no means brown, pour over the wine and boil until the liquid is reduced by half. Add the stock and simmer gently for about 30 minutes.

While the sauce is simmering away, score the skin of the duck breasts with the point of a sharp knife, deeply enough to penetrate into the flesh, and rub with salt and pepper. Grease a roasting tin with the oil and lay the breasts on it, skin side down. Roast for 15–20 minutes, according to how well cooked you like your duck.

Remove the skin from the duck. (It is delicious cut into small strips, fried and sprinkled over a radicchio salad.) Put the duck on a plate and keep warm, covered with foil. Skim off the extra fat from the roasting tin, if there is any. Put the tin over the heat and deglaze with the balsamic vinegar, boiling rapidly for 30 seconds, while scraping the bottom of the pan with a metal spoon. Pour into the sauce.

Blend together the remaining butter and the flour with the prongs of a fork. Add this mixture in small blobs to the sauce, while swirling the saucepan. When the last bit of the mixture is melted, the sauce is ready. Taste for seasoning and transfer to a heated sauce-boat.

Cut the duck breasts into slanting slices and transfer to a warm dish. Spoon over a little of the sauce. Serve the rest of the sauce separately.

PREPARATION

The sauce can be prepared in advance and reheated before the deglazing juices are added. For the duck, see the introduction on page 165.

*
with an
ice-cream
machine

**
without

Gelato di fragola all'aceto balsamico

STRAWBERRY ICE-CREAM FLAVOURED WITH BALSAMIC VINEGAR

---

450 g/1 lb strawberries	*1 tbsp balsamic vinegar*
150 g/5 oz caster sugar	*150 ml/5 fl oz whipping cream*

Wash and hull the strawberries. Dry them with kitchen paper and put them in a food processor with the sugar. Set the processor in motion and add the balsamic vinegar through the funnel.

Transfer the mixture to a bowl, cover it and refrigerate for 2–3 hours. The sugar and the vinegar will bring out the flavour of the fruit. Whip the cream to soft peaks and fold into the strawberry mixture. Put in the ice-cream machine, following the manufacturer's instructions. If you do not have an ice-cream machine, put the mixture in a container and cover it. Stir the mixture once during the freezing. Remove from the freezer half an hour before serving and leave at room temperature.

PREPARATION

This, like any fruit ice-cream, is best eaten within a day of being made.

Autumn Menus

A DINNER FOR 6

Passato di pomodoro
TOMATO SOUP

Fagiano alla Cavalcanti con la polenta
POT-ROAST PHEASANT IN A CAPER, PROSCIUTTO, VINEGAR
AND TRUFFLE SAUCE, WITH GRILLED POLENTA

Crespelle dolci di ricotta
SWEET RICOTTA PANCAKES

The accent of this menu is on elegance, although it is by no means insubstantial.

The tomato soup is fresher and lighter than most. It must be made with best-quality tomatoes, which are still in season when the first pheasants appear. I also recommend home-made vegetable stock, as it brings out the flavour of the tomatoes, while the rice flour gives a less gluey texture to the soup than ordinary flour.

The second course is something quite out of the ordinary. It is adapted from a recipe by one of my favourite cookery writers, Ippolito Cavalcanti, Duca di Buonvicino. You'll find quite a few recipes by Cavalcanti here and there in this book, since I find his *Cucina Teorico-Pratica*, published in 1847, an endless source of inspiration. I have to work hard to adapt the recipes because his quantities are erratic, sometimes extravagant for present-day palates, and are given in the measures used in Naples in the nineteenth century before the metric system was adopted. An example of the extravagance appears in the original recipe for this dish, where the amount of truffle to be added is 1 lb! Even though the truffles were probably not the much-esteemed white truffles of Alba, the *Tuber magnatum*, but only the more common and less flavoursome *Tuber aestivum*, the summer truffle, 1 lb seems somewhat excessive.

In my adaptation I have used truffle paste instead of real truffles. There are several brands of truffle paste, which can be found in the best delicatessens and Italian shops. The cheaper brands contain porcini (ceps) as well as truffle purée, plus butter or oil. Better brands contain only truffle purée and butter or oil.

There is also a new type of preserved truffle which I've been given in Italy but not yet seen elsewhere, in which the truffles, cut into pieces, are suspended in melted butter. This is quite delicious, since you can literally bite into the *cibus deorum*, or food of the gods, as Nero called them. Whatever you use, all these truffle derivatives make a remarkable difference to a dish, something you can verify by dressing some tagliatelle with truffle paste. And don't forget that you need only a very little of this expensive stuff.

Pheasant, these days, is so heavily farmed as to be closer in flavour to chicken than to the original bird of bygone days. Buy from a reputable shop; preferably buy an unplucked and undrawn bird, and ask the shopkeeper to hang it for the right length of time. How long that is is the subject of some contention. Brillat-Savarin wrote that 'the desirable point is reached when the pheasant begins to decompose. Then its aroma develops and mingles with an oil that requires a little fermentation for its distillation, just as coffee requires roasting for its full development.' Without subscribing to Brillat-Savarin's instructions, or to those of Grimod de La Reynière, who suggested that 'a pheasant killed on Mardi Gras should be eaten on Easter Sunday' (that is, forty days later!), I do find that all too often pheasants have an undistinguished taste because they are hardly hung at all. I prefer my pheasants hung for at least two weeks in cold weather, but, asking around, I have discovered that most people these days hang them for no longer than one week. It is a matter of personal preference. A hen bird is smaller than a cock, has a more tender flesh and is just perfect for three people.

I like to serve polenta with pheasant, either in the soft form or as grilled or fried slices. For a dinner party I always prefer grilled polenta. The polenta is made well in advance. It is cut and prepared in the grill pan and needs attention only for the very short time it takes to grill. The recipe for polenta can be found on page 378.

The vegetable accompaniment could be green beans, cooked *al dente, ma non troppo* as seems to be the fashion in most restaurants, and in some private houses too. The sautéed mushrooms with oregano and garlic on page 371 are also suitable, as are the carrots Italian style on page 372.

The pudding is a well-loved old-fashioned one from my childhood, equally loved by my children. For them I had to make it without the rum since, like most children, they could not bear spirits in puddings. I still remember the day when by mistake I used the sultanas which I keep steeped in rum and one of my sons, having eagerly put a spoonful of *crespella* into his mouth, spat it out and burst into tears, howling '*Ma c'è dentro il liquore*' ('There's liqueur in it'). If your children share this dislike, leave out the rum and soak the sultanas in warm milk instead.

These *crespelle* exemplify the quintessential taste of nineteenth-century Milanese cooking, in its perfectly balanced combination of northern Italian spicing with French saucing. Quite a few old northern Italian puddings are based on a sweet béchamel and flavoured with what used to be called Lombard sweet spices – cinnamon, nutmeg and cloves.

I like to make small pancakes when I serve them as a pudding because they are much prettier. The quantities given here will make about 18–20 small pancakes, but if you use a bigger frying pan you may not be able to stretch the batter that far.

*   *Passato di pomodoro*

TOMATO SOUP

4 shallots	salt and pepper
60 g/2 oz unsalted butter	600 ml/1 pint vegetable stock
1 small carrot	3 tbsp rice flour
2 celery stalks	18 fresh basil leaves
1 kg/2 lb ripe tomatoes	freshly grated Parmesan
6 garlic cloves, unpeeled	croûtons (optional)
15 g/½ oz caster sugar	

Chop the shallots and sauté them gently in the butter for 5 minutes. Chop the carrot and the celery and add to the onion. Cook for a further 5 minutes or so.

Meanwhile cut the tomatoes into segments and add to the vegetable *soffritto* together with the garlic, sugar, salt and pepper. Cook for 20 minutes then purée through a food mill. A food processor is not suitable because the tomatoes and the garlic cloves are unpeeled. Add the stock and simmer for a further 15 minutes. Add the rice flour in a thin stream while beating the soup with a small wire whisk or a fork. Cook for 10 minutes over very low heat. Taste and check seasoning.

Pour the soup into six soup bowls. Decorate with the basil

leaves and serve at once. Serve the cheese separately. If you want the soup to be more filling, hand round a bowl of croûtons.

PREPARATION
The soup can be made up to 3 days in advance and refrigerated. It also freezes well.

✳✳ *Fagiano alla Cavalcanti*
POT-ROAST PHEASANT IN A CAPER, PROSCIUTTO, VINEGAR AND TRUFFLE SAUCE

For this dish the prosciutto need not be *prosciutto di Parma*. If you can, buy cheaper prosciutto, cut in two or three thick slices. The truffle paste is available in the best delicatessen and Italian shops.

---

2 plump hen pheasants
a bunch of fresh herbs: sage,
   marjoram, parsley, rosemary
60 g/2 oz unsmoked streaky bacon
salt and pepper
30 g/1 oz unsalted butter
1 onion
4 cloves

1 garlic clove
5 juniper berries, bruised
2 tbsp brandy
150 ml/¼ pint good dry white
   wine
150 ml/¼ pint good strong meat
   stock

For the sauce

120 g/4 oz prosciutto
15 g/½ oz unsalted butter
1 tsp potato flour or arrowroot
150 ml/¼ pint good strong meat
   stock

2 tbsp capers
1 tbsp good red wine vinegar
1 tbsp truffle paste

Remove any stubborn quills from the pheasants, then wipe them clean.

Process the herbs and the bacon until the mixture is all pounded. If you do not have a food processor, chop very finely by hand. Season the birds with salt and pepper inside and out and push the bacon mixture into the cavities. Gently beat the breast bone down with the palm of your hand to give a rounder appearance to the birds. Spread about half the butter all over the breast.

Put the rest of the butter in a casserole, add the onion, cloves, garlic and juniper berries and sauté for 5–10 minutes. Add the pheasants and brown gently on all sides for a few minutes.

Heat the brandy and pour over the birds. Flame the brandy. Meanwhile heat the wine and half the stock and, when the flame from the brandy has died down, add to the pot. Season lightly, cover the pan and cook for about 1¼–1½ hours, until the pheasants are cooked through and the juices run clear when you pierce the thighs with a knife.

To make the sauce, cut the prosciutto into neat matchsticks and sauté in the butter for 2 minutes. Dissolve the potato flour or the arrowroot in a little of the cold stock and then add to the saucepan with the rest of the stock. Rinse the capers and mix into the sauce, together with the vinegar and the truffle paste.

Cook for 15 minutes over very low heat, stirring very frequently, then check the seasoning.

Cut the pheasants into neat joints (four is ideal) and arrange on a heated dish surrounded by the grilled polenta (page 378). Keep warm. Spoon over some of the cooking juices and strain the remaining juices into the prosciutto and caper sauce. Pour the sauce into a sauce-boat.

PREPARATION
The pheasants can be cooked and jointed up to 2 days in advance and refrigerated. Reheat in a low oven with all the cooking juices. Although pheasants freeze very well when uncooked, I don't recommend freezing the finished dish. The sauce can be made up to 1 hour before serving, and kept hot in a bain-marie.

*** *Crespelle dolci di ricotta*

SWEET RICOTTA PANCAKES

If you cannot find good fresh ricotta, use the UHT ricotta sold in tubs in most supermarkets.

For the pancakes

120 g/4 oz flour
pinch of salt
200 ml/7 fl oz semi-skimmed milk

3 large eggs
30 g/1 oz unsalted butter

For the stuffing

60 g/2 oz sultanas
2 tbsp rum
45 g/1½ oz unsalted butter
75 g/2½ oz soft brown sugar
450 g/1 lb ricotta
1 tbsp orange flower water
  (optional)

the grated rind of 1 lemon
½ tsp ground cinnamon
¼ tsp ground cloves
¼ tsp ground ginger
grated nutmeg
2 egg yolks

For the sauce

700 ml/1¼ pints full-cream milk
30 g/1 oz unsalted butter
30 g/1 oz flour

50 g/1¾ oz caster sugar
the juice of 1 orange
2 egg yolks

Prepare the batter. Sieve the flour and the salt into a bowl and add the milk in a thin stream, while beating hard with a small balloon whisk or a fork. Drop in the eggs, one at a time, beating rapidly. Cover the bowl and leave to rest for half an hour or so. You can leave the batter for up to 2 hours if necessary.

When you are ready to make the crêpes, melt half the butter and stir into the batter. The batter should have the consistency of thin cream. Add a couple of tablespoons of water if necessary. Pour the batter into a jug to make it easier to pour.

Smear the bottom of a 15 cm/6 in non-stick frying pan with a little of the remaining butter. Put the pan on moderate heat and heat until hot. Pour about 2 tablespoons of the batter into the pan, tilting the pan to distribute the batter evenly all over the bottom.

Cook until the edge begins to curl and turn golden and then flip the pancake over and cook the other side very briefly. Transfer the pancake to a board.

Draw the pan off the heat after each pancake or it will become too hot and the batter will cook before it can run evenly over the bottom of the pan. Stir the batter and pour it into the pan as before. Repeat this operation until you have used up all the batter, adding a little more butter if necessary.

Put the sultanas in a bowl, pour over the rum and leave for 20 minutes.

Melt the butter and stir in the brown sugar. Push the ricotta through the small-hole disc of a food mill, or through a sieve, into a bowl. Stir in the butter and sugar mixture, the sultanas and the rum, the optional orange flower water, the grated rind of the lemon and all the spices. Fold in the egg yolks and blend everything together thoroughly. Taste and add a little more sugar if needed.

Prepare the sauce. Heat the milk to simmering point. Meanwhile melt the butter and mix in the flour. Cook for 30 seconds, stirring constantly, and then remove the pan from the heat and add the milk very gradually. When all the milk has been added, return the pan to the heat and bring to the boil over gentle heat, stirring the whole time. Mix in the sugar and continue to cook for about 20 minutes, either in a bain-marie or using a heat-diffuser mat. Allow to cool a little and then mix in the orange juice and the egg yolks, one at a time, incorporating them very thoroughly.

Heat the oven to 165°C/325°F/Gas 3.

Butter the bottom of a large oven dish and spread over half the sweet béchamel sauce. Lay a single pancake flat on a chopping board and place on it about 1 tablespoon of the ricotta stuffing. Roll up the pancake and place it in the oven dish. Proceed in this manner until all the pancakes are stuffed and placed next to each other in the dish. Spoon the remaining sauce in between each *crespella* and spread a little over the top.

Bake in the oven for 15 minutes. Remove from the oven and leave the dish to stand for at least 5 minutes before serving.

PREPARATION

The pancakes can be made up to 3 days in advance and refrigerated in a box, layered with clingfilm or greaseproof paper. They also freeze very well for up to 1 month. The stuffing must be prepared no more than 1 day before serving, and the whole dish can be assembled, ready for the oven, up to 6 hours in advance.

A DINNER FOR 6

Peperoni ripieni della zia Renata
PEPPERS FILLED WITH AUBERGINES AND CROÛTONS

Pasticcio di pesce
FISH LASAGNE

Insalata verde
GREEN SALAD (page 368)

Ananas e arancie
PINEAPPLE AND ORANGES

My aunt Renata, a Milanese, had all the characteristics I associate with good cooks. She was plump, cheerful and amusing, but temperamental. Her husband, zio Carlo, was a die-hard Neapolitan forced by circumstance to live in northern Italy. As a child, sitting in his house in drizzling grey Lombardy, I used to listen to his descriptions of the colourful vegetables ripened in the real sun, of the lively fish market at Pozzuoli where at least ten different kinds of clam could be had at any time, and of the abundance of food always ready for anyone who happened to drop in, a sure sign of the hospitality and warmth of the southerners.

These stuffed peppers were one of zia Renata's specialities, and they seem to represent a combination of her cooking skills with zio Carlo's fond memories of luscious sun-ripened vegetables. I was told later that the little croûtons were zia Renata's war-time addition to make the dish more nourishing and to use up any old crumbs of bread, but the addition was so successful that it became an integral part of the dish. The crisp squareness of the croûtons is a pleasant contrast to the soft roundness of the aubergine, both in shape and in texture. The flavours, however, blend harmoniously, an essential requirement for most Italian dishes. Do remember to rinse the capers under cold water to get rid of the vinegar.

To save labour, I tried baking the peppers instead of grilling them, but it does not work as they become too floppy. The best method is to char them over charcoal, which gives them that special flavour. Failing that, put them directly over a flame or, if you cook with electricity, use a hot enough grill to burn the skin without softening the meat too much.

The second course, I'm afraid, calls for a *tour de force* on the part of the cook. Read the recipe and you will see for yourself! But the result is, I think, one of the best pasta dishes ever. Because of the time it takes, and its cost, I like to serve this *pasticcio* as the centrepiece of my dinner. It also makes a most successful buffet dish twinned with a dish of lasagne layered with meat *ragù*. If at all possible, the squid and prawns should be fresh, not frozen.

After these two courses, relax, and bring to the table the best seasonal salad, enhanced by a few leaves of rocket, or a bunch of chopped herbs from the garden. The basic recipe for an Italian green salad is on page 368. Please don't serve the salad with the pasta; serve it afterwards on clean plates.

Cheese is optional. In Italy cheese is seldom served at night because it is too heavy. We have a saying: '*Il formaggio è oro alla mattina, argento a mezzogiorno e piombo alla sera*' ('Cheese is gold in the morning, silver at midday and lead at night').

The pudding is light, fresh, easy and very attractive, but it does need good fruit, since it is not spruced up in any way. When you buy the pineapple make sure that its skin is unblemished and not bruised, and then smell it. If properly ripe it should smell of pineapple. Choose large but thin-skinned oranges. If you are not entirely happy with the fruit you have bought, sprinkle it with a little sugar and a couple of tablespoons of *grappa* or an orange liqueur.

In the last few years I have had many such perfect endings to good dinners in Italy. Fruit desserts are very fashionable in this health-conscious era.

** *Peperoni ripieni della zia Renata*

PEPPERS STUFFED WITH AUBERGINES AND CROÛTONS

---

700 g/1½ lb aubergines
salt
6 meaty peppers, red and yellow
vegetable oil for frying
4 slices good-quality white bread, 1
  or 2 days old, cut into 1 cm/½
  in cubes
6 tbsp extra virgin olive oil

1 garlic clove
1 dried chilli, seeded and crumbled
4 anchovy fillets
7 tbsp parsley, chopped
2 tbsp capers, rinsed and dried
pepper
a dozen black olives for decoration
  (optional)

Peel the aubergines, cut them into 1 cm/½ in cubes and sweat with salt in a colander for at least half an hour.

Meanwhile char the peppers over a direct flame or using a very hot grill. Keep a watch on them and turn them over so that they blacken evenly.

While you are keeping an eye on the peppers, heat the vegetable oil and when very hot add the bread and fry until golden. Retrieve with a slotted spoon and transfer on to kitchen paper to drain.

When the peppers are cool enough to handle, peel them and cut them in half. Remove and discard the cores, seeds and ribs. Place in an oiled ovenproof dish.

Heat the oven to 200°C/400°F/Gas 6.

Rinse the aubergine cubes and dry them with kitchen paper. Heat 4 tablespoons of the olive oil and add the aubergine. Sauté until cooked, about 6 minutes, stirring frequently.

Chop the garlic, chilli and anchovy fillets and add to the aubergine with half the parsley. Cook for 1 minute. Draw off the heat and add the capers and the croûtons. Taste and adjust seasoning.

Fill the peppers neatly with the aubergine mixture. Sprinkle with the remaining chopped parsley and dribble with the remaining olive oil. Bake for 10 minutes. Do not serve the dish straight from the oven; let it rest for half an hour or so, since stuffed vegetables are much nicer just warm. Scatter the olives in the dish before serving.

PREPARATION

The peppers can be grilled up to 3 days in advance and refrigerated. The croûtons can be made up to 2 days in advance and refrigerated. They also freeze well. You can sauté the aubergine up to 2 days in advance and refrigerate it, but the peppers must be stuffed just before going into the oven or the croûtons will become soggy.

***   *Pasticcio di pesce*

FISH LASAGNE

---

1 kg/2 lb mussels
1 small onion
4 garlic cloves
150 ml/¼ pint dry white wine
250 g/9 oz squid
salt and pepper
1 bay leaf
700 g/1½ lb monkfish
450 g/1 lb prawns in their shells

250 g/9 oz fresh scallops,
   preferably the small ones called
   queenies
lasagne made with 2 eggs and
   200–225 g/7–8 oz unbleached
   white flour, or 450 g/1 lb shop-
   bought fresh lasagne, or 350 g/
   12 oz dried egg lasagne

For the white sauce

400 ml/14 fl oz full-fat milk
1 bay leaf

75 g/2½ oz unsalted butter
60 g/2 oz flour

For the tomato sauce

45 g/1½ oz unsalted butter
2 shallots or 1 small onion, very
   finely chopped
1 dried red chilli, seeded and
   crumbled
1 garlic clove, peeled and chopped

about 2 cm/¾ in fresh ginger,
   peeled and very finely sliced
2 tbsp tomato purée
120 ml/4 fl oz dry sherry
75 ml/2½ fl oz double cream
75 ml/2½ fl oz soured cream

First clean and prepare the mussels. Scrub them under running water, knock off the barnacles and tug off the beard. Wash in several changes of water. Throw away any mussels that remain open when tapped on a hard surface; they are dead and must not be eaten.

Put the onion, garlic and wine in a wide pan. Add the mussels, cover with a lid and cook over high heat until the mussels open. Shake the pan frequently. Remove the meat from the shells as soon as they open, but do not force them or they will break. Put the meat in a large bowl and discard the shells. Filter the liquid left in the pan through a sieve lined with muslin or kitchen paper into another large bowl and reserve.

Clean the squid following the directions on page 223. Wash them thoroughly and then cut the sacs into thin strips no more than 5 cm/2 in long. Cut the tentacles into morsels. Put 600 ml/ 1 pint of water in a medium saucepan, add salt and the bay leaf and bring to the boil. Drop in the squid and simmer until just tender. I cannot give a precise time because it depends on the size of the squid. Small squid from the Mediterranean, often frozen, take 5 minutes, while large ones from British coasts, which are fresh and tastier, can take as long as 20 minutes. Lift the squid out of the liquid with a slotted spoon and add to the mussels.

Skin the monkfish and cut into small cubes. Drop into the squid water and cook for 3 minutes. Lift the monkfish out of the water and add to the other fish, reserving the cooking liquid.

Wash the prawns, remove the heads and shells and devein. If large, cut into pieces and add them to the bowl with the fish. Put the heads and shells into the fish cooking liquid and bring to the boil. Simmer for about 5 minutes and then strain into the bowl containing the mussel liquid. Reserve.

Wash the scallops, remove the coral and add it to the fish bowl. Remove the muscle and the intestine and cut the white part of the scallops into horizontal slices. Add to the bowl.

To make the white sauce, measure about 400 ml/14 fl oz of the fish stock and put it in a saucepan. Add the milk and the bay leaf and heat to just below boiling point. Melt the butter in a heavy saucepan and blend in the flour. Cook over low heat, stirring constantly for 40 seconds, remove from the heat and gradually stir in the milk and fish stock mixture. Return the pan to the heat and bring to the boil. Add salt and pepper to taste and simmer over the gentlest heat for at least 20 minutes, stirring frequently.

This kind of flour-based sauce becomes properly smooth and creamy if you cook it for a very long time. If you can, cook the sauce covered in a bain-marie over very low heat for about 45 minutes, or put the saucepan on a flame diffuser. In either case you don't need to watch the sauce; it's enough if you give it a stir every now and then.

Now you can prepare the tomato sauce. Heat the butter gently with the shallot or onion in a small saucepan and sauté until soft. Add the chilli, garlic and ginger and sauté for a further 30 seconds. Stir in the tomato purée and cook for a few more seconds, mixing the whole time, then pour in the sherry and about 100 ml/3½ fl oz of fish stock. Add the two creams. Stir thoroughly, bring to the boil and let the sauce simmer gently for 10 minutes. Mix a couple of tablespoons of the tomato sauce into the white sauce. Add all the fish, cooked and uncooked, to the tomato sauce and simmer for a couple of minutes. Taste and check seasoning.

You now have all the ingredients ready and all you have to do is make the lasagne, if you are indeed making them yourself, and assemble the dish.

Make the pasta dough following the instructions on page 374. Cut out and cook the lasagne as described on page 376. If using bought pasta, follow the packet instructions. When all the lasagne are done, assemble the dish.

Grease a 25 × 20 cm/10 × 8 in oven dish, preferably metal, with a little butter and spread 2 or 3 tablespoons of the tomato sauce over the bottom. Cover with a layer of lasagne, overlapping as little as possible. Spread over 2–3 tablespoons of the fish and its sauce and cover with a second layer of lasagne. Build up these layers until you have used up all the ingredients, making sure you finish with a layer of lasagne on top. Spread the white sauce (which is now pink) all over the top. The dish is now ready to be baked in a preheated oven (190°C/375°F/Gas 5) for about 20–35 minutes, depending on whether it has just been made and is still warm or was made in advance and is therefore cold. When it is ready the sauce on top should be just bubbling, with some patches of crust. Remove from the oven and leave to stand for at least 5 minutes before serving.

PREPARATION
The fish can be prepared up to 1 day in advance, covered and refrigerated. The fish stock must also be refrigerated. The whole dish can be made up to 1 day in advance, covered with clingfilm and refrigerated. I do not recommend freezing; some of the fish will have been frozen in the first place and has not been cooked for long enough.

*
Ananas e arancie
PINEAPPLE AND ORANGES

1 large ripe pineapple	*6–8 large oranges*

Peel the pineapple and slice thickly. Peel the oranges to the quick (i.e. removing all the pith as well) and slice. Remove any pips.

Put the pineapple slices on a large dish. I use a round dish so that everything is round. Cover each pineapple slice with a slice of orange. Cover with clingfilm and refrigerate. Serve straight from the refrigerator.

PREPARATION

I don't like to prepare fruit too long in advance; 6–8 hours is the maximum.

A VEGETARIAN LUNCH FOR 8

Pasta coi finocchi
PASTA WITH FENNEL AND CREAM

La torta di porri
LEEK AND RICE PIE

Insalata verde
GREEN SALAD (page 368)

Formaggio e frutta
CHEESE AND FRUIT

Pasta dishes, other than baked ones, are the most popular first course at any Italian lunch. They are quick and easy to make when you finally manage to get to the kitchen after a busy morning. This menu is in fact ideally suited to just that kind of morning, since the second course can be prepared the day before, and the meal ends with nothing more than the best cheeses and fruit. In Italy puddings are seldom served at lunch, and this is the usual way to end a meal.

The pasta recipe appears in one of my pasta books, *Pasta Perfect*, which has just been reprinted. It is such a success with the friends who have tried it that I decided to include it in this book as well. It is ideal for this menu.

I can particularly recommend the pie. The original was made with courgettes and was given to me by a great friend in Genoa. When I arrived there I heard a thumping noise coming from the kitchen where I found my friend, a distinctly aristocratic lady, bent double, bashing the bottom of the pie dish against the tiled floor. 'This is how the Ligurian peasants dislodge their vegetable pies!' she explained.

When I came back to London the courgettes were tired-looking and very expensive. So I tried making the pie with the young leeks that had just come into the shops and it turned out to be just as delicious. But in the spring and summer when the young English courgettes are available, substitute them for the leeks, adding one white onion to the filling. The quantities and method are the same. The leeks and rice become soft by soaking in the egg and oil mixture, with the result that, when cooked, the filling is moist yet firm. Although these vegetable pies are usually made with *pasta frolla* – shortcrust pastry – in Italy, I think fila pastry is the perfect container. It's also quicker, since you buy it already made! A green salad could follow and the cheese could be served with it.

This menu, which is perfect for any lunch, vegetarian or otherwise, is also well suited to informal suppers.

*   *Pasta coi finocchi*

PASTA WITH FENNEL AND CREAM

---

4 large fennel bulbs, total weight about 1 kg/2 lb	*300 ml/½ pint single cream*
90 g/3 oz unsalted butter	*90 g/3 oz freshly grated Parmesan*
300 ml/½ pint full-fat milk	*700 g/1½ lb shells or other medium size tubular pasta*
salt and freshly ground black pepper	

Cut off and discard the tops and any wilted or bruised parts of the fennel. Reserve the green feathery leaves. Wash and chop them coarsely. Cut the fennel bulbs into quarters, then into wedges about 6 mm/¼ in thick. Wash thoroughly in cold water and dry with kitchen paper.

Heat half the butter in a large, heavy frying pan until it begins to foam. Add the fennel and sauté for 5 minutes. Add the milk and sprinkle with salt. Reduce the heat to very low, cover the pan, and cook until the fennel is tender, about 30 minutes, stirring from time to time. Add a little hot milk or water if the fennel gets too dry.

When the fennel is very tender, break it up with a fork to make a coarse purée. Stir in the cream and season with plenty of pepper. Cook over a very gentle heat for 2 minutes, stirring very often, then blend in half the Parmesan. Cover the pan and set aside.

Meanwhile cook the pasta in plenty of boiling salted water. Turn to page 376 and follow the Agnesi method, which is easier to deal with when you are entertaining. Drain the pasta, then immediately return it to the pan in which it was cooked. Toss immediately with the remaining butter and with the sauce. Turn the pasta into a heated serving dish and sprinkle with the reserved fennel leaves. Serve at once, with the rest of the Parmesan separately in a bowl.

PREPARATION

The sauce can be made up to 2 days in advance and refrigerated in a covered container.

***   *La torta di porri*

LEEK AND RICE PIE

---

700 g/1½ lb leeks	*salt and freshly ground black pepper*
4 eggs	*7 tbsp freshly ground Parmesan*
150 g/5 oz arborio, or other Italian	*cheese*
risotto rice	*225–250 g/8–9 oz frozen fila*
200 ml/7 fl oz extra virgin olive oil	*pastry, thawed*

First prepare the leeks. Cut away and discard all except the white part and the inside of the green part. Cut into very thin rounds, about 3 mm/⅛ in. Wash thoroughly, removing all the earth. If the leeks are large and have a strong smell, meaning that they are rather old, leave them for about an hour in plenty of cold water to which you have added a couple of tablespoons of salt. Drain and put them in a bowl.

Lightly beat the eggs and add to the bowl with the rice, half the oil, two teaspoons of salt, plenty of pepper and the Parmesan. Mix very thoroughly (I use my hands). Set the bowl aside for a couple of hours, but toss again whenever you remember because the liquid sinks to the bottom and you want the leeks and rice mixture to have a fair share of it.

Heat the oven to 180°C/350°F/Gas 4.

Oil a 25 cm/10 in spring-clip tin and lightly flour it. Shake away excess flour. Pour the rest of the oil into a bowl. Carefully unfold the fila pastry leaves, one at a time, taking care to keep the other leaves covered – fila pastry dries out and cracks very easily. Lift out and lay one leaf over the bottom and up the sides of the prepared tin, allowing the ends to hang down over the outside of the tin. Using a pastry brush, brush the leaf all over with a little of the oil and then cover with another leaf of fila pastry. Lay it across the previous one so that the sides of the tin are covered all round. Brush with oil and lay two more leaves in the same way.

Now fill the tin with the leek mixture. Fold the overhanging pieces of fila back over the top, one at a time, to make a lid. If the fila is not long enough, lay four more leaves over the top, brushing each sheet with oil. Cut them to fit inside the tin and fold the overlap over to form a ridge around the edge. Brush each one with oil before you place the next. If necessary cut some of the pieces with scissors, and patch up any that need it so that the filling is evenly covered. Bake for 45–50 minutes.

Let the pie cool for 10 minutes and then remove the side of the tin and turn it over on to an oven tray. Put the pie back in the oven, upside down, for 5 minutes to dry the bottom. Turn on to a lovely round dish ready to serve.

PREPARATION

The pie is best served just warm, a couple of hours after being baked. It is also very good made 1 day in advance, kept out of the fridge and served at room temperature.

A DINNER FOR 8

Passato di sedano
CELERY SOUP

Maiale al latte con la puré di patate
LOIN OF PORK BRAISED IN MILK WITH POTATO PURÉE

Cachi al sugo di lime
SHARON FRUITS WITH LIME JUICE

Italian vegetable soups traditionally consist of a mixture of seasonal vegetables that are cut into small pieces and cooked in stock or water, with some pasta or rice. When the vegetables are made into a purée, as in this soup, it is as a result of French influence. Yet this puréed soup is typically Italian in flavour, since it is rounded out by ricotta instead of cream. The ricotta gives the soup a lighter taste and a rougher texture, emphasized by the addition of the sautéed breadcrumbs, here replacing the more formal croûtons.

A loin of pork braised in milk is a traditional dish from central Italy. I marinate the meat because I find that pork these days is often tough, and sometimes tasteless. My mother, who has been coming to England regularly for many years now, has been saying, equally regularly, *'Ma pensare, che il maiale era squisito in Inghilterra anni fa'* ('To think that pork used to be so good in England years ago'). I live in hope that the trend will change so that we can once again have good pork like those good old days! Perhaps the trend for organic meat, available in some super-markets, will provide the answer. In the meantime, marinating is the solution.

After marinating, my pork is braised in milk, which at the end of the cooking turns into a thick, wickedly rich sauce studded with golden nuggets. With it I serve a potato purée, not too thin this time, to mop up the juices. The carrots Italian style on page 372 are also a good accompaniment.

To cleanse the palate you need fruit, and the Sharon fruits in lime juice are just tart enough to make your tongue tingle a little. Sharon fruits, which were developed in the Sharon Valley in Israel, are one of the few fruits to have improved in recent years.

They are similar to Japanese persimmons but with the advantage that they can be eaten when still firm, as opposed to persimmons which are mouth-contorting if not perfectly ripe. Thus you can eat Sharon fruits, skin and all, as a salad, dressed with a light lemon and oil sauce, or as a dessert dressed with cream and/or yoghurt.

*　　　　　　　*Passato di sedano*

CELERY SOUP

1½ medium heads of celery
75 g/2½ oz butter
2 tbsp olive oil
3 potatoes, cut into small pieces
2 litres/3½ pints home-made stock, preferably Italian broth (see page 378)

salt
4 slices of brown bread, crust removed and very lightly toasted
225 g/½ lb ricotta
freshly ground black pepper
freshly grated Parmesan

Remove the strings and leaves from the celery sticks, wash thoroughly and cut into pieces. Keep the leaves for flavouring other dishes or for chopping into a salad.

Heat 30 g/1 oz of the butter and 1 tablespoon of the oil, and when the butter begins to foam add the celery and the potatoes. Sauté very gently for 5 minutes, stirring frequently.

Meanwhile bring the stock or broth to the boil and pour over the sautéed vegetables. Add salt to taste and simmer for 30 minutes.

While the soup is cooking make coarse breadcrumbs from the toasted bread. A food processor is ideal for the job.

In a small frying pan heat the rest of the butter and oil and, when very hot, mix in the breadcrumbs and fry until all the fat has been absorbed and the crumbs are darker in colour and crisp.

Purée the soup through a food mill or a blender and return to the pan. Bring the soup back to the boil. Draw off the heat. Break up the ricotta with a fork and add to the soup with the pepper. Mix well, taste and adjust seasoning.

Ladle the soup into bowls and hand the fried breadcrumbs and the Parmesan in separate bowls for everyone to help themselves.

PREPARATION

Both the soup and the breadcrumbs can be prepared up to 2 days in advance. They can also be frozen. The ricotta must be added to the reheated soup just before serving.

** *Maiale al latte*

LOIN OF PORK BRAISED IN MILK

1.5 kg/3½ lb loin of pork, boned and rindless but with a thin layer of fat still on
4 tbsp vegetable oil
4 cloves, bruised
pinch of ground cinnamon
sprig of rosemary

3 garlic cloves, peeled and bruised
rock salt and freshly ground black pepper
6–7 peppercorns, bruised
1 bay leaf
30 g/1 oz unsalted butter
450 ml/¾ pint full-fat milk

Tie the joint in several places, if the butcher has not done it for you.

Put the meat in a bowl and add 2 tablespoons of the oil, the cloves, cinnamon, rosemary, garlic, 1 teaspoon of rock salt, the peppercorns and the bay leaf. Coat the pork all over in the marinade, cover the bowl with a lid of some sort and marinate for about 8 hours. Do not put the bowl in the refrigerator unless it is very hot. Turn the meat over in the marinade whenever you remember.

Heat the butter and the rest of the oil in a heavy casserole into which the pork will fit snugly. When the butter foam begins to subside, add the dried joint and brown well on all sides to a rich golden colour.

Heat the milk to boiling point and pour slowly over the meat. Sprinkle with salt and ground pepper, place the lid over the pan slightly askew, and cook for about 3 hours at a steady low simmer. Turn the meat over and baste approximately every 20 minutes. By the end of the cooking the meat should be very tender and the sauce should be a rich dark golden colour, and quite thick. If it is too thin by the time the meat is done, remove the meat to a side dish and boil the sauce briskly without the lid until it darkens and thickens.

Transfer the meat to a carrying board and leave to cool for a few minutes.

Meanwhile skim off as much fat as you can from the surface of the sauce, add 2 tablespoons of hot water and boil over high heat for about 2 minutes, while scraping the bottom of the pan with a metal spoon. Taste and adjust seasonings.

Remove the string and carve the pork into 12 mm/½ in slices. Arrange the slices on a heated dish and spoon the sauce over the slices, or spoon over only a little of the sauce and serve the rest separately in a warm sauce-boat.

PREPARATION

The meat can be cooked up to 3 days in advance and kept, covered, in the refrigerator. It can also be frozen. Thaw completely before reheating. Carve the meat and cover with the sauce. Reheat very gently, covered, in a moderate oven for 15 minutes.

*   # *Cachi al sugo di lime*

SHARON FRUITS WITH LIME JUICE

---

12 *Sharon fruits*	3 *or 4 tbsp caster sugar, according*
4 *limes*	*to taste and the sweetness of the*
	fruit

Wash the Sharon fruits very thoroughly and dry them well. Slice them as you would an orange and lay the slices, slightly overlapping, on a pretty dish.

One hour before you want to eat them, squeeze the limes and pour the juice over the Sharon fruits. Sprinkle with the sugar and leave in the fridge, covered with clingfilm, until you want to serve them.

PREPARATION

The fruits can be cut a few hours in advance and arranged on the serving dish. The dish must be covered with clingfilm. The dressing must be spooned over no more than 1 hour before serving or the Sharon fruits will macerate.

AN AUTUMN DINNER FOR 8

Risotto con la zucca
PUMPKIN RISOTTO

Cervo alla casalinga con la polenta e funghi al funghetto
VENISON STEWED IN ONIONS WITH POLENTA AND SAUTÉED
MUSHROOMS

Coppette di pompelmo e uva
GRAPEFRUIT BOWLS WITH GRAPES (page 101)

Autumn offers an abundance of good produce. For me it is
also the time when it is particularly enjoyable to start cooking
again, after the holidays and the warmer weather. Slow-cooking
dishes are autumnal, well suited to being accompanied by a
golden, steaming polenta. Game is in season, so I designed this
menu round this typically Italian *secondo*. Polenta is the perfect
foil for the succulent richness of the venison, cooked at length in
the oven with plenty of onion. You might think the amount of
onion quite overpowering, but when it is cooked for a long time
very slowly, as it must be, it becomes a golden brown, slightly
caramelized mush which absorbs and at the same time tones
down the gameyness of the meat.

I've chosen mushrooms to go with it, the most autumnal of all
accompaniments. At the time of writing these paragraphs there is a
glut of wild mushrooms in England. While taking my dog for a walk
I have been gathering more than we can eat, and my freezer is full of
them. So I have tried sautéed mushrooms in several ways, and I
have finished going back to the original Genoese recipe for *funghi al
funghetto*, traditionally made with porcini. In the recipe (page 371) I
have suggested using a selection of mushrooms easily available in
most supermarkets. The other accompaniment should be polenta
(page 377), as it always is in Italy. Unfortunately, polenta is not as
popular here as in Italy, so I suggest a celeriac and potato purée or a
Jerusalem artichoke purée as alternatives.

To precede this, a light buttery risotto seems ideal and, being
autumn, risotto with pumpkin is just right. The Hallowe'en
pumpkins, the most commonly available, are not good to eat, as
they have practically no taste. I have used the long trumpet-

shaped Cyprus pumpkin, the sweet dumpling squash, the butter-nut or the onion squash and they are quite good. But the best pumpkin for the risotto is a large, squat pumpkin with very tough green rind and bright orange pulp, often sold in halves, quarters or segments in ethnic markets. This pumpkin is similar to the *zucca Mantovana*, Mantua and its neighbouring countryside being the motherland of pumpkins and the best pumpkin recipes, such as this risotto.

It is quite difficult to choose a good squash or pumpkin. The fruit should be ripe, yet not old, heavy for its size, with a green stem showing no blackening at the foot. The rind should be hard with a bright colour, either yellow, green or mottled, depending on the variety, without any blemish, soft spots or dried ridges. In fact it is easier to buy pieces so that you can see and even taste the inside, which should be bright in colour, fresh-looking and thick. Pumpkins and squashes have an elusive, sweet flavour which is hard to capture. When they are good, this flavour comes to life in a risotto such as this. For me it rates as one of the best dishes of the Lombard tradition, as interpreted here, in my mother's recipe.

In the recipe I give the quantity of the cleaned pumpkin because some, such as the trumpet-shaped one, have hardly any seeds and cottony pulp, while others have a lot of waste.

As the first two courses of this menu are quite nourishing, you will need only fruit to finish the meal. The grapefruit bowls with grapes fit the bill; they are very refreshing as well as being seasonal.

✱✱ *Risotto con la zucca*

PUMPKIN RISOTTO

---

700 g/1½ lb pumpkin, rindless
*   and cleaned*
2.8 litres/4½ pints home-made
*   Italian broth (page 378)*
90 g/3 oz unsalted butter
8 shallots or 3 onions, very finely
*   chopped*
salt

1 tsp sugar
1 large bunch of flat-leaf parsley
600 g/1¼ lb arborio, or other
*   Italian risotto rice*
freshly ground black pepper
120 ml/4 fl oz double cream
90 g/3 oz freshly grated Parmesan

Prepare the pumpkin by removing the seeds, the cottony pulp, if there is any, and the rind. Wash and dry the pumpkin and cut into 1 cm/½ in cubes.

Heat the broth to simmering point.

Heat the butter and the shallots in a large, heavy saucepan and add 1 teaspoon of salt, which will help the onion to soften without browning, and the sugar. Cook for about 5 minutes. Chop the parsley, add half of it to the pan and continue cooking for a further 5 minutes, stirring very frequently.

Now add the pumpkin and cook until just tender. I cannot give a time for this as it depends on which variety of pumpkin or squash you are using. Some take 5–10 minutes, while others take 20 minutes, in which case you will have to add a ladleful of hot broth to the pan. When the pumpkin is just tender right through when pricked with the point of a knife, stir in the rice and sauté for 1–2 minutes until the grains are well coated in the butter. Pour over about 450 ml/¾ pint of simmering broth and stir very thoroughly. Bring the liquid to a lively boil, turn off the heat and cover the pan tightly. You can now leave the rice while you receive your guests, and return to the kitchen about a quarter of an hour before you want to serve dinner.

Bring the broth back to simmering point. Add a knob of butter to the rice, which will have absorbed all the broth and be half cooked. Mix 2 ladlefuls of hot broth into the rice and continue cooking and gradually adding a ladleful of broth at a time until the rice is ready. If you finish the broth before the rice is cooked, add boiling water. This risotto should be more creamy and runny than other risottos, half-way between a thick soup and the usual risotto. Season with pepper and check the salt.

Add the cream and half the Parmesan. Turn the heat off and leave for 1 minute for the cheese to melt and the flavours to blend.

Give the risotto a vigorous stir and heap it up on a heated round dish. Sprinkle the remaining parsley all over the steaming golden mound and serve at once, handing the remaining cheese separately in a bowl.

PREPARATION

See the method, but try to prepare the first part of the risotto no more than 1 hour in advance.

** *Cervo alla casalinga*

STEWED VENISON WITH ONIONS

1.5 kg/3¼ lb venison
2 tbsp olive oil
75 g/2½ oz unsalted butter
1.35 kg/3 lb Spanish onions, sliced
1 tbsp sugar
salt and pepper

300 ml/½ pint strong meat stock
½ tsp ground cinnamon
½ tsp ground cloves
½ nutmeg, grated
300 ml/½ pint dry white wine (if necessary)

For the marinade

600 ml/1 pint dry white wine
2 tbsp olive oil
2 bay leaves
2 carrots
1 large onion

2 celery sticks
2 garlic cloves, peeled and bruised
10 juniper berries, bruised
1 tsp black peppercorns, bruised

Cut the venison into small slices or large strips about 1½ cm/½ in thick. I find that this type of meat becomes less dry and woody if cut into thin strips rather than chunks or cubes. Put the meat in a bowl and add all the ingredients for the marinade. Cover and leave in a cool place overnight. Except in the height of summer there is no need to refrigerate the meat for this short length of time, and, in fact, leaving it at room temperature will help to make the meat more tender.

Next day, heat the oil and butter in a casserole, add the sliced onion, and cook slowly until it softens. Sprinkle with the sugar and turn the heat up. The onion will caramelize slightly and take on a lovely golden brown colour. Season with salt and pepper and add the meat stock and the spices. Cover the casserole and cook over very gentle heat for about 30 minutes, stirring occasionally.

Heat the oven to 150°C/300°F/Gas 2.

Remove the meat from the marinade and dry with kitchen paper. Strain the marinade and discard the vegetables.

Transfer about half the onion from the casserole to a side plate. Lay the venison over the remaining onion in the casserole, season with salt and pepper and cover with the onion previously transferred to the side plate. Heat the marinade and add to the casserole. Add more heated white wine if necessary so that the meat is just covered. Cook in the oven for about 1½–2 hours until the venison is very tender.

PREPARATION

The meat can be marinated up to 3 days in advance, in which case it must be refrigerated. The dish can be prepared up to 2 days in advance and refrigerated. If necessary skim the fat from the surface of the stew before reheating.

DINNER FOR 10

Il fiore di melanzane alla senape
GRILLED AUBERGINES WITH A LEMONY MUSTARD SAUCE

Coniglio con le cipolle
RABBIT WITH ONION AND VINEGAR

Torta di ricotta e mandorle con la salsina di arancia
RICOTTA AND ALMOND CAKE WITH ORANGE SAUCE

I would not call this a particularly elegant menu, because of the inclusion of rabbit with vulgar onion. Yet it is so good and well balanced that I think it can be served at a formal dinner instead of, for instance, the ubiquitous salmon with mayonnaise or the boring old brace of pheasants, where the salmon is all too often farmed and the pheasants frozen. The rabbit is a sure winner as served in this golden onion sauce sharpened by a touch of wine vinegar. Serve the rabbit with a buttery potato purée to mop up the juices and with the lemon-flavoured spinach on page 373.

The dinner opens with a very attractive aubergine dish, looking like a pale sunflower. The flavour, however, has nothing pale about it; the lemony mustard dressing sinks into the grilled aubergine, blending perfectly with its particular kind of taste. Whenever I eat aubergine I am surprised at how well it blends with other ingredients, yet keeping its own individual flavour. It reminds me of a great character actor who is superb in totally different roles and yet they all seem to have been written just for him.

I am sure you must have eaten a ricotta pudding of one sort or another if you are at all keen on Italian cooking, as it is one of the most popular sweets with Italians. But I doubt if you ever had one like this, where the ricotta absorbs the flavour of the almonds and the orange, one of the great duets in the culinary repertoire. The cake can be served as it is, when it is ideal with a cup of tea or with coffee and liqueur after dinner. But at the end of a meal, as here, I prefer to hand round this little orange sauce. Pouring cream is also good with it, especially if you flavour it with a couple of spoonfuls of Grand Marnier and sweeten it with icing sugar.

✱✱ *Il fiore di melanzane alla senape*

GRILLED AUBERGINES WITH A LEMONY MUSTARD SAUCE

1.35 kg/3 lb aubergines
salt
150 ml/¼ pint extra virgin olive
 oil
3 tbsp French mustard

3 tbsp fresh mint, chopped
3 garlic cloves, peeled and chopped
4 tbsp lemon juice
4 tbsp vegetable stock

Wash the aubergines and cut them lengthwise into slices about 8 mm/⅓ in thick. Lay the slices on a slanting wooden board and sprinkle them generously with salt, preferably rock salt. Leave to drain for at least 1 hour, then rinse and pat dry with kitchen paper.

Heat the grill. Line the grill pan with aluminium foil. Brush the foil with a little olive oil and lay the aubergine slices over it. Brush the aubergine with some more oil and put the pan under the grill.

Grill for about 5 minutes on each side until soft and beginning to change colour. If the aubergine slices are charring too quickly, turn the heat down; they are ready when they offer no resistance to the prongs of a fork.

Meanwhile prepare the sauce. Put the mustard, mint, garlic, lemon juice, vegetable stock and a little salt in the food processor. Set it in motion and gradually add the remaining oil through the funnel to make a smooth, well emulsified sauce. Taste and check seasoning.

Choose a lovely round dish. Reserve the best-looking slices of aubergine of the same size. Make a layer of aubergine slices arranged in a circle. Spread a little sauce over it and then cover with another layer of aubergine slices, dressed with the sauce, building up the dish and finishing with the best slices set aside. Reserve a few spoonfuls of sauce. Cover with clingfilm and refrigerate for at least 6 hours.

Before serving, coat with the remaining sauce and decorate the dish with a few sprigs of fresh mint in the middle of the aubergine 'flower'.

PREPARATION

The dish must be prepared at least 6 hours in advance for the flavours to blend. I like to serve it on the following day, when I think it is at its best.

** *Coniglio con le cipolle*

RABBIT WITH ONION AND VINEGAR

You can use either imported domestic rabbit or wild English rabbit. Wild rabbit is tastier but it takes longer to cook – at least 2½ hours, depending on its age. The best thing to do is to cook the rabbit in advance and reheat it before serving.

1.8 kg/4 lb onions, Spanish or white
120 ml/4 fl oz olive oil
salt
150 ml/¼ pint meat stock, or ¼ meat cube dissolved in 150 ml/¼ pint water

4 tbsp sugar
3 kg/6¾ lb rabbit pieces on the bone
120 ml/4 fl oz good red wine vinegar
4 tbsp balsamic vinegar

Slice the onions thinly. Put them in a heavy casserole with the oil, 2 teaspoons of salt and 6 tablespoons of the stock. Cover the casserole with the lid and cook for about 1½ hours over very low heat until the onions are reduced to a golden mush. Turn the heat up to moderate, mix in the sugar and cook for a further 15 minutes to caramelize the onion slightly. Stir frequently.

Heat the oven to 150°C/300°F/Gas 2.

Wash and dry the rabbit pieces and add to the casserole. Check that there is enough liquid before adding them. If necessary add a couple of tablespoons of the stock. Turn the pieces of rabbit over a couple of times and then pour in the wine vinegar. Season with plenty of pepper and with 2 teaspoons of salt.

Cook for 5 minutes over moderate heat, then cover the casserole and place it in the oven. Cook until the rabbit is done. Stir in the balsamic vinegar and cook on top of the stove for a few minutes, turning the pieces over once or twice. Taste and check seasoning. Serve from the casserole or transfer to a heated serving bowl.

PREPARATION

The dish can be prepared up to 3 days in advance and refrigerated. Reheat in a moderate oven for 20 minutes.

*** *Torta di ricotta e mandorle con la salsina di arancia*

RICOTTA AND ALMOND CAKE WITH ORANGE SAUCE

---

150 g/5 oz almonds	*7 eggs, separated*
3 to 4 drops pure almond essence	*the grated rind of 1 orange*
or 5 bitter almonds, peeled and	*3 tbsp Grand Marnier (optional)*
ground	*75 g/2½ oz potato flour*
450 g/1 lb ricotta	*icing sugar*
150 g/5 oz caster sugar	

For the orange sauce

3 large oranges	*½ lemon*
200 g/7 oz granulated sugar	

Butter and line a 25 cm/10 in spring-clip tin with baking parchment.

Heat the oven to 180°C/350°F/Gas 4.

Blanch the almonds (and the bitter almonds, if used) for 30 seconds in boiling water. Peel them, dry them with kitchen paper and chop them in the food processor to a finely-grained texture, though not so fine as ground almonds.

Push the ricotta through a food mill or a sieve into a bowl, add the sugar and beat hard until creamy and smooth. Mix in the almonds, the almond essence (if used) and then the egg yolks, one by one, beating hard after each addition. Mix in the orange rind and the optional liqueur.

Whisk the egg whites until stiff and fold into the ricotta mixture a little at a time, alternatively with the potato flour. Use a metal spoon and a high movement to incorporate more air. Spoon the mixture into the prepared tin and bake for about 40 minutes or until set. A cocktail stick inserted into the middle of the cake should come out very lightly moist. Allow to cool in the tin and then remove on to a round dish. Sprinkle lavishly with icing sugar just before serving.

To make the orange sauce, wash and scrub the oranges thoroughly. Remove the rind, being very careful not to remove the pith while doing so. Cut the rind into julienne strips and put into a small saucepan. Cover with cold water, bring to the boil and cook until they are soft and slightly transparent. Drain.

Put the sugar and 4 tablespoons of water in the same pan and bring very slowly to the boil. When the sugar has dissolved, add the juice of the oranges and of the half lemon. Stir in the strips of rind and simmer for a minute or two. Serve cold in a sauce-boat or a bowl.

PREPARATION

The cake is best made the day it is to be eaten, but if necessary it can be made up to 1 day in advance. The orange sauce can be made up to 1 week in advance and refrigerated in an airtight container.

A BUFFET SUPPER FOR 12

Pappa col pomodoro
BREAD AND TOMATO SOUP

Tiella di pesce di Claudia
APULIAN FISH PIE

Insalata di sedano, carote e mela al sapor di coriandolo
CELERY, CARROT AND APPLE SALAD IN A WINE AND
CORIANDER DRESSING

Torta di riso
RICE CAKE

Insalata autunnale di frutta
AUTUMNAL FRUIT SALAD

I like buffet suppers. When you find the conversation you have been struggling with is grinding to a halt, you can simply say, 'I must go and have some more of that delicious meat', and look for someone more interesting to talk to. And even if you don't get stuck with a bore, it is very pleasant to be able to change eating partners which each course. But at this sort of supper you must serve food that does not need a knife, so that you can sit anywhere, or even stand, and go on eating while you chat. I like to make it a three-course meal, just as if my guests were sitting at table.

This is a menu for an informal supper in early autumn. The soup is made with the summer's last tomatoes, and with bread which anticipates the more wintry bread soups to come. The fish pie includes the first local mussels and the fruit salad is based on the excellent English pears and apples.

The thick bread and tomato soup is well known to the Chiantishire contingent, and is so good that it should be popular with everyone. The best bread to use is *pan pugliese*, which is now available from most delicatessens, Italian shops and large super-markets. When I was in Tuscany recently I had this soup served in hollowed-out *michette*, bread rolls. A very attractive presentation, but one that is perhaps more suitable for serving to a smaller number of guests sitting down at the table. Unfortunately the soft part of the rolls you can buy here is not suitable for using in the soup itself.

The fish pie is a version of an earlier recipe of mine for *tiella di pesce alla pugliese* – baked fish and potatoes in Apulian style – an adaptation made by Claudia Wolfers, a young friend who is a good and enterprising cook. In a clever way she has partly anglicized my *tiella* by adding smoked haddock. The smoked haddock must be Finnan, which is now sold by most fishmongers. Do not attempt to make the dish with other self-styled smoked haddock, which sometimes is not even haddock, nor indeed smoked, having been dyed that dreadful bright yellow and given a smoke flavour artificially.

The special salad I suggest is one I like very much, particularly suitable for an autumnal party. The other salad should be a green salad, of which I give a good basic example on page 368.

The rice cake is as typically Italian as rice pudding is English. The two are based on the same ingredients, but they are treated differently to produce a very different result. *Torta di riso*, of which there are as many variants as there are of rice pudding, is a real cake, firm yet moist. It is served unmoulded and cold, perhaps tepid, but never hot. It is made with Italian rice, which has the property of absorbing the milk, and is flavoured with characteristic Italian flavourings.

The other pudding, the autumnal fruit salad, is a rich mixture of fruit cooked in wine and lavishly flavoured with spices, a dish redolent of the Renaissance, when spices were sprinkled with a generous hand. The two sweets are different, yet they go well enough together to be served on the same plate for people who like mixing food, something that, like all my compatriots, I am not too keen on doing.

*

Pappa col pomodoro

BREAD AND TOMATO SOUP

---

700 g/1½ lb good-quality stale
  white bread, with the crust
  removed
4.5 litres/7¾ pints home-made
  vegetable stock, or 6 vegetable
  bouillon cubes dissolved in the
  same quantity of water
225 ml/8 fl oz extra virgin olive oil
3 onions, chopped

salt
2 tsp sugar
a dozen garlic cloves, peeled and
  very finely chopped
2.25 kg/5 lb fresh tomatoes,
  skinned and coarsely chopped
4 tsp tomato purée
40 g/1½ oz fresh basil leaves
freshly ground black pepper

Break the bread into small pieces and put in a large bowl.

Bring the stock slowly to the boil and pour over the bread. Leave for 15 minutes, stirring occasionally to break up the bread.

Heat the oil with the onion in a saucepan, preferably earthenware, which retains the heat and prevents the onions from burning. Add a teaspoon of salt to the onion to release the moisture, and the sugar. When the onion is soft but not brown, add the garlic, tomatoes and tomato purée. Cook, stirring frequently, for 5 minutes and then add the bread and stock mixture. Cook over gentle heat for 40 minutes, stirring occasionally.

Five minutes before the soup is ready, add the basil and a generous grinding of black pepper. Serve warm or at room temperature, not piping hot.

PREPARATION

You can prepare the soup up to 2 days in advance and keep it in the fridge.

**   *Tiella di pesce di Claudia*

APULIAN FISH PIE

1.8 kg/4 lb mussels
300 ml/½ pint dry white wine
10 garlic cloves, peeled and bruised
2 lemons, cut into segments
300 ml/½ pint skimmed milk
450 g/1 lb smoked Finnan haddock
1 kg/2 lb fresh haddock fillets
1.8 kg/4 lb waxy potatoes
300 ml/½ pint olive oil

salt and pepper
1 kg/2 lb ripe tomatoes
6 tbsp chopped parsley
2 dried chillies, seeded and
    crumbled
225 g/½ lb mature pecorino,
    grated
10 fennel seeds, pounded to coarse
    powder

Scrub the mussels, knocking off any barnacles and tugging off the beards. Wash in many changes of cold water until no sand is left at the bottom of the sink. Nowadays mussels are usually pretty clean because they are farmed on rafts and ropes. Throw away any mussel that remains open when you tap it on a hard surface. It is dead.

Put the wine, 4 of the garlic cloves and the lemons in a large sauté pan. Bring to the boil and boil for 2 minutes. Add about half the mussels, cover the pan with a lid and leave them to steam open. Shake the pan every now and then, to turn the mussels over. When they are open, draw the pan off the heat.

Remove the mussels from their shells and put them in a bowl. Do this over the pan so that you collect the juices. Discard the shells.

Now put the remaining mussels into the pan and do the same again.

Strain the mussel liquor through a sieve lined with muslin into a bowl. Set aside.

Heat the milk, add the smoked haddock and cook for 2–3 minutes. Remove the fish from the milk, skin it and cut into pieces. Skin the fresh haddock fillets and cut into pieces.

Peel the potatoes and cut them into wafer-thin slices. A food processor with the fine blade disc is invaluable for the job. Put the potatoes in a bowl of cold water and rinse them as if you were washing them, to get rid of some of the starch. Drain them, dry them very thoroughly and put them in a bowl. Toss with 2 tablespoons of the oil and season with salt and pepper.

Heat the oven to 200°C/400°F/Gas 6.

Blanch the tomatoes and peel them. Cut them in half and squeeze out some of the seeds and juice by pressing each half gently between your forefinger and thumb. Cut the tomatoes into slices.

Mix together in a bowl the parsley, chillies, pecorino and fennel seeds. Slice the remaining garlic cloves and add to the mixture with some salt to taste.

Grease a large lasagne dish or a shallow oven dish with a little oil. Cover the bottom with half the potatoes. Now make a layer with half the tomatoes. Sprinkle with one third of the herb and cheese mixture and place the smoked fish, the fresh haddock and the mussels on top. Sprinkle with half the remaining herb and cheese mixture and pour over half the remaining olive oil and half the mussel liquor. Cover with the remaining potatoes, then with the remaining tomatoes. Sprinkle with the remaining herb mixture and dribble the rest of the olive oil and the mussel liquor all over.

Cover the dish with a sheet of foil and place in the oven. After 20 minutes remove the foil and continue cooking until the potatoes are tender, about 40 minutes in all. Leave out of the oven for 5 minutes for the flavours to blend, before serving.

PREPARATION

The *tiella* is better made the day it is to be eaten, although the fish can be prepared up to 1 day in advance and refrigerated in a covered container.

* ## Insalata di sedano, carota e mela al sapor di coriandolo

CELERY, CARROT AND APPLE SALAD IN A WINE AND CORIANDER DRESSING

the heart of 2 large white celery heads	*100 ml/3½ fl oz extra virgin olive oil*
7 medium carrots	*the juice of 1 lemon*
2 dessert apples of a sour kind, such as Granny Smith	*salt and pepper*
	3 tbsp fresh coriander, chopped
120 ml/4 fl oz dry white wine	

Wash the tender stalks of the celery and remove any strings if necessary. Slice into very thin strips and put in a bowl.

Peel, wash and dry the carrots. Cut them into matchsticks and add to the bowl. (A food processor with the matchstick disc attached does the work in seconds.)

Peel and cut the apple into the same size matchsticks. Add to the bowl.

Heat the wine, half the oil and the lemon juice and simmer very gently for 5 minutes to evaporate the alcohol. Pour over the vegetables about an hour before you want to serve the salad.

Toss with the rest of the oil and season with salt and plenty of pepper. Sprinkle the chopped coriander leaves over the top just before serving.

PREPARATION

Do not prepare the vegetables more than half an hour before the sauce is poured over them, as they will discolour.

**   *Torta di riso*

RICE CAKE

---

750 ml/1¼ pints full-fat milk	60 g/2 oz pine nuts
180 g/6 oz caster sugar	4 eggs, separated
strip of lemon peel, yellow part only	30 g/1 oz candied orange, lemon and citron peel, chopped
piece of vanilla pod 2.5 cm/1 in long, split in half	the grated rind of ½ lemon
piece of cinnamon stick 5 cm/2 in long	3 tbsp rum
	butter and dried breadcrumbs for the tin
salt	icing sugar for decoration
150 g/5 oz arborio rice	
120 g/4 oz almonds, blanched and peeled	

Put the milk, 30 g/1 oz of the sugar, the lemon peel, vanilla, cinnamon and a pinch of salt in a saucepan and bring to the boil.

Add the rice and stir well with a wooden spoon. Cook, uncovered, over very low heat for about 40 minutes, until the rice has absorbed the milk and is soft and creamy. Stir frequently during the cooking. Set aside to cool.

While the rice is cooking, heat the oven to 180°C/350°F/Gas 4.

Spread the almonds and the pine nuts on a baking tray and toast them in the preheated oven for about 10 minutes. Shake the tray once or twice to prevent them burning. Cool a little and then chop them coarsely by hand or in the food processor, but do not reduce them to powder.

Remove the lemon peel, the vanilla pod and the cinnamon stick from the rice and spoon the rice into a mixing bowl.

Incorporate one egg yolk at a time into the rice, mixing well after each addition. Add the remaining sugar, the nuts, candied peel, grated rind of the lemon and the rum to the rice and egg mixture and combine everything together thoroughly.

Whip the egg whites stiffly and fold into the rice mixture.

Butter a 25 cm/10 in spring-clip tin, line the base of the tin with greaseproof paper and butter the paper. Sprinkle all over with the breadcrumbs and shake off excess crumbs.

Spoon the rice mixture into the prepared tin and bake for about 45 minutes, until a thin skewer or toothpick inserted in the middle of the cake comes out just moist. The cake will also have shrunk from the side of the tin.

Leave the cake to cool in the tin and then remove the clipped band and turn the cake over on to a dish. Remove the base of the tin and the paper, place a round serving dish over the cake and turn it over again. Sprinkle lavishly with icing sugar before serving.

PREPARATION

The cake must be made at least 1 day in advance. It can be kept for a few days in the refrigerator, wrapped in foil. Remove from the refrigerator at least 2 hours before serving, to bring it back to room temperature.

Insalata autunnale di frutta

AUTUMNAL FRUIT SALAD

---

1 bottle sweet white wine
5 tbsp clear honey
the rind and juice of 3 lemons
½ tsp ground ginger
¼ tsp ground cloves
½ tsp grated nutmeg
½ tsp cinnamon
100 g/3½ oz prunes, stoned
300 ml/½ pint tea

100 g/3½ oz sultanas
100 g/3½ oz dried apricots
10 dried figs or 100 g/3½ oz dates,
    stoned and cut into thin strips
450 g/1 lb dessert apples
450 g/1 lb pears
100 g/3½ oz almonds, blanched,
    peeled and cut into slivers
60 g/2 oz pine nuts

For serving

lightly whipped cream or yoghurt (optional)

Put the wine, honey, lemon juice and rind, and the spices in a saucepan. Bring to the boil and simmer very gently for 20 minutes.

Meanwhile put the prunes in a bowl. Cover with hot tea and leave to soak for 20 minutes.

Soak the sultanas, apricots and figs or dates in warm water for 15 minutes, then dry thoroughly and cut the apricots and figs into strips. If you are using dates instead of figs, remove the stones and cut into smaller strips. Do the same to the prunes.

Peel the apples and pears, cut into small cubes and put in a saucepan. Pour over the wine mixture and cook gently until the fruit is tender. Add the dried fruit, the almonds and the pine nuts. Cook for a further 5 minutes, stirring every now and then.

Allow to cool in the pan and then transfer to a bowl. Serve cold, with a bowl of cream or yoghurt if you like.

PREPARATION

This pudding must be made at least 1 day in advance (2 or 3 days would be even better) and chilled. This allows time for the flavours to blend.

A BUFFET SUPPER FOR 12

Minestra di pasta e ceci
CHICK-PEA AND PASTA SOUP

Tiella di carne e patate
MEAT AND POTATO PIE

This menu is similar to the previous one, equally easy to make and equally well suited to eating either standing or with the plate on your lap. I have changed only the first two courses; the salads and desserts can be the same as in the previous menu.

The two menus are also ideal for an informal party of, say, 25 people. You must choose one of the two soups and double the quantities, and then make one fish pie (page 206) and one meat pie exactly as in the recipes. The salads and the puddings should be made in double quantities. Alternatively, and preferably, you could serve one or two extra salads and one or two extra puddings. I would suggest the following: celeriac and radicchio salad (page 284) and fennel and orange salad (page 65); Sharon fruits with lime juice (page 192) and morello cherry jam tart (page 82).

** *Minestra di pasta e ceci*

CHICK-PEA AND PASTA SOUP

---

600 g/1¼ lb dried chick-peas,
   preferably the large ones
1 tbsp bicarbonate of soda
3 tbsp flour
3 tbsp salt
4.5 litres/7¾ pints vegetable stock
4–5 fresh rosemary sprigs
12 garlic cloves, peeled and bruised

180 ml/6 fl oz extra virgin olive oil
600 g/1¼ lb skinned fresh
   tomatoes, seeded
400 g/14 oz small tubular pasta
   such as ditalini
Parmesan cheese
freshly ground black pepper

Put the chick-peas in a bowl and cover with plenty of water.
Mix together the bicarbonate of soda, flour and salt and add

enough water to make a thin paste. Stir this mixture into the bowl with the chick-peas and leave to soak for at least 12 hours. It helps to soften the skin of the chick-peas.

When the chick-peas have doubled their weight they are ready to be cooked. Drain and then rinse them. Put them in a large stockpot, or two smaller stockpots, and add the vegetable stock or the same quantity of water.

Tie the rosemary sprigs in a muslin bag and add to the stockpot. (This will make it possible to remove the rosemary without leaving any needles to float in the soup.)

Add the garlic to the stockpot and pour in half the oil. Cover the pan tightly and bring to the boil. Lower the heat and cook over the lowest simmer until the chick-peas are tender, which can take 2–4 hours. Do not uncover the pan for the first 1½ hours or the chick-peas will harden. For the same reason do not add any salt until the chick-peas are nearly ready.

When the chick-peas are tender, remove the garlic and the rosemary bundle which are floating on the surface of the soup. Purée the tomatoes through a food mill or in a food processor and add to the soup with their juice. Stir well, add salt and pepper to taste and cook for a further 10 minutes or so.

Before you add the pasta, check that there is enough liquid in the pan. You may have to add some boiling water. Now add the pasta and cook until *al dente*. Ladle the soup into soup bowls and pour a little of the remaining oil in the middle of each bowl. Serve immediately, handing the Parmesan round separately.

PREPARATION

You can prepare the soup 2 or 3 days in advance (but do not add the pasta) and chill. You can also freeze it. Add the pasta when the soup is reheated.

** *Tiella di carne e patate*

MEAT AND POTATO PIE

1.35 kg/3 lb braising steak	2 tbsp rosemary leaves
450 g/1 lb pork steak	1/4 tsp grated nutmeg
9 tbsp olive oil	pepper
120 g/4 oz unsalted butter	1 tbsp dried oregano
1 Spanish onion, finely chopped	6 tbsp tomato purée
1 tbsp sugar	300 ml/1/2 pint red wine
salt	180 ml/6 fl oz full-fat milk
3 celery stalks	2 kg/4 1/2 lb waxy potatoes
2 carrots	120 g/4 oz Parmesan, freshly
4 garlic cloves	grated
2 tbsp thyme	1 large bunch of parsley, chopped
6 sage leaves	

If you have a friendly butcher, ask him to remove all the fat and gristle from the beef and pork and to cut the meat into 1½ cm/¾ in cubes. Otherwise you need to do this yourself.

Put the oil, a third of the butter and the onion in a heavy sauté pan (ideally it should be a large earthenware pot). Sprinkle with the sugar and 1 teaspoon of salt and sauté gently until the onion is soft.

Meanwhile chop the celery, carrots, garlic, thyme, sage and rosemary together either by hand or in a food processor. When the onion is cooked, add the vegetable mixture, nutmeg, pepper and oregano to the pan and cook for 10 minutes, stirring frequently. Stir in the tomato purée, cook for 1 minute and then add the meat. Cook until the meat has lost its raw colour, turning it over frequently. Splash with the wine and cook for 10 minutes. Mix in the milk and bring to the boil. Cook over a very gentle heat until the meat is tender, about 40 minutes. If there is too much liquid by the end of the cooking, turn the heat up and boil rapidly to reduce the juice, which should be rich and full of flavour. Taste and check seasoning.

While the meat is cooking, peel the potatoes and cut them into wafer-thin slices. A food processor with the fine blade disc is invaluable for what is otherwise a lengthy job. Put the potatoes in a bowl of cold water and rub the slices together to get rid of some of the starch. Drain and turn the potatoes on to a tea towel. Dry them thoroughly.

Heat the oven to 200°C/400°F/Gas 6.

Butter a large lasagne dish or a shallow oven dish into which the meat should spread to a thickness of about 3–4 cm/1–1½ in. Use two dishes if you do not have one large enough.

Melt the remaining butter in a small pan.

Spread the potatoes over the bottom of the dish, season with salt and pepper and pour over a little of the melted butter. Cover with the meat and sprinkle with half the cheese. Spread the remaining potatoes neatly over the meat and top with the remaining cheese. Spoon the melted butter all over, cover with foil and place the dish in the preheated oven.

Cook for 20 minutes and then remove the foil and continue cooking until the potatoes are done, about 35 minutes in all. Allow the dish to stand for 5 minutes out of the oven before serving, so that all the flavours can blend. Sprinkle the top of the pie with the chopped parsley and bring to the table.

PREPARATION

The meat is better when cooked a day in advance and heated slowly, before being finished with the potatoes in the oven. It can be cooked up to 3 days in advance and refrigerated. It can also be frozen.

Historical Menus

I have always been fascinated by the thought of what people used to eat in the past. My interest in this was once more aroused when I was researching my book *Gastronomy of Italy*, since I had to consult many cookery books written through the centuries to see what ingredients were used. So, for this book, I decided to include a menu from each of the four periods which contributed most to modern Italian cooking, plus one 'Futurist' menu.

The first menu, because it is the earliest, had to be from the only book of Roman recipes, *De Re Coquinaria* by Apicius. It is not known for certain whether Apicius was in fact the author of the book, or whether it was a later compendium of recipes attributed to Apicius.

It was during the Saracen-Sicilian period, some four centuries later, that the foundations of European cooking were laid. The Saracens brought to Italy many spices and vegetables, some of which had previously been known to the Romans. And, even more important, it was in Sicily that these new foods and new methods of cooking came into contact with the indigenous produce and the methods of the earlier civilizations of the Greeks and the Romans. Unfortunately very little writing about cookery has survived from this period, and so I jumped 1,000 years from the Roman era to the Renaissance.

In the fourteenth and fifteenth centuries the great awakening of the mind in Italy was many-sided. Cookery, such an intrinsic part of human life, could not be overlooked, and cookery books began to be written at that time. The recipes in these books have totally captivated me, and I have adapted a certain number to our palates and habits, as you will see throughout this book. I have been fascinated by the similarity of some recipes to modern ones, thus being able to retrace a few favourites to their original source.

These Renaissance cookery books were written by chefs or stewards of grand houses, or of the Vatican, who wrote about the ingredients, how to deal with them, the layout of the kitchen and of the table, the linen, the service, in fact everything connected with cooking and eating. Some books also include menus of the dinners they prepared for visiting monarchs, ambassadors and prelates. One such is the menu of the dinner prepared by Bartolomeo Scappi for his master, Cardinal Lorenzo Campeggi, who was entertaining Charles V 'when his Caesarean Majesty entered Rome in April 1536'. Campeggi's villa was in Trastevere, which was then a suburb of Rome. Many important Romans used to have splendid villas in the suburbs where eminent visitors to the Pope would spend the night before their audience with His

Holiness. Not that these dinners were an ascetic preparation for the awesome meeting of the morrow. Rather, they were a celebration of the excellence and opulence of their host's table, as Scappi's menus testify.

Another fascinating chronicler of glorious meals was Cristoforo di Messisbugo, steward to the fabulously wealthy Cardinal Hippolito d'Este, a brother-in-law of Lucrezia Borgia. Messisbugo's book is not only a recipe book but also an important contribution to social history. He is considered the founder of *haute cuisine*, which France later made its own. I find his recipes rather complicated, however, and I prefer to work from the *Opera* of Scappi.

My other favourite Renaissance writer is Bartolomeo Stefani, chef to another rich and powerful family, the Gonzaga of Mantua. Stefani's simplicity, and his use of herbs in preference to spices, make him a very modern cook, with a light, fresh approach. You will find my adaptation of his pudding, *torta bianca alla bolognese*, on page 232.

The other important period in Italian gastronomy was at the time of Bourbon Naples. Naples became a great cultural centre when the excavations at Pompeii began, in the middle of the eighteenth century, and for some 100 years thereafter it was a Mecca for musicians, literati, artists and young aristocrats from all over Europe. Its *joie de vivre*, its climate and the beauty of its position conspired to make Naples a magnet for the erstwhile jet-set. In 1820, when King Ferdinand entertained the Emperor and Empress of Austria and Prince Metternich, a party was thrown at Capodimonte for 1,000 guests. As Sir Harold Acton writes in his book *The Bourbons at Naples*, 'There were relays of banquets with the rarest fish and the most exquisite viands served in abundance, and any foreign wine asked for was obtainable. The Viennese guests were in ecstasies over Neapolitan *sfogliatelle*, a fine-flaked pastry melting in the mouth, "such stuff as dreams are made on".'

One reason why Naples has contributed much to my cooking (another being my love of Naples) lies in three cookery books written with a strong emphasis on the cooking of the south. They are *Il Cuoco Galante* by Vincenzo Corrado, published in 1778, *L'Apicio Moderno* by Francesco Leonardi, published in 1790, and *Cucina Teorico-Pratica* by Ippolito Cavalcanti, published in 1847. Corrado's book has a fascinating section on vegetables, with some perfect recipes, and one on *timballi* and *pasticci*. In fact the recipe for the main course in my Neapolitan menu comes from this section. Leonardi's work is a vast encyclopedia in six volumes, ranging from the history of Italian cooking to many recipes from foreign countries. He spent some years in Paris and in Russia, where he became chef to Catherine the Great. Cavalcanti was a wealthy aristocrat, but nonetheless he wrote a book that was not only for the rich, incorporating as it does much wise advice and many simple recipes.

The next period, and locality, which I consider fundamental to Italian cooking is the nineteenth century in northern Italy, or more precisely in Piedmont and Lombardy. The cooking of these two regions was greatly influenced by Austria, which dominated Lombardy for more than half the century, and by France. Everything French was the *dernier cri*, to the extent that the wealthy Milanese, who used to spend periods of the year in Paris, would take their chefs to learn *haute cuisine* directly from French masters. Fortunately we have quite a few books written at the time, one by Giovanni Vialardi, who was *chef pâtissier* to the first king of Italy. But the most important book written then, and still considered the Italian masterpiece in this genre, is *La Scienza in Cucina e l'Arte di Mangiar Bene* by Pellegrino Artusi. This book, which by 1963 was in its 800th edition, is still the best-selling cookery book in Italy. It is indeed a joy to read as well as to cook with, and quite a few of my recipes are derived from Artusi's.

My last menu is taken from *La Cucina Futurista* by Filippo Marinetti, written in 1932. Marinetti was primarily a poet, of arguable merit, but his great contribution to posterity was the founding of the Futurist movement. In his book, Marinetti wanted to stimulate our appreciation of the texture, shape and colour of the food, and for this reason ingredients are cooked and presented out of their usual contexts. This led to some uneatable dishes, some negligible dishes and some excellent ones. All, however, are unforgettable.

As an example of Marinetti's idiosyncratic approach to food I give below my translation of the menu for the dinner prepared for him by the manager of the restaurant Penna d'Oca in Milan, entitled 'A Gastronomic Eulogy to Futurism'.

Fat goose
Ice-cream in the moon
Tears of the God 'Gavi' [an Italian
   wine]
Broth of roses and sun
Mediterranean favourite Zig,
   Zug, Zag
Roast lamb in lion sauce
Dawn salad

Blood of Bacchus: 'Ricasoli's soil'
   [named after the original
   grower of Chianti]
Artichoke wheels
Rain of spun sugar
Cinzano exhilarating froth
Fruit from Eve's garden
Coffee and liqueur

I had no difficulty choosing from Marinetti's recipes since my criterion, that of being good to eat, ruled out many of them. Yet because of the shocking, and at times repellent, nature of the recipes, *La Cucina Futurista* is one of the more stimulating and entertaining cookery books of any age.

I have taken gastronomic liberties with most of the recipes I have chosen, to make the dishes more feasible and more acceptable to modern palates. But whenever I have added or substituted an ingredient I have always kept in mind the period when the recipes were originally written, and never brought in any ingredient that was not used at the time.

AN ANCIENT ROMAN DINNER FOR 8

In loligine patina
SQUID IN THE PAN

Porcellum coriandratum
ROAST PORK WITH CORIANDER

Aliter olus molle
PURÉE OF CELERY

Frutta
FRESH FRUIT

The three recipes in this menu come from *De Re Coquinaria*, a collection of Roman recipes compiled during the time of the first Roman Emperors. These recipes to a certain extent constitute the foundations of European cooking, and therefore of American cooking as well.

The authorship of *De Re Coquinaria* is uncertain. There were three gastronomes called Apicius who lived during those years, all so famous for their love of food that by the end of the first century AD the name Apicius had already become the accepted name for the wealthiest Roman gourmets. The Apicius who lived under Tiberius killed himself when he saw his fortune coming to an end. He had spent most of his great wealth on good living and was afraid that the 10 million *sestertii* that remained would place quite unacceptable limits on his way of life. So he arranged his last banquet, and took poison.

The recipes in *De Re Coquinaria* were transcribed anonymously in the third or fourth century AD, and they are the only sure source, however vague, of the eating habits of that period. The book is divided into ten chapters, covering the whole culinary range from wines and syrups to fish, truffles and sauces. The recipes, however, are extremely succinct, with no indication of proportions for the ingredients, and no cooking times or methods. Nor does the book contain information on the laying of the table or the order of the courses.

What we do learn from the book is which ingredients were used and in what combination of tastes. The love of the ancient

Romans for spices and herbs is immediately evident. Whether these were used to disguise unpleasant flavours or for love of spicy and highly-flavoured food we cannot know – probably both.

The first course of my menu, the squid, is flavoured with rue, a herb that has disappeared from modern cooking. Oddly enough, I recently came across a recipe for spaghetti with a rue sauce, created by the great chef Angelo Paracucchi for his restaurant Locanda dell'Angelo near Lerici. Rue has a rather bitter and very aromatic flavour that can swamp everything else. It has to be used with great discretion. It is impossible to buy, but it grows well in any soil and is one of the most decorative plants I know, with its silvery-bluey leaves and compact bush shape. The American John Edwards, who adapted Apicius' recipes, suggests using fresh rosemary instead.

The *secondo* had to be pork, the favourite Roman meat. Cooked in this way, with sweet ingredients juxtaposed with fresh coriander, it is particularly succulent. The accompaniment for the pork is celery, yet another Roman favourite. They must have loved its fragrance, because they used it not only in cooking but even more in garlands and wreaths.

I could not find any sweet that caught my fancy, the few in the book being rather boring custards or omelettes. This is, in fact, quite understandable, since the Romans preferred to eat fruit, which they knew how to produce to perfection.

** *In loligine patina*

SQUID IN THE PAN

'Crush pepper, rue, a little honey, broth, reduced wine and oil to taste, when commencing to boil bind with roux.' (Marcus Gabius Apicius)

1.8 kg/4 lb squid
6 tbsp extra virgin olive oil
120 ml/4 fl oz dry white wine
1 tbsp finely chopped rosemary
*   needles*
1 tbsp finely chopped rue, if
*   available*

2 large garlic cloves, sliced
½ tbsp clear honey
500 ml/1 pint (scant measure) fish
*   stock (see page 379)*
salt and freshly ground black
*   pepper*
1 tbsp flour

The best squid to buy for this dish are those caught around the Cornish coast; they are large and very tasty and they need the lengthy cooking that makes this recipe so perfect.

Ask your fishmonger to clean and skin the squid. If he is not prepared to do so (I feel that in that case I should advise you to find another fishmonger), proceed as follows. Hold the sac in one hand and pull off the tentacles with the other hand. All the contents of the sac will come out too. Cut the tentacles above the eyes. Squeeze out the small bony beak in the centre of the tentacles. Peel off the mottled skin from the sac and the flaps. Remove the transparent backbone from inside the sac and rinse the sac and tentacles thoroughly under running water. Drain in a colander and then dry with kitchen paper. Cut the sacs into 1 cm/½ in strips and the tentacles into small pieces. The squid are now ready for cooking.

Choose a large heavy sauté pan or, better still, a large earthenware pot. The squid should cook spread out, rather than piled up. Heat the oil, add the squid and sauté gently for 5 minutes. When the squid have released their liquid, turn the heat up to evaporate and cook for 2–3 minutes, stirring frequently. Splash with the wine and let it bubble away for a couple of minutes.

Now turn the heat down and mix in the chopped herbs, the garlic and the honey. Cover with the fish stock and bring to the boil. Taste for salt and add some if necessary. (Fish stock is sometimes already salted.) Season with plenty of pepper. Put the lid firmly on the pan or cover with foil tied under the rim of the pan. The squid must cook tightly covered so that the steam is kept in. They must also cook over the gentlest heat. I use a flame disperser. They should be ready in 40–50 minutes, depending on their size. Test for doneness by pricking the squid with a fork; it should offer no resistance to the prongs.

Scoop out the squid, place on a heated serving dish and keep warm, covered with foil. Put the flour in a small bowl and add a few tablespoons of the cooking liquid to make a paste. Blend the paste into the pan and cook for a few minutes, stirring constantly. Check seasonings. Pour the sauce over the squid and serve with plenty of crusty bread. The dish can be served hot, though not too hot, but it is also excellent at room temperature.

PREPARATION
The dish can be prepared totally up to 1 day in advance and chilled in a covered container. Do not serve straight from the fridge.

** *Porcellum coriandratum*

ROAST PORK WITH CORIANDER

'Roast the pig carefully; make a mortar mixture in this way: pound pepper, dill, oregano, green coriander, moisten with honey, wine, broth, oil, vinegar and reduced must. All of this when hot, pour over. Sprinkle over with raisins, pine nuts and chopped onions and so serve.' (Marcus Gabius Apicius)

---

2 tbsp olive oil
1.5 kg/3½ lb boneless rolled leg of
  pork
2 tbsp fresh coriander, chopped

1 tsp dried oregano
2 tsp fresh dill, chopped
8 peppercorns
1 tbsp rock salt

For the sauce

300 ml/½ pint meat stock
200 ml/7 fl oz red wine
1 tbsp red wine vinegar
1 small onion, chopped
2 tbsp pine nuts

3 tbsp sultanas
1½ tbsp honey
4 tbsp olive oil
salt and pepper

Heat the oven to 225°C/425°F/Gas 7.

Put all but 2 tablespoons of the oil in a small roasting tin and coat the meat in the oil. Put the tin in the oven and roast for 15 minutes.

Meanwhile pound together in a mortar (or in a heavy pudding basin) the coriander, oregano, dill, peppercorns and rock salt, moistening with the remaining oil. When the 15 minutes are up turn the heat down to 180°C/350°F/Gas 4. Spread the herb mixture over the meat and replace the meat in the oven. Cook for 1½ hours, basting every quarter of an hour or thereabouts.

For the sauce, put all the ingredients in a saucepan and boil, uncovered, for 40 minutes. The liquid should boil slowly, so that by the end of the 40 minutes there will be plenty left but it will have a rich, concentrated flavour.

When the meat is done, transfer it to a side dish and cover it with foil. Do not worry about it getting cold. Any roast must be left out of the oven before eating for 10 minutes at least, to allow the juices to penetrate the inside of the joint. Skim off as much fat as you can from the surface of the cooking juices. Deglaze the roasting tin with a couple of tablespoons of boiling water and then pour everything into the sauce, scraping down all the bits of herbs.

Carve the meat into 1 cm/½ in slices and spoon a little sauce over the meat. Hand the rest round in a sauce-boat.

PREPARATION

The sauce can be prepared up to 3 days in advance and refrigerated in a covered container. Reheat slowly before you add the deglazed cooking juices.

Aliter olus molle

PURÉE OF CELERY

'Cook celery in soda water, squeeze water out, chop fine. In the mortar crush pepper, lovage, oregano, onion and mix with wine and stock, adding some oil.' (Marcus Gabius Apicius)

2 celery heads	1 tbsp dried oregano
salt	120 ml/4 fl oz white wine
2 tbsp olive oil	225 ml/8 fl oz vegetable stock
1 onion, finely chopped	
1 tbsp lovage, chopped, or 2 tsp celery seeds, pounded	

Remove all the strings from the celery stalks. I find a potato peeler better than a knife for this job. Scrub and wash the stalks and cut into 5 cm/2 in pieces.

Bring a saucepan of salted water to the boil. Add the celery and cook for 5 minutes after the water has come back to the boil. Drain very thoroughly. Chop the celery to a coarse purée. You can use a food processor, although it tends to make the celery too mashed up.

Put all the other ingredients in a saucepan and bring to the boil. Simmer for 10 minutes and then stir in the celery. Cook for a further 10 minutes, stirring frequently. If the purée seems too thin, turn the heat up to evaporate some of the liquid. Taste, check seasoning and serve as an accompaniment to the pork.

PREPARATION

The purée can be prepared up to 1 day in advance and refrigerated in a covered container. Reheat slowly in a heavy saucepan into which you have put 1 tablespoon of olive oil.

A RENAISSANCE DINNER FOR 6

Torta d'herbe da quaresima
A LENTEN SPINACH PIE

Pesce in potaggio
STEWED FISH

Cavolfiore all'olio
BOILED CAULIFLOWER WITH OIL

Torta bianca alla bolognese
RICOTTA AND CREAM CAKE

In 1989 the Victoria and Albert Museum held a special event called *'Una Notte in Italia'* and, as part of this, I gave a cookery demonstration. Because of the historical overtones of the venue I decided to show how to prepare a Renaissance dinner. My dinner was, of course, conceived as a twentieth-century meal and not as a proper Renaissance meal, when each course would have contained many different dishes, all placed on the table at the same time.

The recipe for the *torta* comes from one of the first culinary books to appear in print, the *Libro Novo* by Cristoforo di Messisbugo, who was steward to Cardinal Ippolito d'Este in sixteenth-century Ferrara. The *torta* is a typical example of the cooking of the period, when sweet and savoury ingredients were combined to form a perfect harmony. Sweet ingredients were included in Renaissance, and Roman, recipes in order to enhance the flavour of the food, which sugar does, rather than to sweeten it. Buy Italian spinach, the kind that is in bunches, or very young leaf spinach. The large beet spinach is not suitable.

My choice for the second course is a fish dish, from two recipes by the great Bartolomeo Scappi, who flourished between 1540 and 1570 and was chef to Pope Pius V. The fish Scappi suggests is pike, carp or eel, all great favourites at the time. At my demonstration I used lovely chunks of eel, but I've also made this recipe with hake or halibut steaks, and it works well. I expect it would also be quite good with salmon steak. Most salmon is farmed nowadays and I find its taste not good enough for it to be simply steamed or grilled.

Next in this dinner I would serve a simple salad of boiled cauliflower taken from the *Brieve racconto di tutte le radici di tutte l'erbe e di tutti i frutti* by Giacomo Castelvetro. Castelvetro was born in Modena in 1546 but wrote this booklet in England, where he took refuge after he was banned from Italy, having incurred the wrath of the Inquisition through his leanings towards Protestantism. He dedicated his *Brieve racconto* to his patron, Lucy, Countess of Bedford. The book, which has now been translated into English by Gillian Riley, is not a cookery book but a eulogy of the fruits and vegetables of his native country. There is in Castelvetro's writing all the nostalgia and passion for something once enjoyed, now lost. When I first came across this book in 1975 in the Biblioteca Comunale in Milan I was taken back to the time when I first arrived in England in the early 1950s and the only vegetables were cabbages and lettuces in the summer plus, of course, potatoes and carrots. Nothing has changed, I thought, in 400 years!

Most of the vegetables are cooked in the simplest ways, such as the cauliflower in this recipe. 'We have in this season,' Castelvetro wrote, 'cauliflowers, which take pride of place for goodness and beauty among all the other species of the cabbage family. First cooked in lightly salted water, they are dressed with olive oil, salt and pepper.'

If you want to add a little 'body' to this course, serve some boiled new potatoes, even if they could hardly have figured in a Renaissance menu. Potatoes, which of course came originally from the New World, were hardly eaten in Italy until the nineteenth century.

The sweet, a very delicate soft cake, in effect a cross between a cake and a pudding, is derived from a recipe by Bartolomeo Stefani. Stefani was chef to the Marquis Ottavio Gonzaga of Mantua during the seventeenth century. His fascinating book, *L'Arte di Ben Cucinare*, was published in Mantua in 1662 and has now been reprinted in a facsimile edition by Arnaldo Forni. As well as recipes it contains instructions and advice, information and menus, ending with the menu of an extraordinary banquet served by his patron to Queen Christina of Sweden when she stayed in Mantua on her way to Rome.

The description of the room and table décor make fascinating reading. In the middle of the table there stood a sugar sculpture of Mount Olympus, with the altar of faith, on top of which were two putti holding a royal crown over the Queen's coat of arms. At each end of the table there were four orange trees, with fruit and leaves made of jelly. Between the trees stood two colonnades made of sugar, designed by an architect, one with twelve Corinthian columns and the other with twelve Doric columns. Between one row of columns there stood sugar statues of early warriors, while between the others there were statues of 'the most virtuous men who have ever lived'.

The dinner began with strawberries and marzipan sweetmeats shaped like birds. Fruit was always served first during the Renaissance, because it was supposed to help the digestion. After 400 years this belief is gaining favour again; many dieticians advise eating fruit half an hour before the beginning of a meal. *Plus ça change* . . .

✳✳✳ *Torta d'herbe da quaresima*

A LENTEN SPINACH PIE

'Take washed spinach and put it in a pot and throw in 4 ounces of oil and sauté it well and chop it and put it in a pot with 4 ounces of sugar and 1 ounce of cinnamon and a quarter of pepper and 6 ounces of raisins and 1 pound of figs, cut thin, and half a pound of sultanas and shelled and peeled walnuts and mix everything together well . . . And then you will prepare your case and you will cook following the order of the other lenten pie.' (Cristoforo di Messisbugo)

For the pastry

45 g/1½ oz caster sugar	*½ tsp salt*
¼ tsp powdered saffron or 10 saffron strands	*120 g/4 oz unsalted butter*
250 g/9 oz plain flour	*2 egg yolks*
	1½ tbsp rosewater

For the filling

30 g/1 oz raisins	*30 g/1 oz walnut kernels*
30 g/1 oz sultanas	*3 dried figs*
1.35 kg/3 lb fresh Italian bunch spinach, or 700 g/1½ lb cooked, or frozen spinach	*1 tbsp sugar*
	¼ tsp ground cinnamon
salt and pepper	*½ tsp grated nutmeg*
4 tbsp olive oil	*60 g/2 oz grated Parmesan*
	1 tbsp dried breadcrumbs

For the glazing

1 egg yolk	*pinch of salt*
1 tbsp milk	

First make the pastry the way you usually do, by hand or in the food processor. Pound the sugar and saffron together and mix well into the flour and salt before rubbing in the butter. Mix in the egg yolks and the rosewater. When the dough is ready, wrap it in clingfilm and chill for at least 30 minutes. Soak the raisins and sultanas in a cupful of hot water for 15 minutes or so. Drain and dry thoroughly.

Trim, wash and cook the spinach without putting any water in the pan. The water that clings to the leaves is enough. Add 1 tsp of salt. When the spinach is tender, drain, and as soon as it is cool enough squeeze well between your hands. Sauté it gently in the oil for 10 minutes, stirring frequently to let it *insaporire* – take up the flavour. Chop it coarsely and transfer to a bowl.

Blanch the walnut kernels in a little boiling water for 20 seconds. Drain and remove as much as you can of the bitter skin. Dry the kernels and chop finely, together with the figs. Add to the spinach in the bowl.

Drain and dry the sultanas and the raisins and add to the bowl. Mix in the sugar, cinnamon, nutmeg, salt and pepper. Add the Parmesan, reserving 1 tablespoon, and mix very thoroughly with your hands.

Heat the oven to 190°C/375°F/Gas 5.

Butter an 18 cm/7 in clip-form tin and sprinkle with flour.

Roll out about one-third of the pastry dough into a circle to cover the bottom of the tin. Roll out strips of dough and line the sides of the tin. Sprinkle the bottom with the dried breadcrumbs and the remaining Parmesan. Spoon the spinach mixture into the tin and cover with a disc of rolled-out pastry. Seal the edges and brush with the egg yolk into which you have stirred the milk and salt. If you like, and if you have any pastry left, cut out some pretty shapes, place on the top of the pie and brush with the egg yolk glaze. Pierce the top here and there with a fork to allow the steam to escape.

Bake for 30 minutes, then turn the heat down to 180°C/350°F/Gas 4 and bake for a further 10–15 minutes, until the pastry is lovely and golden. Serve warm or at room temperature, but not hot.

PREPARATION
The whole pie can be made up to 2 days in advance and refrigerated. It can also be frozen successfully, but do not leave in the freezer for longer than 2 weeks or the flavours will evaporate. Remove from the fridge at least 3 hours before serving.

** *Pesce in potaggio*

STEWED FISH

'Cut the fish into thick rolls and cook it with white wine, vinegar, spices and water and cook it as for the trout in Chapter CXVI. It can be served hot or cold.' (Bartolomeo Scappi)

6 fish steaks, about 200 g/7 oz each	1 onion stuck with 3 cloves
225 ml/8 fl oz dry white wine	2 bay leaves
2 tbsp red wine vinegar	2 tbsp sugar
¼ tsp powdered saffron or 10 saffron strands	45 g/1½ oz ground almonds
¼ tsp ground cinnamon	2 tbsp mixed chopped herbs: rosemary, sage, thyme,
¼ tsp ground ginger	marjoram, mint
salt	2 tbsp chopped parsley
15 peppercorns, bruised	30 g/1 oz unsalted butter

Heat the oven to 200°C/400°F/Gas 6.

Put the fish in an oven dish into which it will fit in a single layer.

Heat the wine and vinegar with the spices, seasonings, onion and bay leaves. Add 225 ml/8 fl oz of water and bring to the boil. Boil for 2 minutes and then pour it over the fish. Cover the dish with foil and cook in the oven until ready, about 15–20 minutes, depending on the thickness of the fish steaks.

Transfer the fish to a serving dish and keep warm.

Strain the cooking liquid into a saucepan and reduce over high heat by about half. Add the sugar, ground almonds and herbs, then bring to the boil, turn the heat down and simmer for 10 minutes or so.

Add the butter in little lumps and, when it is all incorporated, transfer into a sauce-boat and serve.

PREPARATION

Fish should always be cooked just before it is eaten. If you are using whole almonds, which is better than buying them ready ground, you can grind them up to 3 days in advance and refrigerate, or you can prepare them up to 2 months in advance and freeze.

* *Torta bianca alla bolognese*

RICOTTA AND CREAM CAKE

'You will take 4 pounds of fat ricotta pounded in the mortar splashed with rose water, adding 12 fresh eggs, 8 ounces of sugar, half an ounce of cinnamon, pounding everything together well and when well swollen, you will grease a pan with butter. You will put in the mixture and you will cook it slowly in the oven and you will serve it hot with sugar on top.' (Bartolomeo Stefani)

---

300 g/10 oz ricotta
1 tbsp rosewater
300 ml/½ pint double cream
120 g/4 oz sugar

½ tsp cinnamon
4 eggs
icing sugar, sifted

Heat the oven to 180°C/350°F/Gas 4.

Pass the ricotta through a food mill or a sieve and mix in the rosewater. Do not use a food processor, as this would not aerate the ricotta. Fold in the cream, the sugar and the cinnamon. Beat the eggs lightly in a bowl and add gradually while beating constantly.

Generously butter a 20 cm/8 in spring-clip tin and line the bottom with greaseproof paper. Butter the paper and spoon the mixture into the tin. Bake in the preheated oven for 50 minutes or until a cocktail stick inserted in the middle of the cake comes out just dry. Remove from the tin and peel off the paper.

Serve warm, sprinkled with plenty of icing sugar.

PREPARATION

The mixture can be prepared up to 5 or 6 hours in advance and refrigerated. If necessary you can even make the cake the day before, although it is nicer just warm.

AN EIGHTEENTH-CENTURY SOUTHERN ITALIAN DINNER FOR 6

Cozze all'Italiana
MUSSELS ITALIAN STYLE

Timballo di maccheroni alla Pampadur
BAKED MACARONI WITH CHICKEN BREAST AND PROSCIUTTO

Mela in tortiglié
APPLE SNOW IN A RING

I t was in Naples in the eighteenth century that what are now the two most Italian of all Italian foods, pasta and tomatoes, became part of everyday eating. In the eighteenth century the Neapolitans, until then known as *mangiafoglie*, leaf-eaters, adopted the traditionally Sicilian pasta and made it their own. And it was in the fertile plain of Campania that the tomato, which first arrived in Europe in the wake of the Conquistadores, found at last the ideal habitat and became the perfect *pomodoro*. It was also during that period that the best Italian cookery books were published in Naples and Rome rather than in the north of Italy, as had been the case previously.

The first two recipes I have chosen for this menu are typically Italian. The *primo* is a favourite dish to this day, and it is often still made as in this Leonardi recipe. Francesco Leonardi was a Roman who finished his successful career as chef to Catherine the Great. He was very knowledgeable about foreign methods, techniques and produce, but he also recorded Italian regional cooking of traditional simplicity, as in this recipe for mussels.

Contrary to what most Italians would do, I have decided to serve a pasta dish as a main course. But this *timballo* is no everyday pasta dish. It is a rich and delectable concoction which the creator of this recipe, Vincenzo Corrado, dedicated to Madame Pompadour, the 'Pampadur' of the title. Corrado was the first author who assimilated the terminology of French gastronomy, which by then had gained supremacy over all other cuisines. He also tried to graft French techniques into the local cuisine. Yet the Italian feeling for simplicity and purity of ingredients is there, especially in the chapter devoted to *'Il Vitto*

Pitagorico', vegetarian food, in which most of the recipes are functional and very appealing to modern palates.

The third book, *Cucina Teorico-Pratica*, from which I have taken the pudding, was written by Ippolito Cavalcanti, Duke of Buonvicino, at the beginning of the nineteenth century. The pudding interested me especially because I could see in it a connection with English nursery food. Perhaps Cavalcanti had the recipe from one of the many English ladies who spent the winter months in Naples. Cavalcanti gave apple snow an appealing shape and decorated it with *erbaggio*, sugar shapes mainly green in colour. I have used chopped pistachio nuts to replace the *erbaggio*. It is a good pudding, and one your friends will love for its familiar flavour, albeit under an elegant disguise.

You must start with a very dry apple purée. If your purée is too wet, put it in a saucepan and heat it, stirring the whole time, until you have achieved a stiff consistency. I give the quantity of the purée, not of the apples, because it depends so much on what apples are used. Many of my readers will want to use their windfalls from the garden, which are usually better than bought fruit, but with windfalls you never know how much waste there will be. Cavalcanti, in spite of his wealth and rank, had a very down-to-earth approach, as can be seen in the fascinating appendix to his book. He gives practical and thrifty advice and I am sure he would have approved of the use of windfalls when there are any.

*   # Cozze all'Italiana

MUSSELS ITALIAN STYLE

'Put in a pan over the fire a little oil, parsley, onion and a point of garlic, everything well chopped, then moisten with half a glass of white wine, reduced by half, and a little water from the mussels, opened in the usual way, let them boil a little and add the mussels, well washed and drained, season with ground pepper, give it a boil and serve with slices of bread underneath.' (Francesco Leonardi, fl. second half of the eighteenth century)

1.8 kg/4 lb mussels	*1 onion*
1 Italian ciabatta *or French loaf*	*3 garlic cloves*
100 ml/3½ fl oz extra virgin olive oil	*200 ml/7 fl oz dry white wine*
	black pepper
1 large bunch flat-leaf parsley	

Scrub the mussels under cold water. Discard any mussel that remains open after you tap it on a hard surface. Tug off the beards, knock off any barnacles and rinse in several changes of water.

Heat the oven to 200°C/400°F/Gas 6.

Cut the bread into fairly thick slices and lay the slices on a baking tray.

Pour the oil into a large saucepan in which you will be able to cook the mussels later. I prefer to use a wide sauté pan in which the mussels can spread out and cook more quickly. If your pan is not large enough use two pans, dividing the ingredients in half, but increasing the amount of oil by 1 tablespoon, and of the wine by 2 tablespoons.

Using a pastry brush, moisten the bread slices with a little of the oil from the pan. Put the baking tray in the oven and bake for 6 to 8 minutes. Turn off the oven, but leave the bread in it to keep warm.

Chop the parsley, onion and garlic together and add to the pan with the oil. Turn the heat on and sauté for 1 minute. Add the wine and the pepper and cook briskly for a couple of minutes to evaporate the alcohol. Transfer the mussels to the pan. Put a lid tightly on the pan and cook until all the mussels are open, which will take 4–5 minutes. Shake the pan often.

As soon as the mussels are open, turn the heat off. If you are using an earthenware pan, bring it to the table, otherwise transfer the mussels and all the juices to a heated terrine, or ladle the mussels directly into individual soup bowls. The toasted bread must be placed in the soup bowls so that the mussels are ladled over it. Serve at once.

PREPARATION

Mussels cannot be reheated. You can scrub and clean them and leave them in a covered bowl up to a few hours in advance. The bread can be toasted up to 2 days in advance, wrapped in foil and refrigerated. Remove from the fridge at least 2 hours before serving.

***   *Timballo di maccheroni alla Pampadur*

BAKED MACARONI WITH CHICKEN BREAST AND PROSCIUTTO

'Have the macaroni cooked in beef stock. Cooked and cooled, it is dressed with roast pig juices and roast capon breasts chopped, chopped prosciutto, pepper and grated cheese; and like that it is placed on the dish and covered with a sauce of yolks of eggs, Parmesan, butter and cream flavoured with cinnamon and, this sauce set in the oven, it is served.' (Vincenzo Corrado, 1734–1836)

---

100 g/3½ oz butter
1 tbsp olive oil
1 rosemary sprig, about 7.5 cm/3 inches long, or 1 tsp dried rosemary
450 g/1 lb boneless pork loin
120 ml/4 fl oz dry white wine
salt and pepper
250 g/9 oz chicken breasts

150 g/5 oz prosciutto, medium sliced
450 g/1 lb large penne or macaroni
60 g/2 oz freshly grated Parmesan
3 tbsp dried breadcrumbs
3 egg yolks
300 ml/½ pint single cream
½ tsp ground cinnamon

Choose a small heavy-based casserole into which the pork will just fit. Put in 30 g/1 oz of the butter, the oil and the rosemary and turn the heat to medium high. As soon as the butter begins to colour, add the pork and brown well on all sides. This will take about 10 minutes.

Turn the heat up to high and pour over the wine. Reduce by half and then turn the heat down to low so that the liquid simmers very gently. Sprinkle with salt and pepper. Cover the pan with a sheet of greaseproof paper and put the lid on slightly askew. Cook for about 1½ hours, turning the meat over every 30 minutes and adding a little water if the pork is cooking dry. When the meat is very tender remove from the pan and reserve for another meal.

Add a couple of tablespoons of warm water to the pan and bring to the boil, scraping the bottom of the pan with a metal spoon to free the cooking residue. Measure the liquid and if necessary add enough water to make up to 120 ml/4 fl oz.

Heat 30 g/1 oz of the remaining butter in a non-stick frying pan. Add the chicken breasts and sauté very gently until done, about 15 minutes, turning the breasts over half-way through the cooking.

Season with a little salt and pepper and add a couple of table-spoons of water if necessary. Transfer the chicken breasts and their juices to a food processor together with the prosciutto, cut into pieces. Process until coarsely ground, not a smooth purée. If you do not have a food processor chop coarsely by hand. Transfer the mixture to a bowl and add the pork juices. Mix thoroughly.

Cook the pasta in plenty of boiling salted water. Drain, turn immediately into the bowl with the meat mixture and add the remaining butter and half the Parmesan. Mix very thoroughly and then taste and adjust seasoning.

Heat the oven to 200°C/400°F/Gas 6.

Butter an oven dish and sprinkle all over with the dried bread-crumbs. Turn the dish upside down and shake off the excess crumbs. Transfer the pasta into the dish and level it down gently.

In a bowl mix together the egg yolks, cream, remaining Parmesan, cinnamon, a little salt and a generous amount of pepper. Spoon this sauce over the pasta and place the dish in the oven. Bake for about 15 minutes until a golden crust forms on the top. Remove the dish from the oven and allow to stand out of the oven for 5 minutes before serving, to allow the flavours to combine.

PREPARATION

The dish can be prepared without the topping up to 1 day in advance. Cover tightly and refrigerate only in hot weather. Spoon over the egg and cream mixture before baking and bake for 5 minutes longer to allow the cold pasta to heat through.

** *Mela in tortiglié*

APPLE SNOW IN A RING

'You will make an apple jam, I mean a compôte of apple, being enough for 12 persons, 3 lb; you will mix in one or two pinches – or perhaps more – of rosolio liqueur, citron, cinnamon and vanilla, according to your taste, and you will arrange the jam on a suitable dish with the utmost care, round and round like a snail; you will whisk 4 egg whites until stiff mixing in 1 lb of sugar; you will cover the ring with this meringue with the blade of a knife, and you will sprinkle it again with sugar and with coloured sugar crystals; and you will place it with hot cinders underneath and with a little live coal above and when the meringue will have formed a crust and will have taken a lovely colour, you will serve it cold.' (Ippolito Cavalcanti, 1787–1860)

600 g/1¼ lb apple purée, sweetened	*the grated rind of 1 lemon*
1 vanilla pod	*3 egg whites*
3 tbsp Maraschino, Alchermes, Rosolio or Crème de Cassis	*75 g/2½ oz sugar*
1 tsp cinnamon	*2 tbsp chopped pistachio nuts*
	200 ml/7 fl oz whipping cream

The apple purée must be dry or it will not keep its ring shape. It should be sweet, to your taste, keeping in mind that it will be covered by a meringue.

Split the vanilla pod in half. Scrape out the seeds, and add them to the purée with the liqueur, cinnamon and lemon rind. Taste and check sweetness and flavouring.

Whisk the egg whites until stiff. Reserve 2 tablespoons of the sugar and add one third of the remainder to the egg whites. Continue whisking and then add half the remaining sugar. Whisk well; the meringue will be beautifully glossy and silky. Now sprinkle the rest of the sugar over the top and fold it into the meringue gently with a metal spoon.

Take a round ovenproof dish and shape the purée into a ring. If your purée is really stiff you can use a forcing bag with a large fluted nose attached. My purée has never been that stiff, because, I expect, the delicious apples from my garden are not of the right sort. But you can try; it would certainly make the sweet look prettier.

Heat the oven to 150°C/300°F/Gas 2.

Cover the apple purée with the meringue, using a thin metal spatula. I never smooth it down too neatly, because I don't like dishes that look too 'manicured'. Sprinkle with the reserved sugar and then with the chopped pistachios. Bake in the oven for 15–20 minutes, until the meringue is set and just coloured.

Leave to cool and then chill. Before serving, whip the cream and use some to fill the hole in the middle. Serve the rest of the cream separately, if you wish.

PREPARATION

The purée can be totally prepared up to 3 days in advance and kept in the fridge in a closed container. The meringue must be prepared and baked no more than 1 hour before serving or it will become soggy.

A NINETEENTH-CENTURY NORTHERN ITALIAN DINNER FOR 8

Zuppa alla santé
VEGETABLE SOUP

Pollastri al riso
POT-ROASTED CHICKENS WITH RICE

Funghi al funghetto
SAUTÉED MUSHROOMS (page 371)

Bavarese lombarda
A BUTTERY MARQUISE FROM LOMBARDY

As I was browsing through my nineteenth-century cookery books when planning this menu, I could retaste in my imagination most of the dishes of my childhood in Milan. Plenty of soups, warming casseroles, large rich braised joints, stewed vegetables and rich puddings. Not much Mediterranean flavour in this cooking, but rather one looking northwards towards Austria with its rich stews and France with its buttery sauces. This is still, fundamentally, the cuisine of northern Italy, into which in the past thirty years the cooking of the south has instilled its lighter and fresher approach.

At home, no dinner was considered a proper dinner by my father if it did not start with a soup. And a proper soup, at that, rich and nutritious and '*non quel consommé che si beve in tazze, e sembra una specie di the*' ('not that consommé that you drink in cups, like some kind of tea').

The soup in this menu is very representative of a soup served at Milanese dinner parties of the period: lighter than a minestrone yet with similar characteristics of flavour and reinforced with bread so that it becomes thick. If you want to make it more elegant, serve small croûtons instead of the large croûtes.

The recipe comes from *Il Cuoco senza Pretese* (*The Unpretentious Cook*), published in Como in 1834. Unfortunately the name of the author is not given. Most of the recipes in this chatty book give precise quantities in pounds and ounces, which were the measures in use in Lombardy before the metric system was adopted around

1860. At the end of each recipe there is a list of costs. This *zuppa alla santé* cost 35 lire – 17 pence. The list in this case does not include the broth, since every self-respecting household always had some broth ready. The recipe speaks for itself in its simplicity. I can only add that it must be made with good Italian-type broth.

The main course is my adaptation from a recipe that appears in *Trattato di Cucina* by the Piedmontese Giovanni Vialardi, published in 1854. It is a large tome, illustrated by the author and divided into nineteen chapters embracing all culinary subjects. One of the chapters, for example, is dedicated to cooking suitable for children and contains a recipe for a *'Pappa'* – pappy food – for a child of three or four hours, 'lacking his or her mother's milk or because of the late arrival of his or her wet nurse'. The recipe is too long, I'm afraid, to find room here. Vialardi's style is rather dull, but his recipes are good, and his drawings for the presentation of the dishes are extremely interesting and very artistic. He was, in fact, a *chef pâtissier* to the first king of Italy, greatly influenced by Carême and other French masters.

The dish in this menu does not need a master for its preparation, nor for its presentation. It is simple enough for any respectable cook and it is very good. Vialardi suggests serving the chicken with a garnish of asparagus or mushrooms. Try my sautéed mushrooms on page 371.

The pudding is one of my favourite recipes by Pellegrino Artusi, possibly the greatest Italian cookery writer, who, although a northerner, was the first to see, late in the nineteenth century, some movement towards the unification of the cooking of Italy following its political unification. The marquise in this menu was indeed often made in Milanese families, as it still is today. Considering the amount of butter it contains and the longevity of many members of past generations of my family, I begin to wonder about the harm butter is supposed to do! This is indeed a rich sweet which I find irresistible, with its subtle eggy flavour enhanced by virtue of the eggs being hard-boiled. At home we children called it, simply, *'Il dolce squisito'*.

*   *Zuppa alla santé*

VEGETABLE SOUP

'Cut into thin slices, and not too long, a few celery stalks, carrots, savoy cabbage, turnips and leeks and fry them in butter for a short time, and then pour them into the broth to finish cooking, and use them later to moisten the bread.' (From *Il Cuoco senza Pretese*, published in 1834)

---

100 g/3½ oz unsalted butter
8 slices *pugliese* bread or other
   good country-type white bread
450 g/1 lb vegetables: potato,
   turnip (if available), onion,
   carrot, celery

2 leeks, white part only
100 g/3½ oz Savoy cabbage leaves
salt and pepper
1.5 litres/2½ pints Italian broth
   (see page 378)
freshly grated Parmesan

Heat the oven to 200°C/400°F/Gas 6.

Melt the butter in a stockpot. Place the bread slices on a baking tray and, using a pastry brush, moisten one side with a little melted butter. Place the tray in the oven for 8 minutes. Turn the heat off and leave the bread in the oven.

Peel and wash the potato, turnip, onion and carrot, keeping them separate. Cut into short matchsticks and dry with kitchen paper. Wash the celery stalks, remove the thread and cut into matchsticks. Thoroughly wash and trim the leeks. Cut them into matchsticks and the cabbage into thin ribbons.

Add the potato, turnip and onion to the stockpot and sauté for 5 minutes over slow heat. Season with a pinch of salt, which will prevent the vegetables browning. They should just soften a little.

Now add the carrot and celery and cook for 3 minutes, still very gently, stirring frequently. Finally add the leek and the cabbage and gently sauté them too, for a minute or two, turning them over and over. While the vegetables are cooking, bring the broth to the boil. Pour the broth over the vegetables, add pepper and cook for 5 minutes or until the potato and turnip are cooked. The other vegetables can be crunchy, but undercooked potato or turnip are definitely unpleasant. Taste and check seasonings.

Put the toasted bread in individual soup bowls and ladle the soup over it. Serve at once, handing the Parmesan round separately.

PREPARATION

If necessary, the soup can be prepared up to 3 days in advance and refrigerated in a covered container. In this case you must turn the heat off as soon as the broth is boiling. Reheat the soup and simmer gently until the vegetables are ready.

✳✳   *Pollastri al riso*

POT-ROASTED CHICKENS WITH RICE

'Cook two young chicken . . . but do not lard them, cooked tender, juicy, of a beautiful colour and serve them with good rice or tagliatelle underneath. Release the cooking juice, purée it through a sieve, defat it, and, reduced as a sauce, pour it over . . . They are served with a garnish of asparagus and mushroom.' (Giovanni Vialardi)

---

120 g/4 oz unsalted butter
1 tbsp olive oil
2 small carrots, cubed
2 onions, sliced
2 celery sticks, cut into strips
small bunch of parsley
2 fresh roasting chickens, weighing
  about 1 kg/2 lb each

salt and pepper
2 tsp fresh rosemary and fresh sage
  leaves, chopped
450 ml/¾ pint good meat or
  chicken stock
300 g/10 oz long grain rice
6 tbsp freshly grated Parmesan

Heat the oven to 200°C/400°F/Gas 6.

Put half the butter, the oil, vegetables and parsley in a heavy casserole into which the two birds will fit snugly. Cook for 10 to 15 minutes over low heat, turning the vegetables over quite frequently.

Meanwhile wash the chickens under cold water and pat dry with kitchen paper. Season each cavity with salt and pepper and with the chopped herbs. Place the chickens over the bed of vegetables, pour over half the stock and season, if necessary, with salt and pepper. Cover with a piece of foil and with the lid. Place the casserole in the oven and cook until the chickens are done, about 1½ hours. Test by piercing a thigh with a skewer. The liquid that runs out should be clear.

Put a large saucepan of water on the heat for the rice.

Carve the chickens into neat pieces and place on a dish. Cover loosely with foil and keep warm in the oven with the heat turned off.

Skim off as much of the fat floating on the surface of the cooking juices as you can. Turn the cooking juices with all the vegetables into a food processor or a blender and blend to a smooth purée. The purée should have the consistency of single cream; if it is too thick add a little of the reserved stock. Taste and check seasonings. Transfer the sauce to a bowl and keep warm in a bain-marie, i.e. by placing the bowl in a saucepan half full of boiling water and covering with a lid.

Cook the rice in the boiling water to which you have added 1½ tablespoons of salt. When the rice is *al dente*, drain well and return immediately to the pan in which it has cooked. Toss with the remaining butter, season with Parmesan and with a few grindings of pepper and then add a few tablespoons of the sauce to coat the rice thoroughly.

Transfer the rice to a large heated serving dish, making a well in the middle. Place the chicken pieces in the well and spoon over the rest of the sauce. Serve at once.

PREPARATION

The chicken can be cooked up to 2 days in advance and refrigerated in a covered container. Carve the chicken before reheating. Reheat in the oven and then make the sauce.

✳✳ *Bavarese lombarda*

A BUTTERY MARQUISE FROM LOMBARDY

'This pudding, named differently by different people, could well be called "the sweet plat du jour" since it is so often served and so much enjoyed in so many families.' (Pellegrino Artusi)

about 150 g/5 oz Madeira cake	12 drops pure vanilla essence
6 large eggs	100 ml/3½ fl oz white rum, such
180 g/6 oz unsalted butter	as Bacardi
180 g/6 oz icing sugar, sifted if necessary	

First make the cake, either according to your usual recipe, or following mine on page 381. A Genoese sponge or a Victorian sponge are also suitable. Use a loaf tin for a better shape of marquise.

Gently lower the eggs with a spoon into a saucepan of boiling water and cook them for 7 minutes exactly. The timing is important because the yolks must be just soft in the middle. Put the saucepan under cold water, leave for 2 minutes and then peel the eggs. Cut them in half and scoop out the yolk (you can use the whites, chopped up, in a salad).

Cut the cake into ½ cm/¼ in thick slices and lay half the slices on a serving dish.

Cream together the butter and the egg yolks and then add the icing sugar, reserving about 3 tablespoons for the decoration, and the vanilla. Blend very thoroughly, using a wooden spatula, or use a food processor for the whole operation.

Pour the rum into a bowl. Moisten the prepared cake with the rum, using a pastry brush. Cover the cake with the cream, spreading it evenly all over. Now place the rest of the cake over the cream and moisten it well with the rum. Cover with clingfilm and chill for at least 3 hours. Just before serving, remove the clingfilm and sprinkle the reserved icing sugar all over the top, using a sugar sifter or pressing it through a fine sieve with a metal spoon.

PREPARATION

Artusi recommends leaving the marquise 'on ice' for 3 hours. I prefer to make it the day before. You can even make it 2 or 3 days in advance. It keeps very well in the fridge.

A FUTURIST DINNER FOR 8

Aerovivanda atlantica
ATLANTIC AIR FARE: AN AEROPLANE ON A PURÉE OF LEGUMES

Trote immortali
IMMORTAL TROUT: TROUT STUFFED WITH CALF'S LIVER AND WALNUT

Pomodori in teglia
BAKED TOMATOES (page 372)

Fragolamammella
STRAWBERRY BREASTS: STRAWBERRY AND RICOTTA PUDDING

Filippo Marinetti (1876–1944) was a Futurist poet, a fascist and a gastronome, in that order. His culinary writings testify to his fascist leanings and his obsession with nationalism and patriotism. He condemned anything of foreign origin, from words to food to ideas. With his friends in the Futurist movement he outraged the public by creating shocking recipes in which he combined conflicting ingredients. A few examples are: candied citrons stuffed with chopped and fried ink-fish, *mortadella* with nougat, and slices of veal with sausages, chestnuts and onions, all sprinkled with chocolate powder.

The most widely publicized of Marinetti's gastronomic activities was his campaign against *la pastasciutta*, which he launched on 15 November 1930 at the Ristorante Penna d'Oca in Milan. 'It is necessary,' he said, 'to annihilate pasta. It is something that is steeped in the past, a symbol of oppressive dullness, plodding deliberation and fat-bellied conceit.' The resulting manifesto became famous all over the world, many newspapers commenting on the importance of the Futurist battle against 'this miserable food'.

Not all Marinetti's culinary ideas are as outrageous as those I have listed, indeed some of the combinations he suggests make good sense. Among them are those I include in this menu, which I have based on his book, *La Cucina Futurista*. I preface my recipes with literal translations of Marinetti's originals, but as you will see I have made a few changes for reasons of practicality.

In the *aerovivanda atlantica* I have used dried peas and I have dressed the purée with olive oil. China orange is a fruit unknown in this country, so I have suggested a kumquat instead. As for the delicious cockscombs, alas, they cannot be bought here, so I have used a courgette cut into a round.

In the case of the *trote immortali*, I decided to stuff the trout with the liver instead of wrapping it round them, because it would be difficult to cook the fish without burning the liver. I also suggest baking the fish rather than frying it so as to make things easier for the cook who has to double as host or hostess. Don't worry if you can't be bothered to remove the bone before stuffing the fish. Just put the stuffing inside the fish cavity and stitch the cavity with a wooden cocktail stick. I often leave the bone in; it gives taste to the fish. But I always peel the walnuts and I do urge you to do the same. It is one of the slowest jobs I know, but it is worth every second. Taste a peeled walnut and an unpeeled one and you'll see what I mean. The baked tomatoes on page 372 and/or the lemon-flavoured spinach on page 373 go well with this dish.

The sweet is fun. The 'breasts' I make never look very beautiful (nor, truth to tell, do my aeroplanes for the first course). Their taste, however, is quite delicious, and very different from the ubiquitous strawberries and cream. I substitute fresh strawberries for the nearly unobtainable candied sort, although I am sure the candied ones would be better.

*   *Aerovivanda atlantica*

ATLANTIC AIR FARE: AN AEROPLANE ON A PURÉE OF LEGUMES

'Purée of legumes (lentils, peas, spinach etc) of a light green colour. On top lay (1 for each diner) some aeroplanes made as follows: puff pastry in a triangular shape (wings); carrots cut lengthwise (fuselage); cockscombs sautéed in butter (rudder). China orange cut into rounds and placed vertically (propeller).' (Filippo Marinetti)

200 g/7 oz brown lentils
200 g/7 oz dried green peas
1 onion
2 bay leaves
salt

150 g/5 oz cooked spinach
120 ml/4 fl oz extra virgin olive oil
2 garlic cloves, peeled and thinly
    sliced
black pepper

For the decoration

225 g/8 oz puff pastry
1 egg for glazing
4 carrots

4 kumquats
1 courgette

Sort through the lentils and the peas and pick out any chaff or small stones. Soak them for 4 hours in two separate bowls. Although often not necessary, I have come to the conclusion that it is always safer to soak pulses because sometimes they have been too long in storage and their skin has hardened too much.

Drain the lentils and put them with half the onion, one bay leaf and some salt in a saucepan. Cover with cold water and cook until the lentils are very tender, about 35–45 minutes.

Drain the dried peas and cook them in the same way as the lentils.

Drain the legumes, removing the bay leaves, and purée them in a food processor or a blender, adding enough of the cooking water to make a very soft purée; it will thicken when cold. Transfer the purée to a bowl and stir in the oil. Add the garlic and a generous amount of pepper. Taste and add salt if necessary. Leave the purée aside to cool.

To make the aeroplanes for the decoration, roll out the puff pastry and cut 16 small triangles out of it. Flour a baking tray and place the pastry triangles on it. Lightly beat the egg with a pinch of salt and brush the triangles with the glaze. Chill for 20 minutes and then bake in a preheated hot oven (220°C/425°F/Gas 7) until brown and puffed, about 15 minutes.

Boil the scraped and washed carrots in salted water until tender. Allow to cool and cut in half lengthwise. Cut the kumquats into rounds and then make a few notches on the round side of each half. Cut the courgette into rounds.

Spread the cold (not chilled) purée on the eight plates. Place half a carrot over the purée on each plate to represent the fuselage. Put a slice of kumquat at the thin end of each carrot for the rudder, a round of courgette, stuck vertically in the purée at the thick end of the carrot for the propeller and a pastry triangle on each side of the carrot for the wings.

PREPARATION

The purée can be made up to 3 days in advance and refrigerated, well covered with clingfilm. It also freezes well. The decorations can also be made in advance, but the dish must be assembled no longer than 1 hour before serving.

***   *Trote immortali*

IMMORTAL TROUT: TROUT STUFFED WITH
CALF'S LIVER AND WALNUT

'Stuff some trout with chopped walnuts and fry them in olive oil. Wrap the trout in very thin slices of calf's liver.' (Filippo Marinetti)

---

8 trout, weighing about 250 g/½ lb each	300 g/10 oz calf's liver, cut into small pieces
4 lemons	6 tbsp olive oil
75 g/2½ oz walnut kernels	4 tbsp chopped parsley
salt and pepper	

If you want to bone the trout, do not have them cleaned by the fishmonger. Split the trout down the back with a sharp pointed knife (I use a boning knife) starting from the head, as close as you can to the backbone. Ease out the backbone, snip it with scissors at the head and tail end, and remove it. Remove the guts and the gills. Wash the fish thoroughly under cold water and dry it very thoroughly. Lay the trout on a board or a dish. Squeeze 2 lemons and dribble the juice over and inside each fish. Season inside and out with salt and pepper. Leave to marinate while you peel the walnuts.

Blanch the walnuts in boiling water for 20 seconds. Drain and remove as much as you can of the bitter skin. Dry them and chop them coarsely.

Heat the oven to 180°C/350°F/Gas 4.

Divide the walnuts into eight portions and push one portion into the cavity of each fish. Divide the calf's liver into eight portions, season it with salt and pepper and put a portion into each fish. Reshape the fish neatly and stitch with one or two wooden cocktail sticks. Cut the remaining 2 lemons into slices.

Grease an oven dish with 1 tablespoon of the oil and lay the fish in the dish. Dribble with the remaining oil and cook in the oven for 20 minutes if boned, 25 minutes if the bone is still in. Lift the trout carefully and place each on to a heated plate. Keep warm.

Pour the cooking juices into a small saucepan. Add 2 table-spoons of lemon juice and reduce over high heat until rich. Taste and adjust seasonings. Spoon the sauce over the fish, sprinkle with some chopped parsley and garnish with the lemon slices.

PREPARATION
The trout can be stuffed and prepared in the tin for baking up to 1 hour beforehand.

✳✳ *Fragolamammella*

STRAWBERRY BREASTS: STRAWBERRY AND RICOTTA PUDDING

'A pink plate, with two erect female breasts made with ricotta, shaded pink with Campari and with nipples of candied strawberries. Other fresh strawberries under the ricotta surface so as to bite into an imagined multiplicity of breasts.' (Filippo Marinetti)

450 g/1 lb fresh strawberries	150 ml/¼ pint double cream
1 tbsp lemon juice	3 tbsp Campari
1 tbsp caster sugar	4 tbsp icing sugar, or a little more
600 g/1¼ lb ricotta	

Rinse the strawberries under cold water, drain and dry them. Set aside 16 of the smallest strawberries and cut the rest into small pieces. Put the cut-up strawberries into a bowl, add the lemon juice and the sugar and leave to macerate for at least 1 hour.

Push the ricotta through a sieve, or a food mill set with the small-hole disc. Add the cream and the Campari and blend very thoroughly. Sieve the icing sugar and mix into the ricotta mixture. Taste and add more sugar to your liking.

Remove about one-third of the ricotta mixture from the bowl and set aside. Mix the strawberries into the remaining ricotta mixture.

Prepare your dessert plates on the work surface. Divide the ricotta and strawberry mixture into 16 mounds, two for each plate. With a moistened spatula smooth some of the reserved ricotta and Campari mixture all over the mounds. Place the small reserved strawberries in the centre of the mounds. You could use an ice-cream scoop, although the mounds will be rather small – you'll have some of the mixture left to make more 'breasts' for second helpings!

PREPARATION
You can make the mounds up to 3 hours in advance and keep them in the fridge.

Winter Menus

A VEGAN LUNCH FOR 4

Pasta asciutta e ceci
PASTA AND CHICK-PEAS

Piatto rustico
STEWED VEGETABLES

Arancie, albicocche e banane al vino
ORANGES, DRIED APRICOTS AND BANANAS IN WINE SYRUP

O ne of my godsons is a vegan, and after I had invited him to lunch the other day I found myself momentarily at a loss as to what I could cook for him. As I looked into my fridge and store cupboard for inspiration I realized that all the possible dishes going through my mind contained either an egg, or a cupful of milk, or two tablespoons of Parmesan . . . all ruled out. Eventually I decided on the following three dishes, and Tom, my godson, seemed delighted with the result.

The first course, on further reflection, was not a problem, since pasta or rice with vegetables was the obvious solution, and for that I have recipes galore. So, narrowing it down, I chose pasta with chick-peas, a nourishing dish which, by the way, can also be made very successfully with *cannellini* beans.

The *piatto rustico* recipe is based on one that had just been given to me by a friend from Umbria, and delicious it certainly is. I decided to serve the vegetables in a hollowed-out round loaf of bread. It looks pretty and gives the dish more substance.

The pudding is fresh yet nourishing, and you can accompany it, for the non-vegan, with the lemon-flavoured meringues on page 381 and/or the almond crescents on page 380.

** *Pasta asciutta e ceci*

PASTA AND CHICK-PEAS

---

150 g/5 oz dried chick-peas
1 tbsp flour
1 tsp bicarbonate of soda
1 tsp salt
1 onion, cut in half
1 bay leaf
350 g/12 oz small tubular pasta,
such as gnocchetti sardi *or*
shells
3 rosemary sprigs
2 garlic cloves, peeled
1 chilli, seeded
6 tbsp olive oil
225 g/½ lb ripe tomatoes, skinned

Put the dried chick-peas in a bowl and cover with cold water. In a small bowl mix the flour, bicarbonate of soda and salt and add enough water to form a thin paste. Add this mixture to the chick-peas and leave for at least 8 hours to soften the skin.

The next day, drain the chick-peas and put them in a heavy pot. An earthenware pot of the sort you can put directly on the heat is the best for cooking pulses. Cover with water to come about 2.5 cm/ 1 in above the chick-peas, add the onion and the bay leaf, and cook, covered, at a gentle simmer until they are tender. This can take up to 3 hours, according to how long the chick-peas have been in store. Check that they stay covered with water. If necessary, add boiling water. Do not add salt to the pan until the chick-peas are nearly done; salt added at the beginning of the cooking will harden them. Do not lift the lid off the pan for the first hour or so; this will cool the water and toughen the skins.

Now, if you have time, you should remove the skins from the chick-peas. The skin comes away very easily, but it is a lengthy job. However, the chick-peas are much better when skinned. The flavour of the *soffritto* – fried mixture – can penetrate the pulp of the chick-peas, and also you won't get unpleasant bits of papery skin between your teeth.

Cook the pasta in plenty of boiling salted water.

While the pasta is cooking chop the rosemary needles, the garlic and the chilli and put them into a large sauté pan with 4 tablespoons of the oil. I use a large, shallow earthenware (again!) dish. Sauté for a minute or so.

Cut the tomatoes in half, squeeze out the seeds and the water and then chop them coarsely. Add to the rosemary and garlic *soffritto* and sauté for a couple of minutes. Add the chick-peas, scooping them out with a slotted spoon in such a way that a little of the liquid goes into the pan with them. Sauté for 5 minutes or so, coating the beans in the *soffritto*.

Drain the pasta when *al dente* and transfer quickly to the pan. Add the rest of the oil and stir-fry for about a minute. Serve immediately from the pan.

PREPARATION

The chick-peas can be cooked up to 2 days in advance and refrigerated. They can also be frozen. The *soffritto* can be made a few hours in advance, and reheated before adding the pasta, which must be cooked at the last minute.

*   # *Piatto rustico*

STEWED VEGETABLES

150 g/5 oz aubergines	400 g/14 oz tin Italian plum
salt	tomatoes
225 g/½ lb potatoes	4 tbsp olive oil
180 g/6 oz courgettes	pepper
180 g/6 oz red peppers	2 tsp dried oregano
200 g/7 oz onions	round loaf of bread, 15–20 cm/
1 garlic clove	6–8 in in diameter

Peel the aubergines and cut into chunks of about 2.5 cm/1 in. Put them in a colander and sprinkle with some salt. Put a plate with a weight over it and leave to discharge their bitter liquid for 1 hour. Then rinse the aubergine under cold water.

Heat the oven to 165°C/325°F/Gas 3.

Peel the potatoes, cut into similar pieces, and do the same with the courgettes and the peppers. Cut the peeled onion into thick slices and the garlic into small slices. Put all the vegetables into a casserole and add the tomatoes, half the olive oil, a teaspoon of salt, a generous grinding of pepper and the oregano. Cover the casserole with a lid and cook in the oven until the vegetables are tender, about 1½ hours.

Remove from the oven and turn the heat up to 200°C/400°F/Gas 6.

Cut the loaf of bread in half and make a container out of the bottom half by scooping out all the soft part. Brush the inside of the bread 'bowl' all over with the rest of the olive oil and put in the oven for about 8 minutes. Transfer the bread bowl to a round dish.

Taste the stewed vegetables and check seasoning. Spoon them with their liquid into the bread bowl and serve at once.

PREPARATION

The vegetables can be stewed up to 2 days in advance and refrigerated. The bread must be filled just before serving or it will become soggy.

*   *Arancie, albicocche e banane al vino*

ORANGES, DRIED APRICOTS AND BANANAS IN WINE SYRUP

250 g/9 oz dried apricots, *preferably Hunza*	*1 tbsp lemon juice* *2 bananas*
300 ml/½ pint dry white wine	*2 oranges*
1 bay leaf	*30 g/1 oz toasted almonds, chopped*
3 tbsp sugar	*(optional)*

Soak the apricots for 1 hour in warm water. Drain. Put the wine, bay leaf and sugar in a heavy saucepan and bring to the boil. Boil gently for 5 minutes after the sugar has dissolved. Add the apricots. Cook until tender, which takes no more than 10 minutes. Remove the bay leaf and add the lemon juice.

When the apricots are cool – not before, or you might break your dish – pour into a glass bowl. Cut the bananas into rounds and mix into the apricots. Peel the oranges to the quick and slice neatly. Reserve some of the best slices, cut the others in half and mix into the other fruit. Lay the pretty slices on the top. Cover with clingfilm and refrigerate for at least 1 hour.

If you are using the toasted almonds, sprinkle them over the top just before serving.

PREPARATION

The apricots can be soaked and cooked up to 2 days in advance, and refrigerated. Add the bananas and oranges no longer than 4 hours before serving. Mix the bananas well to coat them in the syrup or they will discolour.

A DINNER FOR 4

Risotto al Gorgonzola
RISOTTO WITH GORGONZOLA

Coniglio al rosmarino con patate in umido
RABBIT WITH ROSEMARY AND TOMATO SAUCE
AND STEWED POTATOES

Frutta di stagione
SEASONAL FRESH FRUIT

Warming, comforting *risotti* are for chilly days, so I would not serve this dish in the height of summer. Risotto, by the way, is not as easy to make as might be thought. It needs a little practice plus, of course, the right ingredients. Also, it is easier to make in small quantities. For this reason I suggest that, if you are not an experienced risotto maker, you start by making it for four people before attempting larger quantities. This risotto from Lombardy is a favourite of mine for its creamy consistency and its assertive flavour.

Rabbit is now easily available everywhere. It is a white meat, less fat than chicken and therefore healthier, and it lends itself to being prepared in any number of different ways. I buy English wild rabbits when I can and I cook them for longer. The sauce in this recipe is really delicious, with the herby tomato taste everybody associates with traditional Italian cooking. It is a sauce often served in central Italy, where the recipe comes from. If you want to serve another vegetable I would suggest the lemon-flavoured spinach on page 373 or, better still, a lovely green salad afterwards, as in my recipe on page 368.

As for the fruit, my favourite is definitely seasonal and as local as possible. I seldom buy tropical fruits because, with the exception of passion fruit, I find their flavour disappointing and not to my taste. I am sure this is because they haven't ripened on the plant. Unfortunately many fruits from closer lands have also lost some flavour. When you serve fruit you should provide a good selection (with some nuts in the winter) in a lovely glass bowl, which you can put in the middle of the table even from the beginning of the meal.

Any fruit that doesn't need peeling should be washed and thoroughly dried, since nowadays few people in this country bother to provide individual bowls so that each person can rinse their fruit. If you do provide bowls, by the way, don't make the mistake of putting a slice of lemon in the cold water, since this should be done only with the bowls of warm water used for rinsing your fingers after eating fishy and greasy foods with them.

** *Risotto al Gorgonzola*

RISOTTO WITH GORGONZOLA

---

4 shallots or 2 small onions	180 g/6 oz mild Gorgonzola, such
60 g/2 oz unsalted butter	as Dolcelatte, cut into small
salt	pieces
350 g/12 oz arborio, or other	freshly ground black pepper
Italian risotto rice	a lovely bunch of flat-leaf parsley,
150 ml/¼ pint dry white wine	chopped
1.2 litres/2 pints vegetable or	
chicken stock	

Chop the shallots or onions very finely and sauté them in the butter, using a large, heavy saucepan. Add a pinch of salt to release the moisture in the shallots or onions, thus preventing them from browning. Cook gently for 7 minutes or so, stirring frequently.

Meanwhile heat the stock in a separate saucepan to simmering point.

Add the rice to the shallots and stir well for a minute or two, coating the grains in the butter. Turn the heat up and pour over the wine. Let it bubble away and then begin to add the stock little by little. When the stock is absorbed, add another ladleful of simmering stock and continue gradually adding stock until the risotto is ready.

Half-way through the cooking mix in the Gorgonzola, cut into small pieces. Stir constantly until the cheese has melted and then continue cooking the rice, adding the simmering stock little by little. If you have used up all the stock, use hot water to finish the cooking. When adding stock towards the end of the cooking, add only a very little at a time, in case the rice is cooked before it has absorbed all the stock. The rice should cook at a lively simmer, but not too much so.

When the rice is done, tender yet with an inner firmness – about 20 minutes – season with plenty of pepper. If necessary season also with salt, although the saltiness in the cheese may be enough.

Transfer to a heated bowl and sprinkle with the parsley.

PREPARATION

The *soffritto* – the sautéing of the onion – can be prepared in advance and reheated. Apart from that, for a perfect result, you should cook the risotto just before serving it. However, there is a way round that which, I must admit, works quite well. Prepare the *soffritto*. Sauté the rice and then add about 200 ml/7 fl oz of the stock. As soon as the stock is boiling again, turn off the heat and leave with the lid firmly on. When you go back to finish the dish you will find that the rice will be dry and will be half cooked. Add a lump of butter and proceed with the cooking which will now take about 15 minutes.

* *Coniglio al rosmarino*

RABBIT WITH ROSEMARY AND TOMATO SAUCE

1.35–1.5 kg/3–3¼ lb rabbit joints
½ lemon, cut into wedges
2 tbsp olive oil
2 garlic cloves, finely chopped

1 onion, roughly chopped
150 ml/¼ pint dry white wine
salt and freshly ground black pepper

For the sauce

2 or 3 shallots, according to size, or 1 small onion, very finely chopped
the needles from 3 sprigs of rosemary, 12 cm/5 in long, very finely chopped (use fresh rosemary, not dried)
3 tbsp olive oil

450 g/1 lb tomatoes, skinned and seeded, or a 400 g/14 oz tin of plum tomatoes, drained
½–1 dried chilli, according to taste, seeded and very finely chopped
salt

Trim any gristle or fat from the rabbit joints, and rub with the lemon.

Heat the oil in a large, heavy sauté pan and brown the rabbit on all sides. Push it to the side of the pan and add the garlic and the onion. Cook over low heat until the onion is soft, stirring frequently.

Heat the wine in a separate small saucepan.

Bring the rabbit back to the middle of the pan, turn the heat up and splash with the wine. Boil briskly for 1 minute or so to evaporate the alcohol and then season with salt and pepper. Cover the pan and cook for 20 minutes over very low heat. Turn the rabbit over two or three times and, if necessary, add a little hot water during the cooking.

Meanwhile prepare the sauce. In a sauté pan, fry the shallots or the onion and the rosemary gently in the olive oil for 5 minutes. Chop the tomatoes coarsely and add to the pan with the chilli and salt to taste. Cook, uncovered, over low heat for 10 minutes. Adjust the seasonings.

Pour the sauce over the rabbit. Stir quickly, scraping the cooking juices and mixing them into the sauce, and continue cooking until the rabbit is done. Taste and check seasoning. Transfer to a heated dish and serve with the potatoes (see next recipe).

PREPARATION

The rabbit and the sauce can be prepared 1 day in advance and refrigerated. If necessary the dish can be frozen and, when thawed, very gently reheated.

** *Patate in umido*

STEWED POTATOES

---

700 g/1½ lb waxy potatoes	1 tbsp fresh marjoram or 7.5 ml/
30 g/1 oz unsalted butter	½ tbsp dried marjoram
2 tbsp olive oil	1 tbsp tomato purée dissolved in
60 g/2 oz pancetta or unsmoked	100 ml/7 tbsp of hot stock or
streaky bacon, chopped	water
1 onion, finely chopped	salt and freshly ground black
1 garlic clove, finely chopped	pepper

Peel and wash the potatoes, and cut them into 2.5 cm/1 in cubes. Steam them for about 5 minutes.

While the potatoes are cooking, put the butter, oil and *pancetta* in a heavy saucepan and cook for 1 minute. Add the onion and the garlic and sauté gently for 5 minutes, stirring very frequently. Mix in the partly cooked potatoes, turning them over very gently but thoroughly to coat in the fat, and cook for 3–4 minutes.

Add the marjoram, the dissolved tomato purée and the seasoning. Stir well and cook, covered, until the potatoes are tender, turning them over often during the cooking. Use a fork to turn the potatoes over, as this breaks them up less than a spoon, although some are bound to break a little. Taste, adjust seasoning and serve with the rabbit. If you are using an oval dish, put the potatoes alongside the rabbit, or put them in the middle if you have a large round dish.

PREPARATION
Potatoes never take kindly to being reheated, but they can be kept hot for half an hour or so in a very low oven.

A LUNCH FOR 6

Bigoli in salsa
WHOLEWHEAT SPAGHETTI WITH ONION
AND ANCHOVY SAUCE

Trance di nasello al forno
BAKED FISH STEAKS

Spinaci all'agro
LEMON-FLAVOURED SPINACH (page 373)

Formaggio e frutta
CHEESE AND FRUIT

In Italy it is perfectly acceptable, in fact it is considered correct, to serve two courses containing fish, as in this easy-to-prepare meal. The preparation is arranged so that you will need to leave your guests only for the time it takes to cook the spaghetti; it will be even less than that if you cook it following the Agnesi method on page 376.

Bigoli, a speciality of Venice, is the only traditional Italian pasta made with wholewheat. Here I have used wholewheat spaghetti, the nutty flavour of which counterbalances the assertiveness of the anchovy sauce.

My second course, very easy too, is a contrast to the first and yet it is fish again. So we have a harmony, yet at the same time a contrast resulting from the use of a different fish, from the way it is cooked and from the flavourings. I use hake for this dish whenever I can find it, but cod, a fish of the same family, is a perfect substitute. Its culinary merits are at last being recognized. Spinach goes well with this fish, and I recommend the Italian way of preparing it on page 373. Buy bunch spinach or small young leaf spinach. The large spinach beet is not suitable for this dish, nor indeed for any dish, since it is not very good.

Cheese is usually served at lunch parties in Italy, while it is hardly ever served at dinners. The cheese is always followed by a bowl of seasonal fruit. If you want your lunch to be more formal, choose a sweet based on fresh fruit. I would serve the oranges and kiwi on page 39, or the pineapple and oranges on page 184.

* *Bigoli in salsa*

WHOLEWHEAT SPAGHETTI WITH ONION AND ANCHOVY SAUCE

---

75 g/3 oz salted anchovies or
  anchovy fillets
milk
200 g/7 oz Spanish onions, sliced
  paper-thin
7 tbsp olive oil

3 tbsp chopped parsley, preferably
  flat-leaf
salt and freshly ground black
  pepper
500 g/1 lb 2 oz wholewheat
  spaghetti

If you are using salted anchovies, remove the bone and rinse under cold water. Divide into two fillets, put them on a small plate and pour over enough milk to cover. If you are using anchovy fillets, wipe them clean from the oil and cover with milk.

Put the onion and half the oil in a sauté pan large enough to hold the pasta later. Cook slowly until the onion is soft and golden. Add 3 or 4 tablespoons of warm water, stir, and simmer, covered, for 30 minutes, stirring at times. Add a little more water if the sauce becomes too dry. The onion should dissolve and turn almost to a purée.

When the sauce is nearly ready, bring 4 litres/7 pints of salted water to the boil. Drop in the spaghetti and cook until *al dente*. If you prefer, use the Agnesi method of cooking pasta (page 376), which requires less last-minute attention.

While the pasta is cooking, chop the anchovy fillets coarsely and add to the onion sauce with 2 tablespoons of the milk. Mash with a fork to a paste, while cooking for 2 minutes on a very low heat. Mix in the parsley, the remaining oil and the pepper and remove from the heat.

Drain the pasta but do not overdrain, and turn into the pan with the onion and anchovy sauce. Stir-fry for a minute, lifting the spaghetti high into the air so as to coat every strand. Serve at once from the pan or transfer to a heated bowl. No grated cheese is served when pasta is dressed with a fish-based sauce.

PREPARATION
The sauce can be prepared up to 2 days in advance and kept in the fridge. Pasta must always be cooked just before it is served.

*   *Trance di nasello al forno*

BAKED FISH STEAKS

---

6 fish steaks, about 2½ cm/1 in   2 tbsp fresh oregano or marjoram
    thick   salt and pepper
3 shallots, chopped in half   the juice of 1 lemon
3 garlic cloves, bruised   4 tbsp chopped parsley, preferably
6 tbsp extra virgin olive oil   flat-leaf
4 bay leaves

Wash the fish steaks and dry thoroughly with kitchen paper. Roll
them up neatly and tie them round with string, so that they will
keep a nice shape during the cooking.

Put the shallots, garlic, olive oil, bay leaves, oregano or marjoram and salt and pepper in an oven dish large enough to
contain the fish in a single layer. Coat the fish in the mixture on
both sides and leave to marinate for 1 hour, turning the steaks
over once or twice.

About half an hour before eating, heat the oven to 180°C/350°F/
Gas 4. Place the dish in the oven and bake for 20–25 minutes,
turning the steaks over gently half-way through the cooking.

When the fish is done, remove and discard the shallot, garlic
and bay leaves. Dribble with the lemon juice and sprinkle with
the parsley. Serve at once.

PREPARATION

There is no last-minute problem with this dish. Just place it in the
oven about 20 minutes before you want to serve it.

A LUNCH FOR 8

Le tre cicorie in bagna cauda
CHICORY, RADICCHIO AND LITTLE GEM SALAD WITH AN
ANCHOVY AND GARLIC SAUCE

Cotechino allo zabaione
COTECHINO WITH ZABAGLIONE

Lenticchie in umido
STEWED LENTILS

Formaggio e frutta
CHEESE AND FRUIT

This is the ideal menu for a winter lunch or dinner. I have called it a lunch because it is easily prepared, as I think lunches should be, and because there is no pudding. But you can convert it into a dinner by serving something like the walnut and honey pie on page 274 or the autumnal fruit salad on page 210 instead of cheese and fruit.

It is in winter that radicchio and chicory are at their best, and the rich *cotechino* and warming, homely lentils are best suited to a cold winter's day. Indeed this is an excellent New Year's day lunch; in Italy lentils are eaten at the New Year since they are held to bring wealth in the year to come (as many gold coins as lentils!). Pork, too, is for festive occasions, and the combination of the *cotechino* sausage and the lentils is one of the best ever, the lentils cutting across the tasty richness of the *cotechino*.

Please don't shy away from the idea of serving zabaglione as a sauce for the *cotechino*. It is not my invention – I wish it were – but a traditional combination from Modena, a city that offers some of the best food in Italy. It is a perfect match. In Modena they also eat *zampone*, the traditional pig's trotter stuffed with pork meat, with zabaglione. The zabaglione contains a little less sugar than when eaten as a sweet.

Buttered spinach is also a traditional accompaniment to the *cotechino*, and you could serve this as well.

Such a sensational main course is best preceded by a salad. I suggest this radicchio and chicory salad dressed with a sort of *bagna cauda*, which I pour hot on the salad. However, the cauliflower salad on page 289 or the fennel and orange on page 65 would be equally good.

* ## Le tre cicorie in bagna cauda

CHICORY, RADICCHIO AND LITTLE GEM SALAD WITH AN ANCHOVY AND GARLIC SAUCE

Dandelion gives the salad the right degree of bitterness. If you cannot find any, use Little Gem lettuces.

450 g/1 lb chicory	2 dried chillies, seeded and
450 g/1 lb red radicchio	crumbled
1 Little Gem lettuce	150 ml/¼ pint extra virgin olive
8 anchovy fillets	oil
6 garlic cloves, peeled	salt and pepper

Finely shred the chicory, the radicchio and the dandelion or lettuce. Wash them in two or three changes of water and then drain and dry them. Put into a salad bowl.

Cut the anchovy fillets and the garlic in pieces and put them in a mortar with the chillies. Pound to a paste while gradually adding the olive oil. Transfer to a small saucepan or, better, to a small earthenware pot and cook over very gentle heat for 2–3 minutes, while pounding the mixture against the side of the pan. If you have not got a mortar, pound the ingredients in a bowl or directly in the pan, as long as it has a round bottom.

Taste the sauce, add salt if necessary and pepper if you wish, and pour over the salad when still very hot. Toss and serve with plenty of crusty bread.

PREPARATION
The salad can be washed and shredded up to 1 day in advance. Keep it wrapped in a tea-towel in the vegetable drawer of the fridge.

** **   # *Cotechino allo zabaione*

COTECHINO WITH ZABAGLIONE

---

2 cotechini, *about 450 g/1 lb*
  each
4 egg yolks

4 tbsp sugar
150 ml/5 fl oz Marsala

If you have bought *cotechini* which is *precotto* (partly cooked), follow the manufacturer's instructions.

If your *cotechini* are raw, soak them in cold water for a few hours. Prick the *cotechini* with a thin needle in a few places, wrap with muslin, and tie each end with a piece of string. Put them in a saucepan and cover with water. Bring to the boil and cook gently for 2½ hours. Turn the heat off while you prepare the zabaglione.

Using a balloon whisk, beat the egg yolks with the sugar until creamy. Place in a double boiler or over a saucepan of just simmering water and gradually add the Marsala while beating constantly. When the custard thickens, remove from the heat. Transfer to a warm bowl and keep warm in a bain-marie until you bring it to the table.

Carve the *cotechini* into 12 mm/½ in slices and place them, slightly overlapping, on an oval dish. You can cover the dish with foil and keep warm until you bring it to the table.

PREPARATION

Cotechino is one of those marvellous foods that does not need any preparation. The zabaglione takes such a short time to prepare that there is no point in making it beforehand, with the risk of it curdling or of serving it too cold. Do it before you sit at table, and keep it warm.

*   # Lenticchie in umido

STEWED LENTILS

---

450 g/1 lb green lentils
5 tbsp olive oil
1 onion, finely chopped
meat stock, if available

a dozen fresh sage leaves, chopped
2 tbsp cider vinegar
salt and freshly ground black
* pepper*

Spread out a quantity of the lentils and remove any stones or grit. Repeat until you have checked them all. Rinse and drain the lentils. Soak them in cold water for 4–6 hours.

Put the oil and the onion in an earthenware pot or a heavy-bottomed saucepan and sauté on medium heat until the onion is soft.

Heat the stock, if available, or, if you are cooking the *cotechino* at the same time, use some of the liquid in which it is cooking, plus some water.

Add the sage to the onion, stir and then add the lentils. Stir until the lentils are well coated with oil and then add enough stock, *cotechino* liquid or boiling water to cover the lentils, about 1.8 litres/3 pints. Bring the liquid to the boil, turn down the heat, cover the pan and simmer for about 45–60 minutes. The cooking time varies according to how long the lentils have been in store. During the cooking add a little hot water or stock if necessary, so that the lentils will not cook dry. Half-way through the cooking, stir in the vinegar and continue cooking until the lentils are tender. By the time they are cooked they should have absorbed nearly all the liquid.

Add salt and pepper to taste. Mix well, turn the lentils into the dish alongside the *cotechino*, and serve.

PREPARATION

Lentils are better done a day in advance. You don't need to refrigerate them. They can also be frozen.

A VEGETARIAN DINNER FOR 6

Pasticcio di tagliatelle e mozzarella in salsa
BAKED TAGLIATELLE WITH TOMATOES AND MOZZARELLA

Sformatini di carote e patate con contorno di spinaci e crostoni
CARROT AND POTATO TIMBALES WITH SPINACH AND LARGE CROÛTONS

La bonissima
WALNUT AND HONEY PIE

Frutta
FRUIT

The *pasticcio* of tagliatelle is fresh and very Mediterranean, with mozzarella oozing from underneath the ribbon of pasta, and a splash of red sauce flavoured with scented oregano.

In the second course we are in the north-western regions of Italy, Lombardy and Piedmont, whose cuisine feels the proximity of France. The little timbales are the sort of food that is currently appearing in so many fashionable restaurants everywhere. My *sformatini* are made according to an old recipe from my mother's *ricettario* – recipe book. It is a recipe that uses béchamel, which nowadays is the Cinderella among sauces. I cannot understand why béchamel has been demoted; it is a wonderful sauce of many useful properties and excellent flavour. It can be a little tricky to get these *sformatini* to unmould neatly, but if you let the mixture cool slightly they will unmould quite easily. In Italy *sformatini* are usually served without a sauce, but if you want to pass one round, I suggest the fontina and cream sauce on page 121.

With the *sformatini* I like to serve some good young spinach sautéed in butter, and a few large croûtons. I cut slices of good-quality white bread diagonally across and bake them, moistened with melted butter, in a medium hot oven for 7 minutes or so. If you prefer, you can fry bread triangles in butter. Heap the spinach in the centre of a large dish, surround it with the bread triangles and the little timbales, one for each diner plus two in reserve.

The pudding is *La bonissima*, and *bonissima* – meaning very good – it certainly is. The pastry I use is made with the yolks of hard-boiled eggs and some potato flour. It is a soft and buttery pastry, quite different from the usual *pâte sucrée*. It is a difficult pastry to roll out, but if you do it on a sheet of greaseproof paper, as I explain in the method, you will manage quite easily. Of course, you can make your usual pastry with raw egg yolk and sugar, although the final result would be slightly different.

The filling is superb, but care must be taken when buying walnuts. Walnuts go off very quickly because of the high content of oil, which becomes rancid when the walnuts are old. Some of the walnut kernels on sale in this country are not good enough even when they are within their expiry date. Buy the best, the ones from California. Look through the wrapping and check that the kernels are in large pieces and not broken into small pieces and crumbs, a sure sign of age. If, when you open the bag, you find that the walnuts are all in small pieces, take them back to your shop and complain. As you can see, I am waging a war against the poor quality of some food sold in this country.

If you like to enrich the pie, hand round a bowl of *crème fraîche* or double cream with it – *La bonissima* will become *bonissimissima*!

To end the meal, I feel a bowl of seasonal fruit would be perfect.

* *** *Pasticcio di tagliatelle e mozzarella in salsa*
if you make
your own pasta BAKED TAGLIATELLE WITH TOMATOES
AND MOZZARELLA

---

750 ml/1¼ pint tomato sauce
tagliatelle made with 3 eggs and
   300 g/10 oz flour, or 750 g/
   1½ lb fresh shop-bought
   tagliatelle, or 400 g/14 oz dried
   egg tagliatelle
2 Italian mozzarella cheeses, about
   250 g/9 oz net weight
4 tbsp extra virgin olive oil

2 garlic cloves, peeled and very
   finely sliced
1 dried chilli
2 tsp dried oregano
salt and pepper
30 g/1 oz unsalted butter
90 ml/6 tbsp freshly grated
   Parmesan

First make the tomato sauce, using your favourite recipe or the one for Julia's tomato sauce on page 89.

Second, make the fresh pasta (see page 374), if you are going to do so.

Third, coarsely chop the mozzarella, put it in a deep dish and pour over 2 tablespoons of the oil. Add the garlic, chilli, 1 teaspoon of oregano, and a generous grinding of pepper. Leave aside for at least 30 minutes to absorb the oil, though it doesn't matter if you leave it for longer, up to 2 hours.

Having done all these jobs you are ready to assemble the dish, a quick and easy task. Oil a shallow oven dish and heat the oven to 180°C/350°F/Gas 4. Gently heat the tomato sauce, if necessary.

Cook the tagliatelle in plenty of salted boiling water. Remember that if the tagliatelle are fresh they will take only 1–2 minutes to cook. Drain, but do not overdrain, reserving a cupful of the pasta water. Return the pasta immediately to the saucepan and add the butter and the remaining oil. Mix well, then add the hot tomato sauce and the Parmesan.

Remove and discard the chilli from the mozzarella and add the mozzarella to the pasta. Toss very well and, if the pasta appears too dry, add a couple of tablespoons of the reserved water. Taste, adjust seasoning and pour into the prepared oven dish. Sprinkle the remaining oregano over the top, cover with foil and bake for 10 minutes. Allow to sit out of the oven for 3–4 minutes, for the flavours to blend, before bringing the dish to the table.

PREPARATION

The dish can be prepared up to 1 day in advance and refrigerated, well covered with foil. It could be frozen if necessary. However, once again I must emphasize how much nicer pasta is if cooked just before it is eaten. The sauce can be made up to 2 days in advance and refrigerated, or it can be frozen very satisfactorily. The tagliatelle can be made a few days in advance and stored, when completely dry, in an airtight box.

***   *Sformatini di carote e patate*

CARROT AND POTATO TIMBALES

For the potato purée

700 g/1½ lb floury potatoes
150 g/¼ pint full-cream milk
50 g/1¾ oz unsalted butter
3 tbsp freshly grated Parmesan

salt and pepper
grated nutmeg
1 egg + 1 yolk

For the carrot purée

700 g/1½ lb carrots
salt
a thick béchamel made with
   45 g/1½ oz unsalted butter,
   50 g/1¾ oz flour and

225 ml/8 fl oz full-fat milk
1 egg + 1 yolk
3 tbsp freshly grated Parmesan
grated nutmeg
pepper

To assemble

60 g/2 oz unsalted butter

dried breadcrumbs

Wash the potatoes and cook them in their skins. Do not put any salt in the water, as it tends to break them up. At the same time, but in a different saucepan, cook the cleaned carrots in salted water. Drain the vegetables as soon as they are done. Peel the potatoes while still warm and purée them back into the saucepan through the food mill, fitted with the small-hole disc. Heat the potatoes slowly, while stirring constantly, to dry them. Meanwhile heat the milk and then add to the potatoes with the butter, Parmesan, salt and pepper and a generous grating of nutmeg. Beat hard until the purée is smooth. Beat in the egg and the yolk. Taste and check seasonings.

Now prepare the carrot purée. Dry the carrots with kitchen paper and purée them through the food mill back into the saucepan in which they were cooked. Put the saucepan on the heat and dry the purée for a few minutes.

While the potatoes and carrots are cooking make the béchamel. Heat the milk until just beginning to simmer. Meanwhile melt the butter in a heavy saucepan and stir in the flour. Cook for 1 minute and then draw the pan off the heat. Add the milk gradually, while beating vigorously to incorporate it. When all the milk has been absorbed, return the pan to the heat and bring to the boil. Add salt and cook over the gentlest heat for 15 minutes, stirring frequently. Add the béchamel to the carrot purée and allow to cool before you add the egg and the egg yolk. Season with Parmesan, nutmeg and pepper and check the salt.

Heat the oven to 190°C/375°F/Gas 5.

Grease the bottom of eight 100 ml/3½ fl oz ramekins with some of the butter. Cut eight discs out of greaseproof paper the size of the bottom of the ramekins and place them in the ramekins. Generously butter the greaseproof paper and the sides of the ramekins. Sprinkle the ramekins all over with the dried breadcrumbs and shake off excess crumbs.

Melt the remaining butter in a little saucepan.

Half fill the ramekins with the carrot purée, levelling it with the back of a moistened metal spoon. Now spoon the potato purée over the carrot purée and smooth it with the wet spoon. Sprinkle with a little of the breadcrumbs and dribble with a little melted butter. Put the ramekins in a roasting tin. Pour enough boiling water into the tin to come two-thirds of the way up the side of the ramekins. Place the tin in the preheated oven and cook until set, i.e. until a toothpick inserted in the middle of the timbale comes out dry, about 25 minutes.

Remove from the oven and leave for 5 minutes. Run a small spatula round the side of the purée to loosen it from the ramekins and turn each ramekin quickly upside down on to a dish. Shake the ramekins a little and lift them off. Remember to peel off the paper.

PREPARATION

These *sformatini* can be prepared up to 1 day in advance, but they cannot be refrigerated because the flavour of the potatoes changes with chilling.

*** *La bonissima*
WALNUT AND HONEY PIE

For the pastry

150 g/5 oz flour
65 g/2¼ oz potato flour
½ tsp salt
60 g/2 oz caster sugar
150 g/5 oz cold unsalted butter

the yolks of 2 hard-boiled eggs,
  size 2
1 egg yolk
1 tbsp milk

For the filling

150 g/5 oz walnut kernels
150 ml/¼ pint honey
the grated rind of 1 small lemon

4 tbsp dark rum
2 tbsp dried breadcrumbs
1 tbsp caster sugar

For serving

300 ml/½ pint crème fraîche *or*   double cream (optional)

First make the pastry. Sift the two flours and the salt in a mixing
bowl. Add the sugar and the butter cut into small pieces. Rub the
butter into the mixture with the tips of your fingers until the
mixture is like small crumbs. Push the hard-boiled egg yolks
through a sieve, or a food mill set with the small-hole disc,
directly into the bowl. Work the mixture together and then turn
the dough on to a lightly floured surface and gather into a bowl as
quickly as you can. Wrap the dough in clingfilm and refrigerate
for at least half an hour. (If you have a food processor, put the
flours, salt, sugar and butter in the bowl, process for a few
seconds, then add the hard-boiled yolks, cut into small pieces,
and process until a ball forms.)

While the pastry is chilling, blanch the walnut kernels for 30
seconds in boiling water. Remove the skin, lifting them out of the
water a few at a time as they are easier to peel when hot. Put the
peeled kernels on kitchen paper to dry. This is a lengthy and
rather boring job, but as the skin is bitter, removing it makes all
the difference to any dish containing walnuts. But don't worry if
you can't remove all the skin. (Put your favourite tape on, or
enlist your children to help; it is the sort of job they can do quite

well with their nimble little fingers.) Chop the walnuts coarsely, by hand or in the food processor.

Heat the honey in a saucepan and mix in the walnuts and the lemon rind. Cook gently until the mixture is hot and the walnuts are all well coated in the honey. Draw the pan off the heat, add the rum, mix well and leave to cool.

Heat the oven to 180°C/350°F/Gas 4.

Butter an 18–20 cm/7–8 in spring-clip tin and flour lightly all over.

Remove the dough from the fridge and cut off about one third of it. Put a piece of greaseproof paper on the work-top, shake a little flour over it and roll out the third of the dough over the paper. Lift the paper and turn the circle over on to the bottom of the tin. Peel off the greaseproof paper.

Now roll out strips of dough about 5 cm/2 in wide and line the sides of the tin. Sprinkle the breadcrumbs and the sugar over the bottom and then spoon in the filling. Roll out the rest of the dough on to the greaseproof paper and turn it over to cover the pie. Prick it, to make little holes for the steam to escape. With the remaining dough make a piping or narrow tape and place around the edges to seal.

Mix together the egg yolk and the milk and brush the top of the pie all over. If you want, make some cut-out shapes with any remaining pastry to decorate the pie. Brush these as well with the egg yolk mixture.

Bake for about 30–40 minutes until the pastry is a lovely golden colour. Cool in the tin and then transfer the pie to a round dish.

PREPARATION
La bonissima can be prepared up to 2 days in advance.

A DINNER FOR 8

Polenta pasticciata in bianco
BAKED POLENTA WITH CHEESES

Arrosto morto con le patatine
ITALIAN ROAST MEAT WITH ROAST POTATOES

Dolce di marroni dell'Artusi
CHESTNUT AND CREAM PUDDING

When I was in Milan for a brief visit recently it was cold and foggy after months of warm sunny weather. My friends seemed quite pleased with the change and I knew why, since I remembered how I felt when I lived there. After a summer that seemed to consist of an endless succession of scorching days, you really long for the winter with its bright piercing cold, the wet snow and the long evenings when you stroll from one inviting warm shop to the next. Cold weather suits Milan, and Milanese cuisine excels in dishes made for the winter nights.

During my recent visit I had the polenta dish from this menu twice, once for lunch, when it was the *piatto unico* – the only course – and another time for dinner. Traditionally this is the most wintry of all polenta dishes, since it contains Taleggio and Gorgonzola, two cheeses that used to be made in the autumn. They were made when the cows came down from their Alpine pastures, back to their winter sheds in the plains near Bergamo, for the Taleggio, and near Milan, for the Gorgonzola. Alas, there are no longer any cows in Gorgonzola; they had to make way for the pink, green and blue high-rise flats of the sprawling suburbs of Milan. But the cheese is still made in many places in Lombardy, as, also, is Taleggio. Both cheeses are produced industrially all year round, and both are subject to strict controls as to their origins, similar to the DOC applied to wine. Gorgonzola and Taleggio are table cheeses, but they are used in cooking, too, because of their melting properties. In this recipe they add creaminess as well as flavour to the béchamel, into which they are mixed together with Emmental and Parmesan.

The *secondo* is a joint of veal, pot-roasted as are most roasts in Italy. Cooked in this way, the meat dries less and absorbs more of the flavourings with which it cooks. The meat used in Italy is usually *vitellone*, the meat of calves that are already grazing but are no more than three years old. I have found that British veal, now on sale in some butchers and many good supermarkets, compares very favourably with *vitellone* and is an ideal meat for this recipe. *Arrosto* is always accompanied by roast potatoes. Try mine on page 279, and serve a green salad as well.

My *dolce* is not mine at all, but that of the nineteenth-century cookery writer Pellegrino Artusi. It is the best *Montebianco* I know, even prepared with the alteration I had to make. His recipe calls for citron liqueur, which is hard to find even in Milan. So I have substituted dark rum. I would just like to remind you that chestnuts are at their best when they first come into the shops. Buy large, hard, shiny chestnuts. Throw away any that have a rancid smell; you will notice the smell as soon as you begin to peel them. Peeling chestnuts is a labour of love, justified, however, by the result, since fresh chestnuts have a mealy richness that tinned or dried chestnuts lack.

There is no need to make a cut in the shells, as some cookery writers suggest, to avoid the danger of explosion. If you start by submerging the chestnuts in cold water and bring the water slowly to the boil, the chestnuts will not explode and you save yourself the laborious job of slitting the shells.

You can, of course, make your work even easier and buy a tin of ready-shelled whole chestnuts. But because of its simplicity, the excellence of this pudding depends largely on the use of fresh chestnuts. There is now on the market a new kind of product which Philippa Davenport recommended recently in one of her articles in the *Financial Times*. They are ready shelled frozen chestnuts, sold, she wrote, 'under the Colombe label in enlightened delis and supermarkets. It would be foolish to pretend frozen chestnuts are in the same class as fresh ones, but they are the best alternative available to date and they are a truly convenient food.'

✳✳   *Polenta pasticciata in bianco*

BAKED POLENTA WITH CHEESES

---

polenta made with 400 g/
  14 oz maize flour and 2 litres/
  3½ pints water
béchamel made with 1 litre/1¾
  pints full-fat milk, 75 g/2½ oz
  flour and 90 g/3 oz unsalted
  butter
½ tsp grated nutmeg

120 g/4 oz Gorgonzola, cut into
  small pieces
120 g/4 oz Emmental, cut into
  small pieces
120 g/4 oz Taleggio, cut into small
  pieces
60 g/2 oz Parmesan, freshly grated
freshly ground black pepper

Make the polenta as directed on page 377, using the baked method, which is quicker and ideal for this recipe. The polenta must be prepared at least 3 hours in advance so that it can cool through.

When cold, cut the polenta into ½ cm/¼ in slices. If a hard crust has formed at the top, cut it away with a sharp knife.

Now make the béchamel. Heat the milk to simmering point. Melt the butter and blend in the flour. Cook for 30 seconds or so and then draw off the heat and begin to add the milk, a couple of tablespoons at a time. Continue beating and adding the hot milk until all the milk has been properly incorporated. Put the pan back on the heat and bring to the boil, stirring constantly. Season with the nutmeg. Now continue cooking the sauce for about 20 minutes either in a bain-marie or using a flame disperser. Add the Gorgonzola, Emmental and Taleggio. Stir until dissolved and then mix in the Parmesan and the pepper. Taste and add salt if needed; this may not be necessary, since the cheeses may have seasoned the sauce enough. Continue the cooking and stirring until the sauce is smooth and creamy once again. The sauce should be of the same consistency as thin double cream. Add a little more hot milk if it has dried too much during the cooking.

Heat the oven to 200°C/400°F/Gas 6.

Butter a large, shallow oven dish. Spread 2–3 tablespoons of the cheese sauce over the bottom and cover with polenta slices, then spread the cheese sauce over. Make another layer of polenta slices and dress with cheese sauce. I prefer to choose an oven dish in which the polenta will fit in two or three layers. Do not pile the polenta into too many layers or the dish will become stodgy.

Bake for about 15–25 minutes, depending on the number of layers and on whether the dish has been prepared totally in advance and is therefore cold when you put it in the oven. When ready, the top should show patches of golden crust here and there.

PREPARATION

The dish can be prepared up to 1 day in advance and covered tightly. It does not need to be kept in the fridge.

*   # *Arrosto morto*

ITALIAN ROAST VEAL

---

30 g/1 oz unsalted butter
3 tbsp olive oil
1 fresh rosemary sprig, about
    10 cm/4 in long, or 1 tsp dried
    rosemary
3 garlic cloves, peeled and bruised

1.5 kg/3½ lb boned joint of veal,
    preferably top rump, neatly tied
    in several places
150 ml/¼ pint dry white wine
salt
freshly ground black pepper

Heat the butter, oil, rosemary and garlic in a heavy-based casserole in which the meat will fit snugly. When the butter foam begins to subside, remove the garlic, add the meat and brown well on all sides over medium heat. This browning of the meat will take about 15 minutes, and it is essential to do it thoroughly.

Heat the wine in a small saucepan and pour it over the meat. Bring the wine to a lively bubble. Season with salt and cover the casserole with a piece of greaseproof paper and the lid, leaving a small opening for the steam to escape. Turn the heat down to low and cook for about 2 hours, turning the meat over and basting every now and then. If the meat gets too dry, add 2 or 3 tablespoons of hot water during the cooking. The meat is ready when it is easily pierced by a fork. Add pepper, taste the juices and check salt.

Remove the meat from the pan and place on a carving board to cool a little; this will make it much easier to carve.

Add a few tablespoons of warm water to the pan and, while scraping the cooking residue at the bottom of the pan, reduce over lively heat until the juices are rich and syrupy. Strain and keep warm.

Carve the veal into ½ cm/¼ in slices and arrange them, slightly overlapping, on a warm dish. Spoon the juices over the meat and serve at once.

PREPARATION
The roast should be made as short a time as possible before serving, though you can cook it and prepare the juices before your guests arrive, and keep it warm in the oven in the covered casserole. Carve at the last minute.

** *Dolce di marroni dell'Artusi*

CHESTNUT AND CREAM PUDDING

1 kg/2 lb large chestnuts	*120 g/4 oz best-quality bitter*
225 g/8 oz icing sugar	*chocolate*
4 tbsp rum	*600 ml/1 pint whipping cream*

This is the way I peel fresh chestnuts. Wash the chestnuts. Put them in a pan, cover with cold water and bring very slowly to the boil. Cook for 40–45 minutes or until quite soft. To test, fish a chestnut out of the water and squeeze it between thumb and forefinger. It should offer no resistance.

Take a few chestnuts out of the water and peel them by removing the outer skin and the thin brown inner skin. This is rather a lengthy job. If you have children, ask for help; they usually like doing it, as long as the chestnuts are not too hot. Unfortunately it is easier to peel them if they *are* hot, just out of the water!

When they are peeled, purée them in a food mill with the large-hole disc fitted. A food processor is not suitable, as it would mash the chestnuts without aerating the purée. Sift the icing sugar, set aside 2 tablespoons and mix the rest into the chestnut purée together with the rum.

Grate the chocolate in a food processor or through the large holes of a cheese grater. (Hold the piece of chocolate wrapped in foil to avoid it melting from the heat of your hands.) Add to the mixture. Blend everything together.

Choose a large round serving dish and place a saucer in the middle of it.

Now fix the disc with small holes to the food mill. Purée the chestnut mixture through the smaller hole disc, letting it fall directly on the dish all round the saucer. When all the chestnut has gone through, gently push down the purée that has fallen on the saucer and remove the saucer. Do not squash the purée down, it should stay light and fluffy.

Whip the cream, fold in the reserved sugar and fill the hole with it. Pile the remaining cream into a bowl and hand it round, in case some of your guests want a little more.

PREPARATION
The chestnuts can be peeled and puréed through the larger hole up to 3 days in advance and kept in the refrigerator. They can also be frozen, but must be used within 2 weeks or they will become mushy.

A DINNER FOR 8

Tagliatelle con cozze e porri
TAGLIATELLE WITH MUSSELS AND LEEKS

Insalata veronese
CELERIAC, CHICORY AND RADICCHIO SALAD

Formaggio
CHEESE

Torrone molle
SOFT CHOCOLATE NOUGAT

Eight is a good number for the guests, less good for the hosts. It needs a well-planned menu which, like this one, has only one dish to attend to just before eating. This is an informal menu, including dishes that offer contrast in texture and positive well-defined flavours.

In Italy pasta is served only as a first course, except, very occasionally, for some baked pasta dishes. Another maxim is summed up in the saying '*la pasta non aspetta nessuno*' – pasta waits for no one, which means that it must be eaten the moment it is dressed. You can buy fresh tagliatelle or you can use a good Italian brand of dried egg tagliatelle, of which Cipriani is the best. These brands are usually better than the fresh tagliatelle you can buy in shops and supermarkets. But best of all, you can make your own pasta. Mussels and leeks make an excellent combination, and pasta is the liaison that gives the dish more weight.

In the old days I would have hesitated to write a recipe for eight people containing mussels. Who would have stood at the kitchen sink for hours on end to clean 4 lb of dirty, sandy, barnacled and bearded mussels? Nowadays the mussels we buy are usually farmed. The farms are on rafts or ropes, and as a result the mussels are pretty clean when they reach our sinks.

Cheese is seldom served at dinners in Italy, but I think this menu needs a little more substance. There are also many people who love to have some good cheese, and there are so many excellent cheeses on the market, some of the best being English cheeses made with unpasteurised milk. You can hand round the cheese platter with the salad; it is a salad that goes particularly well with cheese. This will also save you having to wash a new set of plates.

The pudding is rich, but, after all, the rest of the meal is not, and it is absolutely delicious and very easy to make.

✷✷   *Tagliatelle con cozze e porri*
✷✷✷   TAGLIATELLE WITH MUSSELS AND LEEKS
if you make
your own pasta

Tagliatelle made with 6 eggs and
  500 g/1 lb 2 oz white flour, or
1 kg/2 lb fresh tagliatelle, or
600 g/1¼ lb dried tagliatelle
1.8 kg/4 lb mussels
300 ml/½ pint dry white wine
1 kg/2 lb leeks (buy small ones if

you can; they are younger and
  therefore sweeter).
100 g/3½ oz unsalted butter
salt and freshly ground black
  pepper
300 ml/½ pint double cream

If you are making your own tagliatelle do this first, following my instructions on page 374.

Clean and prepare the mussels. Put them in the sink or a large basin of cold water. Scrub them hard with a stiff brush, knock off any barnacles and tug off the beard. Wash thoroughly, drain, and throw away any mussel that remains open when tapped on a hard surface; it is dead and must not be eaten. You should cook this quantity of mussels in two batches. Use a large pan with a tight-fitting lid, so that the mussels can spread out properly. Pour the wine into the pan and add the mussels. Cover and cook over high heat until the mussels open. Shake the pan frequently.

Remove the mussels from the shells as soon as they open, but do not force them open or they will break. Discard the shells and cook the second batch of mussels. Now filter the liquid at the bottom of the pan into a saucepan through a sieve lined with muslin. Reduce the liquid over high heat until about 300 ml (½ pint) is left. Set aside.

The next step is to prepare the leeks. Trim them, cutting away the roots and about 4–7 cm/2–3 in from the top, depending how fresh they are. Cut all the white part of the leeks, and the tender green heart, into thin rounds. Wash very thoroughly, removing any grit stuck between the leaves. Drain.

Put about three-quarters of the butter in a very large sauté or frying pan. Heat until the butter has melted and then add the leeks and cook, turning them over in the butter, for 5 minutes. Cover the leeks with a sheet of buttered greaseproof paper, put the lid on the pan and cook very gently for about 45 minutes, until the leeks become a purée. Keep a watch on the cooking and add a couple of tablespoons of the filtered mussel liquid whenever the leeks are too dry. Add the mussels and the rest of the mussel liquid. Taste and add salt and a generous amount of pepper.

Now you can cook the pasta, keeping in mind that fresh pasta takes less time to cook than dried. While the pasta is cooking, heat the cream in a small saucepan. When the pasta is *al dente*, drain, but do not overdrain, reserving a cupful of the pasta water. Transfer the pasta immediately to a heated bowl.

Add the remaining butter, the hot cream and the lovely sauce. Toss thoroughly and, if the dish appears too dry, add a few tablespoons of the reserved pasta water. Serve immediately.

PREPARATION

The leeks can be cooked up to one day in advance and refrigerated. The mussels could also be cleaned and opened one day in advance. Put them in a bowl with the strained liquid, cover with clingfilm and refrigerate. The tagliatelle must be cooked just before serving.

*   *Insalata veronese*

CELERIAC, CHICORY AND RADICCHIO SALAD

---

1 medium size celeriac
3 chicory heads

3 medium size radicchio heads

For the dressing

45 ml/3 tbsp lemon juice
5 ml/1 tsp English mustard
*   powder*

120 ml/4 fl oz extra virgin olive oil
salt and pepper

First make the dressing. Put the lemon juice in a bowl and mix in the mustard. Add the oil in a very thin stream while beating with a fork to emulsify. Season to taste.

Peel the celeriac and cut into julienne strips. (This is easily done in a food processor with the julienne disc.) Toss with some of the dressing and put in a bowl. Cover with clingfilm and leave in the refrigerator for 2–3 hours.

Cut the chicory and the radicchio into 1 cm/½ in strips. Wash and dry thoroughly and toss with the remaining dressing. Put the celeriac in the middle of a serving dish and spoon the salad mixture around it.

PREPARATION

The celeriac can be cut and dressed the day before and refrigerated. The salad can be washed and cut a few hours in advance and kept, wrapped in a clean tea-towel, in the vegetable drawer of the fridge.

*   # *Torrone molle*

SOFT CHOCOLATE NOUGAT

---

225 g/8 oz unsalted butter, at room
    temperature
225 g/8 oz granulated sugar
120 g/4 oz best cocoa powder
1 whole egg + 1 yolk

120 g/4 oz almonds
120 g/4 oz plain biscuits, e.g.
    digestives
3 tbsp dark rum

Cream together the butter and sugar until light and fluffy. Add the cocoa, spoonful by spoonful, and beat hard until it has been completely incorporated. This takes a little time and some beating. Use a food processor if you have one.

Lightly beat together the egg and the yolk and add to the butter-cream, stirring until they are well blended.

Blanch the almonds for 30 seconds in boiling water. Peel them and then chop them coarsely. Add to the butter-cream mixture. Crumble the biscuits with a rolling pin and add to the mixture together with the rum. Mix very thoroughly.

Line a 600 ml/1 pint loaf tin with greaseproof paper and spoon the mixture into it. Press it down well to eliminate any air pockets and level the top with a spatula. Cover with clingfilm and refrigerate for at least 4 hours.

To serve, turn the *torrone* out on to an oval dish. I like to decorate it with candied violets and almonds, or to surround it with whipped cream piped through a forcing bag set with a fluted nozzle. The *torrone* is served cut, with a sharp knife, into slices about 1 cm/½ in thick.

PREPARATION

The *torrone* can be made up to 2 days in advance and refrigerated. It can also be frozen.

A DINNER FOR 10–12

Insalata di cavolfiore alla salsa bianca
CAULIFLOWER SALAD WITH ANCHOVY AND
PINE NUT DRESSING

*Bollito misto con salsa rossa, salsa verde, salsa di api e
mostarda di Cremona*
BOILED MEATS WITH RED SAUCE, GREEN SAUCE,
HONEY AND WALNUT SAUCE AND *MOSTARDA* OF FRUIT

Arance caramellate
CARAMELIZED ORANGES

La torta di Julia
CHOCOLATE AND NUT CAKE (page 139)

The centrepiece of this dinner is the *bollito misto*, which is the ideal dish when you have a lot of people to feed, since, at its best, it contains many different kinds of meat. *Bollito misto* is made in all northern Italian regions; if you go there, do keep a look-out for a restaurant that serves it – a sure sign of a top-class establishment. A trolley with many compartments will be wheeled to your table and from it you can choose a thick slice of beef, a small chunk of veal, a leg of chicken, a slice or two of *cotechino* and one of tongue, plus a few boiled vegetables. All the meats are immersed in steaming stock, giving off a rich and intense aroma that holds promise of the delights to come.

I was brought up on *bollito misto*. It appeared on the table of our home in Milan every Monday, so that there was stock in the kitchen for most of the week. When I came to live in England meat was still scarce (it was rationed until 1954, nine years after the end of the war) and cuts suitable for *bollito misto* were unobtainable. But slowly things improved and my mind turned to one of my favourite dishes. At first my husband, with the English 'boiled beef and carrots' in mind, was dubious about this dish of which I spoke with such enthusiasm. But soon, as more and more of the right cuts became available, my *bollito* began to be accepted with pleasure, until eventually *bollito misto* became a family favourite.

Bollito misto is a convivial dish which must be offered in generous quantities, accompanied by at least two sauces and the delicious *mostarda di frutta*. There are quite a few *mostarde* on the market, but the most popular and easily available kind is *mostarda di Cremona*. Called also *mostarda di frutta*, it consists of various fruits, previously candied and then preserved in a thick syrup of white wine and honey highly spiced with mustard. Truth to tell, I am quite happy to do without the other sauces and have only *mostarda*, but as it is not to everyone's taste I am including recipes for the three best sauces to go with *bollito misto*. The honey and walnut sauce is quite delicious, by the way.

My recipe for *bollito misto* is for ten to twelve people, but you can of course scale it down, by omitting the *cotechino* for instance. When I do *bollito* for the family, I cook only a piece of flank or brisket and one or two *ossibuchi*. The trimmings are the same, although I would do only one sauce, or just put my best olive oil on the table, plus the jar of *mostarda di Cremona*, and let everybody get on with it. *Bollito misto* is always accompanied by boiled vegetables, potatoes, carrots and onions being the most common.

The first course of this menu is a cauliflower salad that I have adapted from a recipe by Vincenzo Corrado, a Neapolitan cookery writer of the eighteenth century. Cauliflower and anchovy have always been a successful combination of flavours. Here they are joined by the delicate resinous flavour of pine nuts, which also provide a contrast of texture.

For pudding I have chosen a melt-in-the-mouth chocolate cake. The recipe comes to me from my daughter, the Julia of the title. It is one which even I, not at all a chocolate lover, find irresistible. The *arance caramellate* are for the discreet eaters, or for the very greedy who like to indulge in two puddings.

* *Insalata di cavolfiore alla salsa bianca*

CAULIFLOWER SALAD WITH ANCHOVY AND PINE NUT DRESSING

---

3 medium cauliflowers
150 ml/¼ pint extra virgin olive
  oil
120 g/4 oz pine nuts
6 salted anchovies or 12 anchovy
  fillets

2 tbsp white wine vinegar
3 tbsp lemon juice
salt and pepper
6 tbsp chopped parsley

Divide the cauliflowers into small florets. Wash the florets thoroughly and then cook them in plenty of salted water until tender. How long cauliflower should cook is entirely up to you. As an Italian, I like my cooked vegetables properly cooked and not the way they are served today in so many places. What I mean by 'properly cooked' is that they should be tender when pricked with a fork, but not soft. It is at that stage, and only then, that vegetables begin to develop their full flavour.

Drain thoroughly and spread the florets out on kitchen paper. Pat them dry and transfer to a bowl or a dish. Toss them gently with 2 tablespoons of the oil while the cauliflower is still hot, so that it can absorb the oil better.

Roast the pine nuts for a couple of minutes in a non-stick pan to bring out the flavour. Clean and rinse the salted anchovies or drain the anchovy fillets from the oil. Put them in a mortar with the pine nuts. Pound the mixture with the vinegar, lemon juice, salt and pepper, using the pestle. Stir in the oil with a fork to form an emulsion. The sauce can also be made in a food processor.

Spoon the sauce over the cauliflower, cover with clingfilm and leave for 1 hour. Serve at room temperature with a sprinkling of chopped parsley for garnish, and plenty of good bread.

PREPARATION

The cauliflower can be cooked, and the sauce prepared, up to 1 day in advance, but do not pour the sauce more than 1 hour before serving or the cauliflower will 'cook' in the sauce.

✱✱ *Bollito misto*

MIXED BOILED MEATS

---

1 large onion, stuck with 1 clove
2 celery sticks
1 leek
2 carrots
1 kg/2 lb beef flank or brisket
3 fresh ripe tomatoes, or tinned
   tomatoes without their juice
5–6 peppercorns, lightly crushed

a few parsley stalks
salt
450 g/1 lb shoulder of veal, boned,
   or 2 large ossibuchi
½ a fresh chicken, preferably a
   boiling hen
1 cotechino, about 450 g/1 lb

Put the onion, celery, leek and carrots in a saucepan, cover with cold water and bring to the boil. Add the beef and bring back to the boil. Lower the heat – the stock should just be simmering. Remove the scum that comes to the surface during the first few minutes of cooking. Add the tomatoes, peppercorns, parsley and some salt. Cover the pan and simmer for 1½ hours.

Add the veal and simmer for a further hour. Put in the chicken and cook for 1 to 1½ hours, depending on whether it is a roaster or a boiler. If you are using a pre-cooked *cotechino*, follow the manufacturer's instructions. If the *cotechino* is uncooked, follow my instructions given in the recipe for *cotechino allo zabaione* on page 267.

When you serve the *bollito*, lift one piece of meat at a time out of the stock and carve only as much as you need to go round for the first helping. Keep the rest in the stock, as this prevents the meat getting dry. If you have also cooked the *cotechino*, transfer it to the stockpot with all the other meats.

Put the carved meat on a large heated platter and bring it to the table, with dishes of boiled potatoes, boiled carrots, boiled onions and any other seasonal roots all cooked separately, and little bowls of the sauces (see the following recipes).

PREPARATION

You can cook the *bollito misto* one day in advance, but do not put in the chicken. Bring the *bollito* back to the boil and add the piece of chicken about 1½ hours before serving.

*

Salsa rossa

RED SAUCE

3 tbsp olive oil	3 garlic cloves, peeled
450 g/1 lb tomatoes, cut into quarters	1 or 2 dried chillies, according to taste, seeded
1 tsp tomato purée	1 clove
2 onions, coarsely chopped	1 pinch of cinnamon
1 carrot, coarsely chopped	salt
1 celery stick, coarsely chopped	1 tbsp red wine vinegar

Put half the oil and all the other ingredients except the vinegar in a saucepan with a very heavy bottom. I use an earthenware pot of the sort you can put directly on the heat. Cook over the gentlest heat for 1–1½ hours, adding a little hot water if necessary.

Purée through a food mill or a sieve. If you use a food processor, you must skin the tomatoes before you cook them.

Return the purée to the pan and add the rest of the oil and the vinegar. Cook for a further 30 minutes, then taste and check seasoning. The sauce is now ready, but let it cool a little before you serve it. You can also serve it at room temperature.

PREPARATION

This sauce can be prepared up to 3 days in advance, covered and refrigerated. It also freezes very well.

*

Salsa verde

GREEN SAUCE

---

30 g/1 oz fresh white breadcrumbs
1–1½ tsp red wine vinegar
1 garlic clove
30 g/1 oz parsley, preferably flat-
   leaf
4 tbsp tarragon
2 tbsp capers
half a dozen cornichons (very small
   gherkins – if unobtainable, use 1
   extra tbsp capers)

1 hard-boiled egg, shelled
6 anchovy fillets or 3 salted
   anchovies, boned and rinsed
2 tsp Dijon mustard
150 ml/¼ pint extra virgin olive
   oil
pepper
salt

Put the breadcrumbs in a bowl and pour the vinegar over them.
Set aside.

Peel the garlic clove, cut it in half and remove the hard central
core, if necessary. This is the part that has a pungent instead of a
sweet flavour.

Chop the parsley, tarragon, capers, cornichons, hard-boiled
egg, anchovies and garlic together. Put this mixture into another
bowl.

Squeeze out the vinegar from the bread and add the bread to
the mixture in the bowl, working it in with a fork. Add the
mustard and then gradually add the olive oil, beating the whole
time. Season with a good deal of pepper. Taste and add salt if
necessary; the anchovies and capers may have given enough salt
to the sauce. You might like to add a little more vinegar; it
depends on the strength of your vinegar and how you like the
sauce.

The whole sauce can be made in the food processor.

PREPARATION

Salsa verde can be made up to 3 days in advance and kept,
covered, in the fridge.

* *Salsa di api*

HONEY AND WALNUT SAUCE

Buy the walnuts from a good supplier. Look through the plastic wrapper and check that the kernels are in large pieces, preferably no smaller than quarters. They should not be crumbled, as this is a sure sign of walnuts that are too old. Stale walnuts have a rancid taste that will ruin any dish.

---

30 g/1 oz walnut kernels
3 tbsp home-made stock
3 tbsp clear honey

1½ tbsp English mustard, prepared

Heat a small saucepan of water to boiling point. Add the walnuts and blanch for 20 seconds. Drain and peel them, not an easy task but one that makes all the difference to the final result, as walnut skins have a bitter taste.

Put the walnuts in a food processor, add the stock and the honey and process to a coarse purée. Add the mustard and process again for a few seconds to mix it in thoroughly.

PREPARATION

The sauce can be prepared up to 2 days in advance and kept, covered, in the fridge.

* *Arance caramellate*

CARAMELIZED ORANGES

10–12 thin-skinned oranges, seedless if possible
200 g/7 oz granulated sugar

3 tbsp Grand Marnier or Cointreau

Scrub the oranges and dry thoroughly. Remove the zest of 3 of the oranges very thinly, leaving all the pith on the fruit. Cut 3 strips of skin from a fourth orange. Put all the oranges in the freezer to harden while you make the syrup.

Cut the zest from the 3 oranges into julienne strips about 25 mm/1 in long and put them in boiling water. Boil for 5 minutes to get rid of the bitter taste. Drain and refresh under cold water and set aside.

Put the sugar, the 3 orange strips and 150 ml/¼ pint of water in a small saucepan and cook over low heat. When the syrup begins to boil, turn the heat up slightly and continue boiling until the syrup begins to turn pale gold at the edge of the pan. Now remove the orange strips and add the juliennes. Boil for 5 minutes, stirring constantly, until the juliennes become slightly transparent and syrupy-looking. Add the liqueur, stir and draw off the heat.

Take the oranges out of the freezer and peel carefully with a small sharp knife, removing every scrap of pith. Cut the oranges across into thin slices and put them in a glass bowl or deep dish. Do this over a plate so that you can collect the juice and pour it over the oranges at the end.

Spoon the syrup and the juliennes over the oranges and chill for at least 2 hours.

PREPARATION

You can cut the oranges and make the syrup up to 1 day in advance, and keep, covered, in the fridge. Pour the syrup over the oranges no longer than 6 hours before serving them.

Special Occasion Menus

The six occasions I have chosen for this section all merit special treatment, and I have devised six special menus accordingly. The occasions are: Christmas dinner, New Year's Eve supper, St Valentine's day dinner *à deux*, Easter lunch, a birthday dinner and an alfresco lunch for a glorious summer's day.

A CHRISTMAS DINNER FOR 10

Mousse di prosciutto cotto della Signora Gay
TRUFFLE-FLAVOURED HAM MOUSSE

Stracciatella al sapor di limone
LEMON-FLAVOURED EGG AND PARMESAN SOUP (page 157)

Tacchino arrosto alla milanese con le patate
STUFFED ROAST TURKEY WITH ROAST POTATOES

Le caramellone natalizie con crema allo zenzero
CHRISTMAS CRACKER STRUDELS WITH GINGER CUSTARD

Our 1990 Christmas dinner provided a good opportunity for a 'dress rehearsal' for this menu, since I had to hand in the manuscript of this book just a few days later. All, I am glad to say, went well.

First came the ham mousse, the provenance of which you can read on page 133. I follow the mousse with a light soup (page 157), perfect for a soothing rest before the onslaught that follows.

The turkey is my version of the original Milanese turkey we used to eat at the pre-war Christmas dinners at the home of our aunt and uncle. They were marvellous parties. The grown-ups, presided over by Nonna Irene, looking like a miniature Queen Mary in widow's weeds and rows of pearls to her waist, sat at a vast table, while we children sat at a smaller table in a corner of the room. I was the youngest of all, a very light eater and totally overwhelmed by the occasion. My memories of the food are sketchy. I remember only red monsters with frightening claws, glistening brown turkeys, and on one of the sideboards a huge dome-shaped *panettone* surrounded by dishes and dishes of candied fruits, dried fruits, chocolates, chestnut truffles, marrons glacés, grapes, mandarins, quince cheese and fruit jellies, at all of which I would just pick occasionally. Not yet awakened to the delights of gastronomy, I preferred the cacophony of the saucepan-banging we indulged in, in the little saucepan room, to the despair of the deafened grown-ups.

Back to my 1990 Christmas dinner, which was spartan by comparison, yet quite ample for our shrunken stomachs and complex enough for our non-existent domestic staff. I made two stuffings for the turkey, both based on original Milanese stuffings. The fruit stuffing for the cavity is there simply to keep the meat moist during the cooking; it is not much good to eat. But, having bought a fairly small turkey, I had extra stuffing which I cooked as in the recipe here, and it made a very good relish to go with the turkey. The chestnut stuffing also is too much for a small bird, but it makes the most delicious forcemeat croquettes.

With the turkey I served roast potatoes flavoured with bay leaf, as in the recipe on page 369, and Brussels sprouts and parsnips. I love parsnips but not Brussels sprouts, whose cabbagey taste I find overpowering. So I partly boiled the parsnips and the sprouts and sautéed them separately in butter. I then placed them together in an oven dish, flavoured them with grated Parmesan and covered them with a velouté sauce. The mealy sweetness of the parsnips counteracted the strong brassica flavour of the sprouts, just as chestnuts do when added to sprouts.

I used always to serve Christmas pudding when my children were young; I do not think they liked it particularly, but they liked the tradition. In the recent past, breaking with English tradition, I have served the chestnut purée and cream pudding on page 280, or just an orange jelly, plus the *panettone*, *torrone* and other delicacies traditional to my Milanese Christmas.

This year I tried these small strudels. The recipe comes from Francesca Davoli, a talented young Roman cook who I am sure will soon make her name in the Italian gastronomic field. The appearance of these strudels shaped like Christmas crackers would already be enough to testify to Francesca's talent, but it is the custard which, figuratively, sets the crackers alight. It is a zesty, spicy sauce, yet light and refreshing, a perfect foil to the rich flavour of the strudel filling.

By the end of such an ample dinner, however, not everyone is in a state to face a cracker strudel, or even half a strudel. So I always make a mandarin or orange jelly as well. This year I chose a Yorkshire recipe by Elisabeth Luard for the jelly, and it was quite delicious.

*** *Mousse di prosciutto cotto della Signora Gay*

TRUFFLE-FLAVOURED HAM MOUSSE

---

a thick béchamel made with 15 g/½ oz butter, 1 tbsp flour and 150 ml/¼ pint full-fat milk
325 g/11 oz best lean ham

2–3 tsp truffle paste
120 ml/4 fl oz whipping cream
pepper

For the aspic jelly

600 ml/1 pint good meat stock
4 tbsp dry sherry or dry Marsala
2 egg whites

about 10 g/⅓ oz gelatine powder or 4 gelatine leaves (as necessary)

First make the aspic jelly, a much easier job than you might think. All you need is some stock, thoroughly skimmed of fat and full of flavour, plus the ability to proceed with precision. Put the egg whites and the sherry in a saucepan and add the cold stock. Bring the liquid to the simmer while beating with a balloon whisk. Then stop beating, turn the heat down to minimum and leave for about 15 minutes. The stock should not boil but should just break some bubbles on the surface.

Now strain the stock very carefully through a sieve lined with a piece of muslin folded double. Taste and check salt, remembering that food served cold needs more seasoning. If you have made the stock with all the right ingredients for an aspic jelly – beef, chicken carcass, pork rind and calf's foot or pig trotters (plus onion skin for the colour) – you may find that it does not need any added gelatine. To test it, put a tablespoon of stock on a saucer in the freezer for 10 minutes. If it sets, no gelatine is needed. If not, dissolve some of the gelatine in a little of the stock and stir well into the rest. If you are using gelatine leaves, soften the leaves in cold water and then dissolve in the stock. Test again until you achieve the right consistency.

Pour enough jelly into a 1.25 litre/2 pint loaf tin, to come about 2 cm/¾ in up the side of the tin. Put the tin into the fridge for the jelly to set while you prepare the mousse.

Make the béchamel in the usual way, but do not add any salt.

Cook very gently for 15 minutes or so, using the bain-marie method or a flame disperser. When ready, cool in a bowl of iced water.

Put the ham in the food processor and process until very finely chopped. Transfer to a bowl and mix in the truffle paste. Truffle paste varies from brand to brand. You might need 2 or 3 teaspoons. Just taste after you have added a little and add more if you want the truffle flavour to come through more positively. Add the béchamel as soon as it is cold, and lastly add the whipped cream. Season with a generous amount of pepper; salt should not be necessary.

Take a 600 ml/1 pint loaf tin and press the mousse into it, taking care to eliminate any air pockets. Put the tin in the fridge to cool thoroughly. When the jelly in the first tin is set, slide a palette knife round the ham mousse. Turn the tin containing the mousse on to a plate and then turn into the larger tin with the aspic layer; the mousse should fall into the larger tin. Pour some of the jelly which is not set around the mousse, cover with clingfilm and refrigerate.

Before your guests arrive, unmould the aspic on to an oval dish. This is easily done if you immerse the tin in a bowl of hot water for 15–20 seconds. Keep in the fridge until the last minute and decorate the dish with a sprig of bay, or a sprig of holly or ivy if you are serving it at Christmas.

PREPARATION
The whole dish can be prepared up to 3 days in advance and refrigerated.

***   *Tacchino arrosto alla milanese*

STUFFED ROAST TURKEY

At last there are good turkeys on the market again. I find the 'bronze' turkey very good, with lean and succulent meat.

---

1 'bronze' turkey of about 6–7 kg/ 11–13 lb undressed weight, with the liver reserved for the stuffing	90–120 g/3–4 oz unsalted butter
	6–8 rashers unsmoked streaky bacon
salt and pepper	1 tbsp white flour
the two stuffings (see the following recipes)	

For the stock

the neck, gizzard and heart of the turkey	1 celery stalk
1 carrot	4 or 5 parsley stalks
1 onion	6 peppercorns
1 bay leaf	1 tsp salt
	150 g/¼ pint red wine

First make the stock. Put all the ingredients for it in a saucepan and cover with *cold* water by 5 cm/2 in. Simmer gently for 2 hours, then strain through a metal sieve. Set aside.

Wipe the turkey thoroughly inside and out with kitchen paper and season it well with salt and pepper. Loosely pack the fruit stuffing in the cavity. Close the opening with a thin skewer. Stuff the neck end of the turkey loosely with the meat and chestnut stuffing and sew up the flap of skin with thick cotton. Spread about two-thirds of the butter all over the turkey, especially over the breast, which is the driest meat.

Heat the oven to 230°C/450°F/Gas 8.

Lay a large sheet of foil over a large roasting tin and place another sheet across it. Put half the remaining butter, cut up into small pieces, over the foil. Lay the bird in the prepared tin and cover its breast with the streaky bacon. Wrap the foil loosely round the bird, leaving a pocket of air on top.

Bake for 45 minutes and then turn the heat down to 165°C/ 325°F/Gas 3 and continue cooking until the bird is done. To test, insert a small pointed knife into the thickest part of the thigh. The juice that runs out should be clear, not bloody. A turkey of this size should take about 3½ hours. About half an hour before the end of the cooking time, unfold the foil and cut it all around. Push the bacon down the side of the tin.

Turn the heat up to 200°C/400°F/Gas 6. Baste the turkey and put it back in the oven to let the breast get brown and shining. When the turkey is lovely and brown, transfer it and the bacon rashers to a dish, cover with foil and leave out of the oven for at least 30 minutes. This will allow the juices that have come to the surface to sink back into the meat.

Blend the flour with the remaining knob of butter and set aside.

Meanwhile, prepare the gravy. A good turkey should have left very little fat. If, however, you see some in the roasting tin, skim off as much of it as you can. Heat the cooking juices and add some stock, according to how much gravy you like to serve. Boil for a minute or two and then add the *beurre manié* – the butter and flour mixture – in small pieces, beating with a small balloon whisk. Taste and add salt and pepper as you wish. Transfer the gravy to one or two sauce-boats.

Bring the turkey to the table. Remember to give each diner some chestnut and meat stuffing, but not the fruit stuffing.

PREPARATION
You can prepare the turkey up to 2 hours before you need to put it in the oven. Do not refrigerate. The stock can be made as soon as you have the turkey.

** *Ripieno di castagne*
PORK AND CHESTNUT STUFFING

---

225 g/½ lb chestnuts
120 g/4 oz pancetta
200 g/7 oz onion
200 g/7 oz celery, stalk and leaves
2 garlic cloves, peeled
a small handful of parsley, preferably flat-leaf
a dozen fresh sage leaves
1 tbsp fresh rosemary needles
30 g/1 oz unsalted butter

30 g/1 oz fresh white breadcrumbs
225 g/½ lb lean minced pork
225 g/½ lb Italian, French or any other pure pork, mild sausage, skinned and crumbled
the turkey liver, cleaned and chopped
3 tbsp freshly grated Parmesan
salt and pepper

First cook and peel the chestnuts. (I explain how to do this in the recipe for the chestnut purée and cream pudding on page 280.)

Coarsely chop the *pancetta*, onion, celery, garlic, parsley, sage and rosemary. If you use a food processor, do not reduce the mixture to a mush.

Melt the butter in a large frying pan and add the *pancetta* mixture, breadcrumbs, minced pork and sausage and stir-fry for 5 minutes. Add the liver and cook for a further 5 minutes. Stir frequently to *insaporire* – let the mixture take the flavour.

Transfer to a bowl and add the Parmesan, plenty of freshly milled pepper, and salt to taste. Mix in the chestnuts. I cut the large ones in half, or even in quarters. Taste and adjust seasoning. Loosely pack the stuffing into the neck end of the turkey and sew up the flap of skin.

If you have some stuffing left over, chop it well in a food processor, adding one egg for binding. Shape small croquettes, the size of golf balls, and roll them in flour. Put the croquettes in the fridge to get firm.

About 30 minutes before you want to serve the dinner, place the croquettes on a generously oiled oven tray. Brush them with more oil and bake for 30 minutes.

PREPARATION
This stuffing can be prepared up to 2 days in advance and refrigerated in a closed container. It can also be frozen, but use within 2–3 weeks or the chestnuts will become mushy.

*   Ripieno di frutta*
FRUIT STUFFING

I use half the fruit mixture to stuff the cavity of the turkey, to keep it moist during the cooking, and the other half to make a zesty fruit relish to hand round cold with the turkey.

2 oranges	4 garlic cloves, peeled
1 lemon	300 ml/½ pint good red wine
450 g/1 lb fresh cranberries	1 tsp ground mace
2 dessert apples, peeled and cubed	1 tsp ground clove
3 onions, preferably red, sliced	150 g/5 oz brown sugar
a dozen prunes, stoned and cut into strips	salt and pepper

Wash and dry one of the oranges and grate the rind into a large bowl. Peel the two oranges and the lemon to the quick. Separate the segments and, with a small knife, remove any white pith and the papery skin between the segments. Add the clean pulp to the bowl, together with all the other ingredients. Cover with clingfilm and leave to macerate for 1–2 hours.

Pack half the mixture into the cavity of the bird and sew up the hole with a thin skewer or with thick thread and a needle.

Place the rest of the mixture in a saucepan and stew gently for about 1 hour. Stir occasionally, and add a couple of tablespoons of water if it gets too dry. The mixture will become all rich and gluey, rather like chutney, by the end of the cooking. Taste and adjust salt and pepper.

PREPARATION
You can prepare the fruit the day before, but do not macerate in the wine for longer than 2 hours.

*** *Le caramellone natalizie con crema allo zenzero*

CHRISTMAS CRACKER STRUDELS WITH GINGER CUSTARD

---

3 tart dessert apples, e.g. Granny Smiths	1 tsp cinnamon
	3 tbsp caster sugar
2 tbsp lemon juice	30 g/1 oz dried breadcrumbs
100 g/3½ oz sultanas	120 g/4 oz unsalted butter
1 tbsp dark rum	300–350 g/10–14 oz frozen fila pastry, thawed
60 g/2 oz walnuts, peeled and chopped	icing sugar

For the ginger custard

90 g/3 oz root ginger	4 large egg yolks
500 ml/18 fl oz full fat milk	90 g/3 oz sugar

First prepare the custard. Peel the root ginger and grate it through the coarse holes of a cheese grater.

Bring the milk to simmering point and stir in the ginger. Draw the pan off the heat immediately and leave to infuse for about 1 hour. Strain the milk mixture through a fine strainer. Discard the ginger and return the milk to the pan.

Put the egg yolks in a bowl and gradually add the sugar while beating with a hand-held electric beater or a wire whisk. Beat for 2–3 minutes, until the mixture is pale yellow and forms a ribbon.

Meanwhile bring the strained milk up to simmering point again. Pour it slowly over the egg mixture while continuing to beat. Transfer the mixture to a heavy saucepan and place it over a moderate heat. Cook, stirring slowly and constantly with a wooden spoon and reaching all the corners at the bottom of the pan, until the sauce thickens enough to coat the back of the spoon, which will take about 15 minutes. To see whether it is ready, dip the spoon in the custard and draw your finger across the back of it. If a clear line remains, the custard is ready. If you have a jam thermometer, check that the temperature is no more than 80°C/170°F.

Withdraw the pan from the heat and place it in a basin of cold water to cool quickly. Beat for the first minute and then occasionally. When cold, cover with clingfilm and chill.

Peel the apples, quarter and core them. Cut each quarter in half lengthwise and then slice them thinly across. Put them in a pudding basin and add the lemon juice, sultanas, rum, walnuts, cinnamon, sugar and dried breadcrumbs. Mix very thoroughly.

Melt 30 g/1 oz of the butter in a non-stick frying pan. Add the apple mixture and sauté gently for 5 minutes, turning it over often to *insaporire* – take the flavour. Set aside for about 1 hour for the flavours to blend.

Melt the remaining butter in a small saucepan. Brush an oven tray with a little butter.

Unroll the fila pastry and cut out four leaves about 15 × 12 cm/ 6 × 5 in. Keep the rest of the fila pastry covered or it will dry out and crack. Place a leaf of fila on the work top and brush with melted butter. Place the other three leaves on top of the first, brushing generously with butter between each leaf. Spread one small tablespoon of the filling on the top leaf, leaving 2½–4 cm/ 1–1½ in at the end of the longer side uncovered. Roll up the pastry along its length to form a miniature Swiss roll. Twist the pastry ends like a cracker, and crimp them. Place on a buttered oven tray. Repeat this process to make the other nine crackers. Refrigerate to chill the pastry for about 45 minutes.

Heat the oven to 190°C/375°F/Gas 5.

When the oven is hot, bake the crackers for 20 minutes, until they are golden.

When the crackers have cooled slightly, sprinkle with icing sugar and serve, while still warm, with the ginger custard handed round separately in a bowl. If you prefer, place the crackers on individual dessert plates and spoon a little custard around them.

PREPARATION

The custard can be prepared up to 4 days in advance and kept in the refrigerator. The crackers, like strudel, are best eaten freshly baked and warm. However, they can be made up to 2 days in advance and kept wrapped in foil. Reheat in a warm oven for 10 minutes.

NEW YEAR'S EVE SUPPER FOR 10

Bresaola con la rucola
BRESAOLA WITH ROCKET (page 119)

Il gran raviolo
ONE EGG RAVIOLI IN CLEAR BROTH

Zampone allo zabaione con le lenticchie
ZAMPONE SAUSAGE IN A ZABAGLIONE SAUCE WITH STEWED
LENTILS (page 267)

Bomba di panna e marrons glacés
CREAM AND MARRONS GLACÉS *BOMBE*

Ananas e arancie
PINEAPPLE AND ORANGES (page 187)

The most memorable New Year's Eve supper I ever had was years ago in Naples. It was not long after the end of the war, when the scars of war were healing and people were beginning to enjoy life again. I went south from Milan to see the New Year in with family friends who had teenage children of my age.

New Year's Eve in southern Italy is a major event. Fireworks go off in all directions and car horns hoot mercilessly, but even then I was not prepared for what happened just a few minutes after we had toasted in the New Year. Our friend Mariarosa got up from the table, picked up her chair, went over to the window, opened it, and proceeded to throw her chair down on to the street below. Her brother and sister did the same with some of the crockery on the table, which I hasten to add was not their best Capodimonte. I ran to the window to witness the spectacle of Neapolitans hurling their oldest chattels into the street; they were having a good clean-up to welcome in the year 1948. Later in the night the poor people from *i bassi* – the slums – would come around and pick what could be salvaged from the rubble. I am told that nowadays this custom, which also existed in Rome, has almost died away, with only a few old crocks being thrown out.

In this menu I have been able to include one item from the supper I enjoyed on that memorable night: the *zampone*. The other dishes would have been local in origin, pies made with local vegetables, as well as cheeses and sausages. There would also have been delicious little sweet things, many of them fried at the last moment, so again not well suited to this menu. My menu, a mainly northern Italian one, is in fact very easy, only the soup requiring final attention.

I thought it a good idea to start with something that can be bought, prosciutto or *bresaola*, serving them with rocket and Parmesan, both, with their pungent flavour, good stimulants to the appetite. The recipe for this dish is on page 119. To make the dish more festive, cut about 150 g/5 oz of good Parmesan or *grana padana* into slivers and scatter over the dish. And if you want to add an exotic and really delicious touch, replace 1 tablespoon of olive oil with the same amount of truffle-flavoured oil, which can be bought in specialized shops and enlightened delicatessens.

The soup is slightly complicated, yet much less so than the traditional Italian New Year's soup, *cappelletti in brodo*. *Cappelletti* are small pasta shapes, and they take hours to make even if you are an experienced pasta maker. The soup I suggest is ideal, one beautiful large *ravioli* floating in a bowl of clear broth. The making of these large ravioli is a little tricky, but if you practise two or three times beforehand you should be able to come up trumps on the day. This is the only difficult dish in this menu.

Zampone is the traditional festive dish in northern Italy. It consists of pure pork mince, flavoured with nutmeg, cinnamon and cloves, pushed into a boned pig's trotter. The ingenuity of its casing arose from the exigencies of the people of Modena during the siege of that city by the papal army in 1511. There was plenty of minced pork but, until someone thought of the trotter, no way of making a sausage. Outside Italy *zamponi*, like *cotechini*, are produced industrially and sold pre-cooked, so that they need only to be heated. They are not as utterly delicious as the farm-produced *zamponi* you can buy in Italy, but they are an excellent product which I do recommend.

The accompanying zabaglione is the traditional sauce with which *zampone* is served in Modena. It may strike you as odd, but I have found that even the most inveterate English palate has succumbed to its charm. The heady alcoholic sweetness of the zabaglione cuts through the richness of the *zampone*. At a New Year's Eve supper *zampone* is always accompanied by lentils, which are considered an augury of future prosperity, each lentil representing a gold coin, or at least the wish for one. I would also serve a dish of buttery spinach, another traditional accompaniment to *zampone*. You will need two *zamponi* for ten people. To cook *zampone* in a zabaglione sauce, follow the instructions for the *cotechino* on page 267.

One of the two sweets in the menu is fresh and refreshing, the other is rich and luscious. I make the *bombe* with the broken marrons glacés that can be bought in Italy. They are sold in tubs by the large manufacturers at a quarter of the price of the perfect ones. Still, even if you are not planning a trip to Italy for the purpose of making this saving, I am sure the excellence of this pudding will justify the cost of its ingredients. It is a sumptuous pudding, particularly suitable for a New Year's meal, when no expense should be spared.

✳✳✳   *Il gran raviolo*

ONE EGG RAVIOLI IN CLEAR BROTH

---

350 g/¾ lb cooked spinach or
  frozen leaf spinach, thawed
90 g/3 oz unsalted butter
300 g/10 oz fresh ricotta
100 g/3½ oz freshly grated
  Parmesan
½ nutmeg, grated
salt and freshly ground black
  pepper

10 small eggs
2.5 litres/4½ pints Italian broth
  (see page 378)
pasta dough made with 5 eggs and
  500 g/1 lb 2 oz white flour and
  1 tsp olive oil

Squeeze all the liquid out of the spinach with your hands and chop it finely.

Melt the butter in a sauté or frying pan and add the spinach. Turn it over and over until it has absorbed all the butter, and cook for about 5 minutes. Transfer to a bowl and add the ricotta, 8 tablespoons of Parmesan, the nutmeg, and salt and pepper to taste. Mix very thoroughly with your hands. Taste and check seasoning.

Now make the pasta dough following the instructions on page 374. Roll it out thinly. If you are using the machine, you must roll out as wide a sheet as the machine can take. Roll out to the last but one notch. If you are rolling out by hand and you are not an experienced pasta-maker, you should divide the dough into five balls and roll out one ball at a time, while keeping the rest of the dough wrapped in a clean cloth.

Cut the rolled-out dough into 10 cm/4 in rounds using a saucer or a tartlet tin. Fill each ravioli before you proceed to roll out more dough, or the dough will dry out and you will not be able to seal the ravioli. Place about 2 tablespoons of the spinach and ricotta mixture on every other round. Shape the mixture into a ring, leaving 1½ cm/⅔ in clean edge all round, and room for the egg yolk in the middle. Break one egg and very carefully discard or reserve the white. Tip the yolk gently, and without breaking it, into the clear centre of the ring of spinach mixture. Using a pastry brush, moisten the edges of the round with cold water. Place one of the unfilled rounds on top, make sure that no air is trapped inside, and seal the edges tightly together.

Roll out more dough, fill it as before, and continue until you have prepared all 10 large ravioli.

Divide the broth between two large sauté pans and bring to the boil. Using a fish slice, transfer as many ravioli as you can into the pans without them overlapping. Cook for 5 minutes after the broth has come back to the boil. Keep the broth simmering rather than boiling fast, or the ravioli may break. The difficulty of this dish is to have the pasta properly cooked while keeping the egg yolks soft and runny.

Lift each ravioli out of the broth very carefully and place in a heated soup dish. Cover with a little of the broth and keep warm while you finish cooking all the ravioli. Top up each bowl with the remaining broth and serve with the remaining Parmesan handed round in a bowl.

PREPARATION
Try to prepare the ravioli as late as you possibly can, or the pasta will dry too much and take longer to cook. The egg yolks inside will then be overcooked. The ravioli must not be made more than 1 hour in advance. They must be cooked at the last moment.

*   *Bomba di panna e marrons glacés*

CREAM AND MARRONS GLACÉS *BOMBE*

---

300 g/10 oz marrons glacés
5 tbsp dark rum
90 g/3 oz best bitter chocolate

700 ml/1¼ pint whipping cream
6 tbsp icing sugar, sieved
3 egg whites

Cut the marrons glacés into small pieces and put them in a bowl. Add the rum and leave to macerate for half an hour or so.

Meanwhile cut the chocolate into small bits. I find it best to do this by hand with a broad-bladed knife, as a food processor tends to reduce part of the chocolate to powder.

Whip the cream, mix in the icing sugar, the marrons glacés with the rum and the chocolate pieces.

Whisk the egg whites until stiff and fold into the mixture.

Spoon the lovely mixture into a 1½ litre/2½ pint *bombe* mould, or any other dome-shaped container of that capacity. Cover with the lid or with foil and put in the freezer for at least 6 hours. Remove from the freezer half an hour before serving.

PREPARATION

The *bombe* can be made and frozen up to 1 week in advance, although it gradually loses flavour. Ideally it should be made up to 1 day before it is eaten.

AN EASTER LUNCH FOR 8

Salame e uova sode
SALAME AND HARD-BOILED EGGS

La torta pasqualina
EASTER PIE

Cosciotto di agnello arrosto con le cipolline
ROAST LEG OF LAMB WITH SMALL ONIONS

Insalata bianca e verde
LAMB'S LETTUCE, ROCKET AND FENNEL SALAD (page 150)

Colomba pasquale
EASTER CAKE

My Easter lunch borrows recipes from many different regions. The antipasto, however, is the traditional Easter antipasto served in most regions, matching the new season's salami with the ancient tradition of eating eggs on Easter Sunday. In the past, eggs were eaten in large quantities on that day because, as a result of abstinence during Lent, everyone had a surplus of eggs. There were plenty to eat, and plenty more to give to friends who did not keep hens. Chocolate, porcelain, wooden or even Fabergé Easter eggs are all an embellishment of something that was once a necessity.

For eight people you need 450 g/1 lb of different salami – Milano, Napoli and Varzi – and eight hard-boiled eggs, which must be shelled and cut in half lengthwise.

The *torta pasqualina* is the Genoese Easter dish, just as lamb is that of the Romans. The traditional cooking of Liguria is based largely on vegetables. Meat used to be very scarce and appeared only in the shape of a hen or, more often, a rabbit, neither of them festive food in Italy. The Ligurian women created the most superb dishes from the most easily available ingredients, in this case Swiss chard, which by Easter time was just ready to be cut. There are two versions of the *torta pasqualina*, one, more modern and mundane, filled with Ligurian artichokes, the other, the original, filled with Swiss chard and a curd cheese called *quagliata*.

The pastry is made with flour, oil and water, a similar mixture to that used for fila pastry. This kind of pastry without any eggs, and the way it is stretched, is a speciality of Liguria, and one is bound to wonder whether the Genoese sailors did not bring back the know-how from their journey to the eastern Mediterranean, where they must have encountered fila pastry. When I discussed this with Claudia Roden we became aware of the similarity not only in the ingredients of the two pastries but also in the actual operation of stretching the dough.

Years ago I was shown how to make *torta pasqualina* in a friend's villa in Santa Margherita, in Liguria. Albina, the cook, showed me how to stretch the dough by first rolling it with the long Italian rolling-pin, then stretching it first with one hand and then with the other. The whole operation was performed with such grace and dexterity that it reminded me of a ritual Arab dance. In Savona, on the western Riviera, they make thirty-three layers of pastry, one for each year of Christ's life, but Albina made only twenty layers, as they do in Genoa. Having been fascinated by the demonstration, I decided that I would take the easy way out and use fila pastry! My recipe here is based on the one in the classic book of Ligurian cooking, *La Cuciniera Genovese* by Giobatta and Giovanni Ratto, which has been in print since the last century.

Just as eggs are historically connected with Easter, so is lamb. Originally symbolic of Jewish rites, lamb later became symbolic of the Christian Eucharist. Lamb in Italy is very young at Easter time and is often cooked whole on the spit and served with an olive sprig stuck in the middle. English lambs are bigger, and a leg is usually ample for eight people.

I have chosen this recipe from a lovely old book that I found in my mother's bookcase. I have to confess that the book is no longer there, having mysteriously transferred itself to my collection. The book, published in 1863, is called *Il Cuoco Milanese* (*The Milanese Cook*) and its subtitle says it is 'An indispensable cooking manual for families of every class'. Perhaps 'indispensable' is an overstatement, but the book is full of good recipes. The lamb should be cooked for 3 hours according to the recipe, but we are now used to meat that tends to be on the undercooked side, so I cut the time to 2 hours. This will give you a cooked roast, not a pink one, which is better for this kind of slow roasting with wine and onions. You can always shorten the timing if you like your lamb pink. The meat juices are sharpened by the juices of the lemon and oranges. Choose oranges that are not too sweet, such as the late varieties from Calabria or from Valencia or, if still around, the delicious Tarocco from Sicily.

With the lamb I would serve a bowl of buttery new potatoes. Lamb's lettuce is the traditional Easter salad in Italy, but here it is so outrageously expensive that you might like to mix it with something else, as I do in my lamb's lettuce, rocket and fennel salad on page 150, and serve it after the meat.

Colomba is a traditional cake from Lombardy, made in the shape of a dove – *colomba* in Italian. It has a light dough similar to *panettone*, but without any sultanas or candied fruit. It is covered with sugar crystals and almonds. Its origins, variously claimed by Milan and Pavia, are legendary, as are those of many old Lombard dishes. The Milanese legend is based on the appearance of two doves over the war chariot of the Lombard League in 1176 during the battle of Legnano against the German Emperor, Frederick Barbarossa. The Lombards won, and since then the dove has been a memento of this victory.

The Pavia legend concerns a young girl who baked such a delicious cake in the shape of a dove for the Longobard Alboin that he spared her – and only her – from abduction among the twelve virgins he demanded when he conquered Pavia in 572. Alboin was one of the most cruel kings, as all Italian children know from a poem by Carducci. He ordered his wife, Rosamunda, to drink wine from her dead father's skull.

> 'Bevi Rosmunda
> Tu lo baciasti prima ch'ei mora,
> bacialo ancora.'

('Drink Rosamunda, you kissed him before he died, kiss him once more.') Not a nice king at all. However, the virgin baker evaded his rapacity, and all thanks to her delicious *colomba*.

Whichever story you believe, *colomba* is a soft, sweet bread, or cake, which for me has one of the most nostalgic aromas. When we used to spend Easter at our flat in Venice, we would go and buy our *colomba* after Mass on Easter Sunday from a bakery near the Campo San Barnaba. The whole of the Dorsoduro was pervaded by its vanilla scent.

Italians do not make this type of traditional food at home because buying it is part of the tradition. On Easter Sunday everybody goes to Mass in their best clothes, and then to the *pasticceria* to buy a delicious *colomba* and have an *aperitivo* with their friends. If you feel that you should redeem your soul, and slave in the kitchen, I suggest you make the irresistible but easy to prepare *cassata siciliana* on page 33, which is the Easter sweet in Sicily, and leave the *colomba* to the experts.

***   La torta pasqualina

EASTER PIE

1.8 kg/4 lb Swiss chard	*450 g/1 lb fresh ricotta*
salt and freshly ground black	*350–400 g/12–14 oz frozen fila*
pepper	*pastry, thawed*
120 ml/4 fl oz olive oil	*60 g/2 oz freshly grated Parmesan*
2 garlic cloves, peeled and bruised	*60 g/2 oz unsalted butter*
3 tbsp chopped marjoram	*6 eggs*

Strip off the green part of the leaves of the chard. Cut the stalks into thin strips. Wash and turn them into a pan half full of boiling salted water.

Cut the green part of the leaves into thin strips and wash them. Add to the pan 5 minutes after the stalks. Cook until both the stalks and the leaves are tender. Drain thoroughly, and as soon as it is cool enough, squeeze out all the liquid with your hands.

Pour 2 tablespoons of the oil, the garlic and the marjoram into a frying pan. When the aroma of the garlic rises, remove and discard it. Add the chard and sauté for 5 minutes, stirring frequently. Season with lots of pepper and leave to cool.

Heat the oven to 180°C/350°F/Gas 4.

Tip the ricotta into a bowl and break it all up with a fork into thick crumbs.

Grease a 25 cm/10 in spring-form tin with a little of the oil. Fit 10 sheets of fila pastry, one on top of the other, so that the edges fold over the sides of the tin. Brush each sheet with some of the oil. Keep the rest of the pastry covered while you put the sheets in place, because fila pastry dries up and cracks very quickly. Spread with the chard, the crumbled ricotta, half the Parmesan and a generous amount of pepper.

Form five hollows around the edge and one in the centre of the filling. Place a knob of butter in each hollow and then break an egg into the hollow, taking care that the yolk remains whole. Sprinkle with the remaining Parmesan and cover with 10 sheets of fila, cutting them so that they fit neatly into the tin, and brushing each sheet with oil. Turn the overhanging fila over the top and roll it over to form a ridge round the edge. Brush generously with oil and place the tin in the oven.

Bake for half an hour and then turn the heat up to 200°C/400°F/ Gas 6 and bake for a further 20 minutes to crisp the top.

Let the *torta* cool in the tin, then remove the band and transfer the *torta* and the bottom of the tin to a serving platter.

PREPARATION

Torta pasqualina can be baked up to 1 day in advance and reheated in a low oven for long enough to crisp up the pastry. It is eaten warm or at room temperature.

✳✳ *Cosciotto di agnello arrosto con le cipolline*

ROAST LEG OF LAMB WITH SMALL ONIONS

---

30 g/1 oz pancetta *or unsmoked*
   streaky bacon
3 garlic cloves
2.25–2.7 kg/5–6 lb leg of lamb
300 ml/½ pint good, but light,
   Italian red wine

450 g/1 lb small white onions
1 tsp sugar
the juice of 1 lemon
the juice of 2 oranges
salt and pepper
30 g/1 oz unsalted butter

For the marinade

7.5 ml/½ tbsp coarse salt
4 tbsp olive oil
fresh herbs, for example 1 sprig of
   parsley, a few celery leaves,

1 sprig of rosemary, 2 or 3 sage
   leaves, 2 sprigs of thyme,
   1 sprig of marjoram
6 peppercorns, bruised

Chop the *pancetta* and the garlic. Make a few deep slits in the lamb along the grain of the meat and push little pellets of the mixture into the slits.

Rub the lamb with salt, place it in a roasting tin and pour over the olive oil. Add the herbs and peppercorns and leave to marinate for 24 hours. The dish should be kept in a cold place, but not in the refrigerator. Unless the weather is hot and sultry you can keep it, covered, in the kitchen.

Heat the oven to 180°C/350°F/Gas 4.

Pour the wine over the lamb and place in the oven. Baste the meat every 30 minutes or so.

Put the onions in a pan, cover with cold water and bring to the boil, then drain them. This will make them easier to peel and help spare your tears. Remove the outside skin and any dangling roots, but do not remove any layer of onion or cut into the root: this is what keeps them whole during the cooking.

About 1 hour after you put the lamb in the oven, add the onions. Put the tin back in the oven and continue cooking until the meat is to your liking. A joint of this size will need about 2 hours, because when cooked in this way the lamb should be well cooked, not pink.

Remove the leg from the tin and set aside to rest while you prepare the sauce. Any large joint should be left to rest for at least 10 minutes before carving, for the juices to penetrate the meat.

Lift out the onions with a slotted spoon and put them into a small heated dish or bowl.

Strain the cooking juices into a clean saucepan. Skim off as much fat as you possibly can – a boring job, but quite necessary for a delicate gravy. Heat the cooking juices and add the sugar and the juice of the lemon and the oranges. Taste and adjust seasonings. When the sauce is simmering, add the butter in little pieces and let it dissolve, while swirling the pan. Transfer to a heated sauce-boat.

Now you are ready to carve the joint at the table and hand around the onions, the sauce and the other vegetables.

PREPARATION

No roast can be successfully reheated.

A ST VALENTINE'S SUPPER FOR 2

Prosciutto e melone

Animelle al Marsala coi pisellini
SWEETBREADS GLAZED IN MARSALA WITH GARDEN PEAS

Crema di frutti della passione
PASSION FRUIT FOOL

The most important thing about the preparation of a tête-à-tête supper is that whatever has to be done at the last minute should take as little time as possible. You certainly do not want to disappear into the kitchen for half an hour, leaving your heart-throb all alone. Nor, at this stage of the relationship, do you want to have him/her to help in the kitchen.

The *primo* is the simplest and most delicious Italian *primo* there is, as long as the prosciutto and the melon are good. If you can, buy *prosciutto di Parma* or *di San Daniele* from a retailer who will slice it for you, instead of buying already sliced and vacuum-packed prosciutto. 225 g/½ lb of prosciutto is ample for two people.

Nowadays it is easy to buy melons all the year round. The difficulty is telling whether the melon is good before you buy it. Although weight, aroma, and softness at the bottom end are all supposed to be signs of a good melon, they are not always reliable. When I serve this dish I like to remove the melon rind completely and place the slices on a dish surrounding the prosciutto.

I chose sweetbreads for a *secondo* because they are a most delicious and delicate luxury. Another reason was that they have the prettiest name of any food, both in English and Italian. *Animelle*, a delightful-sounding word, means little souls. For this recipe I prefer to use lamb's sweetbreads, which are easier to buy than calf's sweetbreads. Even the frozen New Zealand ones are quite good. Sweetbreads are the thymus gland of a young animal, which shrivels up in adulthood. Because they are so delicate they are best cooked very simply, as in this recipe. The sweetbreads, sautéed in butter, are then cooked in Marsala until they become glazed and succulent. The cooking is quick, about 10 minutes; the preparation is tiresome, but it can be done well in advance.

A bowl of tagliatelle tossed in butter is an unorthodox accompaniment by Italian standards. But I have no hesitation in recommending it because the two ingredients are a perfect match. The traditional accompaniment to sweetbreads are peas or mangetout, and I would follow tradition and serve them gently stewed in stock with a knob of butter.

The pudding is as easy as it is irresistible, with the elusive orange-blossom flavour of passion fruits. Passion fruits are at their best when they begin to shrivel up. If they are still smooth when you buy them, keep them on the window-sill until ready, but do not forget them or they will shrivel up too much.

**

Animelle al Marsala

SWEETBREADS GLAZED WITH MARSALA

225 g/½ lb lamb sweetbreads	*2 tbsp white flour*
2 tsp lemon juice or wine vinegar	*salt*
45 g/1½ oz unsalted butter	*6 tbsp Marsala or sweet sherry*
3 fresh sage leaves	*freshly ground black pepper*

Place the sweetbreads in a bowl and cover with cold water. Leave to soak for at least 1 hour, to purge them of their blood. Drain and rinse them. Put them in a saucepan, add water to cover and add the lemon juice or vinegar. Bring to the boil and simmer gently for 2–3 minutes, until the sweetbreads have become white and firm. Drain them and rinse under cold water.

As soon as they are cool enough to handle, remove any tubes or bits of hardened blood. Put them between two plates with a weight on top and leave for at least 3 hours, or overnight, in the refrigerator. When it is time to cook them, divide them into nuggets and dry thoroughly with kitchen paper.

Heat the butter with the sage in a sauté pan in which the sweetbreads will fit in a single layer.

Put the flour and ½ a teaspoon of salt in a plastic bag, add the sweetbreads and shake the bag to coat them with the flour. Turn the bag upside down over a sieve and shake the sieve to remove excess flour. When the butter foam is beginning to subside, throw in the floured nuggets and sauté quickly until brown. Splash with the Marsala and continue cooking for 6–7 minutes until they are dark and glazed. Season with salt and pepper. Taste and check the juices for seasoning; they should be rich and syrupy.

If you are serving the sweetbreads with tagliatelle, place a ring of buttered pasta on a heated serving dish or on two heated plates and spoon the sweetbreads and all their delicious juices in the centre.

PREPARATION

The sweetbreads can be blanched and placed under a weight up to 1 day in advance, and refrigerated. If you like, cook them up to half an hour in advance and keep them warm in a covered pan placed over a bowl of very hot, but not boiling, water.

* *Crema di frutti della passione*

PASSION FRUIT FOOL

6 passion fruits	*3 tbsp icing sugar, sifted*
1 tbsp sweet sherry	*1 egg white*
150 ml/¼ pint double cream	

Cut the passion fruits in half and scoop out the inside into a bowl. Add the sherry and set aside for at least 1 hour.

Whip the cream until stiff and fold in the sifted icing sugar. Whisk the egg white and fold 3 tablespoons into the whipped cream. Combine the passion fruits with the cream mixture, cover with clingfilm and refrigerate for at least 1 hour.

Place two long-stemmed glasses in the fridge. Before serving, give the cream mixture a quick whip and spoon into the chilled glasses.

PREPARATION

The passion fruits can be prepared up to 1 day in advance and refrigerated in a covered bowl. The whole dessert can be made up to 2 hours in advance.

A BIRTHDAY DINNER FOR 6

Risotto allo spumante
RISOTTO WITH CHAMPAGNE

Faraona allo spumante
GUINEA-FOWL COOKED IN CHAMPAGNE

Sorbetto allo spumante
CHAMPAGNE SORBET

Asking around among friends, I have found that most men prefer small dinner parties. The reason they give is that with six people there is likely to be a single conversation round the table in which everyone takes part. My husband shares this preference, so for his birthday, after making more elaborate plans, I usually finish by asking only four friends.

Perhaps, then, this menu shows signs of sex discrimination, since women usually prefer larger parties. But the other reason why I designed the birthday menu for only six people is gastronomic rather than social, namely that this delicious and festive risotto, like any other, is easier to make in not too large a quantity.

The three recipes are simple ones in which, to match the occasion, champagne replaces wine. However, as well as adding a festive element, champagne gives a pleasantly tingly taste that you cannot achieve with a still wine. A sparkling white wine, such as Prosecco, would give the same result, so you do not need to open your best vintage champagne.

My experience is that the only good guinea-fowl are the French ones. Perhaps this situation will have changed by the time you read this, but whatever guinea-fowl you buy, be sure of your supplier and do not buy frozen birds. The baked tomatoes on page 372 and/or the potato and carrot timbales on page 272 are suitable vegetables.

With regard to the sorbet, I should point out that a sorbet made with wine does not freeze hard, and melts quickly. For this reason, put the glasses or bowls in the freezer before filling them with the sorbet. After you have filled them put them straight back in the freezer and leave them there until you want to bring them to the table. If raspberries are not in the shops, use other fruit, cut up into very small cubes. During the winter I choose juicy pears or seedless grapes. In desperation I have also used the ubiquitous but attractive kiwi. The almond crescents on page 380 are especially good with this sorbet.

** *Risotto allo spumante*
RISOTTO WITH CHAMPAGNE

60 g/2 oz unsalted butter	champagne, spumante or
1 tbsp olive oil	sparkling wine
3 shallots, cut in half	450 g/1 lb arborio, or other Italian
salt	risotto rice
1.5 litres/2½ pints Italian broth	4 tbsp freshly grated Parmesan
(see page 378)	pepper, preferably white
300 ml/½ pint non-vintage	

The ideal saucepan for risotto is large and wide with a heavy round bottom. Choose the nearest you have to this ideal and put in it 45 g/1½ oz of the butter, the oil and the shallots. Add a little salt and sauté the shallots until gold all round. Lift them out with a slotted spoon and discard. Because the flavour of this risotto should be dominated by the champagne, the onion flavour has to be minimal.

Meanwhile heat the broth to simmering point. Heat the champagne for 5 minutes in a separate saucepan. Add the rice to the melted butter and sauté for 1 minute, stirring several times to coat the grains in the butter. Splash with half the champagne and let it bubble away. Add a ladleful of the simmering broth. Keep the broth over the lowest possible heat, with the lid on to prevent evaporation.

Continue cooking the rice while adding the simmering broth by the ladleful whenever the rice begins to become dry. Stir very frequently to prevent the rice sticking to the bottom and sides of the pan. Good Italian rice takes about 20 minutes to cook from the moment the first ladleful of broth is added. When the rice is cooked – it should be firm but tender – stir in the remaining champagne, previously heated for a couple of minutes.

Draw the saucepan from the heat and add the remaining butter, the Parmesan and some pepper, which should be white so as not to spoil the appearance of this ivory-coloured risotto. Transfer to a dish and serve at once.

PREPARATION

Risotto should be prepared just before serving. If this is difficult, prepare the risotto no longer than 1 hour in advance, as far as the stage where you add the first ladleful of broth. Add 2 ladlefuls of simmering broth instead of 1, stir very well, cover the pan tightly and turn off the heat. When you return to the dish you will find that the rice has absorbed all the broth and is half cooked. Reheat the rice and the broth and proceed to cook the rice as instructed above.

** *Faraona allo spumante*

GUINEA-FOWL COOKED IN CHAMPAGNE

90 g/3 oz unsalted butter	6 tbsp vegetable oil
4 shallots, very finely chopped	9 tbsp flour
salt and pepper	450 ml/¾ pint champagne
2 guinea-fowl	120 ml/4 fl oz double cream

Heat the butter and the shallot in a heavy sauté pan or oval casserole that will be large enough to accommodate loosely all the pieces of guinea-fowl. Add a pinch of salt and sauté until the shallot is soft. Set aside.

Cut each guinea-fowl into eight pieces: two wings, two drumsticks, two thighs and two pieces from each breast. Cut off the pinions and keep them with the backs to be used for stock on another occasion. Remove any feathers and wipe the joints all over with kitchen paper.

Put the vegetable oil in a frying pan and turn the heat to medium high. Spread the flour on a board and lightly dredge the guinea-fowl pieces in the flour. Shake off excess flour and, when the oil is hot but not smoking, slip as many pieces as will fit loosely into the pan. Fry until a fine gold crust has formed and then turn the pieces over and fry the underside. When the pieces are done on all sides, transfer them to the pan or casserole containing the shallot. Season with salt and pepper and fry another batch, if necessary.

When all the pieces are done, place the pan or casserole over a medium heat. Turn the pieces over once and after about 2 minutes pour over the champagne very slowly. Bring to the boil, turn the heat down to very low and cover the pan. Cook for about 40 minutes, turning the guinea-fowl pieces over every now and then. When the thighs feel tender when pricked with a fork, transfer all the pieces to a heated serving dish and cover with foil to keep warm in a warm oven.

Turn the heat up and deglaze the pan with a couple of tablespoons of hot water. Scrape the bottom of the pan with a metal spoon to release any bits, while reducing the cooking juices by a third. Turn the heat down to low and stir in the cream. Mix thoroughly, taste and adjust seasoning. Bring slowly to the boil. When the cream has thinned down, the sauce is ready. Spoon a little of the sauce over the birds and pour the rest into a heated sauce-boat to hand round separately.

PREPARATION

The birds can be cooked up to 3 days in advance and refrigerated. Reheat very slowly and make the sauce just before serving.

Sorbetto allo spumante

*
with an
ice-cream
machine

***
without

CHAMPAGNE SORBET

---

250 g/9 oz caster sugar	non-vintage champagne
1 orange	225 g/½ lb raspberries
600 ml/1 pint spumante or	

Reserve 4 tablespoons of the sugar and put the rest in a heavy saucepan. Wash the orange thoroughly under running water to remove any pesticide or wax. Cut the peel from half the orange, using a swivel-action potato peeler, being careful to leave the bitter white pith on the orange. Add to the pan with the sugar, together with 250 ml/9 fl oz of water. Heat gently at first until the sugar has completely dissolved, then turn the heat up and boil for 5 minutes. Set aside to cool.

Squeeze the orange. When the syrup is cold, add the juice through a fine strainer.

Remove and discard the orange peel. Put the syrup and the bottle of champagne in the refrigerator until you want to make the sorbet.

Start the ice-cream machine. Pour the syrup and the champagne into the machine and churn until the mixture has frozen to a firm consistency. Scrape the sorbet into a bowl, cover with clingfilm and place in the freezer until you want to serve it. If you do not have an ice-cream machine, set the freezer to the lowest temperature. Put the mixture in a bowl (metal is better because it conducts the cold faster) and freeze until the edges are icy. Whisk until smooth and return to the freezer. Keep whisking at 2-hourly intervals until the mixture is smooth. If you use a food processor for re-whisking, let the mixture freeze hard and then break it down into chunks and process until smooth.

A couple of hours before serving, divide the raspberries between six long-stemmed glasses and sprinkle with the reserved sugar. Place the glasses in the refrigerator. Spoon the sorbet into the glasses just before serving.

PREPARATION

The sorbet must be made up to 6 hours in advance, but no more than 4 days ahead or the flavour will vanish.

AN ALFRESCO LUNCH FOR 10

Schegge di pecorino e Parmigiano con le olive verdi
WEDGES OF PECORINO AND PARMESAN WITH GREEN OLIVES

Spaghettini eccitanti
THIN SPAGHETTI IN A PIQUANT TOMATO SAUCE

Tre frittate
THREE ITALIAN OMELETTES

Verdure alla griglia
GRILLED VEGETABLES

Frutta di stagione
SEASONAL FRUIT

T he English can't bear to be shut indoors when the sun comes out in the summer. There is always the feeling that it might be the last sunny day of the year. They are right to enjoy the sun because an English summer's day in the country, or in a garden, allows you to enjoy the most perfect weather I know: not too hot or too bright, with a gentle breeze that carries the soft scents of nature. So the table is laid outside, and the meal is geared towards simplicity and rusticity, which is where an Italian menu such as this one fits the bill perfectly.

I thought the occasion called for cheeses with green olives to be served with the pre-prandial wine, something that is often done in Italy. Then to the table for the 'titillating spaghetti'. This is a recipe I had from a friend who prepared the dish for us when we arrived at her house in Lerici. The view from Grazia's house is breathtaking. It dominates the cosy little harbour littered with small boats to the west, while to the east it is dominated by the great expanse of the sea. In that balmy Mediterranean night the spaghetti seemed superb, although afterwards I was afraid that perhaps the secret of its success was the setting in which I had eaten it. But when, after a year, I decided to give it a try, I found to my delight that it was an excellent dish anywhere. However, it must be made with good olive oil and plain olives kept in brine, with no flavouring.

Sun-dried tomatoes have been used in southern Italy for centuries. What is new is that they have been taken up by fashionable people and restaurants in northern Italy, and then in England and America, and launched as a discovery. Sun-dried tomatoes are plum tomatoes, cut in half and dried on wooden slats in the sun. You see them outside every house in the south, under nets to protect them from the flies. The liquid evaporates slowly in the heat, leaving a dried fruit with a concentrated, sweet flavour. They are used here in the spaghetti sauce, but they most commonly appear as a dish in an antipasto, dressed with olive oil and a little garlic.

For *secondo* I suggest you bring to the table the cold *frittate*. A *frittata* is an Italian omelette, and is more like a thin Spanish *tortilla* or a Middle Eastern *eggah* than an omelette. It can be plain, dressed with Parmesan, or mixed with a variety of ingredients, of which the three in this menu are examples. I find the *frittata* with tuna and peppers most appealing visually, and also gastronomically provided it is made only with the best real tuna, tinned and packed in olive oil, rather than the cheap brands of skipjack tuna. When I was first given the recipe for this *frittata* by a great friend and a good cook, I was reminded of the mouth-watering description of such an omelette written by Brillat-Savarin in his *The Philosopher in the Kitchen*. The omelette was given to Madame Récamier by a *curé* she was visiting on a day of abstinence. He must have been delighted when the lovely Madame Récamier said, 'I have never seen such an appetizing omelette on our worldly tables.' I hope your *frittata* will arouse such a comment. Other good *frittate* are made with sautéed fennel, mushrooms and even cooked spaghetti. As you can see, *frittate* offer a great many ways of recycling left-overs.

For vegetables, try the grilled mixture; they are particularly delicious when grilled on a barbecue. A second suitable accompaniment is the tomato, cucumber and pepper salad on page 129.

Informality and rusticity being the theme of the party, a bowl of seasonal fruit is highly appropriate for the finale.

Schegge di pecorino e Parmigiano con le olive verdi

WEDGES OF PECORINO AND PARMESAN WITH GREEN OLIVES

This is not so much a recipe as an idea.

---

450 g/1 lb soft pecorino	*grana padano*
450 g/1 lb Parmesan, preferably	*450 g/1 lb green olives*

Buy the cheeses from a reliable shop which has a good turnover, and ask to taste them to make sure they are good. For eating, as opposed to cooking, I prefer a pecorino and Parmesan that are young and less strong. I would choose a young Tuscan or Sardinian pecorino and a *grana padano*, a similar cheese to Parmigiano-Reggiano, which is better for grating and cooking.

Cut the cheeses into large chunks and serve them with the green olives.

---

* # Spaghettini eccitanti

THIN SPAGHETTI IN A PIQUANT TOMATO SAUCE

The dish is equally good hot or cold.

---

250 g/½ lb sun-dried tomatoes	*10 garlic cloves, bruised*
250 ml/9 fl oz red wine vinegar	*a dozen basil leaves*
250 ml/9 fl oz extra virgin olive oil	*150 g/5 oz black olives in brine*
4 or 5 dried chillies, according to	*800 g/1¾ lb* spaghettini
taste, seeded and crumbled	*salt*

Put the sun-dried tomatoes in a bowl. Heat the vinegar with the same quantity of water and when just boiling pour it over the tomatoes. Leave to soak for 2–3 hours.

Drain the tomatoes, lay them on a wooden board and dry each one thoroughly. Cut them into thin strips and put them in a bowl large enough to hold the *spaghettini* later. Alternatively, use two bowls, dividing all the ingredients between them. Add the oil, chillies, garlic and basil. Stone the olives, cut into strips and add to the bowl.

Cook the spaghettini in plenty of salted water. If you are serving it cold, drain it when it is even more *al dente* than you would like for eating it hot. Overcooked cold pasta is really unpleasant. Turn the pasta into the bowl or bowls and toss very thoroughly, lifting the strands up high so as to separate them. Leave to infuse for 2 hours or so, then fish out the garlic and discard.

If you are serving the pasta hot, prepare the dressing 2 hours in advance for the flavours to blend, and cook and add the pasta just before serving.

PREPARATION

The tomatoes can be soaked and sliced up to 2 weeks in advance; they should be kept in a jar under olive oil. The olives, too, can be prepared in advance and kept under olive oil. You can use the preserving oil to dress the *spaghettini*.

** *Frittata di cipolle*

ONION *FRITTATA*

300 g/10 oz Spanish onions or white onions	4 tbsp freshly grated Parmesan cheese
2 tbsp olive oil	pepper
salt	30 g/1 oz unsalted butter
5 eggs	

Cut the onions into very thin slices and put them with the oil into a 20 cm/8 in non-stick frying pan. Add 1 teaspoon of salt to help the onion release its moisture and cook very slowly until the onion has wilted. Stir frequently and add a couple of tablespoons of hot water if necessary. The onion should turn a lovely golden colour, but not get brown. Set aside to cool.

Break the eggs into a bowl and beat them lightly until well blended. Scoop the onion out of the pan, leaving behind the oil, and mix gently but thoroughly into the eggs. Stir in the Parmesan, a generous grinding of pepper and a sprinkling more of salt.

Wipe the frying pan clean with kitchen paper, add the butter and heat it until foaming. Pour the egg mixture into the pan, stirring it with a fork while pouring so that the onion will not sink to the bottom. Do not stir the mixture further, just turn the heat down to very low and leave it for 15 minutes. By the end of this time the eggs will have set and only the top surface will be runny.

There are two ways to cook the top. The method that gives a better result is to turn the *frittata* over by first freeing the sides with a spatula and then turning it over on to a round dish or a lid. Slide the *frittata* back into the pan and brown the other side for no longer than 1 minute. The second method, which is easier but tends to harden the surface too much, is to pass the pan under the grill for 1 minute, just long enough to set the top. Transfer it to a dish or a wooden board lined with kitchen paper to absorb the extra fat.

Leave the *frittata* to cool and then cut into lozenges. To do that, cut it across in strips about 4 cm/1½ in wide and then cut across the other way.

✳✳ *Frittata di zucchine*
COURGETTE *FRITTATA*

---

350 g/¾ lb courgettes	*5 eggs*
salt	*pepper*
2 tbsp olive oil	*1 tbsp dried oregano*
2 garlic cloves, peeled and finely sliced	*6 tbsp freshly grated Parmesan*
2 tbsp chopped parsley	*30 g/1 oz unsalted butter*

Put the courgettes into a sink of cold water. Wash them thoroughly, dry them with kitchen paper and cut them into 1 cm/½ in cubes. If you have time, put the cubes in a colander, sprinkle with salt and leave for half an hour. This will release some liquid. Dry the courgettes and set aside.

Put the oil, garlic and parsley in a 20 cm/8 in non-stick frying pan. When the aroma of the garlic rises, remove it and add the courgettes. Cook until lightly browned, about 10–15 minutes, stirring frequently.

Meanwhile lightly beat the eggs in a bowl until the yolks and the whites are properly blended. Season with salt and pepper, oregano and Parmesan.

When the courgettes are done, lift them out with a slotted spoon and transfer them to the bowl with the eggs. Now follow the instructions in the previous recipe, onion *frittata*, from the third paragraph, 'Wipe the frying pan clean . . . ', to the end.

**   *Frittata di peperoni e tonno*

PEPPERS AND TUNA FISH *FRITTATA*

---

2 sweet peppers, preferably of	*a 200 g/7 oz tin of tuna, packed in*
different colours	*olive oil or natural brine*
1 Spanish onion, very thinly sliced	*12–15 sweet green olives, stoned*
4 tbsp olive oil	*and cut into narrow strips*
salt	*freshly ground black pepper*
5 eggs	

Wash and dry the peppers. Cut in half, remove the core, seeds and ribs and cut into thin, short strips.

Put 3 tablespoons of the oil in a pan, add the onion and the pepper and sprinkle with salt (this will help to release the liquid, and prevent the vegetables burning). Cover with a buttered paper and a tight-fitting lid. Leave to sweat until very soft – about 40 minutes. Keep a watch on the pan and add a couple of tablespoons of water whenever the vegetables are cooking dry.

Lightly beat the eggs and add the tuna, finely shredded, the olives and pepper to taste.

When the vegetable mixture is ready, leave it to cool a little and then add to the egg mixture, scooping it out of the pan with a slotted spoon. Leave the cooking juices in the pan. Mix everything together very thoroughly.

Put the rest of the oil in a 20 cm/8 in non-stick pan. When the oil is hot, add the egg and vegetable mixture. Turn the heat to very low and cook until the underneath is set but the top is still runny, about 15 minutes.

Now follow the instructions in the recipe for onion *frittata* (pages 330–31), from the fourth paragraph, 'There are two ways . . . ', to the end.

***   *Verdure alla griglia*

GRILLED VEGETABLES

---

2 aubergines	pepper
salt	225 g/½ lb large mushrooms
4 courgettes	4 peppers
150 ml/¼ pint extra virgin olive oil	

For the sauce

30 g/1 oz pine nuts	a small bunch of parsley
30 g/1 oz basil leaves	150 ml/¼ pint extra virgin olive oil
4 garlic cloves	salt and pepper

Wash and dry the aubergines. Cut them across into slices about 8 mm/⅓ in thick and put them in a colander. Sprinkle liberally with salt and leave them to sweat while you prepare the other vegetables.

Heat the grill and oil a grill pan or baking tray. To save time, fill the pan or tray with as many of the following vegetables as will fit, so that they cook together. You should follow the sequence given below, to allow for the different cooking times needed.

Wash and dry the courgettes, cut off the ends, and cut them lengthwise into 10 mm/½ in thick slices. If the slices are too long, cut them across in half. Put them in the grill pan, pour some drops of olive oil over them, sprinkle with salt and pepper and and grill them on both sides.

Rinse the aubergines and pat them dry. Put them in the pan as soon as there is room. Pour some olive oil over them and season only with pepper, since you have already salted them. The aubergines will take only 4–5 minutes on each side. They should be tender when pricked with a fork. Undercooked aubergines are unpleasant, but overcooked ones tend to acquire a bitter taste.

Wipe the mushrooms and detach the stems, which you can use for another dish. Grill the mushroom caps, moistened with olive oil and seasoned with salt and pepper. The mushrooms are the quickest to cook.

I prefer to char the peppers directly over a flame, turning them over and over so that all the skin is charred. As soon as they have cooled down, peel them by wiping them with kitchen paper. Do not wash them under running water, as that will wash away the tasty juices. Cut them in half, remove the core, seeds and ribs and cut them into wide strips.

Now you can arrange all the vegetables prettily either on a very large dish or, preferably, on two dishes, so that you can place one at each end of the table.

For the sauce, toast the pine nuts in a non-stick frying pan until just golden, shaking the pan very frequently. Put them in the food processor with the basil, garlic and parsley and process, pulsing until chopped very coarsely, while adding the oil through the beaker. Add salt and pepper and then check the seasoning. Spoon over the vegetables 1 hour or so before eating. If you do not have a food processor, pound the pine nuts, basil, garlic and parsley in a mortar moistened with 2 or 3 tablespoons of the oil. Add the oil while beating with a small wire whisk or with a fork.

PREPARATION
All the vegetables can be grilled up to 1 day in advance. Keep them, separated and covered, in the refrigerator. The sauce can be made up to 2 days in advance and chilled.

My Five Favourite Menus

These are the gastronomic equivalents of my Desert Island Discs. Like choosing eight records, narrowing it down to a choice of five menus meant concentrating singlemindedly on what I like best. That soon brought three favourites into sharp focus: fish, fruit and rich puddings.

My penchant for creamy puddings is just as Italian as that for fish and fruit. I am sure everyone who has lived in Italy must have noticed how rich Italian sweets can be. The reason is simple. We eat sweets only rarely, certainly no more than once a week, so that when we do we want the full treatment.

A vivid childhood memory is of the excitement every Sunday when my father brought home the *paste* – small cakes – for lunch. The thrill of unwrapping them was followed by transports of delight as my teeth sank into the chosen favourite.

There were voluptuous fat meringues, elegantly shaped *bignés* coated with different icings, dark shining *africani*, and *cannoli, cannoni e cannoncini* encircled by rings of pastry and oozing cream, chocolate or custard. There were also pretty fruit tartlets but, not deceived by their prettiness, I used to bag the richer *paste* before my brother Guido could get them. I still love *paste*, and I love to look at them in the smart pâtisseries of Turin and Milan.

My love of *paste* has now, perforce, been transferred to puddings; I very much enjoy a really good pudding at the end of a dinner party. Here are a few good recipes, some richer than others, but all simple enough to make.

A DINNER FOR 4

Soffiato di riso all'aragosta
SOUFFLÉ OF RICE AND LOBSTER

Petti di pollo farciti di carciofi
CHICKEN BREASTS STUFFED WITH ARTICHOKES

Pere alla crema del Lario
PEARS STEWED IN RED WINE WITH LIQUEUR-FLAVOURED
CREAM (page 17)

This menu is ideal for serving to friends for whom you'd like to cook something special, something they could otherwise only enjoy at a restaurant, and at a great price too. It is also a perfect dinner for a formal occasion.

The first course speaks for itself. It is not difficult to make since it is not a real soufflé; the rice and the lobster keep the mixture up, so that you don't have to worry about ending up with a *soufflé tombé*.

The chicken breasts are also quite straightforward; the only job you might have to practise is preparing the artichokes. But before you begin to prepare them you must know which ones to buy. I say this because all too often I see globe artichokes in British supermarkets and greengrocers that are so old, brown, dried up and wrinkled that I despair. Buy lovely green artichokes showing no brown patches. Ideally they should be tightly closed and have leaves attached to the stalk that are silvery-green and alive-looking. Don't buy artichokes that are so tightly wrapped in clingfilm that you can't see what they are like. If you cannot find fresh artichokes – the best months are February, March and April – don't attempt to make this dish. (Or go to Italy in February, as I do for Carnival week, and come back with a suitcase of artichokes, with or without thorns, large or small, purple, green or yellow, but all beautifully fresh!) Sautéed potatoes make a good accompaniment to this dish.

** **   *Soffiato di riso all'aragosta*

SOUFFLÉ OF RICE AND LOBSTER

---

1 cooked lobster	3 eggs, separated
200 g/7 oz long grain rice	2 tbsp chopped dill
salt	4 tbsp Parmesan cheese
45 g/1½ oz unsalted butter	pepper
100 ml/3½ oz double cream	1 tbsp dried breadcrumbs

Ask the fishmonger to split the cooked lobster in half. Remove all the meat from the lobster carapace, not forgetting the small claws. Do this over a bowl so as to collect the juices. Cut the lobster meat into small cubes.

Meanwhile cook the rice in boiling salted water. As soon as it is ready, drain and refresh under cold water. Put it back into the saucepan and add the butter, cream, egg yolks, dill and all but 1 tablespoon of the Parmesan. Mix thoroughly, then gently mix in the lobster and its juices. Taste and add salt and pepper.

Heat the oven to 200°C/400°F/Gas 6.

Butter a 2 litre/3½ pint soufflé dish generously and sprinkle with the remaining Parmesan mixed with the breadcrumbs.

Whisk the egg whites until stiff but not dry, and fold them gently into the rice mixture with a metal spoon. Spoon the mixture into the dish and bake for 25–30 minutes.

PREPARATION

You can prepare the lobster meat 1 day in advance and refrigerate it. The rice should not be cooked longer than 6–8 hours in advance and must not be refrigerated. As with potatoes, chilling alters its flavour. The dish can be assembled about half an hour before it goes into the oven.

∗∗∗   *Petti di pollo farciti di carciofi*
CHICKEN BREASTS STUFFED WITH ARTICHOKES

---

4 chicken breasts
juice of ½ a lemon
salt and pepper
flour

45 g/1½ oz unsalted butter
200 g/7 fl oz good chicken or meat
   stock

For the artichokes

2 globe artichokes, about 450 g/1 lb
1 lemon, cut in half
4 tbsp olive oil
salt and pepper

1 tbsp chopped fresh mint leaves
1 garlic clove, peeled and chopped
4 ripe tomatoes, blanched and
   skinned

Slice the chicken breasts lengthwise, on one side only, almost through to the other side, so that they open like a book. Put them on a dish, sprinkle with the lemon juice and season with salt and pepper. Leave to marinate for no longer than 1 hour, while you prepare the artichokes (see page 341).

Cut the prepared artichokes into quarters and remove the fuzzy choke and the prickly purplish leaves at the base. Slice the artichokes into thin wedges, so that one edge remains attached to the bottom. Put in a bowl of acidulated cold water.

Remove all the tough outside part of the stalks. Cut the tender inside, which is very good, into rounds. Add to the acidulated water as you cut them.

When everything is done, dry the artichokes thoroughly.

Put the oil and the artichoke wedges and rounds in a heavy sauté pan. Season with salt and pepper and brown gently for 3 minutes, turning them over frequently. Mix in the chopped mint and the garlic and sauté for a further couple of minutes.

Cut the tomatoes in half and squeeze out the seeds and the water. Chop the tomatoes coarsely and add to the pan. Add a couple of tablespoons of hot water and cook, with the lid tightly on, for about 30–40 minutes, adding more water whenever the artichokes begin to catch. At the end of the cooking the artichokes should feel quite tender all through when pricked with a fork, and there should be no liquid left in the pan except for the oily tomato sauce.

Dry the chicken breasts with kitchen paper and put them on a board or on your work surface. Lay a large spoonful of artichoke mixture on one half of each of the breasts. Fold each breast over and stitch it with one or two wooden cocktail sticks along its length, not across. Coat each breast very lightly in flour to which you have added half a teaspoon of salt.

Heat the butter in a large pan and when it is sizzling, but before it turns brown, add the chicken breasts and fry gently on each side. Meanwhile heat the stock in a small saucepan. When the chicken breasts are pale gold, pour over half the stock and continue cooking over low heat for 15 minutes, adding a table-spoon or two of hot stock if necessary. Taste and adjust season-ing.

Remove the cocktail sticks from the chicken breasts, transfer them to a heated dish and spoon over the cooking liquid.

PREPARATION

The dish can be prepared totally up to 1 day in advance and refrigerated. Add a little knob of butter when you reheat it. Alternatively the artichokes, which are the lengthy job, can be prepared and cooked up to 2 days in advance and refrigerated. They can also be frozen.

How to prepare artichokes

Before you start, rub your hands with ½ a lemon to protect them from the artichoke juice, which would otherwise make them black. Cut off the artichokes at the base and rub the cut parts with the lemon. Hold the artichoke in one hand and with the other break off the tough outer leaves. It is hard to say how many layers of these tough leaves must be discarded, since it depends on the age and quality of the artichoke. Next, snap off the green part of each leaf by bending it back with a sharp movement. This leaves the tender part attached to the bottom. Continue snapping off the tough tops until you get to the central cone of paler leaves.

With a very sharp knife cut off about 2½ cm/1 in straight across the top of the cone. What is left is nearly all edible, without the stringy parts that will remain uneatable however long you cook them. Every time you cut this edible part, rub immediately with the lemon and drop into a bowl of cold water to which you have added the juice of ½ a lemon.

A DINNER FOR 6

Ravioli di pesce
FISH *RAVIOLI*

Gamberi imperiali in salsa all'abruzzese
PRAWNS IN A PIQUANT TOMATO SAUCE

Insalata agra di barbabietola
BEETROOT, GRAPEFRUIT AND WATERCRESS SALAD

Gelato di albicocca
APRICOT ICE-CREAM

This is an elegant menu for fish-lovers, which opens grandly with *ravioli* filled with a mixture of white fish and ricotta plus a little cream to give it lightness.

Until twenty years ago *ravioli* were seldom other than *di grasso*, filled with meat, or *di magro*, filled with ricotta and spinach. With the advent of the *nuova cucina*, *nuovi ravioli* appeared everywhere, some more successful than others. *Ravioli di pesce* are to my mind the best of the newcomers, combining in a very Italian way three basic ingredients in the best tradition: pasta, fish and ricotta. The only catch is that they are none too quick to make. But *ravioli* never were everyday cooking. In my home in Milan *tortellini* and *ravioli* were made no more than three or four times a year: always at Christmas, for Sabato Grasso (the last Saturday in Carnival), and around November, when pumpkins were in season for the delicious *ravioli di zucca*, large ravioli filled with a purée of pumpkin, *mostarda di Cremona* and a touch of crumbled *amaretti*. And at home there was usually a cook to make them!

My *ravioli di pesce* are a perfect preamble to the second course, with its stronger note on the same theme, fish. In the last few years more and more fishmongers have been selling raw prawns. They are frozen tiger prawn tails from the East. If you are lucky you can sometimes find raw fresh prawns, usually with the head still on, called either gambas or king prawns. They are ideal for this recipe, an old one from Abruzzi. The fish flavour of the prawns is emphasized by a touch of anchovy purée, and enveloped in the classic Mediterranean ambience of tomato and garlic. To this is added chilli, the characteristic spice of Abruzzi cooking. The secret for success with this dish is that the prawns and the tomatoes should cook for a very short time, so that their original fresh flavour comes through intact.

You can serve some boiled long grain rice tossed with olive oil to mop up the sauce of the prawns. After that you need a salad, and for a change from the usual *insalata verde*, green salad, I suggest this beetroot, grapefruit and watercress salad which is cleansing, refreshing and fruity.

The first beetroots are just appearing in the shops when apricots are at their best. I have made the apricot ice-cream with raw apricots and with poached ones. I prefer the second method, because fruit bought in a country where it does not actually grow does not have enough flavour. The poaching in syrup and orange juice brings out the little flavour the fruit has. The *amaretto* liqueur is optional, but it does contribute a dark almondy flavour which goes well with the apricots.

Hand round a dish of almond crescents (page 380) if you wish. They are very good and they go well with the ice-cream.

***   # *Ravioli di pesce*

FISH RAVIOLI

Home-made pasta made with 200 g/7 oz unbleached white flour, 2 large eggs and 15 ml/ 1 tbsp olive oil

For the filling

60 g/2 oz unsalted butter
1 shallot, very finely chopped
300 g/10 oz white fish fillet, such as Dover sole, turbot, John Dory, sea bass or sea bream
1 tbsp anchovy purée

100 ml/3½ fl oz dry white wine
150 g/5 oz ricotta
4 tbsp double cream
3 tbsp freshly grated Parmesan
2 egg yolks
salt and pepper

For the sauce

90 g/3 oz unsalted butter
3 tbsp chives, very finely cut

freshly grated Parmesan

First prepare the filling. Heat the butter and the shallot and cook for 5 minutes, stirring and pressing the shallot against the side of the saucepan to release the flavour. Meanwhile clean, trim and cut the fish into very small pieces and add to the pan together with the anchovy purée. Cook until the fish becomes opaque – no longer than 2 minutes. Turn the heat up and splash with the wine, then boil rapidly until the wine has totally evaporated. Flake the fish coarsely, transfer to a bowl and allow to cool for a few minutes. Add the ricotta, cream, Parmesan and egg yolks. Season with salt and pepper and mix very well. Set aside while you make the pasta, following the instructions on page 374.

Cut off a quarter of the dough, leaving the rest wrapped in clingfilm. Thin the dough down in the pasta machine notch by notch as far as the last but one notch, as described on page 375. If you are rolling out by hand, roll the dough out as thin as you possibly can. Cover all but a strip of the *sfoglia* (pasta dough) with a tea-towel to prevent it drying out.

Place small-teaspoon dollops of the filling in a straight line along the length of the strip of *sfoglia*, spacing them about 4 cm/ 1½ in apart and the same distance from the edge. Fold the *sfoglia* over the filling and, using a pastry wheel, trim the edges where they meet. Then cut the *sfoglia* into squares between each mound of filling. Separate the squares and squeeze out any air. Seal them tight with moistened fingers. In dry climates or hot kitchens I recommend applying a narrow strip of cold water with a pastry brush all round the edges, and in between each dollop of filling, before folding the *sfoglia* over the filling.

Place the *ravioli* on clean dry tea-towels. Do not let them touch or they will stick together. Cut off another quarter of the dough, knead in any trimmings from the previous batch and thin the strip down as before. If you are rolling out by hand, keep the *sfoglia* you are not working on well covered or it will dry up and become brittle. Continue making more *ravioli* until you have used up all the filling and/or all the dough. Leave them uncovered until they are properly dry; you can then cover them with another cloth.

Bring a large saucepan full of water to the boil. Add 1½ tablespoons of salt and 1 tablespoon of olive oil. Drop the *ravioli* gently into the pan and bring the water back to the boil. Adjust the heat so that the water boils gently; if it boils too fast the *ravioli* may break. Cook until they are done, about 4–5 minutes, stirring gently every now and then. The best way to tell if they are done is to try one: the pasta should be still firm to the bite, *al dente*, at the edge. Lift the *ravioli* out with a slotted spoon, pat dry with kitchen paper, and transfer them immediately to a heated and buttered bowl.

While they are cooking, melt the butter for the sauce in a small saucepan. Add the chives and pour over the *ravioli*. Serve at once, handing round some Parmesan in a separate bowl if you want.

PREPARATION

The *ravioli* can be prepared up to 1 day in advance and refrigerated. They must be placed, sprinkled with semolina, in plastic containers between sheets of greaseproof paper. *Ravioli* stored in this way can also be frozen, although I do not recommend it because, like other food, pasta loses its fresh flavour when frozen. Cook them when still frozen.

You can cook the *ravioli* just before the meal and keep them in a very low oven while you eat the first course. They should be lightly covered with foil, so that they can breathe but will not dry out too much.

✳ *Gamberi imperiali in salsa all'abruzzese*

PRAWNS IN A PIQUANT TOMATO SAUCE

25–30 king prawns or tiger
  prawns
4 garlic cloves, peeled and finely
  chopped
1 large bunch of flat-leaf parsley
1 or 2 dried chillies, according to
  taste, seeded
6 tbsp extra virgin olive oil
2 tsp anchovy purée

450 g/1 lb fresh ripe tomatoes,
  preferably plum tomatoes,
  peeled, seeded and very coarsely
  chopped
120 ml/4 fl oz dry white wine
salt
freshly ground black pepper
  (optional)

Rinse the prawns, shell and devein them.

Chop the garlic, parsley and chillies either by hand or in a food processor.

Put the oil in a large sauté pan (I use a round earthenware pan) and add the parsley mixture. Sauté for 1 minute over low heat, stirring very frequently, and mix in the anchovy purée. Add the prawns and the tomatoes. Turn them over once or twice in the pan and then splash with the wine and cook for 5 minutes. Season with salt and black pepper if you like. If you have a nice-looking sauté pan, serve directly from it.

PREPARATION

You can prepare the prawns and the parsley mixture in advance. You can even make the *soffritto* (the fried mixture) beforehand, but you must cook the prawns just before serving. You can cook them while someone else collects the dirty plates of the first course from the table.

*   ## *Insalata agra di barbabietola*

BEETROOT, GRAPEFRUIT AND WATERCRESS SALAD

5 medium size beetroots, cooked	*1½ grapefruit*
4 tbsp extra virgin olive oil	*6 spring onions*
salt and pepper	*2 bunches watercress*

Peel and slice the beetroots. Put them in a bowl and toss them with 2 tablespoons of the olive oil, a little salt and a lot of pepper. Pile them on a dish.

Peel the grapefruit, divide into segments and remove the thin transparent skin. Cut each segment in half and scatter over the beetroot, together with the white bulb of the spring onions, cut into thin rounds.

Wash and dry the watercress. Remove the long stalks but leave in nice short sprigs.

Surround the beetroot mound with the watercress. Dribble the remaining olive oil over the watercress and sprinkle with salt and pepper.

PREPARATION

The vegetables and the grapefruit can be prepared up to 1 day in advance. The dish can be arranged up to 1 hour in advance and covered with clingfilm, but dress the watercress just before serving.

Gelato di albicocca

*
with an
ice-cream
machine

**
without

APRICOT ICE-CREAM

---

450 g/1 lb fresh apricots
100 g/3½ oz sugar
the juice of 1 orange

150 ml/¼ pint whipping cream
1 tbsp icing sugar
2 tbsp amaretto *liqueur*

Wash the apricots, cut them in half and remove the stones.

Put the sugar, orange juice and 4 tablespoons of water in a heavy pan. Bring gently to the boil and simmer for 3 minutes or so, stirring very frequently to dissolve the sugar. Add the apricots to the pan. Cover the pan and cook until soft.

Pour the contents of the pan into a food processor or a liquidizer and process or blend to a coarse purée.

Lightly whip the cream with the icing sugar. Mix in the *amaretto* and the apricot purée. Transfer the mixture to an ice-cream machine and freeze, following the manufacturer's instructions. If you do not have one of these invaluable machines, freeze to a slush, whisk thoroughly and put back in the freezer until set.

Remove the ice-cream from the freezer and place in the fridge about 1 hour before serving.

PREPARATION

Any fruit ice-cream or sorbet loses flavour if made too long in advance. Try to make it no more than 2 days before you want to serve it.

DINNER FOR 6

Zuppa di pan gratto
FISH SOUP WITH BREADCRUMBS, CREAM, EGG YOLKS AND
PARMESAN

Branzino farcito di Joan
SEA-BASS STUFFED WITH SCALLOPS, SHRIMPS
AND BLACK OLIVES

Insalata verde
GREEN SALAD

Il tiramisú di Edda
WHITE MASCARPONE TRIFLE: A SUMMER *TIRAMISÚ*

Italian meals are normally conceived as a whole; various courses
complement each other, and their flavours are in harmony. A
delicate-tasting sea-bass must be preceded by a delicate course
into which the flavour of the fish might well be introduced. So,
having seen beautiful sea-bass at my fishmonger, I planned this
very elegant menu for my small dinner party around it.

The soup is derived from a recipe in *Cucina Teorico-Pratica*, by
Ippolito Cavalcanti, Duke of Buonvicino, which was published in
1837. This book is one of the two most authoritative works on
Neapolitan cooking, the other being *Il Cuoco Galante* by Vincenzo
Corrado. In his book, Cavalcanti presents twenty-five menus for
each of four basic ingredients: meat, fish and seafood, eggs, and
vegetables. The menus bear witness to the harmony I have
spoken of. The soup I chose, which is included in the egg section,
can be made, as Cavalcanti suggests, with chicken or fish stock. I
have chosen the fish version, which I prefer when the next course
is fish, but if you have good chicken stock ready, use that.

In Britain sea-bass is easily available in late spring and in the
summer, when a certain number swim up to our southern shores.
It is the king of fish for the Italians and the French, who love its
firm flesh, free of bone, and its delicate flavour. Sea-bass is
usually grilled, boiled, or roasted as in this recipe. Here I have
boned the fish before stuffing it, which makes it more attractive to
serve and more agreeable to eat. You can cut through the fish so

that each diner will have a slice of fish with its succulent stuffing inside. If you have an amenable and friendly fishmonger, a great asset in life, he will bone the fish for you. The dish is superb even when the bone is left in; just push the stuffing into the cavity and stitch with cocktail sticks. In this case you will need less stuffing.

This dish is a classic of grand Italian cooking, the centrepiece of many dinners and buffet parties, just as salmon is here. The recipe comes from my cousin, Joan, Italian in spite of her name, at whose house I have enjoyed many elegant, and excellent, dinners. The same recipe is also perfect using sea bream, a less expensive fish.

Serve some new potatoes with the fish, and afterwards pass round a bowl of mixed green salad, an example of which is to be found on page 368.

The finale of the dinner is a lovely white *tiramisú*. To my mind this is much nicer than the usual *tiramisú* flavoured with coffee and brandy, which, although of recent origin, is now to be found on the menu of every Italian restaurant. This is a lighter, fresher version created by a Venetian friend, Edda Bellini, and christened 'a summer *tiramisú*' by another friend, and colleague, Betsy Newell. You can make your own sponge fingers or buy Italian *savoiardi*. Shop-bought sponge fingers are too sweet and not absorbent enough.

* # *Zuppa di pan gratto*

FISH SOUP WITH BREADCRUMBS, CREAM, EGG YOLKS AND PARMESAN

---

4 slices of good quality white bread, 1 cm/½ in thick	3 egg yolks
45 g/1½ oz unsalted butter	120 ml/4 fl oz double cream
1 tbsp oil	3 tbsp lemon juice
1.35 litres/2¼ pints fish broth (page 379)	45 g/1½ oz freshly grated Parmesan
5 tbsp dried white breadcrumbs	salt and pepper
	4 tbsp chopped parsley

Remove the crust from the bread and cut into small cubes.

Heat the butter and the oil in a frying pan until very hot. Add the bread and fry until golden. Transfer with a slotted spoon to a triple thickness of kitchen paper to drain.

Bring the fish broth to the boil. Add the dried breadcrumbs, stirring constantly. Simmer for 5 minutes.

Meanwhile beat the egg yolks lightly with a fork. Add the cream, lemon juice, Parmesan and plenty of pepper and continue beating until well blended. Draw the soup off the heat and beat in the egg and cream mixture. Taste and add salt if necessary.

Ladle the soup into heated bowls, sprinkle with the parsley, and serve at once, with the croûtons in a bowl.

PREPARATION

Once you have the fish broth ready, the soup takes less than 5 minutes. You can prepare the croûtons well in advance; they even freeze well.

*** *Branzino farcito di Joan*

SEA-BASS STUFFED WITH SCALLOPS, SHRIMPS AND BLACK OLIVES

1 sea-bass, weighing about 1.8 kg/ 4 lb	2 tbsp chopped parsley
120 g/4 oz shrimps	2 tbsp capers, rinsed and dried
4 scallops	2 tbsp brandy
10 black olives	6 tbsp extra virgin olive oil
	salt and pepper

If your fishmonger has not been amenable enough to bone the fish for you, this is how you should proceed if you wish to bone it yourself. With a boning knife, extend the slit in the fish's belly all the way from the head to the tail. Using your fingers and a small knife, prise loose the rib bones that are embedded in the upper belly of the fish. Then proceed down the belly and loosen all the backbone, scraping any flesh off it. Now bend the head of the fish backwards sharply to snap it off from the backbone. If it does not snap, cut it with poultry scissors. Do the same at the tail end. Check that all the scales have been properly removed. Wash the fish and let it drain while you prepare the stuffing.

Peel the shrimps over a bowl to collect the juices. Cut the

bodies into small pieces and put them in the bowl. Wash and dry the scallops, cut them into pieces and add to the bowl.

Stone the black olives and cut them into strips. Add to the bowl together with the chopped parsley, capers and brandy. Add 30 ml/2 tbsp of the oil, some salt and a generous grinding of pepper. Mix very thoroughly and leave to infuse for about 1 hour.

Heat the oven to 200°C/400°F/Gas 6.

Grease a large sheet of foil with 15 ml/1 tbsp of the oil. Place the foil on a baking tray or roasting tin long enough to hold the fish without bending it.

Dry the fish and lay it flat, skin side down, on the foil. Season both sides with salt and pepper and then pile the stuffing on one half of the open fish. Close the fish as if it were a book and sew it down the belly. Loosely wrap the fish up by twisting over the edge of the foil all round, making sure that the corners are tightly sealed too. Place in the oven and bake for 40 minutes.

Remove from the oven and allow to stand in the sealed foil while you serve and eat the soup. Transfer the fish, still in the foil, to a large oval dish and bring to the table. Cut round the twisted edges of the foil. Cut the fish across into slices and serve, spooning some of the cooking juices over the fish.

PREPARATION
The fish can be stuffed, sewn and wrapped for baking up to 1 hour in advance.

** *Il tiramisú di Edda*

WHITE MASCARPONE TRIFLE: A SUMMER *TIRAMISÚ*

---

small meringues, made with 2 egg whites and 120 g/4 oz caster sugar	90 ml/3 fl oz white rum, such as Bacardi
2 eggs, separated	90 ml/3 fl oz milk
90 g/3 oz caster sugar	18 savoiardi or home-made sponge fingers
325 g/11 oz mascarpone	

Heat the oven to 140°C/275°F/Gas 1.

First make the meringues. Remember that the egg whites must be at room temperature before you start whipping them.

Line a baking tray with parchment paper.

Whisk the egg whites until firm. Sieve half the sugar across the surface and beat it in until the mixture looks glossy and smooth. Sieve another half of the remaining sugar over the surface and fold it in with a large metal spoon. Fold in the rest of the sugar.

Using two spoons or a forcing bag fitted with a large round nozzle, place small rounds of the mixture, well spaced, on the baking tray.

Dredge the surface of the meringues very slightly with extra sugar and bake until firm and a light golden colour. Before lifting them off the tray, check that the underside has dried. If still soft, leave them a little longer. Set aside 7 or 8 of the prettiest meringues and crumble the others.

Now make the trifle. Beat the egg yolks with the sugar until pale and mousse-like. Fold in the mascarpone gradually and then beat until it has been incorporated. Whisk only 1 of the egg whites until firm (discard the second egg white or keep for another recipe) and fold into the mascarpone cream.

Mix the rum and the milk in a soup plate. Dip the biscuits in the mixture just long enough for them to soften. Lay about 9 moistened biscuits in an oval dish. Spread over about one-third of the mascarpone cream. Sprinkle with the meringue crumbs. Dip another 9 biscuits into the rum and milk mixture and arrange them on top of the meringue crumbs. Spread over about half the remaining cream. Cover with clingfilm and refrigerate. Put the remaining cream in a closed container and refrigerate.

Before serving, smooth the remaining cream all over the pudding and decorate with the pretty meringues you have set aside.

PREPARATION

Tiramisú, whether white or brown, should be made 1 day in advance and served chilled.

DINNER FOR 8

Minestra di cavolfiore
CAULIFLOWER SOUP

Brasato cotto a crudo con la polenta
BRAISED BEEF WITH POLENTA

Funghi al funghetto
MUSHROOMS WITH OREGANO AND GARLIC (page 371)

Bônet
AMARETTI PUDDING

Last year I was given a small cookery book from sixty years ago, a book totally unknown to me, which I read the same day, taking notes and marking useful tips, while savouring the wonderful dishes the writer seemed to be conjuring up before my eyes. The little book is called *La Cucina Elegante* and was written by E. V. Quattrova. This is not, as I thought, a *nom de plume*, even though it means four eggs! It is in fact the name of a society lady of the 30s. Her little book contains excellent and, as its title declares, elegant recipes as well as advice on how to entertain, how to seat the guests and how to instruct the cook (less of a problem these days). Many pages have charming drawings by two well-known Italian artists of the time. This recipe for cauliflower soup, like many in the book, is easy to prepare.

The main course is braised beef with a difference. *Brasato*, a very popular dish in Italy, consists of a single joint which, usually, is first sautéed or sealed and then cooked slowly in wine and/or stock and/or tomato sauce. This recipe, which comes from my mother's recipe book, is the only one I know in which the meat, after being marinated overnight, is cooked *a crudo* – raw, in a covered pan, with all the other ingredients including the onions also raw. I find the flavour of the meat lighter than that of a *brasato* cooked in the orthodox way, and the whole operation is definitely quicker, a great plus.

I serve polenta (see page 377) to mop up the juice of the *brasato*, and the carrots on page 372. If you want a second vegetable, I suggest the sautéed mushrooms with oregano and garlic on page 371.

The pudding is a really soft dark pudding with a rich flavour and a silky texture. It is a speciality of Piedmont, as its name testifies. *Bônet*, pronounced 'boonayt', means bonnet, and the pudding is so named because the copper mould in which it is cooked is a round mould shaped like a bonnet. You can use any sort of shape, although a bonnet-shaped mould is prettier. I have also made *bônet* in a ring mould, filling the hole with cream. The cream is my addition; I find it lightens the pudding and combines perfectly with the almond-caramel flavour.

*   *Minestra di cavolfiore*

CAULIFLOWER SOUP

1 large white cauliflower, about 600 g/1¼ lb	*4 egg yolks*
1.8 litres/3 pints Italian broth (page 378)	*150 ml/¼ pint double cream*
30 g/1 oz rice flour	*45 g/1½ oz unsalted butter*
	salt and pepper
	croûtons for serving

Cut the cauliflower into florets, discarding the green leaves and the core, and wash.

Bring the broth to the boil and add the florets. Cook until *al dente*, but tender, and then lift them out of the stock.

Now you need a food mill fitted with a disc with large holes, so that the cauliflower will be grainy and not puréed. Otherwise chop the florets by hand. A food processor will give the wrong texture. Push the florets through the food mill directly back into the stock.

Put the rice flour in a small saucepan and add 2 ladlefuls of hot stock. Cook for 10 minutes. Withdraw from the heat and mix in the yolks, one at a time. Stir this mixture into the soup and remove the soup from the heat. Heat the cream and mix it in with the butter, cut into small pieces. As soon as the butter has melted, pour the soup into individual soup bowls and serve with croûtons.

PREPARATION

The stock can be made days or weeks in advance and then defatted and frozen. It keeps well in the fridge for up to 48 hours, but no longer, unless you bring it back to the boil and simmer it for about 5 minutes.

The soup can be prepared 2 days in advance, but the egg mixture, cream and butter must be added shortly before serving.

The croûtons can be prepared days or weeks in advance and frozen in plastic bags.

✻✻ *Brasato cotto a crudo con la polenta*

BRAISED BEEF WITH POLENTA

1.8 kg/4 lb beef, preferably chuck steak, in a single piece and neatly tied	*streaky bacon*
	a selection of fresh herbs: 4 sage leaves, 2 sprigs of rosemary,
3 garlic cloves	*4 sprigs of thyme, a small bunch*
salt and pepper	*of parsley*
1 bay leaf	*1 large onion*
3 tbsp olive oil	*75 g/2½ oz unsalted butter*
30 g/1 oz pancetta or unsmoked	*300 ml/½ pint red wine*

Rub the meat with 2 of the garlic cloves and the salt and pepper. Place it in a bowl with all the garlic and the bay leaf and then pour over the oil. Cover and leave overnight. I never put meat in the fridge to marinate unless the weather is very hot. Meat is often hung for too short a time, so that it benefits from a few hours at room temperature.

Chop the *pancetta* or bacon and the herbs. Add salt and pepper and lard the meat by making small incisions with a sharp-pointed knife and pushing small lumps of the herb and *pancetta* mixture into the meat, along the grain.

Cut the onion into thick slices and put them into a casserole, preferably oval, with 60 g/2 oz of the butter. Season with a little salt and pepper. Lay the meat on top of the onion and cover the pan tightly.

Put the casserole on a medium heat and cook for 5 minutes. Turn the meat over and continue cooking for 30 minutes, keeping the lid on. If the onion begins to catch, lower the heat slightly.

Heat the wine and add to the pan. Cover the pan and cook over very low heat for about 2½ hours, by which time the meat should be done. Remove the meat to a chopping board and cover with a piece of foil while you prepare the sauce.

Taste the cooking juices. You may need to reduce them over high heat. This depends on the water content of the meat; if you have a good butcher this should not be necessary. Purée the cooking juices through a sieve or in a food processor and return to the pan. Gradually add the remaining butter cut into small pieces and cook until the last piece has melted.

Carve the meat into slices about ¼ in thick. I use an electric knife, which I find invaluable when it comes to carving braised meat. Lay the meat on a hot serving dish and spoon over a little of the sauce. Serve the rest of the sauce separately in a heated sauce-boat.

PREPARATION

You can carve the meat and prepare the sauce up to 30 minutes in advance. Put the slices back into the casserole and cover with the sauce. Keep warm in a cool oven. You can cook the meat the day before and reheat it whole in a hot oven, well covered, for 20 minutes.

*** # Bônet

AMARETTI PUDDING

---

300 ml/½ pint single cream	*3 tbsp unsweetened cocoa powder*
300 ml/½ pint full-fat milk	*1 tbsp dark rum*
5 eggs	*1 tbsp amaretto liqueur*
90 g/3 oz caster sugar	*300 ml/½ pint whipping cream*
150 g/5 oz amaretti biscuits	

For the caramel

60 g/2 oz caster sugar	*1 tsp lemon juice*
2 tbsp water	

First make the caramel. Heat the oven to 165°C/325°F/Gas 3 and place a 1 litre/2 pint mould in it to heat for 5 minutes.

Put the ingredients for the caramel in a small saucepan and bring to the boil over medium heat. Do not be tempted to stir;

leave it alone and the sugar will dissolve. The lemon juice will prevent crystals forming on the edge of the syrup. When the syrup begins to turn dark brown, withdraw it from the heat and pour it into the heated mould. Tip the mould in all directions to coat the sides and bottom evenly. It is necessary to heat the mould because if it is cold, the caramel may set before you can cover the whole surface of the mould with it. Set aside while you make the pudding.

Add the cream to the milk and bring to simmering point. Beat the eggs with the sugar until frothy and light. Pour the milk mixture over the eggs in a slow stream from a height so as to cool the liquid, beating constantly.

Crush the *amaretti* biscuits in a food processor, or with a rolling-pin and mix into the egg and milk mixture together with the cocoa, the rum and the liqueur. Beat thoroughly, using a balloon whisk rather than an electric hand beater, which would scatter bubbles of mixture all over your kitchen.

Pour the mixture into the prepared mould. Place the mould in a roasting tin and add enough very hot (but not actually boiling) water to come half-way up the side of the roasting tin. Place the tin in the preheated oven and cook for about 1 hour until the *bônet* is set. To test if it is ready, insert the thin blade of a knife into the middle of the pudding. It should come out dry.

Remove from the oven and let the *bônet* cool in the mould. When cold, place the mould in the fridge and leave for at least 3 hours. To unmould, loosen the pudding all round with a palette knife. Place a round dish over the mould and turn the mould over on to the dish. Give a few sharp jerks to the dish and then lift the mould away. Put the mould back over the *bônet* to protect it and refrigerate until you are ready to serve it.

Whip the cream and pipe it round the pudding or, if you are using a ring mould, fill the central hole with it.

PREPARATION
Bônet is better made 1 or 2 days in advance, for the flavours to blend, and refrigerated. It can also be frozen, but do not leave too long in the freezer or the flavour will evaporate.

A LUNCH FOR 10

Spaghettini aglio, olio e peperoncino
THIN SPAGHETTI WITH GARLIC, OIL AND CHILLI

Il polpettone di tonno della Mamma in salsina all'uovo
TUNNY FISH ROLL WITH EGG AND CREAM SAUCE

L'insalata di Luisetta
A MIXED SALAD OF VEGETABLES, GRAPEFRUIT AND PRAWNS

Pomodori al basilico
TOMATOES WITH BASIL

Formaggio
CHEESE

Gelato di fragola all'aceto balsamico
STRAWBERRY ICE-CREAM FLAVOURED WITH BALSAMIC
VINEGAR (page 168)

Sorbetto di limone al sapor di basilico
LEMON SORBET FLAVOURED WITH FRESH BASIL (page 106)

I am not, in general, too fond of lunch parties; they break the day in two, leaving a second half that seems to lack any firm focus. But in the summer, when there is the prospect of being able to sit in the garden, a lunch party is sometimes called for. The menu will be simple, with a cold *secondo* and no pudding, except for one or two ice-creams which have been made one or two days before.

The first course of my favourite lunch is definitely pasta, not only because I love it but also because it requires the minimum of work. And these *spaghettini* make the simplest of all pasta dishes, yet one of the most popular with southern Italians, who are experts in the matter.

After that I like to serve two *secondi* which go beautifully together. One is my mother's tunny fish roll and the other is a rich vegetable and prawn salad, a recipe given to me by Luisetta Fioruzzi who is one of the best Milanese hostesses, which, I can tell you, is saying something. I had to alter the recipe slightly, however, since the artichokes used in her recipe are found only in Italy. They are artichokes from Liguria, rather thin and with thorns at the end of each leaf. Tender and sweet, they are eaten raw, either dipped leaf by leaf into a golden pool of olive oil or very thinly sliced in a salad.

My mother's *polpettone* is different from the more usual one made with a tunny fish and potato mixture. The mixture here is tunny fish, eggs and Parmesan, seasoned with nutmeg, an unusual but extremely successful combination of flavours. It is important to buy good tinned tuna packed in olive oil; the Italian and Spanish brands are the best and are worth their higher price. They are available in the best delicatessens and specialist shops, or by post from The Oil Merchant, 3 Haarlem Road, London W14. The common brands of tuna sold in most supermarkets contain skipjack and not real tuna. The *polpettone* can be covered with a thin mayonnaise or with an egg and lemon sauce, as in this menu. It is a delicate sauce and a welcome change from a mayonnaise.

Tomatoes that are ripe, soft and juicy, cut in half, dribbled with the best olive oil and sprinkled with a few torn basil leaves have always been a firm favourite of mine. Other salads to serve would be a lovely green salad such as that on page 368, or the tomato, cucumber and pepper salad on page 129.

A cheese platter follows, and in its turn is followed by two ice-creams. The first is an exquisite strawberry ice-cream flavoured with balsamic vinegar, and the second is a lemon sorbet with an indefinable flavour given to it by a few basil leaves.

* *Spaghettini aglio, olio e peperoncino*

THIN SPAGHETTI WITH GARLIC, OIL AND CHILLI

---

1 kg/2 lb thin spaghettini
salt
150 ml/¼ pint extra virgin olive
   oil

6 garlic cloves, peeled and sliced
2 or 3 dried chillies, according to
   taste, seeded and crumbled

Cook the pasta in plenty of boiling salted water. You may prefer to cook it following the Agnesi method on page 376, which requires less careful attention.

Meanwhile put the oil, garlic and chillies in a frying pan large enough to hold all the pasta. Cook for 1 minute over low heat. As soon as the garlic aroma rises, the sauce is ready. Draw off the heat immediately or the garlic may burn, and this would ruin the taste.

When the pasta is ready, drain it through a colander, reserving a cupful of the water. Transfer the pasta immediately to the frying pan. Stir-fry for a minute or so, lifting the *spaghettini* high into the air so that every strand is beautifully glistening with oil. Add a couple of tablespoons of the reserved pasta water if the dish seems a bit too dry. Serve at once, preferably straight from the pan.

No cheese is needed for this typically Neapolitan quick pasta.

PREPARATION
This dish, like every pasta dish, must be made at the last minute. *Spaghettini* cook in about 6 minutes.

✳✳✳ *Il polpettone di tonno della Mamma*

TUNNY FISH ROLL

400 g/14 oz tinned tuna, drained (buy best Spanish or Italian tuna)	salt and freshly ground pepper
	200 ml/7 fl oz wine vinegar
	200 ml/7 fl oz dry white wine
3 whole eggs plus 1 yolk	10–12 sprigs parsley
2 hard-boiled eggs, coarsely chopped	2 small onions, sliced
	3 tbsp olive oil
100 g/3½ oz freshly grated Parmesan	1 tsp lemon juice
2 pinches of grated nutmeg	black olives, lemon slices and capers to garnish

Flake and mash the tuna in a bowl. Add the eggs, hard-boiled eggs, Parmesan, nutmeg and plenty of pepper. Taste and check salt. Mix thoroughly.

Moisten a piece of muslin under cold water, wring it out until just damp, and lay it out double on the work surface. Place the tuna mixture on the cloth and roll it into a log shape, about 8 cm/ 3 in in diameter. Pat it all over to eliminate air pockets. Wrap the muslin around it and tie both ends with string.

Place the roll with the vinegar, wine, parsley, onions and a little salt in an oval casserole into which the roll will just fit. Add enough water to cover the roll by about 1 cm/½ in. Cover the casserole and bring to the boil. Cook, over very low heat, for 45 minutes.

Remove the tuna roll from the casserole and place it between two plates. Put a weight on top and leave to cool for at least 2 hours.

When the roll is cold, unwrap it carefully and cut into 1 cm/½ in slices. Arrange the slices, very slightly overlapping, on a dish. Mix together the olive oil and lemon juice and spoon over the slices 2 hours before serving. Coat lightly with the egg and cream sauce from the following recipe and garnish with black olives, lemon slices and capers. If you prefer, hand the sauce round separately in two small bowls and let people help themselves.

PREPARATION

The *polpettone* can be made and cooked up to 2 days in advance and kept, wrapped, in the refrigerator. Slice it, bring back to room temperature and dress it with the oil and lemon.

* # Salsina all'uovo

EGG AND CREAM SAUCE

This sauce is also good with stewed or boiled fish, with vegetables or with poached chicken.

5 egg yolks	5 tbsp lemon juice
1 tsp English mustard powder	6 tbsp extra virgin olive oil
salt and pepper	120 ml/4 fl oz double cream

Whisk the yolks in a bowl. Add the mustard powder, salt and pepper and lemon juice and put the bowl over a saucepan half full of simmering water.

Add the oil slowly while whisking constantly, and continue whisking until the sauce thickens. Be careful not to let it boil or the egg will curdle. Draw off the heat and beat in the cream. Return to the bain-marie and cook for a further couple of minutes.

Transfer the bowl to a basin of cold water and leave to cool.

PREPARATION
The sauce can be prepared up to 1 day in advance and refrigerated. Remove from the fridge at least 2 hours before you use it to coat the tunny fish roll.

**   *L'insalata di Luisetta*

A MIXED SALAD OF VEGETABLES, GRAPEFRUIT AND PRAWNS

---

750 g/1½ lb prawns, preferably raw	*2 pink grapefruit*
1 bunch of rocket	*225 g/½ lb very small young courgettes*
the heart of 1 curly endive	*150 ml/¼ pint extra virgin olive oil*
225 g/½ lb green beans, steamed or boiled	*6 tbsp raspberry vinegar, if available, or cider vinegar*
the hearts of 2 celery heads	*salt and pepper*
6 small tomatoes	

If you are using raw prawns, cook them in a vegetable stock made with water and flavoured with 1 carrot, ½ an onion, 1 stick of celery, a bay leaf, 2 sprigs of parsley, fennel tops or dill, peppercorns and a little salt, adding a little olive oil and some white wine. They take only 2 minutes to cook.

Clean, trim and wash the rocket and the white heart of the endive. Cut into very fine strips and lay on a large oval dish. Cut the beans into 4 cm/1½ in pieces, the celery into very thin strips and the tomatoes into thin segments and place them over the green salad.

Peel the grapefruits to the quick, remove the membrane between the segments and scatter the grapefruit flesh over the dish.

Wash and dry the courgettes and cut into thin rounds. Add to the dish.

Shell the prawns and de-vein if necessary. Keep about half a dozen of the best for garnish; cut the others into small pieces and put them here and there among the vegetables.

Beat the oil and vinegar together in a bowl with a fork, add salt and pepper and pour all over the salad. Decorate with the reserved prawns and serve at once.

PREPARATION

All the vegetables can be prepared up to 4 hours beforehand, but they should be laid on the dish no longer than 1 hour in advance. The salad must be dressed just before serving.

* *Pomodori al basilico*

TOMATOES WITH BASIL

This is hardly a recipe. You need about 2 dozen ripe but firm tomatoes; when they are in season I buy plum tomatoes, which are tastier and contain fewer seeds and less water. Blanch them in boiling water for 15 seconds, then plunge them into a bowl of cold water. Skin them and cut them in half. Squeeze out some of the seeds by pressing each half between your thumb and first finger. Sprinkle some salt into each half and place, cut side down, on a wooden board to drain. Place the board in the refrigerator and leave for at least 1 hour.

Dry the tomatoes inside and out and put them on a large platter. Dribble 120 ml/4 fl oz of your best olive oil all over them and season with a generous grinding of black pepper. Place 1 small basil leaf or a piece of a larger one on each tomato. Place a thin slice of garlic on top of the basil, so that people who do not like garlic can see it and leave it. Serve chilled.

PREPARATION

You can prepare the tomatoes up to 6 hours in advance and keep them upside down on a board in the fridge. Dress before serving.

Basic Recipes

This section contains fourteen basic recipes. Some are needed as a base for dishes in other parts of the book, while others are recipes for the classic vegetable dishes served as an accompaniment in many of the menus.

*
serves 6–8

La mia insalata verde

GREEN SALAD WITH HERB DRESSING

Buy a selection of the following salads: Cos and round lettuce, Belgian chicory, lamb's lettuce, Little Gem, curly endive and a radicchio head for colour. I am not very keen on Lollo Rosso, but if you like it use a few leaves. I would never add Webb or Iceberg, as they have the wrong texture and a cabbagey taste that does not go with the other salads.

Having picked, washed and thoroughly dried the salad, cut the leaves into shreds or small pieces; only lamb's lettuce should be left whole. I find the current fashion for serving large whole leaves totally wrong for two good reasons: first, you cannot possibly toss the salad well enough to coat it properly with the dressing; second, one or two leaves will fill your plate – especially if the salad is served on small side plates – when you would have liked to help yourself to more. To this basic selection, add a bunch of rocket. I shred rocket so that its peppery flavour can be detected in every mouthful.

Now for the dressing of my choice. I use herbs from the garden: 2 leaves of sorrel, 2 or 3 leaves of spring borage, a few basil leaves, a dozen blades of chives, lovage leaf and a little fresh oregano or marjoram. All these herbs are chopped with a little garlic – 1 small clove for 8 people is more than enough. Before you chop the garlic, cut it in half and remove the green inner core, which has a strong and sharp flavour.

Put the chopped herb mixture in the salad bowl and add about 2 tablespoons of good red wine vinegar, 2 teaspoons of sea salt and a generous amount of black pepper. Now add gradually about 8 tablespoons of extra virgin olive oil, while beating with a fork. The proportion of vinegar to oil depends on personal taste, on the fruitiness of the oil and on the acidity of the vinegar; my quantities are a rough guide. I sometimes like to add 1–1½ teaspoons of Dijon mustard, not an Italian habit, but one I am delighted to borrow from France.

Add about half the salad to the bowl, toss thoroughly and then add the rest of the salad. The secret of a good salad is to be patient and mix very well (in Italy it is said that 36 times is the magic number!), otherwise the first people to help themselves will have dry rabbit food, while the last will have a soup.

PREPARATION
The salad can be prepared up to 1 day in advance and kept in the refrigerator, wrapped in a clean cloth. The herb dressing must be prepared up to 1 hour in advance to allow the flavours to blend, but the salad must be tossed at the last minute.

* serves 6

Patate arrosto

ROAST POTATOES

I find this unorthodox method of roasting potatoes ideal when I have friends to dinner. They cook, covered, in the oven so that I can forget about them, and they are very good. You can flavour them with rosemary, bay leaves or fennel seeds.

24–30 small new potatoes, all	*salt and pepper*
perfect	*1 sprig fresh rosemary, or 2 bay*
3 tbsp olive oil	*leaves, or 1 tsp fennel seeds,*
4 garlic cloves	*pounded*

Scrape the potatoes. Wash them in a basin of cold water and dry thoroughly.

Heat the oven to 200°C/400°F/Gas 6 and place an oven dish in it to heat up.

Pour the olive oil into a large frying or sauté pan into which the potatoes will fit in a single layer, and add the garlic. Place the pan on medium high heat and when the garlic becomes pale gold, remove it. Slip in the potatoes and fry them for 7–8 minutes, shaking the pan frequently, so that they form a golden crust all over.

Transfer the potatoes and the little oil left at the bottom of the pan to the oven dish. Season the potatoes with salt and pepper and add the herb of your choice. Cover the dish with its lid or, tightly, with foil. Bake until the potatoes are done, about 30–40 minutes.

PREPARATION
Potatoes cooked this way keep warm in the turned-off oven for a good half hour.

** Patate trifolate

serves 6–8

POTATOES WITH PARSLEY

1.35 kg/3 lb waxy potatoes
2 tbsp olive oil
60 g/2 oz unsalted butter
4 tbsp chopped parsley, preferably
   flat-leaf

3 garlic cloves, bruised
salt and freshly ground black
   pepper

Peel the potatoes and rinse them. Cut them into small cubes of about 1½ cm/¾ in and dry them thoroughly.

Heat the oil and the butter with the parsley and the garlic in a large frying pan. When the butter foam begins to subside, remove the garlic and add the potatoes. Cook over medium heat for about 8 minutes, turning them over and over until they are well coated and are just beginning to brown at the edges.

Turn the heat down to very low and add 120 ml/4 fl oz of hot water. Mix well, cover the pan tightly with a lid and cook for about 30 minutes. Shake the pan and stir occasionally during the cooking. Use a fork to stir, as it is less likely to break the potatoes. If the potatoes get too dry add a little more hot water.

When the potatoes are tender, add salt and pepper to taste. It is better to add the salt at the end of the cooking, because it tends to make potatoes disintegrate. Mix well, taste and check seasoning.

PREPARATION
Potatoes should not be reheated. But if necessary you can cook them up to 1 hour in advance and keep them in the tightly covered pan. They will keep warm for quite a time. Before serving, heat them up over high heat for 5 minutes, stirring very frequently.

*
serves 6

Funghi al funghetto

SAUTÉED MUSHROOMS WITH OREGANO
AND GARLIC

This is my adaptation of a recipe that appears in the classic book *La Cuciniera Genovese* by Giobatta and Giovanni Ratto, which is now, after a century, in its eighteenth edition.

The mushrooms used in the recipe are, of course, fresh porcini. As these are very difficult to find in this country, I suggest you use a selection of what you can buy or what you can pick, if you know which ones to pick. Freshly picked mushrooms will give your dish a better flavour.

---

700 g/1½ lb mixed mushrooms: *cultivated*, champignons de Paris, *oyster*	*5 tbsp olive oil*
	salt
	2 tbsp dried oregano
4 garlic cloves	*pepper*

Clean the mushrooms by wiping them with kitchen paper. Slice them thinly.

Chop 2 of the garlic cloves very finely. Thread a wooden cocktail stick through the others so that you can find them easily and remove them at the end of the cooking.

Put all the garlic and the oil in a large sauté pan. Add the mushrooms and salt and cook at a lively heat, stirring frequently, until all the liquid that comes out at the beginning has evaporated. Season with the oregano and with pepper.

Continue cooking for 15 minutes, taking care that the mushrooms do not stick to the bottom of the pan. If they do, add a couple of tablespoons of water and stir well. Fish out the garlic cloves and serve immediately.

PREPARATION

Mushrooms should not be refrigerated because they lose their flavour. You can cook them up to 1 day in advance and reheat them, uncovered, over low heat before serving.

Pomodori in teglia

BAKED TOMATOES

*
serves 6–8

10 ripe tomatoes	*2 tbsp dried breadcrumbs*
salt and pepper	*5 tbsp extra virgin olive oil*
4 tbsp chopped flat-leaf parsley	

Wash and dry the tomatoes and cut them in half. Gently squeeze out some of the seeds or fish them out with the point of a coffee spoon. If you have time, sprinkle them with salt and lay them on a board, cut side down, then leave them in the fridge for 1 hour or so. It does not matter if you leave them for longer.

Heat the oven to 190°C/375°F/Gas 5.

Grease an oven dish, preferably metal, with some of the oil. Dry the inside of the tomatoes with kitchen paper and put them in the oven dish, cut side up.

Mix the parsley and the breadcrumbs together, season with salt and pepper and spoon a little of the mixture over each tomato half. Dribble with the rest of the oil and bake for 15 to 20 minutes, until just soft.

PREPARATION

You can bake the tomatoes up to 1 day in advance and reheat them gently in the oven. Alternatively you can serve them at room temperature; they will be just as good, if not better.

Le carote di Ada Boni

CARROTS ITALIAN STYLE

**
serves 8

This is a recipe from the great classic, *Il Talismano della Felicità*, by Ada Boni.

1 kg/2 lb carrots	*2 tsp flour*
60 g/2 oz unsalted butter	*350 ml/12 fl oz stock, or ½*
salt and pepper	*bouillon cube dissolved in the*
1 tsp sugar	*same amount of water*

Scrape the carrots. Wash them and cut them into 5 cm/2 in pieces. Cut each piece into quarters lengthwise and remove, if necessary, the inner hard core. Cut each quarter into matchstick-sized segments.

Melt the butter in a large sauté pan, add the carrots and sauté gently for 5 minutes. Season with salt, pepper and sugar and sprinkle with the flour. Stir well and cook for 1 minute. Add the stock, which should just cover the carrots. Bring to the boil and cover with a tight-fitting lid.

Turn the heat down and cook very gently for about 30 minutes, stirring every now and then. By the end the carrots should be soft. Taste and adjust seasonings.

If there is still too much liquid when the carrots are ready, transfer them to a serving dish with a slotted spoon and reduce the cooking juices rapidly. Pour the juices over the carrots.

PREPARATION

The carrots can be cooked up to 1 day in advance. Keep them in the same sauté pan. They do not need to be refrigerated. Reheat very gently before serving.

*

serves 6–8

Spinaci all'agro

LEMON-FLAVOURED SPINACH

1.35 kg/3 lb bunch spinach (or leaf spinach but not beet spinach)	*7 tbsp extra virgin olive oil* *2 garlic cloves, peeled and bruised* *the juice of 1 large lemon*

Cut off the roots and/or the longer stems of the spinach. Put it in a bowl of water, shake it around and leave for a few minutes for the earth to fall to the bottom. Scoop out the spinach and change the water two or more times, until no more earth settles on the bottom of the bowl. Bunch spinach, if you are using it, needs more washing than leaf spinach because it holds some earth in the curls of its leaves. Transfer the spinach to a saucepan with no water other than that which clings to the leaves. Add 1 teaspoon of salt, cover the pan, and cook over high heat until the spinach is cooked, turning it over frequently.

When the spinach is properly cooked – test by eating a leaf with a stem – drain it and rinse under cold water. Drain it again and squeeze out all the liquid with your hands. Cut it into chunks.

Put the oil and garlic in a frying pan, add the spinach, and sauté it over gentle heat for 10 minutes, stirring frequently. Do this on low heat, since you only want to flavour the spinach with the oil, and to heat it. Remove the garlic, pour over half the lemon juice and toss thoroughly. Taste and adjust seasoning, and add more lemon juice to your liking.

PREPARATION

The whole dish can be made up to 1 day in advance, in which case it must be refrigerated. The spinach can be reheated in the oven. Alternatively the spinach can be cooked in advance and then sautéed before serving. Don't worry if it is not hot; it is also perfect warm.

✳✳✳   *Pasta*

makes enough pasta
for 2–3 people

Here is my recipe for making the traditional pasta from Emilia-Romagna. This is the pasta Italians like best to make because it is the best pasta. It is a pasta you can bite into and one that holds its cooking point well. Use the best free-range eggs for a stronger flavour.

---

2 free-range eggs, size 2
200 g/7 oz white flour
   (approximately – it is not
   possible to give an exact
   quantity because it varies

according to the flour's
absorption capacity, the size of
the eggs and the humidity of the
atmosphere)

Put the flour on the work surface and make a well in the centre. Break the eggs into the well. Beat them lightly with a fork and draw the flour in gradually from the inner wall of the well. When the eggs are no longer runny, draw in enough flour to enable you to knead the dough with your hands. You may not need all the flour; push some to the side and add only what is needed. Alternatively you might need a little more from the bag, which you should keep at hand. Work until the flour and eggs are thoroughly amalgamated and then put the dough to one side and scrape the work-top clean. Wash and dry your hands.

Proceed to knead the dough by pressing and pushing with the heel of your palm, folding it back, giving it half a turn and repeating these movements. Repeat the movements for about 7–8 minutes if you are going to make your pasta by hand, or 3–4 minutes if you are going to use a machine. Wrap the dough in clingfilm and let it rest for at least 30 minutes, though you can leave it for up to 3 hours.

Rolling out pasta by hand

Unless you have a *mattarello* – a long thin Italian rolling-pin – and a lot of practice you will find this a difficult task. If you do not have a *mattarello*, roll out the dough in two or more batches, keeping the rest of the dough wrapped in a clean cloth. It is particularly hard in humid places or in drafty and overheated kitchens. Here I condense a very long process into a short paragraph of instructions.

Dust the work surface and the rolling-pin with flour. Stretch the dough, working away from you, while turning the widening circle of dough so that it keeps a circular shape. The *sfoglia* – the sheet of rolled-out dough – must be rolled out until it is no thicker than 1 mm/¹⁄₁₆ in. In theory it should be transparent. This thinning process must be done very quickly, in 8–10 minutes, or the *sfoglia* will dry out, lose its elasticity and become impossible to roll thin.

Rolling out pasta by machine

The hand-cranked type of machine is very good and inexpensive. I strongly advise you to buy one and you will be amply repaid within a few weeks. You will be able to produce good tagliatelle for six people in half an hour at a quarter of the price of shop-bought fresh pasta and of a quality you could never find in a shop. I prefer the old-fashioned hand-cranked machine to the sophisticated but noisy electric ones, of which there are several at various prices.

Follow the manufacturer's instructions, but do remember to knead the dough by hand for at least a few minutes, even if the instructions say that the machine can do that for you.

Tagliatelle and *tagliolini* can be cut by hand or in the machine. There is also an attachment for *ravioli* which is quite good, although I prefer to make them by hand. Other shapes must be made by hand and I have explained how to make them in the relevant recipes. When making tagliatelle and *tagliolini* the *sfoglia* – the rolled-out dough – must be allowed to hang a little to dry, or the strands will stick to each other. It is difficult to say how long it needs, as it depends on the temperature and humidity of the atmosphere, but it should be dry to the touch and just beginning to become leathery. Stuffed pasta must not be left to dry.

Lasagne are easy to prepare. Cut out the pasta into rectangles of about 12 × 8 cm/5 × 3 in and cook them, no more than six or seven pieces at a time, in a large shallow pan of salted boiling water to which you have added a tablespoon of oil to prevent them sticking to each other. As soon as the lasagne are cooked, lift them out of the water and plunge them into a bowl of cold water which you have placed near the burner. Fish them out of the bowl and lay them on clean kitchen cloths. Pat them dry with kitchen paper. When all the lasagne are done, assemble the dish.

The cooking of pasta

It is easy to cook pasta, but it can be ruined by carelessness. We say in Italy, '*Gli spaghetti amano la compagnia*' ('Spaghetti loves company'). You should never leave the kitchen while pasta is in the pot. Timing is crucial. Pasta needs to be cooked in a large pot and a lot of water, at least 1.2 litres/2 pints to 150 g/5 oz of pasta.

Bring the water to the boil, then add about 1½ tablespoons of cooking salt. Slide all the pasta into the boiling water, stir with a wooden fork or spoon to separate the pasta shapes, and cover the pan so that the water returns to the boil as soon as possible. Remove the lid and adjust the heat so that the water boils briskly but does not boil over. Cook until *al dente*, then drain and dress immediately with the sauce. If the sauce is not ready, toss with a little butter or olive oil.

The Agnesi method

When I went to Imperia many years ago to see over the Agnesi pasta factory, the late Vincenzo Agnesi told me the way he liked to cook pasta. Here is what I call the Agnesi method, which I find more suitable when I have friends to dinner, since the pasta does not become overcooked if you leave it a minute too long in the pot. It also produces a dish of pasta that retains the characteristic flavour of semolina. The method is only suitable for dried pasta.

Bring a large saucepan of water to the boil, add salt to taste and then add the pasta and stir. When the water has come back to the boil, cook for 2 minutes, stirring frequently. Turn off the heat, put a Turkish towel cloth over the pan and close with a tight-fitting lid. Leave for the same length of time that the pasta would take to cook by the normal method, i.e. if it were still boiling. When the time is up, drain the pasta.

One final instruction: never overdrain pasta. This applies in particular to long pasta such as spaghetti and tagliatelle, since the other shapes have holes and hollows in which they retain a few drops of water. In Naples, the motherland of spaghetti, long pasta is lifted from the water with a long fork instead of being drained through a colander. In this book, in the various recipes where it applies, I have suggested keeping aside a cupful of the pasta water, a few tablespoons of which you might need to add to the sauce to achieve the correct fluidity.

** *Polenta*

makes enough soft
polenta for 6 helpings

---

300 g/10 oz coarse-ground maize (corn meal)	*2 tsp salt*

Choose a large, deep, heavy saucepan and fill it with 1.8 litres/ 3 pints of water. When the water comes to the boil, add the salt. Turn the heat down and add the flour in a very thin stream, letting it fall through your nearly closed fist while, with the other hand, stirring constantly with a long-handled wooden spoon. Cook the polenta for at least 40 minutes, stirring constantly for the first 10 minutes and then every minute or so.

When ready, transfer the polenta into a bowl, previously moistened with cold water. Leave it to rest for a few minutes and then turn the bowl upside down on to a large round platter or a wooden board covered with a white napkin. The polenta will fall on to it and look, as it should, like a golden mound. (If some of the polenta sticks to the bottom of the pan, cover with water and leave for a few hours. The polenta can then be easily washed away.)

Polenta can also be made in the oven, a less laborious method. In this case the proportion of flour to water must be increased. Bring the salted water to simmering point. Add 350 g/12 oz of maize flour in a thin stream, bring slowly to the boil and boil the mixture for 5 minutes, stirring constantly. Pour it into a buttered oven dish, cover with buttered foil and bake for 1 hour at 190°C/ 375°F/Gas 5.

Grilled polenta

Prepare the polenta in either of the ways instructed above. Pour it out on to a dish or a board and spread it out to a thickness of about 5 cm/2 in. When the polenta is cool, cut it into 1 cm/½ in slices. Brush the slices with olive oil and grill on both sides until a crust forms.

Sliced polenta is also excellent fried in butter or olive oil until a light crust forms on each side.

✶✶   *Il brodo*

makes 1.5–2 litres/
2½–3½ pints   ITALIAN BROTH

Italian broth, which is needed for making a good risotto or a delicate clear soup, is much more delicate than English or French meat stock. *Brodo* is made from beef and veal, with some chicken and a few bones, in the proportion of two-thirds meat to one-third bones. Lamb and pork are never included. I buy 2 *ossibuchi*, a piece of beef flank, a few chicken wings or a small carcass.

1.5 kg/3¼ lb assorted meat	*a handful of mushroom peelings or*
1 onion, cut in half and stuck with	*stalks*
3 cloves	*½ dozen parsley stalks*
1 or 2 carrots, cut in pieces	*1 bay leaf*
2 celery stalks, cut in pieces	*1 garlic clove, peeled*
1 fennel stalk or a few feathery	*1 ripe tomato, quartered*
fennel tops, if available	*6 peppercorns*
1 leek, cut in pieces	*1 tsp salt*

Put all the ingredients in a stock pot. Add about 3 litres/5 pints of cold water, or enough to cover, and bring to the boil. The water must be cold to start with, so that the meat and vegetables can slowly release their juices. Set the lid very slightly askew so that the steam can escape. Turn the heat down to the minimum for the stock to simmer. The best stock is made from liquid that cooks at a temperature of 80°C/175°F, rather than 100°C/220°F, the boiling point. Using a slotted spoon, skim off the scum that comes to the surface during the first quarter of an hour of cooking. Cook for about 3 hours.

Strain the broth through a large strainer lined with muslin. Leave to cool and then put in the refrigerator.

Remove the fat that solidifies on the surface. At the end of the operation, when a few specks of fat are hard to remove, heat the broth and then lay a piece of kitchen paper on the top of the broth and drag it gently across the surface. All the bits will stick to the paper.

Taste, and if you think it is a bit too mild, reduce over high heat, remembering, however, that the broth may taste mild because it contains a minimal amount of salt. Cover with clingfilm and keep in the fridge for up to 3 days or in the freezer for up to 3 months.

Before you use the broth to make the clear soups in this book it should be clarified. Put 2 egg whites and 4 tablespoons of sherry in a pot. Beat in the cold stock while the pan is on the heat. Bring to the simmer while beating constantly. Now let the broth simmer very gently for 15 minutes without touching it.

Strain the broth through a large sieve lined with a piece of muslin folded double. The broth is now ready for the soup.

*   *Brodo di pesce*

FISH BROTH

1.35 kg/3 lb white fish bones and heads	2 tomatoes, quartered
	6 garlic cloves, unpeeled
3 tbsp olive oil	1 dozen peppercorns
1 large onion, quartered	1 tsp salt
2 carrots, thickly sliced	4 sprigs flat-leaf parsley
a handful of fennel tops	2 bay leaves
2 celery stalks, thickly sliced	300 ml/½ pint dry white wine

For a good fish broth you must use only white fish. With any luck your fishmonger will give you some sole bones and heads, haddock, hake, etc. Make up the rest with some inexpensive fish such as whiting. Cut off and discard the gills in the heads of the fish as they would give the stock a bitter taste. Rinse the fish carcasses.

Heat the oil, vegetables and garlic in a stockpot and sauté gently for 7–8 minutes. Rinse the fish, add to the pan and sauté for 5 minutes to *insaporire* – give it flavour. Add 3 litres/5 pints of cold water, the peppercorns, parsley, bay leaves and salt. Bring to the boil and skim well. Simmer for 15 minutes, then pour in the wine and simmer for a further 15 minutes. Strain through a large sieve lined with a piece of muslin. Cool, then skim again if necessary and blot off any surface fat, using kitchen paper.

Transfer the broth to a clean pan and reduce over high heat until you have only 1.35 litres/2¼ pints left.

*** *Cornetti alle mandorle di Vera*

VERA'S ALMOND CRESCENTS

makes 35 biscuits

This is an excellent recipe from my Italian friend Vera Colling-wood. The biscuits are good served with fruit puddings or ice-cream.

150 g/5 oz unsalted butter	150 g/5 oz plain flour
60 g/2 oz ground almonds	6 drops pure vanilla essence
45 g/1½ oz caster sugar	icing sugar

Cream the butter, almonds and sugar until pale and fluffy. Stir in the flour with a wooden spoon and add the vanilla essence. (The mixture can also be made in the food processor.)

Roll into sausage shapes, 15 cm/6 in long by 1–1½ cm/½–⅔ in in diameter, on a board sprinkled with flour, and with floured hands. Wrap the sausages in foil and chill for 30–45 minutes.

Heat the oven to 150°C/300°F/Gas 2.

Cut the sausages into 6½ cm/2½ in long pieces with a sharp knife. Roll lightly in the floured palms of your hands, or on the floured board, and shape into small crescents.

Butter and flour a large baking tray and lay the crescents on it, spacing them at 2½ cm/1 in intervals. Bake until very lightly coloured – about 25 minutes. Allow to cool a little and then transfer to a rack. Do this very gently because these biscuits are very friable. When the biscuits are cold, dredge them with sifted icing sugar and store in an airtight tin between layers of grease-proof paper.

✳✳ *Meringhine al limone*

makes about
25 meringues   LEMON-FLAVOURED MERINGUES

---

2 egg whites, at room temperature   *the grated rind of 1 lemon*
120 g/4 oz caster sugar

Heat the oven to 165°C/325°F/Gas 3.

Put the egg whites in a copper, ceramic or stainless steel bowl. The bowl must be very clean, as egg whites are particularly sensitive to the presence of fat. For this reason, do not use a plastic bowl.

Beat the egg whites until stiff. Add half the sugar and continue beating until glossy, then fold in the remaining sugar and the rind of the lemon.

Line two baking trays with parchment paper. Butter the paper and, using a forcing bag or a spoon, lay small blobs of the whipped mixture on the tray, keeping them 5 cm/2 in apart.

Bake until dry and just golden, about half an hour. Cool on a wire rack, and when cold store in an airtight tin.

✳✳ *Pan di Spagna*

makes a cake of
about 180 g/6 oz   FATLESS SPONGE

---

2 eggs, separated   *50 g/1¾ oz superfine plain flour*
60 g/2 oz caster sugar   *½ tsp salt*

Preheat the oven to 180°C/350°F/Gas 4.

Butter a 500 ml/1 pint loaf tin generously, dust with flour all over and shake off the excess.

Whisk the egg yolks with the sugar until pale yellow and forming soft peaks. Use an electric hand beater if you have one, but not a food processor, which does not work for this recipe. Sieve the flour with ¼ teaspoon of the salt at least twice, letting the flour drop from a height to aerate it.

Put the egg whites and the rest of the salt in a very clean bowl and whisk until stiff but not dry.

Scoop out a couple of tablespoons of the egg white and drop them over the egg yolk and sugar mixture. Sprinkle with 2 tablespoons of the flour and delicately fold into the yolk mixture with a metal spoon. Repeat, adding a little of each at a time and folding them in until all the egg white and flour have been incorporated. Use a light movement, raising the spoon high so as to aerate the mixture. Stop folding as soon as the mixture becomes homogeneous.

Pour the mixture into the prepared tin and bake for about 30 minutes until the cake is spongy to the touch and has shrunk from the sides of the tin.

Loosen the cake from the sides of the tin with a palette knife and turn on to a wire rack. Leave to cool completely and then wrap with foil or store in a cake tin.

PREPARATION
This cake is best used within 1 day of making, although it can be made well in advance and frozen, wrapped in foil. Allow to defrost completely before using.

Index

Note: Page numbers in **bold** type indicate actual recipes.

Acton, Sir Harold, 218
Aerovivanda atlantica, **245–8**
Agnello arrosto alla moda del rina-scimento, 35–6, **38–9**
Agnesi, Vincenzo, 376–7
Al dente (general), 13–14
Alfresco lunch, 297
Aliter olus molle, 221, 222, **225–6**
Almond crescents, 25, 114, 145, 253, 323, 343, **380–81**
Amaretti, 40, 41
Amaretti pudding, 353, 354, **356–7**
Ananas e arancie, 178, 179, **184**, 262
Anello di tagliolini in salsa di zucchine, 40, **42–3**
Animelle al Marsala coi pisellini, 319–20, **320–21**
Apicius, *De Re Coquinaria*, 217, 221–2, 224, 225
Apple snow in a ring, 233, 234, **237–8**
Apricot ice-cream, 342, 343, **347**
Apulian fish pie, 203, 204, **206–7**
Arance caramellate, 287, 288, **293–4**
Arancie, albicocche e banane al vino, 30, 253, **256**
Arancie e kiwi, 35, **39**, 262
Arista alla toscana, 67, **70–71**
Arrosto morto, 276–7, **279–80**
Artichokes (general), 338, 341

Artusi, Pellegrino, *La Scienza in Cucina e l'Arte Mangiar Bene*, 219, 240, 277
Asparagi alla milanese, 13–14, **16–17**
Asparagus (general), 13–14
Asparagus with fried eggs and Parmesan, 13–14, **16–17**
Atlantic airfare: an aeroplane on a puree of legumes, **245–8**
Aubergine cannelloni with tomato sauce, 98, **100–101**
Aubergines, grilled with a lemony mustard sauce, 198, **199**
Autumnal fruit salad, 203, 204, **210**

Baked fish steaks, 262, **264**
Baked green lasagne, 72, **76–7**
Baked macaroni with chicken breast and prosciutto, 233, **236–7**
Baked macaroni with sausage and garlic, 72, **74–5**
Baked pasta and aubergine, 103, **104–5**
Baked polenta with cheeses, 276, **278–9**
Baked sea bream with tomatoes and basil, 160, 161, **162–3**
Baked tagliatelle
with ham and peas, 72, **79**
with tomatoes and mozzarella, 269, **270–71**
Baked tomatoes, 8, 245, **372**

Balsamic-vinegar-flavoured dinner, 164–8
Basil-flavoured dinner, 160–63
Basil-flavoured lemon sorbet, 103–4, **106–7**, 160, 161
Bavarese lombarda, 239, 240, **243–4**
Bean and pasta soup with radicchio, 29, **30–31**
Beef
  braised, with polenta, 353, **355–6**
  braised in vinegar and cream, 56, **58–9**
  cured fillet of, with rocket, 118, **119–20**, 308, 309
Beetroot, grapefruit and watercress salad, 342, 343, **346**
Berriedale-Johnson, Michelle, 29
Bigoli in salsa, 262, **263**
Birthday dinner, 297
Bocconcini di coda di rospo alla puré di lenticchie, 24–5, **26–7**
Bollito misto, 287–8, **290**
Bolognese feast, 72–83
Bomba di panna e marrons glacés, 308, 310, **312**
Bônet, 353, 354, **356–7**
Bonissima, la, 72, 74, 269, **274–5**
Braised beef with polenta, 353, **355–6**
Braised quails in a nest of *paglia e fieno*, 150–51, **152–3**
Branzino farcito di Joan, 348–9, **350–51**
Brasato cotto a crudo con la polenta, 353, **355–6**
Bread, 24, 108
  grilled, with olive oil, garlic and tomato, xiii, 67, 108, **109–10**
  and tomato soup, 203–4, **205**
Breaded pork chops, 145, **147–8**
Bresaola con la ruccola, 118, **119–20**, 308, 309
Bresaola with rocket, 118, **119–20**, 308, 309
Brillat-Savarin, Anthelme, *The Philosopher in the Kitchen*, 328

Broad beans and pecorino cheese, 67, 68
Brodo, 156, **378–9**
Brodo di pesce, **379–80**
Broth *see* Italian broth, fish broth
Bruschetta toscana, xiii, 67, 108, **109–110**
Budino alla pesca, 93, **96–7**
Buttery marquise from Lombardy, 239, 240, **243–4**

Cachi al sugo di lime, 189, **192**
Cannellini beans and tomato sautéed in oil, 67, **71**
Cannelloni di melanzane in salsa, 98, **100–101**
Caponatina di melanzane, 60, **61–2**
Cappelletti alle erbe, 13, **14–16**
Caramelized oranges, 287, 288, **293–4**
Caramellone natalizie con crema allo zenzero, 298, 299, **306–7**
Carote di Ada Boni, 172, **372–3**
Carpaccio di salmone, 113, 114, **116**, 132
Carrot and potato timbales, 269, **272–3**
Carrot, celeriac and orange salad, 145, **148–9**
Carrots Italian style, 172, **372–3**
Cassata Siciliana, 29, 30, **33–4**, 60
Castelvetro, Giacomo, *Brieve racconto. . .* , 228
Cauliflower
  salad with anchovy and pine nut dressing, 266, 287, 288, **289**
  soup, 353, **354–5**
Cavalcanti, Ippolito, Duca di Buonvicino, *Cucina Teorico-Pratica*, 171, 218, 219, 234, 237
Celeriac, chicory and radicchio salad, 73, 282, **284–5**
Celery, purée of, 221, 222, **225–6**

Celery, carrot and apple salad in a wine and coriander dressing, 203, 204, **207–8**

Celery soup, 189, **190–91**

Cervo alla casalinga, 193, **196–7**

Champagne sorbet, 322–3, **325–6**

Cherries stewed in wine, 118, 119, **123–4**

Chestnut and cream pudding, 276, 277, **280–81**, 299

Chicken
  and spinach roll flavoured with basil, 18, **20–22**
  breasts in a seventeenth-century sweet-and-sour sauce, 40–41, **43–4**
  breasts stuffed with artichokes, 338, **340–41**
  with garlic, 87, **91–2**
  liver canapés, xiii, 67, **69**
  soup, with hard-boiled eggs and parsley, 18, **19–20**

Chick-pea and pasta soup, **211–12**

Chicory, radicchio and little gem salad with an anchovy and garlic sauce, 265, **266**

Chocolate and nut cake, 132, 134, **139–40**, 287, 288

Christmas, 342
  cracker strudels with ginger custard, 298, 299, **306–7**
  dinner, 297, 298–307

Cicoria belga all'aceto balsamico, 164, 165, **166–7**

Ciliege cotte al vino, 118, 119, **123–4**

Clear soup with hard-boiled eggs and parsley, 18, **19–20**

Coda alla vaccinara, 53, **54–5**

Coffee granita, 3, **6–7**

Colomba pasquale, 313, 315–16

Conchiglie rosse ripiene di spaghettini in insalata, 132, **137**

Coniglio al rosmarino, 257, **259–60**

Coniglio con le cipolle, 198, **200**

Coppette di frutta al caramello, 156, **158–9**

Coppette di pompelmo con l'uva, 98, **101–2**, 193, 194

Cornetti alle mandorle di Vera, 25, 114, 145, 253, 323, 343, **380–81**

Corrado, Vincenzo, *Il Cuoco*, 218–19, 233–4, 236

Cosciotto di agnello arrosto con le cipolline, 313, 314–15, **317–18**

Costolette di maiale, 145, **147–8**

Costolettine di agnello alla griglia, 3, **5–6**

Cotechino allo zabaione, 265, **267**

Cotechino with zabaglione, 265, **267**

Courgette and tomato salad, 24, **25–6**, 73

Courgette *frittata*, **331–2**

Cozze all'Italiana, 233, **234–5**

Cream and marrons glacés *bombe*, 308, 310, **312**

Crema di frutti della passione, 319, 320, **321**

Crespelle dolci di ricotta, 171, 172–3, **176–7**

Crostata di conserva di amarena, 72, 74, **82–3**

Crostini alla toscana, xiii, 67, **69**

Croûtons (large), 269

Cuoco Milanese, Il, 314

Cuoco senza Pretese, 239–40, 241

Cured fillet of beef with rocket, 118, **119–20**, 308, 309

Dentice al forno, 160, 161, **162–3**

Dolce di marroni dell'Artusi, 276, 277, **280–81**, 299

Duck breasts with balsamic vinegar, 164, 165, **167–8**

Easter
  cake, 313, **315–16**
  lunch, 297, 313–18
  pie, 313–14, **316–17**

Edwards, John, 222

Egg and cream sauce, 358, 359, **361–2**

Egg, Parmesan and parsley
　　dumplings in stock, 53, **57–8**
Eighteenth-century southern Italian
　　dinner, 233–8
Equipment, xiv-xv

Fagiano alla Cavalcanti con la polenta,
　　171–2, **174–5**
Fagioli all'uccelletto, 67, **71**
Fatless sponge, **381-2**
Faraona allo spumante, 322, **324–5**
Fave e pecorino, 67, 68
Fennel, Belgian chicory and orange
　　salad, 60, **65–6**
Fennel and Parmesan salad, 72, 73,
　　81
Fennel wedges with olive oil, 53, **54**
Filetti di pesce con le scaglie di patate,
　　93, **95**
Filetti di San Pietro in salsa di broccoli,
　　103, **105–6**
Finocchi in pinzimonio, 53, **54**
Fiore di melanzane alla senape, 198, **199**
Fioruzzi, Luisetta, 358–9
Fish
　　broth, **379-80**
　　fillets with potato scales, 93, **95**
　　lasagne, 178, 179, **181–3**
　　pie, Apulian, 203, 204, **206–7**
　　ravioli, 342, **343–5**
　　soup with breadcrumbs, cream,
　　　　egg yolks and Parmesan, 348,
　　　　349–50
Flat spaghetti with peas and cream,
　　3, **4–5**
Fontina and cream sauce, **121–2**, 269
Fragolamammella, 245–6, **249–50**
Frittata di cipolle, **330–31**
Frittata di peperoni e tonno, 328, **332**
Frittata di zucchine, **331–2**
Frittate (general), 327, 328, **330–32**
Fruit salad
　　in a caramel sauce, 156, **158–9**
　　with lemon granita, 24–5, **28**, 132,
　　　　134

Fruit stuffing, 299, **304-5**
Funghi al funghetto, 8, 172, 193, 239,
　　353, **371**
Fusilli and green beans in tomato
　　sauce, 113–14, **115**
Fusilli e fagiolini al pomodoro, 113–14,
　　115
Futurist dinner, 245–50

Gamberi imperiali in salsa all'abruzzese,
　　342–3, **345–6**
Gastronomy of Italy, 217
Gelato
　　di albicocca, 342, 343, **347**
　　di fragola all'aceto balsamico, 164,
　　　　168, 358
　　di mascarpone, **23**, 165
　　di ricotta, 132, 134, **138–9**
Gnocchetti alla purè di fagioli bianchi,
　　125, **126–7**
Golden dinner, 145–9
Gran raviolo, 308, 309, **310–11**
Granita al caffè, 3, **6–7**
Grapefruit bowls with grapes, 98,
　　101–2, 193, 194
Green and white dinner, 150–55
Green bean and tomato salad, 72, **80**
Green beans, 41, 113–14, 160–61,
　　161–2
Green salad
　　general, 73, 178, 185, 257, 348,
　　　　359, **368–9**
　　with herb dressing, **368–9**
Green sauce, 287, 288, **292**
Grilled aubergines with a lemony
　　mustard sauce, 198, **199**
Grilled bread with olive oil, garlic
　　and tomato, 108, **109–10**
Grilled lamb cutlets, 3, **5–6**
Grilled polenta, 165, 172, 353, **377–8**
Grilled radicchio and chicory, 50, **52**
Grilled vegetables, 327, 328, **333–4**
Guinea-fowl cooked in champagne,
　　322, **324–5**
Guy's tomato sauce, 87–8, **90**

Ham mousse, truffle-flavoured, 132, 133–4, 298, **300–301**
Historical menus, 215–50
Honey and walnut sauce, 287, 288, **293**

Ice-cream, 53
  apricot, 342, 343, **347**
  mascarpone, **23**, 165
  ricotta, 132, 134, **138–9**
  strawberry, flavoured with balsamic vinegar, 164, **168**, 358
  see also Sorbets
Immortal trout: trout stuffed with calf's liver and walnut, 245, 246, **248–9**
In loligine patina, 221, **222–3**
Insalata
  agra di barbabietola, 342, 343, **346**
  autunnale di frutta, 203, 204, **210**
  bianca e verde, 3, 150, 151, **153–4**, 313
  di carote sedano di Verona e arancie, 145, **148–9**
  di cavolfiore alla salsa bianca, 266, 287, 288, **289**
  di fagiolini e pomodori, 72, **80**
  di finocchi, cicoria belga e arancie, 60, **65–6**
  di finocchio al Parmigiano, 72, 73, **81**
  di Luisetta, 358, 359, **362–3**
  di pasta, fontina, noci e sedano, 132, **136–7**
  di pomodori, cetrioli e peperoni, 73, 125, 126, **129**, 328, 359
  di sedano, carota e mela al sapor di coriandolo, 203, 204, **207–8**
  di zucchine e pomodori all'aceto balsamico e alla menta, 24, **25–6**, 73
  verde, 73, 178, 185, 257, 348, 359, **368–9**
  Veronese, 73, 282, **284–5**
Italian broth, 156, **378–9**
Italian cookery, history of, 217–19
Italian roast veal, 276, **279–80**

John Dory fillets with broccoli sauce, 103, **105–6**
Julia's tomato sauce, 88, **89**

Lamb, Patrick, 29
Lamb
  grilled cutlets, 3, **5–6**
  roast leg with a saffron and balsamic vinegar sauce, 35–6, **38–9**
  roast leg with small onions, 313, 314–15, **317–18**
Lamb's lettuce, rocket and fennel salad, 3, 150, 151, **153–4**, 313
Lasagne
  baked green, 72, **76–7**
  fish, 178, 179, **181–3**
Lasagne verdi al forno, 72, **76–7**
Leek and rice pie, 185–6, **187–8**
Lemon-flavoured dishes
  dinner, 156–9
  egg and Parmesan soup, 156, **157**, 298
  meringues, 253, **381**
  spinach, 24–5, 160, 161, 257, 262, **373–4**
Lemon granita, 24–5, **28**, 132, 134
Lemon sorbet flavoured with fresh basil, 103–4, **106–7**, 160–61, 358
Lenten spinach pie, 227, **229–30**
Lenticchie in umido, 265, **268**
Lentils (general), 24–5
Leonardi, Francesco, *L'Apicio Moderno*, 218, 219, 233, 234
Linguine coi piselli alla panna, 3, 4–5
Loin of pork braised in milk with potato purée, 189, **191–2**
Luard, Elisabeth, 299

Macaroni
  baked with chicken breast and prosciutto, 233, **236–7**
  baked with sausage and garlic, 72, **74–5**
  pie, 60, **63–5**

Maccheroni gratinati con la luganega e l'aglio, 72, **74–5**
Macedonia di frutta con la neve al limone, 24–5, **28**, 132, 134
McGee, Harold, *Curious Cook*, 13–14
Maiale al latte con la puré di patate, 189, **191–2**
Manzo alla California, 56, **58–9**
Marinetti, Filippo, *La Cucina Futurista*, 219–20, 245, 246, 248, 249
Martino, Maestro, *Libro de Arte Coquinaria*, 35
Mascarpone alle due salsine, 40, **45–6**
Mascarpone ice-cream, **23**, 165
Mascarpone with elderflower and rose geranium sauces, 40, **45–6**
Meat and potato pie, 211, **213–14**
Meats, mixed boiled, 287–8, **290**
Mela in tortiglie, 233, 234, **237–8**
Menu planning, ix–xiii
Meringhine al limone, 253, **381**
Meringued peaches, 125, 126, **130–31**
Mia insalata verde, La, **368–9**
Milanese dinner, 56–9
Minestra di cavolfiore, 353, **354-5**
Minestra di pasta e ceci, **211–12**
Minestra mariconda, 56, **57–8**
Minestrina delicata, 18, **19–20**
Mixed boiled meats, 287–8, **290**
Mixed salads of vegetables, grapefruit and prawns, 358, 359, **362–3**
Monkfish morsels with lentil purée, 24–5, **26–7**
Morello cherry jam tart, 72, 74, **82-3**
Mostarda di Cremona, 287, 288
Mostarda of fruit, 287, 288
Moulded cream pudding, 150, 151, **154–5**
Moulded risotto with vegetables, **8–10**
Mousse di prosciutto cotto della Signora Gay, 132, 133–4, 298, **300–301**

Mushrooms with oregano and garlic, 8, 172, 193, 239, 353, **371**
Mussels Italian style, 233, **234–5**

Neve al limone, La, 24–5, **28**, 132, 134
New Year's Day, 265
New Year's Eve supper, 297, **308–12**
Nineteenth-century northern Italian dinner, 239–44
Noci, uva e grana, 108, **112**

Omelettes, 327, 328, **330–32**
One egg *ravioli* in clear broth, 308, 309, **310–11**
Onion *frittata*, **330–31**
Oranges, dried apricots and bananas in wine syrup, 30, 253, **256**
Oranges and kiwi fruit, 35, **39**, 262
Oxtail and celery braised in white wine, 53, **54–5**

Pan di Spagna, **381–2**
Pancakes, sweet ricotta, 171, 172–3, **176–7**
Panettone col mascarpone, **56–7**
Panettone with mascarpone, 56–7
Panforte e vinsanto, 67, **68**
Panna cotta, 150, 151, **154–5**
Pappa col pomodoro, 203–4, **205**
Passato di pomodoro, 171, **173–4**
Passato di sedano, 189, **190–91**
Passion fruit fool, 319, 320, **321**
Pasta
  general, 374–7
  Agnesi method, 376–7
  cooking, 376
  rolling out, 375–6
Pasta, fontina, walnut and celery salad, 132, **136–7**
Pasta al sugo, **87–8**
Pasta and chick-peas, 253, **254–5**
Pasta asciutta e ceci, 253, **254–5**
Pasta coi finocchi, 185, **186–7**
Pasta e fagioli alla contadina, 29, **30–31**

Pasta Perfect, 185

Pasta with fennel and cream, 185, **186–7**

Pasta with butter bean purée, 125, **126–7**

Pasta with tomato sauce, **87–8**

Pasticcio di pasta e melanzane in bianco, 103, **104–5**

Pasticcio di pesce, 178, 179, **181–3**

Pasticcio di tagliatelle e mozzerella in salsa, 269, **270–71**

Patate arrosto, **369**

Patate e fagiolini al pesto, 160–61, **161–2**

Patate in umido, 257, **260–61**

Patate trifolate, **370**

Peaches with raspberry sauce, 113, 114, **117**

Peach mould, 93, **96–7**

Pears stewed in red wine with liqueur-flavoured cream, 13–14, **17**, 132, 134, 338

Pecorino cheese with raw broad beans, 150, **151**

Pecorino con le fave, 150, **151**

Penne ai quattro formaggi, 72, **78**

Penne with four cheeses, 72, **78**

Peperoni all'aceto, 108, **111–12**

Peperoni ripieni della zia Renata, 178–9, **180–81**

Peppers and tuna fish *frittata*, 328, **332**

Peppers filled with aubergines and croûtons, 178–9, **180–81**

Peppers in vinegar, 108, **111–12**

Pere alla crema del Lario, 13–14, **17**, 132, 134, 338

Pesce in potaggio, 227, **231**

Pesche al sugo di lampone, 113, 114, **117**

Pesche in camicia, 125, 126, **130–31**

Petti di anatra all'aceto balsamico, 164, 165, **167–8**

Petti di cappone alla Stefani, 40–41, **43–4**

Petti di pollo farciti di carciofi, 338, **340–41**

Pheasant (general), 171–2, 174–5

Piatto rustico, 253, **255–6**

Pineapple and oranges, 178, 179, **184**, 262

Platina, *De Honesta Voluptate et Valetudine*, 35

Plums baked in wine, 18–19, **22–3**

Polenta, 165, 172, 353, **377–8**
    baked with cheeses, 276, **278–9**
    and sautéed mushrooms, 193

Polenta e funghi al funghetto, 193

Polenta pasticciata in bianco, 276, **278–9**

Pollastrelli all'aceto balsamico, 8, **11**

Pollastri al riso, 239, 240, **242-3**

Pollo all'aglio, 87, **91–2**

Polpettone di tonno della Mamma, 358, 359, **360–61**

Pomodori al basilico, 68, 358, 359, **363**

Pomodori in teglia, 8, 245, **372**

Porcellum coriandratum, 221, 222, **224–5**

Pork and chestnut stuffing, 299, **303–4**

Portrait of pasta, 72–3

Potato and almond cake, 118, 119, **122–3**, 132, 134

Potatoes and green beans with pesto, 160–61, **161–2**

Potatoes with parsley, 370

Pot-roasted chickens with rice, 239, 240, **242-3**

Pot-roast pheasant in a caper, prosciutto, vinegar and truffle sauce, with grilled polenta, 171–2, **174–5**

Prawn and bean salad, 98, **99–100**, 132

Prawns in a piquant tomato sauce, 342–3, **345–6**

Prosciutto e melone, **319**

Prugne al vino, 18–19, **22–3**

Puddings (general), xii–xiii, 337

Pumpkin risotto, 193–4, **194–5**
Purée of celery, 221, 222, **225–6**

Quaglie nel nido, 150–51, **152–3**
Quantities (general), xiv
Quattrova, E.V., *La Cucina Elegante*, 353

Rabbit with onion and vinegar, 198, **200**
Rabbit with rosemary and tomato sauce, 257, **259–60**
Radicchio alla trevisana, 50, **52**
Ratto, Giobatta and Giovanni, *La Cuciniera Genovese*, 314
Ravioli
  fish, 342, **343–5**
  il gran raviolo, 308, 309, **310–11**
  stuffed with herbs and ricotta, 13, **14–16**
Ravioli de pesce, 342, **343–5**
Red mullet with prosciutto and rosemary, 125, 126, **128**
Red sauce, 287, 288, **291**
Renaissance dinner, 227–32
Ricchi e i poveri, I, 98, **99–100**, 132
Rice cake, 203, **208–9**
Ricotta and almond cake with orange sauce, 198, **201–2**
Ricotta and cream cake, 227, 228, **232**
Ricotta ice-cream, 132, 134, **138–9**
Ricotta pancakes, sweet, 171, 172–3, **176–7**
Ripieno di castagne, 299, **303–4**
Ripieno di frutta, 299, **304–5**
Risotto, 257
  moulded, with vegetables, **8–10**
  pumpkin, 193–4, **194–5**
  saffron, 145, **146–7**
  with champagne, 322, **323–4**
  with gorgonzola, 257, **258–9**
  with mussels, 50, **51–2**
Risotto al gorgonzola, 257, **258–9**
Risotto allo spumante, 322, **323–4**
Risotto coi peoci, 50, **51–2**

Risotto con la zucca, 193–4, **194–5**
Risotto con le verdure in forma, 8–9, **9–10**
Risotto giallo, 145, **146–7**
Roasted chicory with balsamic vinegar, 164, 165, **166–7**
Roast leg of lamb
  with a saffron and balsamic vinegar sauce, 35–6, **38–9**
  with small onions, 313, 314–15, **317–18**
Roast pork with coriander, 221, 222, **224–5**
Roast potatoes, **369**
Roast poussins with balsamic vinegar, 8, **11**
Roden, Claudia, 314
Roman dinner, ancient, 221–6
Roman late supper, 53–5
Rotolo di spinaci al burro e formaggio, 118–19, **120–22**

St Valentine's day dinner, 297
Saffron risotto, 145, **146–7**
Salads, 73, 132, 134
  autumnal fruit, 203, 204, **210**
  Beetroot, grapefruit and watercress, 342, 343, **346**
  Carrot, celeriac and orange, 145, **148–9**
  Cauliflower, 266, 287, 288, **289**
  Celeriac, chicory and radicchio, 73, 282, **284–5**
  Celery, carrot and apple, 203, 204, **207–8**
  Chicory, radicchio and little gem, 265, **266**
  Courgette and tomato, 24, **25–6**, 73
  Fennel and Parmesan, 72, 73, **81**
  Fennel, Belgian chicory and orange, 60, **65–6**
  Green bean and tomato, 72, **80**
  Green salad, 73, 178, 185, 257, 348, 359, **368–9**

Lamb's lettuce, rocket and fennel, 3, 150, 151, **153–4**, 313

Pasta, fontina, walnut and celery, 132, **136–7**

Prawn and bean, 98, **99–100**, 132

Radicchio leaves filled with thin spaghetti, 132, **137**

Tomato, cucumber and peppers, 73, 125, 126, **129**, 328, 359

Vegetables, grapefruit and prawn, 358, 359, **362–3**

Salame and hard-boiled eggs, **313**

Salame di pollo e spinaci al sapor di basilico, 18, **20–22**

Salame e uova sode, **313**

Salmon Carpaccio, 113, 114, **116**, 132

Salsa di api, 287, 288, **293**

Salsa rossa, 287, 288, **291**

Salsa verde, 287, 288, **292**

Salsina all'uovo, 358, 359, **361–2**

Sautéed mushrooms with oregano and garlic, 8, 172, 193, 239, 353, **371**

Scappi, Bartolomeo, 217–18, 227, 231

Scarpazzone lombardo, 29–30, **31–2**

Schegge di pecorino e Parmigiano con le olive verdi, 327, **329**

Sea-bass stuffed with scallops, shrimps and black olives, 348–9, **350–51**

Sea-bream, baked with tomatoes and basil, 160, 161, **162–3**

Secrets from an Italian Kitchen, 13, 164

Sformatini di carote e patate, 269, **272–3**

Sharon fruits with lime juice, 189, **192**

Sicilian *cassata*, 29, 30, **33–4**, 60

Sicilian dinner, 60–66

Sienese fruit and spice cake with *vinsanto*, 67, 68

Soffiato di capelli d'angelo, 93, **94–5**

Soffiato di riso all'aragosta, 338, **339**

Soft chocolate nougat, 282–3, **285–6**

Sorbet, 53–4, 322–3

champagne, 322–3, **325–6**

lemon-flavoured, with basil, 103–4, **106–7**, 160, 161, 358

see also ice-cream

Sorbetto allo spumante, 322–3, **325–6**

Sorbetto di limone al basilico, 103–4, **106–7**, 160, 161, 358

Soufflé of rice and lobster, 338, **339**

Spaghetti

flat, with peas and cream, 3, **4–5**

radicchio leaves filled with thin, 132, **137**

thin, in a piquant tomato sauce, 327, 328, **329–30**

thin, with garlic, oil and chilli, 358, **359–60**

wholewheat with onion and anchovy sauce, 262, **263**

Spaghettini eccitanti, 327, 328, **329–30**

Spaghettini aglio, olio e peperoncino, 358, **359–60**

Spinach, 269

and pasta roll with melted butter, and Parmesan, 118–19, **120–22**

tourte, 29–30, **31–2**

Spinaci all'agro, 24-5, 160, 161, 257, 262, **373–4**

Squid in the pan, 221, **222–3**

Stefani, Bartolomeo, *L'Arte di Ben Cucinare*, 41, 218, 228–9, 232

Stewed fish, 227, **231**

Stewed lentils, 265, **268**

Stewed pears with liqueur-flavoured cream, 13–14, **17**, 132, 134, 338

Stewed potatoes, 257, **260–61**

Stewed vegetables, 253, **255–6**

Stewed venison with onions, 193, **196–7**

Stracciatella al sapor di limone, 156, **157**, 298

Strawberry breasts: strawberry and ricotta pudding, 245–6, **249–50**

Strawberry ice-cream flavoured with balsamic vinegar, 164, **168**, 358

Stuffed roast turkey with roast potatoes, 298–9, **302–3**

Sugo di Guy, 87–8, **90**
Sugo di Julia, 88, **89**
Sweet and sour aubergine, 60, **61–2**
Sweetbreads glazed in Marsala with
    garden peas, 319–20, **320–21**
Sweet ricotta pancakes, 171, 172–3,
    176–7
Sweetmeats, 40

Tacchino arrosto alla milanese, 298–9,
    302–3
Tagliatelle
    baked, with ham and peas, 72, **79**
    baked, with tomatoes and
        mozzarella, 269, **270–71**
    with artichokes, 35, **36–7**
    with mozzarella, anchovy fillets
        and parsley, 108, **110–11**
    with mussels and leeks, 282,
        283–4
Tagliatelle coi carciofi, 35, **36–7**
Tagliatelle con cozze e porri, 282, **283–4**
Tagliatelle di Guido, 108, **110–11**
*Tagliatelle gratinate al prosciutto cotto e
    piselli*, 72, **79**
Tagliolini ring in a creamy courgette
    sauce, 40, **42–3**
Thin spaghetti in a piquant tomato
    sauce, 327, 328, **329–30**
Thin spaghetti, radacchio leaves
    filled with, 132, **137**
Thin spaghetti with garlic, oil and
    chilli, 358, **359–60**
Tiella di carne e patate, 211, **213–14**
Tiella di pesce di Claudia, 203, 204,
    206–7
Timballo del Gattopardo, 60, **63–5**
Timballo di maccheroni alla Pampadur,
    233, **236–7**
Tiramisú di Edda, 348, 349, **351–2**
Tomato, cucumber and peppers, 73,
    125, 126, **129**, 328, 359
Tomatoes with basil, 68, 358, 359, **363**
Tomato soup, 171, **173–4**
Torrone molle, 282–3, **285–6**

Torta
    bianca alla bolognese, 218, 227, 228,
        232
    d'herbe da quaresima, 227, **229–30**
    di cioccolato di Julia, 132, 134,
        139–40, 287, 288
    di patate e mandorle, 118, 119,
        122–3, 132, 134
    di porri, 185–6, **187–8**
    *di ricotta e mandorle con la salsina di
        arancia*, 198, **201–2**
    di riso, 203, **208–9**
    pasqualina, 313–14, **316–17**
Tourte, spinach, 29–30, **31–2**
Trance di nasello al forno, 262, **264**
Tre cicorie in bagna cauda, 265, **266**
Triglie alla marchigiana, 125, 126, **128**
Trote immortali, 245, 246, **248–9**
Truffle-flavoured ham mousse, 132,
    133–4, 298, **300–301**
Tunny fish roll, 358, 359, **360–61**
Turkey, roast, 298–9, **302–3**
Tuscan lunch, 67–71
Tuscan roast pork, 67, **70–71**

Veal in a tuna sauce, 132, 133, **135–6**
Veal with lemon and cream, 156, **157–8**
Vegan lunch, 253–6
Vegetable soup, 239–40, **240–41**
Vegetarian dishes, xii
Venetian lunch, 50–52
Venison stewed with onions, 193,
    196–7
Vera's almond crescents, 25, 114,
    145, 253, 323, 343, **380–81**
Verdure alla griglia, 327, 328, **333–4**
Vermicelli soufflé, 93, **94–5**
Vialardi, Giovani, *Trattato di Cucina*,
    219, 240
Vitello al limone, 156, **157–8**
Vitello tonnato alla Milanese, 132, 133,
    135–6

Walnut and honey pie, 72, 74, 269,
    274–5

Walnuts, grapes and Parmesan, 108, **112**

Wedges of pecorino and Parmesan with green olives, 327, **329**

White mascarpone trifle: a summer *tiramisú*, 348, 349, **351–2**

Wholewheat spaghetti with onion and anchovy sauce, 262, **263**

Zabaglione, cold, 145, **149**

Zabaglione with strawberry purée, 8–9, **12**

Zabaione con la puré di fragole, 8–9, **12**

Zabaione gelato, 145, **149**

Zampone allo zabaione con le lenticchie, 308, **309**

Zampone sausage in a zabaglione sauce with stewed lentils, 308, **309**

Zuppa alla santé, 239–40, **240–41**

Zuppa di pan gratto, 348, **349-50**